INSIDE
ODBC

D0536350

KYLE GEIGER

with programming by
Brian Tschumper and
Jason Zander

Microsoft Press

PUBLISHED BY
Microsoft Press
A Division of Microsoft Corporation
One Microsoft Way
Redmond, Washington 98052-6399

Library of Congress Cataloging-in-Publication Data
Geiger, Kyle, 1958-
    Inside ODBC / Kyle Geiger.
       p.   cm.
    Includes index.
    ISBN 1-55615-815-7
    1. Database management. 2. ODBC. I. Title.
QA76.9.D3G43   1995
005.74--dc20   95-18867
                                     CIP

Printed and bound in the United States of America.

1 2 3 4 5 6 7 8 9 QBP 0 9 8 7 6 5

Distributed to the book trade in Canada by Macmillan of Canada, a division of Canada Publishing Corporation.

A CIP catalogue record for this book is available from the British Library.

Microsoft Press books are available through booksellers and distributors worldwide. For further information about international editions, contact your local Microsoft Corporation office. Or contact Microsoft Press International directly at fax (206) 936-7329.

Acquisitions Editors: Dean Holmes, David Clark
Project Editor: Katherine A. Krause
Technical Editor: Dail Magee, Jr.

TABLE OF CONTENTS

CHAPTER THREE

Client/Server Architecture   **73**

CHAPTER FOUR

ODBC Architecture   **99**

PART II: PROGRAMMING WITH ODBC

CHAPTER SEVEN

Getting Started with ODBC Programming   **273**

CHAPTER EIGHT

ODBC at Work   **307**

APPENDIX

ODBC and Standards Groups   **461**

PREFACE

In the beginning there was data, and the data was without form, and darkness was upon the face of the earth.

And Codd[1] said, "Let there be a relational data model." And it was so.

And Codd said, "Let the data be separated from the application program data structures, giving data independence." And it was good.

And DBMS vendors said, "Let us be fruitful and multiply." And it was so.

And users said, "Let us obtain applications to access the data from all DBMS vendors."

And the application developers became downcast, saying, "Yea, I must walk through the valley of the shadow of each vendor's precompiler or call level interface, communications stack, and protocol." And it was not good.

So the SQL Access Group and X/Open said, "Let us facilitate the implementation of ISO standards, and so provide technology for database interoperability." And it was so.

And it came to pass that three technologies emerged: embedded SQL, RDA, and a call level interface.

And Microsoft said, "Let us implement the call level interface, and let us work with DBMS vendors and application writers to interoperate." And it was so. And it was good.

And that was how ODBC came to be.

Welcome to *Inside ODBC*, the book designed to give you both a conceptual understanding of ODBC and some practical hands-on experience with ODBC programming. Accordingly, this book is divided into two major parts. Part I (Chapters 1 through 6) is the conceptual part; it introduces ODBC, provides a lot of background information relevant to understanding ODBC, and contains a fair amount of detail about the design of ODBC. Part II (Chapters 7 through 9) is for programmers; it starts out with very simple ODBC programs and progresses to very complex ones. The final chapter, Chapter 9, is a preview of coming attractions—a look at what is likely to be included in

---

1. Dr. E. F. Codd, considered to be the creator of the relational data model. Dr. Codd's seminal paper, "A Relational Model of Data for Large Shared Data Banks," was first published in the *Communications of the Association of Computing Machinery* (CACM) in June 1970.

future versions of ODBC. Although Chapter 9 is in Part II, it isn't just for programmers. Anyone who is curious about how ODBC will be enhanced in the future will want to read it.

Overall, the flow of the book is from the general to the specific. Each chapter expands the set of topics and gives more details on concepts previously introduced.

Chapter 1 introduces and defines ODBC. It also describes ODBC's original design requirements and gives a brief overview of the major technical highlights of ODBC. Chapter 2 is about different kinds of database systems and programming models and how they influenced ODBC. Chapter 3 discusses client/server architecture (or more accurately what *I* mean by client/server architecture) and its impact on ODBC. Chapter 4 starts getting into the details of ODBC itself. The architecture of ODBC is described in depth and many functional areas of the programming interface are explained. Chapter 5 goes into even more detail about some crucial ODBC topics. This chapter completes the conceptual treatment of ODBC. Chapter 6 concludes Part I with a behind-the-scenes look at an actual ODBC driver. Many of the concepts in the first five chapters can be seen in action in this chapter.

Chapter 7, the first chapter in Part II, contains four simple C programs that use ODBC. Most of the basic programming techniques common to ODBC programs are used in these examples. Chapter 8 describes 11 more complete sample programs that demonstrate many elements of the ODBC programming interface. All the source code for the examples in Chapters 7 and 8 is included on the companion CD. Chapter 9, as stated above, gives a brief glimpse into what's ahead for future versions of ODBC.

Finally, the appendix describes the various standards bodies that have had a role in the design of ODBC.

At various points in Part I you will find shaded "Inside Story" sidebars. These sidebars have two purposes. The first is to give you some of the early history of ODBC; the second is to break up the technical material in the chapters with something a bit more lighthearted.

Who Should Read this Book

I had two audiences in mind when I wrote this book. The first audience is made up of people who work with databases. Many people have heard of or read about ODBC at trade shows or in the trade press, but there hasn't been much in the way of a detailed explanation of what ODBC is and how it works. People who work with databases—users, application developers, DBMS vendors, MIS professionals, independent software vendors, database administrators, and database consultants—need a solid conceptual understanding of

ODBC so that they can effectively deploy software that uses ODBC in their organizations. Part I is written for this audience.

The second audience is made up of programmers who want to use ODBC to write database applications or utilities. The CD that comes with this book includes more than 20,000 lines of source code in 15 sample programs in three programming languages (C, C++, and Visual Basic). Part II will be helpful regardless of whether you are a relative newcomer just starting to write programs using ODBC or an experienced professional.

Acknowledgments

As you will see when you read the "Inside Story" sidebars, ODBC has been influenced by a large number of very talented people from many companies in the computer industry. So also has this book. I've tried to list those who have made a significant contribution either to ODBC or to this book. For those I've missed, please accept my apologies. Your contributions are appreciated and reflected in the success of ODBC nonetheless.

Starting at the beginning, I'd like to thank the original "gang of four" who labored mightily over the original specification: Jeff Balboni and Larry Barnes of Digital Equipment; Don Nadel, Tom McGary, Peter Wilkins, and Peter O'Kelly of Lotus Development Corporation; Tom Haggin and Ed Archibald from Sybase; and Bob Muglia from Microsoft. Extra thanks to Don Nadel and Tom Haggin for reviewing the "Inside Story" sections to ensure that I told it the way it really was.

Special thanks to Lowell Tuttman of Microsoft, who was probably the only person who believed in ODBC more than I did in those early days. Thanks, Lowell, for communicating the ODBC vision to DBMS vendors, Windows ISVs, the SQL Access Group, and the rest of the database community, and for being such a good friend during the tough times. And thanks also go to Colleen Lambert and Peter Petesch, who carried the ODBC marketing banner so effectively later on.

The entire ODBC team at Microsoft deserves recognition for putting "legs" on the ODBC specification. Without the valiant efforts of the program managers, product managers, developers, testers, technical writers, and product support people, ODBC would still be just a piece of paper. Thank you for building a quality developer's kit and for keeping up with the innovations in the database industry.

Special thanks go to Mike Pizzo of Microsoft, who has not only been a primary technical contributor to ODBC within Microsoft but has been Microsoft's eyes and ears on the various standards bodies (X/Open SQL Access Group, ANSI, and ISO). Mike has probably had more direct influence on

ODBC in the last two years than just about anyone else. Mike's comments on Chapter 9 and the Appendix were especially helpful, as were the comments from Murali Venkatrao and Alam Ali.

Thanks also go to Ron Bourret at Microsoft, primary technical writer for the *Microsoft ODBC 2.0 Programmer's Reference*, whose careful critiques of most of the chapters of *Inside ODBC* helped keep me on track, and whose humor is always a source of encouragement. Amrish Kumar of the Microsoft SQL Server group provided many helpful comments on Chapter 6 regarding the Microsoft SQL Server drives for Microsoft SQL Server version 6.

Kathy Krause and Dail Magee, Jr., of Microsoft Press were wonderful to work with on this project. Not only are they excellent editors, but they also helped make writing this book fun. I'd also like to thank this book's principal compositor, Barbara Remmele, for the many hours she spent making this book look good and read well; the principal proofreader, Lisa Theobald, for her attention to detail and her sensitive copy editing; the illustrator, Michael Victor, for taking the time to make the art look just right; and everyone else at Microsoft Press who helped make this book a reality.

Although many people outside Microsoft have made valuable contributions to ODBC, two individuals deserve recognition for their efforts to keep the de jure and de facto standards (ISO CLI and ODBC) moving in the same direction. Paul Cotton at Fulcrum Technologies and Frank Pellow at IBM have been and continue to be movers and shakers in the standards world for the CLI, providing innumerable innovations and corrections to ODBC. Paul's detailed comments on early drafts of this book and Frank's help with IBM-specific material were greatly appreciated. Thanks also to Margaret Li of IBM, who provided the IBM precompiler output for Chapter 2.

Thanks also go to Merrill Holt and Peter Vasterd at Oracle for their help with the Oracle precompiler example in Chapter 2, to Andy Mendelsohn at Oracle for answering my queries on Oracle's transaction processing, and to the other Oracle folks who had a significant impact on ODBC's early design: Gary Hallmark, Sandeep Jain, and Richard Lim.

Brian Tschumper and Jason Zander from Microsoft wrote nearly all the code in the sample programs in Chapter 8, and it is completely accurate to say that Part II of this book would not have happened without them. They have been delightful to work with, and if you are a programmer who will look at the source code on the CD, I'm sure you'll appreciate their well-written code (except, that is, in the places where I messed it up!).

Finally, and most important, I'd like to thank my wonderful wife, Kimberly, for putting up with the long hours it took to finish this book on time, and most of all for her faithful dedication to the most important job in the world: being a homeschool mom to our four children.

INSIDE ODBC

In Part I, all the major concepts of ODBC are explained, with a good bit of background and discussion of database architecture provided so that you can see why ODBC is designed the way it is. Although this is the conceptual rather than the programming part of the book, I don't hesitate to use code if it is necessary to get the point across.

My primary purpose for Part I is to give you a thorough introduction to ODBC: what it is, the motivation for creating it, the problems it solves, and how it works at a general level. My secondary purpose is to provide the necessary background about the architectural framework of database systems and the programming models for accessing them so that you can see how ODBC fits into that framework. Ultimately, I hope that this part of the book explains ODBC in enough detail so that you can see how or if ODBC will be useful to you or your company.

ODBC: The Database Connectivity Solution

Ten years ago, the idea that you could use a software application to access a database and, without programming, use that same application to access other kinds of databases was unheard of. ODBC has made such database access not only possible but commonplace. In this first chapter, we'll define ODBC, describe the problems it was designed to solve, and explore the major elements of ODBC's design.

1.1 What Is ODBC?

Open Database Connectivity (ODBC) is a standard application programming interface (API) for accessing data in both relational and nonrelational

---

GLOSSARY

API (application programming interface) A set of related functions that a computer programmer uses to obtain some kind of service from another piece of software. Programmers of Windows-based applications use the Windows API to create windows, draw text on the screen, access files, and perform all other services provided by Windows. Despite the use of the word *application* in this term, applications might not be the only software using an API; lower-level software components such as network drivers also have APIs, but these components are not "applications" and are not (typically) used directly by applications. See also the definition of CLI (call level interface) on the next page for an alternative definition of API.

database management systems (DBMSs). Using the ODBC API, applications can access data stored in a variety of personal computer, minicomputer, and mainframe DBMSs, even when each DBMS uses a different data storage format and programming interface. To accomplish this DBMS independence, ODBC's architecture "componentizes" database access, providing a logical separation between the application and the DBMS. Conceptually, the ODBC API is for database access what the Microsoft Windows API is for video displays; Windows-based applications do not have to include specialized code for each video adapter and display—they use the Windows API, and Windows itself provides the device independence.

ODBC is based on the call level interface (CLI) specification of the X/Open SQL Access Group, which is likely to become an ANSI and ISO standard by the end of 1995. Basing ODBC on a standard was important for at least two reasons. First, every major DBMS vendor participates in the standards process, providing a forum that allows the vendors to specify the requirements of each DBMS product and that encourages experts from each DBMS vendor to develop technical solutions. Second, a formal standard carries commercial significance because government procurement agencies and some large companies require vendors to comply with certain standards if they want to bid on contracts.

GLOSSARY

DBMS (database management system) The software that manages access to structured data. For example, IBM DB2, Microsoft SQL Server, Oracle 7 Server, and Sybase SQL Server are DBMSs. In this book I use the term DBMS more generally to include PC database products such as Microsoft Access, FoxPro, and Borland Paradox, as well as any other software that can provide data access services.

CLI (call level interface) A set of function calls (just like API, defined previously). However, CLI is used in the SQL standards world to describe an interface that is not embedded SQL, which is also referred to as an API. Embedded SQL is an alternative programming interface in which SQL statements are intermixed with normal program syntax and transformed by a precompiler into function calls to the DBMS runtime library.

ANSI (American National Standards Institute) The primary formal standards-making body in the United States. ANSI defines standards for all kinds of things, including computer languages and bicycle helmet safety. ANSI is part of the U.S. Department of Commerce and is the national standards body representing the United States at ISO meetings.

In addition to its influence in the formal standards process, ODBC is becoming the informal standard for database connectivity through its use in many software products. Application developers like the degree of database independence that ODBC provides, and information systems people from companies of all sizes have found that ODBC eases the complex requirements they face when integrating disparate applications with diverse sources of data.

Here are some of the uses of ODBC in the computing industry today:

- By 1994 all major Microsoft applications and development tools supported ODBC. Microsoft Excel, Word, Access, Visual Basic, FoxPro, Microsoft SQL Server for Windows NT, and Visual C++ all use ODBC technology to access a variety of DBMSs. If you have any of these products installed on your computer, you probably have ODBC too.[1]

GLOSSARY

X/Open SQL Access Group An industry consortium of DBMS vendors whose objective is to enable SQL-based products from multiple vendors to work together. Founded in 1989 as the SQL Access Group, the group merged with X/Open in late 1994 and continues to pursue its objective as a technical working body within X/Open. X/Open Company is a consortium of companies that promotes multivendor computing guidelines by publishing portability guides.

ISO (International Organization for Standardization) A worldwide federation of national standards bodies that sets standards for a wide variety of technologies, including computer languages and animal shipping crates. (I am not making this up. Jim Melton, editor of the ANSI and ISO SQL specifications, reports that ISO has committees "whose sole purpose is to specify standards for bolt, nut, washer, and screw factors.... There's another for paper sizes and composition, surface reflectance, etc.") In addition to ANSI, national standards bodies include BSI (British Standards Institute) and DIN (Deutsches Institut für Normung). See the Melton and Simon book listed at the end of this chapter for information about standards organizations and how they function.

---

1. To find out for sure, go to the Control Panel in Windows. If you see an icon labeled *ODBC*, you've got it.

■ Support for ODBC is not limited to Microsoft. Nearly all DBMS vendors and major independent software vendors (ISVs) support ODBC, including Lotus (Approach), Powersoft (PowerBuilder), IBM (the AS/400 and DB2/6000 drivers), Oracle (the Oracle driver), Novell (AppWare), and Borland (Interbase). The fact that many of Microsoft's competitors support ODBC is a testament to its widespread adoption as an industry standard.

■ ODBC has had a long and favorable relationship with several standards organizations. The X/Open SQL Access Group, ANSI, and ISO are all currently working on advancing the core elements of the ODBC API through their respective organizations. At times it has been difficult to tell who is leading and who is following in the development of the API. The truth is that the development of ODBC has been one of the most cooperative efforts I've ever witnessed. Innovations existing in ODBC have been adopted into the formal standard, and in turn, inventions of the standards groups have been incorporated into new releases of ODBC.

■ Versions 2.*x* of ODBC provide excellent tools for building 32-bit database applications with new Microsoft operating systems, including Windows NT and Windows 95. Object-oriented programming can be accomplished using either the C++ classes included with ODBC versions 2.*x* or the more powerful database objects for ODBC bundled with Visual C++, as well as many development tools provided by other manufacturers. Visual Basic for Applications, which is included with Microsoft Excel 5, also includes direct programming support for ODBC.

■ ODBC is a cross-platform solution. From its conception ODBC was designed to work on various operating systems (and with various programming languages). Portability is a primary concern of the standards bodies that work on the CLI. Microsoft has licensed the source code for ODBC to third parties who have provided or will soon provide ODBC on the Macintosh, a variety of UNIX platforms, OS/2, and other operating systems. Some DBMS vendors already use ODBC as their native programming interface. IBM, Watcom, and Informix have been among the first to do so.

The use of ODBC is widespread. But why? In the next section we'll look at some of the reasons.

1.2 What's the Problem?
The Need for Database Connectivity

Why is ODBC used by so many products in so many ways? For what problem is ODBC the solution?

Every solution should address a real-world problem. This probably seems obvious, but we in the computer business sometimes forget this point and can all too easily get wrapped up in the technology for its own sake because it is fun and interesting. This part of the chapter describes the real-world computing problems that ODBC solves. It begins by describing the need for a database connectivity solution from three perspectives: users (the people who use computers in an effort to make their businesses more productive), application developers (including vendors who produce application development tools), and DBMS vendors. Each perspective has some overlap with the others, but each also has some unique characteristics worth noting.

1.2.1 The User's Perspective

In 1988, when thinking about a database connectivity standard first began at Microsoft, it was already apparent that applications—both Microsoft's and those produced by the ISV community—needed to have access to the data that customers use to run their businesses. This is largely the result of a trend that started in the late 1980s and has continued to this day: more and more companies are incorporating low-cost PCs and graphical user interfaces such

---

GLOSSARY

ISV (independent software vendor) A company that produces a software product. Lotus is a large ISV; Joe's Screen Door and Software Enterprises is a small ISV. (Yes, I made up that second one, but you get the point.)

User A person who uses a computer to accomplish a task related to his or her business or personal interest. In this section the term more specifically means someone in a corporation who must use one or more applications that access a DBMS. Examples of user tasks include making sales forecasts with a spreadsheet using actual sales data from a corporate mainframe, updating inventory data when new shipments arrive, and adding new employees to a personnel database.

---

as Windows into their working environments and have realized huge productivity gains as a result. However, one rather significant problem remains: the actual data used to drive a business is typically not on a PC. (And even when it is, it can be in any one of many different file formats.) In fact, the data that users want to manipulate in their spreadsheets (or data entry forms or report writers) spans nearly every existing hardware platform, operating system, network, and DBMS. Users have access to many powerful tools but do not have a convenient way to manipulate their real data.

In addition to this, the use of various computing systems in medium and large companies has evolved in such a way that different DBMSs are often deployed in various parts of the organization. At the same time, the companies are experiencing an increasing need to share information among these different systems. Sometimes different DBMSs are deployed because a particular application best fits one department's needs and that application works only with a particular DBMS. Sometimes different DBMSs are deployed because of the specific functionality or performance characteristics of the database server itself. And sometimes it is simply a case of users within each department buying and using what they know. It is not uncommon to find that one department within an organization has specific expertise for a DBMS that is different from what another department has.

For example, a corporation might keep its sales and financial information on an IBM mainframe with DB2 while the manufacturing system uses RDB on a VAX. To access the manufacturing information and the sales information in a single application (to track the effect on sales of a change made in manufacturing, for instance), both DB2 and RDB would have to be queried.[2]

As stated earlier, there has also been an increasing desire to use new PC-based tools (Microsoft Excel or Lotus 1-2-3, for example) for analysis. How can the increasingly powerful desktop PC applications be most effectively integrated with data on local area network (LAN) servers, minicomputers, and mainframes? How can the components of database applications be simplified in a distributed computing environment of PCs and other computers (which came to be known as *client/server* computing)?

---

2. Actually, a third DBMS could also be involved in this situation. To avoid taxing the sales and manufacturing DBMSs with queries from this analysis application, another system could be used to download data from the sales and manufacturing systems during off-hours. It might be another RDB or DB2 system, but then again it might be Sybase or Oracle. In the latter case, the need for a common programming interface becomes even more evident.

As we sought the answers to these and other questions, the analysis of the user's needs unfolded and several more needs became clear.

■ **Users need flexible, more universal extraction tools.** Pure analysis applications (which are not required to create or modify shared data) use data extraction tools that export data from a variety of data sources to some common PC format (text or Xbase, for example) or to a departmental DBMS on the LAN. Then the application of choice can read the common format and do the analysis. However, customers are finding that it isn't always easy to know in advance what subset of the data they want to look at. That is, when they run the extraction tool, they almost always specify a query to get only the data that they are interested in at the time (such as sales figures for the past month). Many times further analysis is needed (for example, to see how the past month's sales compare to those of the same month a year ago), and they have to go back to the extraction tool, load the data into the application, and do the analysis. Although it is clearly workable, this process is cumbersome when the user doesn't know up front all the questions he or she wants to ask about the data. This situation has led to the development of ad hoc query tools, of which there are several now on the market. Thus even pure analysis applications need to be able to easily access data in a wide variety of environments and formats.

■ **Users need line-of-business applications that can be developed and modified quickly.** The mainstream line-of-business database applications (applications for customer list processing, order entry, inventory management, and payroll, for example) derive ease-of-use

---

GLOSSARY

Ad hoc query tool An application that leads the user through the formulation and execution of a query. Such applications are useful when the user does not have a specific query in mind. Typical ad hoc query tools step the user through the selection of tables, identification of columns to be displayed, and the designation of criteria to be used on the columns to display only the rows needed. The query is executed, the results are displayed, and further refinements are made to the query until the required data is found. Examples of ad hoc query tools include Microsoft Query, Intersolv Q+E, Andyne GQL, Fairfield Software Clear Access, and Brio DataPrism.

benefits from graphical user interfaces, but the extraction tool methodology described earlier does nothing to help them because, obviously, it has no update capability. Although in most cases such an application is targeted at a single DBMS and can therefore best use the native API and development tools supplied by the DBMS vendor, some applications must be targeted at multiple DBMSs simply because multiple DBMSs exist within the corporation. Often the companies have solved this problem by developing one application to access one DBMS and a different application to access another DBMS. A common programming interface for both DBMSs reduces training costs and development time.

■ **Users need a solution that works with existing technologies as much as possible.** It is not acceptable to propose a solution that requires wholesale replacement of network hardware and/or software. The solution must allow for a smooth migration between DBMSs without requiring a rewrite of the applications.

■ **Users need a solution that exploits all the features of each DBMS.** A "lowest common denominator" solution is not acceptable for any but a very few cases.

■ **Users need high performance.** The solution must be equal or nearly equal in performance to the native programming interface for a DBMS.

■ **Users need simplicity.** If there is one thing that everyone in the computer industry agrees on, it is that the present database access situation is too complicated. Users need to have less to worry about, not more. A standard database connectivity solution should reduce some of the complexities involved in accessing data. The solution should shield the user from the underlying complexities of network software, protocol stacks, and the various naming conventions of servers and DBMSs. In general, it should hide the details of how to connect the application at the desktop to the data source, regardless of the data source's location.

Without a common programming interface to access multiple DBMSs, users are faced with a plethora of APIs, technologies, and each vendor's own database connectivity solution. This situation is depicted in Figure 1-1.

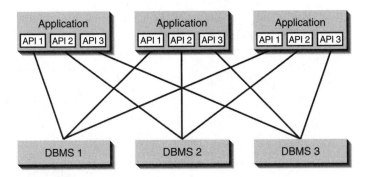

Figure 1-1.
The user's perspective of the need for database connectivity.

1.2.2 The Application Developer's and the Development Tool Developer's Perspective

The needs of the people who write applications (application developers, typically within a company) and the needs of the people who produce the tools for the application developers to use (development tool developers) overlap somewhat with the needs of the people who actually use the applications to accomplish a task (users). However, a few other needs are unique to the developer community.

■ **Developers want to eliminate DBMS vendor lock-in.** If an application developer can use a standard API rather than a DBMS vendor's native API, the developer has to do less work to allow the application to use another DBMS or to write a single application that uses multiple DBMSs at the same time.[3] From the application developer's perspective, access to multiple DBMSs is centered on the application, as shown in Figure 1-2 on the following page.

---

3. Despite this savings, today this is not quite true. The top DBMS vendors have enough market presence that developers will still use the native APIs for their DBMSs in a few cases. But as the implementations of the standard API improve to be on par with the performance and functionality of the DBMS vendors' native APIs, it will become harder and harder for application developers to justify devoting resources to multiple native APIs.

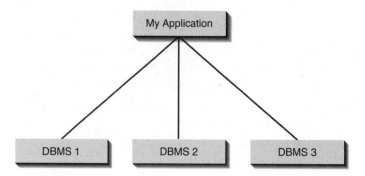

Figure 1-2.
The application developer's perspective of the need for database connectivity.

■ **Developers need to be able to build line-of-business applications using rapid application development (RAD) tools that target different DBMSs.**   With the increasing popularity of RAD tools (for example, Powersoft's PowerBuilder, Gupta's SQL Windows, and Microsoft Visual Basic) that ease the construction of line-of-business applications, the burden of supporting multiple DBMSs shifts from the corporate application developer to the producers of these development tools. That is, although a particular developer using a database development tool would almost always target a single DBMS, another developer using the same tool might need to access a different DBMS. Database development tool developers are thus forced into either writing to every DBMS vendor's native API or abstracting their programming interface into something that can be used to access multiple DBMSs. All development tools at the time of this writing (to my knowledge) have the latter: a common, database-independent API. Thus every development tool developer must invent such an API or use some other standard API such as ODBC.

■ **Developers need application prototyping that allows access to multiple DBMSs.**   A developer writing an application that is to be deployed in a client/server environment will find that the development process is simplified if he or she can use a local data store (such as dBASE) to prototype the overall structure of the application and then retarget the application to the client/server system (for example, Microsoft SQL Server) later. Again, it would certainly be possible to write to one API for the local data store and to another when the move to the client/server system is made, but this is a difficult and cumbersome process at best. It is far better to have a single API, with a consistent model but different implementations underneath, so that the number of changes the application has to make when the target DBMS changes is minimized.

■ **Developers of distributed applications need access to multiple DBMSs.** A similar situation exists for distributed applications in which both a local and a server-based data store are used in the final production system. This arrangement is becoming more commonplace as data is collected in the field on notebook computers and PDAs and then resynchronized with data on corporate servers at night. This situation is also an issue for wide area networking environments in which changes to data must propagate to different DBMSs on different platforms. While the solution is more properly achieved with replication, an API common to multiple data sources can make this technical challenge less daunting when multiple DBMSs are involved.[4]

■ **Developers require full functionality and high performance.** Application developers need a standard programming interface that is not restricted to a "lowest common denominator" approach—that is, it is important that applications not be forced to use only the features common to all DBMS products. The consistent feedback

---

GLOSSARY

Distributed application An application whose components exist in multiple computers within an organization or that uses data stored in more than one computer.

PDA (personal digital assistant) A handheld personal computer not much larger than a calculator. The Apple Newton and Motorola Envoy are PDAs.

Replication The copying of data from one computer to another so that changes made to the data on one computer are made on other computers, and vice versa.

---

4. One example of this is Microsoft SQL Server 6, which uses ODBC as the underlying API for its replication services. Another is the Oracle Transparent Gateway (announced in early 1995), which supports distributed application development and uses ODBC to access other UNIX DBMS products.

from developers is that *they* need to be the ones who will make the choice about how interoperable their applications will be. The choice should not be predetermined by the architecture or programming interface of the database connectivity solution. Therefore, any solution has to allow all the functionality and features of any given DBMS to be exploited, even if using some features would mean that the application might not work with a different DBMS.

1.2.3 The DBMS Vendor's Perspective

On the one hand, DBMS vendors (companies such as Oracle, Sybase, IBM, and Microsoft that produce DBMS products) see some value in the notion of database connectivity to help meet the increasing need to support things like distributed, heterogeneous query processing (for example, the processing of join tables from DB2, Oracle, and Microsoft SQL Server in a single query). The announcement of the DataJoiner product by IBM in May 1994 is a good indication that there is indeed some interest on the DBMS vendors' part to add distributed database capabilities to their products.

On the other hand, it is hard to justify that there is really a "need" for database connectivity on the client side from the perspective of the DBMS vendors. In fact, quite the opposite is true. Each DBMS vendor wants to be the one and only DBMS for all customers. Once a customer invests in writing to the proprietary interface for the DBMS, that customer tends to be locked in more and more tightly to the DBMS, since changing DBMSs would mean changing programming APIs, which requires another huge development effort on the customer's part. This DBMS-centered view is shown in Figure 1-3.

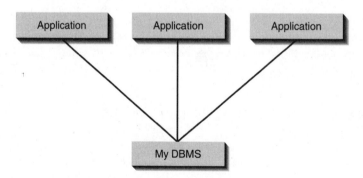

Figure 1-3.
The DBMS vendor's perspective of the need for database connectivity.

The DBMS vendor's perspective is the inverse of the application developer's perspective described in the previous section: the DBMS vendor needs to convince as many developers of applications and development tools as possible to work with its DBMS, which in turn expands the solutions available for the customer.

Given the description above, the needs of the DBMS vendors are defined in the following list:

- **DBMS vendors need to satisfy their customers.** For the DBMS vendors, the "need" for database connectivity really comes from other quarters: their customers. It is the customers themselves who either have multiple DBMSs already installed or don't want to be locked into a single DBMS vendor's database, native programming interface, or development tools. Second, the promise of client/server computing brings with it the idea that applications are separate from the database server, so users expect to be able to choose applications and application development tools as well as database servers, even if those software components are from different vendors. The prospect of choosing particular tools for particular needs is appealing—pick the best report writer, the best forms tool, and so forth. When a wealth of tools is available for a particular DBMS, that system becomes more attractive to customers. Thus the DBMS vendors are motivated to get many applications to work with their DBMSs. As I stated earlier, each DBMS vendor prefers applications to accomplish this with its DBMS's native API. But since that "lock-in" approach isn't desirable from the customer's perspective, it ends up being in the best interest of the DBMS vendors to support a database connectivity solution.

- **DBMS vendors need to comply with standards.** Another important issue for DBMS vendors is that of standards compliance. Most DBMS vendors want to comply with American (ANSI) and international (ISO) database standards for the simple business reason that U.S. government agencies (and in many cases customers outside the United States) require vendors to comply with these standards if they want to bid on contracts. In the case of the SQL standard, the DBMS vendors seek to influence the standard both to enhance its usefulness from a purely technical perspective and to champion the cause of their own technical agendas. The call level interface is just another example of an area in which DBMS vendors need to be involved, precisely because someday a government agency might mandate compliance to it. The "need," therefore, is to ensure that the interface is technically adequate and that the DBMS vendors' interests are met so that vendors can effectively bid on contracts.

■ **DBMS vendors need to reduce "API war" marketing.** Rather than trying to evangelize the ISV community to write to a DBMS's native API, why shouldn't DBMS vendors share the evangelism effort with the rest of the industry by supporting a standard database connectivity interface? That way, the DBMS vendors can focus on, and compete on, server features and performance, which is more at the core of their business anyway. In this type of environment, the DBMS vendors would gain some economies of scale from a marketing perspective. Ultimately, because of the number of applications that want to use a common API, it is in the best interest of each DBMS vendor to ensure that its product has a good implementation of the API so that the applications will work with the product.

1.3 A Design Overview of ODBC

To conclude this chapter, I'll cover a few of the major design points of ODBC. The points raised here are very high-level and address many of the needs described in the previous section; the details of how ODBC meets these needs will be covered in later chapters as we delve further into how ODBC works.

1.3.1 ODBC Is a Programming Interface That Uses SQL

One of the basic questions a database application must address is how the application will specify to the DBMS the data that is to be used and how that data is to be manipulated. From its earliest days, the design of ODBC rested heavily on the assumption that SQL (structured query language) would be widely supported by DBMS vendors. However, it wasn't only SQL by itself that was important, but the whole idea of the relational data model—that is, that data can be described by the simple abstraction of tables with rows and columns and that relationships between tables can be described by the values that match in related columns. With only those concepts, it is possible to model almost any kind of data and its interrelationships.

When the intent is to try to access all kinds of data—even data in formats that are not considered relational or that don't support SQL—it is important to have an underlying model that can support the most generality possible. This simple model of tables, rows, and columns succeeds in almost every case. Why? Because even if the data source isn't a relational database, the data items can be represented as a list with rows and columns of data, in which each row has the same number and type of columns but contains different values. In the most general case, even a single data value can be represented as a table with one row and one column. Once this is understood, it is a short step to recognizing that SQL could be implemented "on top of" almost any kind of data source and thus the data source could be accessed just as any traditional SQL database would be accessed. Literally anything that can be represented as a set of rows and columns can be accessed via SQL (although only a subset of the entire language might be appropriate). Even things that aren't usually considered databases, such as plain text files, can fit into this model.

Because SQL is a language, it is more extensible than non-language–based solutions. That is, it is much easier to execute a statement with a new keyword or type of expression than it is to recode an application to use a new kind of data structure.

1.3.2 ODBC Shields Application Writers from the Complexity of Connecting to a Data Source

A second basic question for application writers is how the user can access a DBMS if it is running on another machine across a network. Application writers and users quickly encounter a formidable amount of complexity when they try to determine how to configure and manage the myriad networking topologies, naming conventions, and what we generally call the "plumbing" of getting computer A and computer B to talk to each other.

GLOSSARY

SQL (structured query language) A language used by nearly every commercially available DBMS for the retrieval and manipulation of data.

ODBC shields application programmers from the details of the underlying database and communications software needed to access the target data. ODBC defines an abstraction called a "data source," which is a name that should have meaning to the end user (for example, "Personnel," "Sales," or "Inventory"). ODBC maps this name to the appropriate implementation (called a "driver" by ODBC), network software, server name or address, and context within the DBMS. When security information such as user ID and password is required, ODBC is flexible enough to either prompt the user directly or allow the application programmer to display the necessary prompts. The goal was to make it easy for the application programmer to get the end user connected to the appropriate source of data without having to become a networking expert.

1.3.3 The ODBC Architecture Allows Multiple Applications to Access Multiple Data Sources

A third basic question is how a single application can use data sources of various types without having to be recompiled for each type of data source and, similarly, how multiple applications can use the same data source at the same time. The answer to the first half of this question lies in using Windows dynamic-link libraries (DLLs), which can be loaded at runtime. To use a different type of data source, the user must simply install a new DLL.

To support multiple concurrent applications, to provide concurrent access to multiple drivers, and to support the "data source" abstraction defined above, ODBC defines an architecture that consists of applications, a Driver Manager, ODBC *drivers* (implementations of the ODBC API that support a particular DBMS), any necessary networking software to enable access across the network to the DBMS, and finally the DBMS itself. Figure 1-4 depicts the ODBC architecture with some example applications and ODBC drivers.

It is the ODBC Driver Manager that provides the linkage between the applications and the drivers, allowing many applications to access data through many drivers. The Driver Manager loads and unloads one or more drivers on behalf of one or more applications. When an application needs to access a data source, the Driver Manager loads the correct driver by looking up its filename using the data source name specified by the application. The Driver Manager determines the ODBC function calls that are supported by the driver and saves their memory addresses in a table. When an application calls a function in a driver, the Driver Manager determines to which driver the function call should be routed and calls it. In this way, multiple drivers can be managed simultaneously and the application programmer doesn't

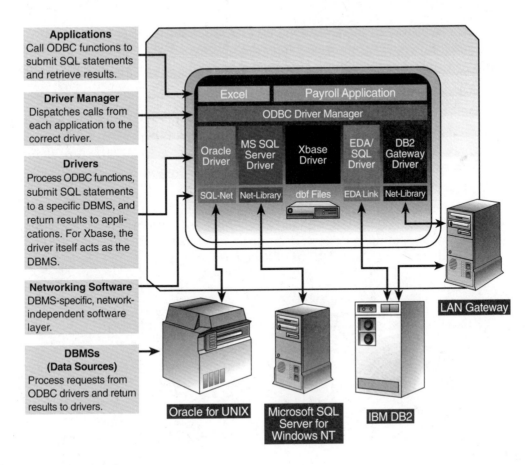

Applications
Call ODBC functions to submit SQL statements and retrieve results.

Driver Manager
Dispatches calls from each application to the correct driver.

Drivers
Process ODBC functions, submit SQL statements to a specific DBMS, and return results to applications. For Xbase, the driver itself acts as the DBMS.

Networking Software
DBMS-specific, network-independent software layer.

DBMSs (Data Sources)
Process requests from ODBC drivers and return results to drivers.

Figure 1-4.
ODBC architecture.[5]

have to be bothered with the details of managing each driver. Also, an application can use ODBC at the same time as another without having to be aware of it.

1.3.4   ODBC Provides an "Adaptive" Programming Model

The final basic question we will cover here is how to let ODBC provide functionality that can be used with all DBMSs while still allowing an application to exploit the capabilities of a single DBMS. The answer is to provide interrogation functions that an application can use to determine a DBMS's capabilities

---

5. Although ODBC could support such a frightfully well-connected PC, no one in their right mind would actually have a real-world need to connect two applications to five data sources simultaneously. It's a great marketing slide, though!

dynamically. The interrogation functions allow an application to ask a driver whether certain features are supported in the DBMS. The application programmer can then choose which capabilities to use either by hard-coding choices at development time or by coding the application to make these choices at runtime.

For example, a graphical query-building application could ask a driver if outer joins are supported and, if so, could allow the user to select a type of join (inner vs. outer) or, if not, could disable a menu item. There are almost 100 different options and settings that ODBC allows an application to ask a particular DBMS about.

In summary, ODBC frees application programmers from having to code their applications to different programming interfaces when access or portability to multiple DBMSs is required. The alternative—coding to each DBMS vendor's native API—is depicted in Figure 1-5.

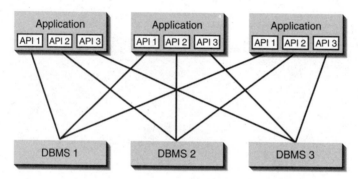

Figure 1-5.
Accessing multiple DBMSs without ODBC.

ODBC simplifies the "API confusion" by providing a single programming interface for multiple DBMSs, as shown in Figure 1-6.

Now you have seen some of the problems that ODBC was designed to address and have had an overview of the ODBC design philosophy. In the next two chapters, we're going to explore some of the technical characteristics of different kinds of DBMSs in order to set the stage for a more complete look at ODBC's architecture.

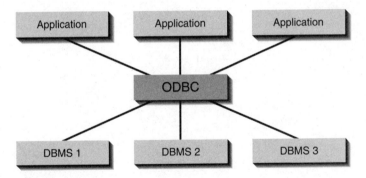

Figure 1-6.
Accessing multiple DBMSs with ODBC.

REFERENCES

Richard D. Hackathorn. *Enterprise Database Connectivity.* Wiley & Sons, 1993. This book is a must for anyone wanting to get the big-picture view of database connectivity (of which ODBC is just one small piece).

Jim Melton and Alan R. Simon. *Understanding the New SQL: A Complete Guide.* Morgan Kaufman Publishers, 1993. This book is a wealth of practical information for anyone interested in the SQL-92 standard. I mention it here mostly for its Appendix F, which has an excellent description of national and international standards organizations.

C H A P T E R   T W O

Database Architectures and Programming Models

This chapter departs a bit from the discussion of ODBC to provide some background material you'll need to gain a complete understanding of the ODBC technology: a description of current database technologies and their associated programming models. Recall that in Chapter 1 we identified the need for a standard database API to work with a broad range of DBMSs. (And let me emphasize that by DBMSs I mean not just traditional products such as Oracle but also desktop database products such as FoxPro and Paradox.) Clearly an attempt to design an API to access "all data" is a tall order. In this chapter we look into some of the different styles of data access that ODBC's designers had to take into consideration.

Specifically, in this chapter we look at the architectures of three broad categories of database products[1] and the application programming model for the underlying architecture in each category. The three categories are:

- Traditional relational DBMSs such as Microsoft SQL Server, Oracle, DB2, RDB, Informix, and Ingres

---

1. Actually, some of the products in these categories are not strictly "database products." In practice, a database can be nothing more than a tabular list in a simple text file, spreadsheet, or word processing document. If the data has a consistent format of rows and columns, it can be treated like a table in a relational database.

■ File management systems (simple flat files) and the additions made to them to provide better data access capabilities (ISAMs)

■ Desktop databases such as Microsoft Access, dBASE, FoxPro, and Paradox

In the descriptions of these models, this chapter demonstrates how the programming models for each category show a definite preference for certain kinds of functionality at the expense of others. Finally, this chapter discusses the impact these different architectures had on the design of ODBC and how ODBC supports (or does not support) certain features of each programming model.

2.1 Traditional Relational DBMSs

For the purposes of this topic we will use a simplified description of traditional relational database system and application architecture consisting of the following six components.[2] The structure is shown in Figure 2-1.

■ **User interface.** What the end user sees on the screen.

■ **Application.** The software that performs specific tasks on behalf of the end user. It uses the database API to accomplish data access tasks. The application is also responsible for interacting with the end user by providing the user interface.

■ **Database API.** The code that interacts with the DBMS. Usually the database API provides some way of delivering SQL statements to the DBMS and returning results to the application. ODBC is a database API, as are Oracle OCI, Sybase DB-Library, and embedded SQL.

GLOSSARY

ISAM (indexed sequential access method) An embellishment to a simple sequential disk file that adds an index or indexes to expedite searching and sorting on columns of data.

---

2. For a less simplified view of system architecture, see Chapter 4 of Richard D. Hackathorn's *Enterprise Database Connectivity* (Wiley & Sons, 1993), in which he describes eight components rather than the six presented here.

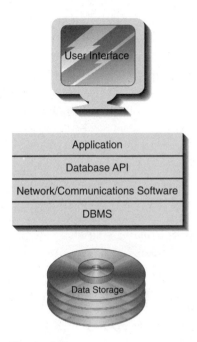

Figure 2-1.
Traditional relational database system architecture.

■ **Network/communications software.** The software that enables two physically separate computers to communicate with each other. Included in this category is the software for local area networks, wide area networks (such as phone lines), and terminal emulation. There are typically many layers of software and many underlying protocols in this component, but we're not concerned with them in this book. The interface between the database API and the network/communications component does (generally speaking) little more than open and close a connection to another computer and read and write a stream of information across that connection. (There is, of course, a network/communications component on all computers connected to each other, but in this book I usually show the network/communications component only when its presence pertains to the discussion.)

■ **DBMS.** Software that executes commands to access the data in data storage. Usually a DBMS includes an SQL parser, an optimizer, an execution module, and many other components that provide data management services (for example, security, transactions, and recovery). Sometimes referred to as simply "the server," the DBMS is usually what we think of when we refer to Microsoft SQL Server running on Microsoft Windows NT, Oracle running on UNIX, or DB2 running on MVS. I use the term DBMS again later in the discussion of desktop database products. Desktop DBMSs such as FoxPro, Microsoft Access, and Paradox also execute commands but lack many of the sophisticated means found in the products mentioned above for handling multiple concurrent users, transactions, and other features.

■ **Data storage.** Where the actual data is stored; typically a hard disk.

The next few pages describe two computing systems in which the preceding six components are used and how the two systems differ. The descriptions are pretty high-level, but the impact of the systems' designs on the database API and on ODBC's design will become clear when we go through the programming models for each.

2.1.1 Centralized Systems (Usually Mainframes)

The typical architecture of a relational DBMS on a mainframe is very centralized. The application, database API, DBMS, and data storage share the same resources (CPU, memory, and disk). Applications interact with the end user via terminals connected to the mainframe. The terminals are usually limited to a character-based display of information. This structure is depicted in Figure 2-2.

In this architecture there is effectively no way to use the graphical user interface (GUI) capabilities and processing power of the PC (if the terminal is indeed a PC). The mainframe is the sole source of computing power. The terminal protocol is limited to screen-painting primitives, such as those that move the cursor to a specified position on the screen, paint characters, and send keystrokes to the mainframe.[3] For database applications, however, this

---

GLOSSARY

Terminal protocol The information that flows between a terminal and a mainframe. Popular terminals and their associated protocols include VT 100, VT 52, and IBM 3270.

---

3. That's why you see the network/communications software component grayed in Figure 2-2. Generally the functionality for handling the terminal protocol is built into the hardware of the terminal; there is no general-purpose CPU that can execute a communications module.

architecture offers some real advantages: there is no networking to worry about, and the application and the DBMS can work closely together to support very high performance via static SQL. (See section 2.1.3.1 for a description of static SQL.)

The tight coupling of the application with the DBMS generally makes portability of such an application to another DBMS difficult, but the performance benefits of this arrangement are numerous. ODBC was not designed to work in this type of architecture, although it can be used with an architecture in which the mainframe is treated as a great big DBMS machine that does not run the application. Separating applications from the DBMS is one fundamental part of ODBC and, in fact, of client/server systems in general. Let's look at those next.

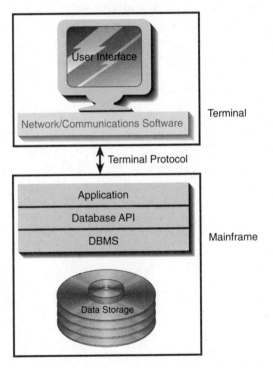

Figure 2-2.
Mainframe database system architecture.

2.1.2 Client/Server Systems

As with mainframe systems, each client/server system uses a centralized DBMS on (typically) one computer. The DBMS is responsible for processing SQL statements and accessing the data. But a client/server system differs from a mainframe in that it places the application program and the database API on a separate computer and uses the network to connect to the DBMS.

The key point is that the application program is now separate from the DBMS—it has separate memory, its own processor, and usually its own local hard disk. It communicates with the DBMS across the network with a stream of information known as the *data protocol,* which is simply an encoded form of the SQL request and result data that flows between the two computers. The user interface component is also managed separately from the computer that runs the DBMS. The computer that runs the application, provides the user interface, and uses the database API is usually called the *client.* The computer that runs the DBMS is called the *server.* Figure 2-3 depicts the six components we started with arrayed in a client/server system.

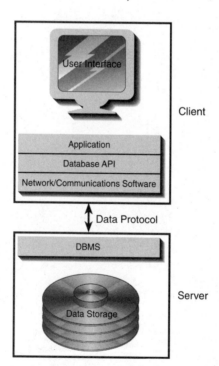

Figure 2-3.
Client/server system architecture.

Figure 2-4 shows some specific examples of DBMSs and the components that fit into this model.

Virtually every relational DBMS can be divided into such a client/server architecture. This could even include mainframe systems, if, as I stated at the end of the last section, they are treated as only DBMS machines and not as computers that run application code.

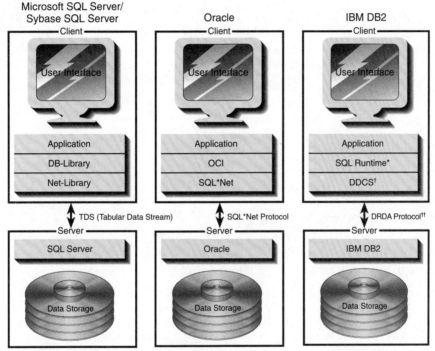

*   Until recently, most applications using IBM DBMSs used embedded SQL (see section 2.1.3.1), as shown here. Now IBM also has a CLI (see section 2.1.3.2). IBM's CLI equivalent to DB-Library and OCI is actually based on ODBC. When the CLI is used, IBM's SQL Runtime and the IBM CLI have a special peer-to-peer relationship that is not shown here.

†   The DDCS (Distributed Database Connection Services) component is used only for OS/2 and UNIX clients. Otherwise, the network/communications software is considered to be part of SQL Runtime.

†† IBM also supports a kind of DRDA "lite" called DB2RA. It is typically used when an IBM mainframe is not the client or server. For example, if the server in this diagram was DB2 for MVS running on the mainframe, DRDA would be used, but if the server was DB2 for OS/2 or DB2 for AIX, DB2RA would typically be used.

Figure 2-4.
Three examples of client/server architecture.

One fundamental point you should note from this discussion with re-gard to designing a standard database API is that the method of interaction between the application and the DBMS in these systems is via SQL. The programming models might use SQL in very different ways (as we'll see in the next section), but in all models the DBMS processes SQL statements and sends results (status information, errors, and data) to applications.

2.1.3 Programming Models for Relational Systems

The design of ODBC was heavily influenced by the SQL standards and the commercial implementations of SQL DBMSs. In this section we look at the programming models for database access found in the SQL standards and in most DBMS products. These models are viable alternatives to ODBC. Along the way I mention how each programming model influenced ODBC and how ODBC compares to it. Specifically, we look at three programming models: embedded SQL, call level interfaces (CLIs), and fourth-generation languages (4GLs).

2.1.3.1 Embedded SQL

The term *embedded SQL* refers to SQL statements that are embedded in another programming language, such as C or COBOL. The programming language is called the *host language* in the SQL standard. (The latest SQL standard, which is called SQL-92, has "embeddings" for seven languages: C, COBOL, FORTRAN, Ada, PL/I, Pascal, and MUMPS.) This embedding is necessary because the SQL language is not a complete programming language by itself. For example, standard SQL does not have any constructs for flow of control (such as if-then-else statements, looping constructs, and goto statements). However, adding these extensions to SQL is a current work item for the next SQL standard. As an aside, some products have implemented flow-of-control extensions to their SQL dialect, most notably Sybase and Oracle, the latter with version 7. However, SQL statements are more typically used to perform data access functionality and are intermixed with a third-generation programming language (3GL) such as the seven mentioned above for all other application tasks. Before any application code containing embedded SQL can be compiled, it must be precompiled so that the embedded SQL can be converted into something that will be syntactically valid for the host programming language. In most cases, the embedded SQL is translated into function calls to the runtime library of the DBMS's proprietary programming interface.

Embedded SQL has two main forms that are widely implemented: *static* and *dynamic*. In static SQL all of the SQL statements are defined at the time the application program is written. That is, the structure of the SQL statements does not change (is "static") while the application is running. In dynamic SQL, on the other hand, the SQL statements can be constructed "dynamically" by the application at runtime. There is also a small extension to dynamic SQL called *extended dynamic SQL* that adds one more feature to dynamic SQL.

Unfortunately, the terms "static SQL" and "dynamic SQL" are not consistently used and can be very confusing. For example, you won't find the term "static SQL" anywhere in the SQL standard—static SQL is usually considered to be just plain SQL, and dynamic SQL is an extension that appeared for the first time in the SQL-92 standard. However, many products had dynamic SQL capabilities long before the SQL-92 standard was published. Confusion also exists because some products implement static SQL in different ways. For example, IBM supports static SQL by binding the SQL statements to the database at compile time, whereas Oracle actually processes the SQL statements dynamically at runtime. However, both programming models are of the static SQL type. Perfectly clear, right? The examples below will attempt to dispel the confusion.

Static SQL   As mentioned, in static SQL all the SQL statements are defined at the time the application program is written. It is possible to change such things as a comparison value within an SQL statement, but not the structure of the statement itself. For example, you could not add a table to or remove a column from the SQL statement, nor could you add another condition.

Getting data to and from the database into variables in the programming language and performing comparisons that involve programming language variables and SQL expressions are accomplished using *host variables*. Host variables are known to both the host language compiler and the SQL precompiler. They are declared in a special section of the code so that the precompiler knows their names and types. Within an SQL statement, each host variable is preceded by a colon so that the appropriate substitution of the value of the variable can be made at runtime.

Figure 2-5 on the following page shows an example of an embedded SQL program written in C. As with all "toy" examples, a lot of detail is left out, but this example is complete enough to show the main concepts. The example program inserts two rows into a hypothetical employee table called EMP, which has columns for employee name and department number. After the two employee rows are inserted, all rows matching one department number are retrieved. Note how the host variables DEPT, NAME, and DNUM are used in lines 19, 23, and 27.

```
1   /* Declare host variables */
2   EXEC SQL BEGIN DECLARE SECTION;
3   short DEPT;
4   char NAME[26];
5   short DNUM;
6   EXEC SQL END DECLARE SECTION;
7    /* Include error handling code */
8    /* SQLCA stands for SQL Communications Area */
9   EXEC SQL INCLUDE SQLCA;
10
11  main()
12  {
13  /* Insert some data into the sample table */
14  EXEC SQL INSERT INTO EMP VALUES ('JOE', 100);
15  EXEC SQL INSERT INTO EMP VALUES ('SALLY', 100);
16  EXEC SQL COMMIT WORK;
17
18  /* Prompt user for department number to look at */
19  GetInput(&DEPT);
20
21  /* Show all rows matching input department number */
22  EXEC SQL DECLARE C1 CURSOR FOR
23      SELECT EMPNAME, DEPTNO FROM EMP WHERE DEPTNO = :DEPT;
24  EXEC SQL OPEN C1
25  while (SQLCODE == 0)
26      {
27      EXEC SQL FETCH C1 INTO :NAME, :DNUM
28      }
29  EXEC SQL CLOSE C1
30  } /* main() */
```

Figure 2-5.
Embedded SQL in C.

To see how an embedded static SQL program really works, let's take a look at what happens with the application and the database.

Step 1: The Application Is Precompiled and Compiled   An embedded SQL application is compiled in two stages: first the application is precompiled by the precompiler provided by the DBMS vendor, and then the output of the precompiler is compiled by the normal compiler for the host programming language.[4] The output of the precompiler is the same as the original

---

4. Some development tools integrate these two stages, but two transformations are still performed on the original source code.

program, but the embedded SQL statements (every line that begins with EXEC SQL) are replaced by function calls to the runtime library provided by the DBMS vendor.

Precompilation is handled quite differently by different vendors. Take IBM and Oracle, for example. IBM's precompiler actually makes a connection to the DBMS, and the precompiler and DBMS interact in several ways:

1. The syntax of the SQL statements is sent to the DBMS and checked by the DBMS's parser. Errors are returned just as if there was a syntax error in the original application program.

2. The semantics of the SQL statements are checked by the DBMS. The DBMS verifies that any table names referenced actually exist in the database, that the column names of the referenced tables are correct, that the user has the necessary privileges to perform the operation specified (although this step can be deferred until execution time), and that the data types of the host variables are compatible with the columns referenced. (For example, the DBMS makes sure that a floating-point host variable isn't being compared or assigned to a character column.) The DBMS usually performs these steps by querying the system tables (sometimes called the *catalog*) to check for the table and column names and their associated data type information.

3. If the SQL statements don't have errors, they are optimized for maximum performance. The SQL optimizer decides how it will execute each statement by determining which indexes to use, the order in which to perform operations, which algorithms to use to access the data, and so on. The optimizer then uses this information to generate an *access plan*. The access plan is stored in the database itself, and the SQL text is for all practical purposes not used again.

4. Back in the application code, the relevant sections of the access plan are stored as arguments of the function calls generated by the precompiler. At runtime, then, the only things passed to the DBMS for each SQL statement from the application are a message that tells the DBMS to execute a section of the access plan and the value of any host variables used in the statement.

This complete process is shown in Figure 2-6 on the following page.

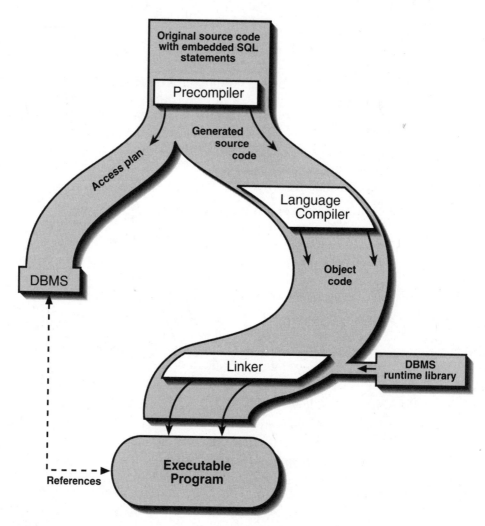

Figure 2-6.
Building an application with embedded static SQL (IBM).

Figure 2-7 shows some of the generated output from the IBM DB2/6000 precompiler given the program shown in Figure 2-5. I have removed some of the code to focus on the main issues. Note how the original embedded SQL statements are retained as comments in the generated source code.

```
1   /* EXEC SQL BEGIN DECLARE SECTION; */
2     short DEPT;
3     char NAME[26];
```

Figure 2-7.
Output from IBM DB2/6000 precompiler.

Figure 2-7. *continued*

```
4    short DNUM;
5   /* EXEC SQL END DECLARE SECTION; */
6    /* Include error handling code */
7    /* SQLCA stands for SQL Communications Area */
8   /* EXEC SQL INCLUDE SQLCA; */
9   #include "sqlca.h"
10   struct sqlca sqlca;
11    main()
12    {
13    /* Insert some data into the sample table */
14   /* EXEC SQL INSERT INTO EMP VALUES ('JOE', 100); */
15    {
16      sqlastrt(sqla_program_id, &sqla_rtinfo, &sqlca);
17      sqlacall((unsigned short)24,2,0,0,0L);
18      sqlastop(0L);
19    }
20   /* EXEC SQL INSERT INTO EMP VALUES ('SALLY', 100); */
21    {
22      sqlastrt(sqla_program_id, &sqla_rtinfo, &sqlca);
23      sqlacall((unsigned short)24,3,0,0,0L);
24      sqlastop(0L);
25    }
26   /* EXEC SQL COMMIT WORK; */
27    {
28      sqlastrt(sqla_program_id, &sqla_rtinfo, &sqlca);
29      sqlacall((unsigned short)21,0,0,0,0L);
30      sqlastop(0L);
31    }
32    /* Prompt user for department number to look at */
33    GetInput(&DEPT);
34    /* Show all rows matching input department number */
35   /* EXEC SQL DECLARE C1 CURSOR FOR
36       SELECT EMPNAME, DEPTNO FROM EMP WHERE DEPTNO = :DEPT; */
37   /* EXEC SQL OPEN C1; */
38    {
39      sqlastrt(sqla_program_id, &sqla_rtinfo, &sqlca);
40      sqlaaloc(2,1,1,0L);
41        {
42          struct sqla_setd_list sql_setdlist[1];
43          sql_setdlist[0].sqltype = 500; sql_setdlist[0].sqllen = 2;
44          sql_setdlist[0].sqldata = (void*)&DEPT;
45          sql_setdlist[0].sqlind = 0L;
46          sqlasetd(2,0,1,sql_setdlist,0L);
47        }
```

(continued)

35

Figure 2-7. *continued*

```
48      sqlacall((unsigned short)26,5,2,0,0L);
49      sqlastop(0L);
50  }
51    while (SQLCODE == 0)
52      {
53  /* EXEC SQL FETCH C1 INTO :NAME, :DNUM; */
54  {
55      sqlastrt(sqla_program_id, &sqla_rtinfo, &sqlca);
56      sqlaaloc(3,2,2,0L);
57        {
58          struct sqla_setd_list sql_setdlist[2];
59          sql_setdlist[0].sqltype = 460; sql_setdlist[0].sqllen = 26;
60          sql_setdlist[0].sqldata = NAME;
61          sql_setdlist[0].sqlind = 0L;
62          sql_setdlist[1].sqltype = 500; sql_setdlist[1].sqllen = 2;
63          sql_setdlist[1].sqldata = &DNUM;
64          sql_setdlist[1].sqlind = 0L;
65          sqlasetd(3,0,2,sql_setdlist,0L);
66        }
67      sqlacall((unsigned short)25,5,0,3,0L);
68      sqlastop(0L);
69  }
70      }
71    } /* main() */
```

Lines 17, 23, and 48 are the function calls that actually execute the statements. Note that there is no SQL text anywhere in these functions, but instead there are integer values that specify the access plan number and the section within the access plan for the particular statement being executed. In a sense, this IBM model makes the application an extension of the DBMS itself because the SQL part of the application is stored in the DBMS and referenced only by number at runtime.

If we build this same application with Oracle, the generated source code from the precompiler is very different from that of the IBM example. The Oracle example differs in that there is no generation of an access plan at compile time. Instead, the SQL strings themselves are stored in the generated code from the precompiler and are sent to the DBMS at runtime. Figure 2-8 shows the output from the precompiler using Oracle's Pro*C 2.1.1. This precompiler is available with release 7.2 of the Oracle DBMS. This output was precompiled on SunOS 4.1.3. As with the previous example, I have removed or rearranged some of the generated code for clarity and to make the comparison to the IBM example easier.

```
1   /* EXEC SQL BEGIN DECLARE SECTION; */
2      short DEPT;
3      char NAME[26];
4      short DNUM;
5   /* EXEC SQL END DECLARE SECTION; */
6    /* Include error handling code */
7    /* SQLCA stands for SQL Communications Area) */
8   /* EXEC SQL INCLUDE SQLCA;
9    (SQLCA header file goes here)
10   */
11  static const char *sq0004 =
12      "select EMPNAME ,DEPTNO  from EMP where DEPTNO=:b0";
13  main()
14  {
15     /* Insert some data into sample table */
16     /* EXEC SQL INSERT INTO EMP VALUES ('JOE', 100); */
17  {
18     sqlstm.stmt = "insert into EMP values ('JOE',100)";
19     sqlstm.iters = (unsigned int  )1;
20     sqlstm.offset = (unsigned int  )2;
21     sqlstm.cud = sqlcud0;
22     sqlstm.sqlest = (unsigned char  *)&sqlca;
23     sqlstm.sqlety = (unsigned short)0;
24     sqlcex(&sqlctx, &sqlstm, &sqlfpn);
25  }
26       /* EXEC SQL INSERT INTO EMP VALUES ('SALLY', 100); */
27  {
28     sqlstm.stmt = "insert into EMP values ('SALLY',100)";
29     sqlstm.iters = (unsigned int  )1;
30     sqlstm.offset = (unsigned int  )16;
31     sqlstm.cud = sqlcud0;
32     sqlstm.sqlest = (unsigned char  *)&sqlca;
33     sqlstm.sqlety = (unsigned short)0;
34     sqlcex(&sqlctx, &sqlstm, &sqlfpn);
35  }
36       /* EXEC SQL COMMIT WORK; */
37  {
38     sqlstm.iters = (unsigned int  )1;
39     sqlstm.offset = (unsigned int  )30;
40     sqlstm.cud = sqlcud0;
41     sqlstm.sqlest = (unsigned char  *)&sqlca;
42     sqlstm.sqlety = (unsigned short)0;
43     sqlcex(&sqlctx, &sqlstm, &sqlfpn);
44  }
```

Figure 2-8.   *(continued)*

Output from Oracle (version 7.2) precompiler.

Figure 2-8. *continued*

```
45        /* Prompt user for department number to look at */
46      GetInput(&DEPT);
47
48      /* Show all rows matching input department number */
49      /* EXEC SQL DECLARE C1 CURSOR FOR
50          SELECT EMPNAME, DEPTNO FROM EMP WHERE DEPTNO = :DEPT; */
51
52      /* EXEC SQL OPEN C1; */
53      {
54        sqlstm.stmt = sq0004;
55        sqlstm.iters = (unsigned int  )1;
56        sqlstm.offset = (unsigned int  )44;
57        sqlstm.cud = sqlcud0;
58        sqlstm.sqlest = (unsigned char *)&sqlca;
59        sqlstm.sqlety = (unsigned short)0;
60        sqlstm.sqhstv[0] = (unsigned char *)&DEPT;
61        sqlstm.sqhstl[0] = (unsigned int  )2;
62        sqlstm.sqindv[0] = (             short *)0;
63        sqlstm.sqharm[0] = (unsigned int  )0;
64        sqlstm.sqphsv = sqlstm.sqhstv;
65        sqlstm.sqphsl = sqlstm.sqhstl;
66        sqlstm.sqpind = sqlstm.sqindv;
67        sqlstm.sqparm = sqlstm.sqharm;
68        sqlstm.sqparc = sqlstm.sqharc;
69        sqlcex(&sqlctx, &sqlstm, &sqlfpn);
70      }
71
72      while (SQLCODE == 0)
73      {
74          /* EXEC SQL FETCH C1 INTO :NAME, :DNUM; */
75      {
76        sqlstm.iters = (unsigned int  )1;
77        sqlstm.offset = (unsigned int  )62;
78        sqlstm.cud = sqlcud0;
79        sqlstm.sqlest = (unsigned char *)&sqlca;
80        sqlstm.sqlety = (unsigned short)0;
81        sqlstm.sqhstv[0] = (unsigned char *)NAME;
82        sqlstm.sqhstl[0] = (unsigned int  )26;
83        sqlstm.sqindv[0] = (             short *)0;
84        sqlstm.sqharm[0] = (unsigned int  )0;
85        sqlstm.sqhstv[1] = (unsigned char *)&DNUM;
86        sqlstm.sqhstl[1] = (unsigned int  )2;
87        sqlstm.sqindv[1] = (             short *)0;
88        sqlstm.sqharm[1] = (unsigned int  )0;
89        sqlstm.sqphsv = sqlstm.sqhstv;
```

Figure 2-8. *continued*

```
90          sqlstm.sqphsl = sqlstm.sqhstl;
91          sqlstm.sqpind = sqlstm.sqindv;
92          sqlstm.sqparm = sqlstm.sqharm;
93          sqlstm.sqparc = sqlstm.sqharc;
94          sqlcex(&sqlctx, &sqlstm, &sqlfpn);
95  }
96         }
97  } /* main() */
```

You can see in lines 18, 28, and 54 the SQL strings assigned to variables in a structure. In lines 24, 34, and 69 these variables are used in the function call *sqlcex*, which actually executes the statements, sending the SQL text to the Oracle DBMS at runtime for execution.

Step 2: The Application Is Run   As mentioned, at runtime there is quite a contrast between the IBM and Oracle implementations of an embedded SQL application. In the IBM implementation, the work of parsing and optimizing the SQL is done at compile time, whereas in the Oracle implementation, the parsing and optimizing is done at runtime. At runtime, the IBM implementation sends only a reference to the access plan created for that application, whereas the Oracle implementation passes SQL strings. Depending upon the program, passing SQL strings could have a huge effect on the performance of the DBMS and could result in a great deal of information being sent across the network.

I call the IBM implementation "true static SQL." It is a model that cannot be handled by a call level interface unless the DBMS supports stored procedures or something similar (as the IBM DRDA packages do). But I'll say more about this later when we discuss call level interfaces in section 2.1.3.2.

One might conclude from the preceding discussion that IBM's implementation is superior to Oracle's. But it is not that simple, especially in a distributed environment in which different clients need to connect to different servers on a regular basis. True static SQL works best when everything is on the same machine, such as a mainframe. Things get a little more complicated when the application is developed separately from the DBMS. Remember that the precompiler works intimately with the DBMS to verify the SQL, and that with true static SQL this is done at compile time. But what happens when the application is built by another person or another company that doesn't have access to the customer's DBMS? How will the precompiler be able to ask the DBMS to do the usual processing of SQL?

To deal with this more distributed development situation, the IBM implementation requires a separate step, called "binding," which is performed at runtime. In this step, the generation of the access plan is deferred until runtime. However, once the application is bound, it does not need to be bound again unless the program is modified.

In addition to the performance benefits of the static SQL approach, one of the nicest features of embedded SQL is that all the type checking and conversions can be done automatically by the precompiler, and the application doesn't have to do anything explicit (other than declare a host variable of the appropriate type). The other SQL programming models require the application programmer to explicitly describe the types of data at runtime so that the database API will know how to convert the data appropriately. In the static SQL model, the precompiler knows the data types of variables because it is dealing with source code and the associated symbol table, which is similar to what the language compiler will use. And for the IBM implementation in which the DBMS is accessed at compile time, the types of the columns in the database are also known. In this case all the necessary conversions can be supplied by the precompiler in the generated code.

Dynamic SQL   In contrast to static SQL, in dynamic SQL the SQL statements can be constructed *dynamically* by the application at runtime. This approach is necessary when the application doesn't know all the operations it will be required to perform against the database in advance, or when the number of possible combinations of operations is so great that it is easier to build the SQL strings in the program dynamically rather than encode all possible combinations in static SQL. However, even with dynamic SQL the precompiler approach is still used. Instead of host variables, dynamic SQL uses *parameters* that can be embedded within the SQL statements and substituted with values later. (An SQL parameter is a question mark that is used in the same place within the SQL statement as a host variable.) Figure 2-9 shows a sample dynamic SQL program.

```
BEGIN DECLARE SECTION
char SQL[100];
short DEPT;
char NAME[26];
short DNUM;
end declare section
```

Figure 2-9.
Sample dynamic SQL program.

Figure 2-9. *continued*

```
main()
{
EXEC SQL INCLUDE SQLCA;
EXEC SQL INCLUDE SQLDA;

/* Create a simplified employee table */

EXEC SQL CREATE TABLE EMP (EMPNAME CHAR(25), DEPTNO SMALLINT);

if (SQLCODE != 0)
        /* Handle errors... */

strcpy(sql, "INSERT INTO EMP VALUES ('JOE', 100)");
EXEC SQL PREPARE S1 FROM :SQL;
EXEC SQL EXECUTE S1;
strcpy(sql, "INSERT INTO EMP VALUES ('SALLY', 100)");
EXEC SQL PREPARE S1 FROM :SQL;
EXEC SQL EXECUTE S1;
EXEC SQL COMMIT WORK;

/* Prompt user for department number to look at */
DEPT=GetInput(DEPT);

/* Show all rows matching input department number */
strcpy(sql, "SELECT EMPNAME, DEPTNO FROM EMP WHERE DEPTNO = ?");
EXEC SQL PREPARE S1 FROM :SQL;
EXEC SQL DECLARE C1 CURSOR FOR S1;
EXEC SQL OPEN C1 USING :DEPT;
while (SQLCODE == 0)
        {
        EXEC SQL FETCH C1 INTO :NAME, :DNUM;
        }
}
```

Note how the SQL statements themselves (except the DECLARE CURSOR statement) are first placed into program variables and then "prepared" via the PREPARE command in SQL. What happens to these PREPARE statements at runtime is exactly what happens in the static SQL example at compile time: the statements are parsed, checked for syntactic and semantic correctness, and optimized by the database engine; then an access plan is generated within the database. And, as in the static SQL model at compile time, the statements are not actually executed at this point but when either EXECUTE or OPEN is executed.

This example doesn't really show the power of the dynamic SQL approach for ad hoc queries—it is really just a recasting of the first example, which more naturally lends itself to static SQL. An interactive program that allows the user to enter an SQL statement and execute it would provide a better example, but such a program would be too lengthy to show here. For now, it is worthwhile to point out the main differences with respect to these two programming models.

In static SQL the specification of a statement and its execution are indistinguishable (for example, EXEC SQL INSERT INTO EMP VALUES ('JOE', 100) actually does the insertion when this statement is encountered in the program), but in dynamic SQL the specification and execution are done in two explicit steps. In dynamic SQL the PREPARE command is used to specify the SQL statement; then the EXECUTE command executes noncursor operations, or the OPEN command executes a SELECT statement that returns multiple rows.

One of the interesting effects of this two-step process is that the statement, once prepared, can be executed multiple times without having to be prepared again. Remember how in static SQL the access plan is stored in the database at compile time? In the case of dynamic SQL the access plan is generated when the program executes the PREPARE command. Execution speed is identical to that of the static SQL case once the initial PREPARE command has finished. But precisely because there is an explicit command for execution, there is nothing stopping the application from just issuing EXECUTE statements multiple times. It is worth noting that this difference may not be as significant as it first appears. If you put either the static SQL statement *or* a single dynamic SQL EXECUTE statement in a loop (with appropriate conditions to perform the SQL), the effect is exactly the same. Here is a set of examples to illustrate. The following code from the first static SQL example

```
EXEC SQL INSERT INTO EMP VALUES ('JOE', 100);
EXEC SQL INSERT INTO EMP VALUES ('SALLY', 100);
EXEC SQL INSERT INTO EMP VALUES ('BILL', 200);
```

could just as easily be written as

```
while(GetInput(name, &dnum))
    EXEC SQL INSERT INTO EMP VALUES (:name, :dnum)
```

where the function *GetInput* gets the values for name and department number from the user (or from a file or anywhere else). This also assumes that *GetInput* returns TRUE as long as there is more input to process and FALSE when it is finished.

The dynamic SQL version is very similar:

```
EXEC SQL PREPARE S1 FROM "INSERT INTO EMP VALUES (?, ?)"
while(GetInput(name, &dnum))
    EXEC SQL EXECUTE S1 USING :name, :dnum
```

But let's say that we aren't doing insertions, which by their nature do not vary, since the table into which they are being made isn't going to change much. Consider instead a case in which we want to update the employee table in a variety of ways: to make name changes, department changes, and salary increases for all employees in certain departments, for example. The application program will use our *GetInput* function to prompt the user for the kind of update to be done, but this time the return value will also indicate which kind of operation will be done, or it will return 0 when it is finished.

Here is the program fragment in static SQL:

```
while (operation = GetInput(&EMPID, NEWNAME, &DNUM))
    switch (operation) {
        case NEW_NAME:
            EXEC SQL UPDATE EMP SET NAME = :NEWNAME
                WHERE EMPID = :EMPID
        break;
        case NEW_DEPT:
            EXEC SQL UPDATE EMP SET DEPTNO = :DNUM WHERE EMPID = :EMPID;
        break;
        case NEW_SALARY:
            EXEC SQL UPDATE EMP SET SALARY = SALARY * 1.10
                WHERE DEPTNO = :DNUM;
        break;
        case DEL_EMP:
            EXEC SQL DELETE EMP WHERE EMPID = :EMPID
        break;
    }
```

The equivalent dynamic SQL program would be straightforward. But now consider a simple extension: what if the application needs to be able to handle any number of multiple employees and departments with a single statement? For example, for two departments to receive raises, the static SQL statements would be

```
EXEC SQL UPDATE EMP SET SALARY = SALARY * 1.10
    WHERE DEPTNO IN (:DNUM1, :DNUM2);
```

or the slightly less elegant

```
EXEC SQL UPDATE EMP SET SALARY = SALARY * 1.10
    WHERE DEPTNO = :DNUM1 OR DEPTNO = :DNUM2;
```

With three departments, the statements would be

```
EXEC SQL UPDATE EMP SET SALARY = SALARY * 1.10
    WHERE DEPTNO IN (:DNUM1, :DNUM2, :DNUM3);
```

Get the picture? The application program would have to deal with a formulation of the static SQL statement for each possible number of departments or, more likely, pick a maximum and assign the unused department numbers to NULL, resulting in the awkward

```
EXEC SQL UPDATE EMP SET SALARY = SALARY * 1.10
    WHERE DEPTNO IN (:DNUM1, :DNUM2, :DNUM3, :DNUM4, :DNUM5, :DNUM6);
```

Of course, we could simply loop on the update statement and use the same update over and over within a single transaction, but this would increase network traffic and decrease concurrency within the database itself because locks would be held longer. Finally, consider what would happen if we wanted to update another column besides salary or if we wanted to construct a SELECT statement that returned a different set of columns or expressions depending on user input.

Wouldn't it be a lot simpler if the application could simply generate the appropriate SQL based on the actual user input? This is where dynamic SQL can be very handy. For this contrived example, the application could construct an SQL statement with the correct number of parameters, put it in a variable, and then prepare the statement. This requires the use of a data structure called the SQLDA (SQL Descriptor Area), which allows for dynamic numbers of parameters to be described in an SQL statement. The SQLDA is used by most current DBMS products. The SQLDA is populated with values in the same fashion as a normal C structure. It should be noted, however, that SQL-92 contains a more elegant method than the SQLDA: *descriptors* that can be read and written directly from SQL. (See Chapter 9 for more about descriptors.)

The fully generalized use of dynamic SQL allows for almost complete flexibility in generating SQL statements under program control. The SQLDA is used to handle the number and types of data elements in SQL statements. Host variables for input (for example, a comparison in an SQL statement) and output (for example, FETCH INTO :A, :B) are replaced by references to elements in the SQLDA. Dynamic SQL also allows applications to discover the types and lengths of columns (or expressions) that have been output from a query by using the DESCRIBE statement after the query has been prepared. There is an analogous DESCRIBE INPUT statement, which tells the application the number and types of all parameters in an SQL statement after the statement has been prepared, but this, unfortunately, has not been widely implemented.

The point here is that the use of dynamic SQL gives the end user more choices in what can be done. The clearest example of a case in which this is needed is when the end user must make decisions about what operations to do based on information in the database itself. The columns that are available in a sales table; the conditions that are necessary to update, delete, or view the data; and how the information is aggregated are all things that might not be known when an application program is originally built, and it might be impractical to specify static SQL formulations for every possible combination.

This is not to say that static SQL is somehow inferior. Not at all. The choice between the two just depends on how much the application and end user know about the structure of the data and the queries that will need to be executed. If the application programmer needs flexibility, it makes the most sense to use dynamic SQL. On the other hand, if the information is fixed, the application programmer will find the static SQL option to be simpler and better performing.

Cursors in Dynamic SQL   Basic to an understanding of dynamic SQL is an understanding of how cursors are handled. (See the definition of *cursor* at the bottom of this page.) The subject can be confusing because in addition to supporting cursors, the SQL standard also defines a special-purpose method for returning exactly one row to an application, and the terminology of the two methods is often confused. The statement that returns one row only is called a *select statement,* and the statement that returns multiple rows is called a *cursor,* even though both statements use the verb SELECT. The one-row-only statement is commonly referred to by two other names: *singleton select* and *select into.* In embedded SQL, a singleton select statement is of the form

```
SELECT expression_list INTO host_variable_list FROM table_list [WHERE ...]
```

GLOSSARY

Cursor In database terminology, the mechanism that allows the individual rows resulting from a query to a DBMS to be processed one at a time, in a fashion similar to processing records in an ordinary disk file. The mechanism is called a cursor because it indicates the current position in a results set, just as the cursor on a computer screen indicates the current position in, for example, a document.

This statement will return an error if more than one row is returned. The singleton select method is extremely useful for two common application programming tasks: using foreign keys to do lookups in tables and computing aggregates such as grand totals.

For example, in a system set up according to the classic order entry schema of customers, orders, items, and parts, the item table might have a foreign key called PARTNO that references the parts table. To validate a part number that is keyed in and to retrieve the name of the part when a new item for an order is entered, the singleton select statement is very handy:

```
SELECT PARTNAME INTO :PNAME FROM PARTS WHERE PARTNO = :PARTENTRY
```

Because PARTNO is the primary key in the parts table, it is guaranteed to return only one row.

Computing aggregates is also a good use for the singleton select statement:

```
SELECT SUM(SALES), AVG(SALES) INTO :TOTSALES, :AVGSALES FROM SALES
    WHERE REGION = 'NW'
```

The beauty of this SQL statement is that it is concise and is almost as easy to use as an assignment statement in the host programming language. I bring up this particular SQL construct in detail because it is one that the call level interface approach of ODBC does not distinguish from SELECT statements that return multiple rows, although it could by combining some elements of dynamic SQL with the singleton select syntax.[5]

GLOSSARY

Foreign key A column or columns in one table used to reference a unique column or columns in another table to model a one-to-many or one-to-one relationship between the two tables. Typically the column referenced by the foreign key is the primary key of the referenced table.

Primary key A column or columns in a table whose values uniquely identify the rows in that table.

---

5. Those of you already familiar with ODBC programming might be interested to see how this would be done. By replacing host variables in the singleton select syntax with parameters, the semantics can be preserved. For example, the example could be formulated as SELECT SUM(SALES), AVG(SALES) INTO ?, ? FROM SALES WHERE REGION = 'NW' as long as bindings were established for the parameters. The difficulty here is that neither SQL-92 nor any DBMSs to my knowledge support SELECT INTO as a dynamic SQL statement, so the statement would have to be detected by the driver and converted into a form that the DBMS could execute dynamically.

The form of the select statement that returns multiple rows (the cursor statement) is expressed in three steps. In static SQL, first a cursor must be declared:

```
DECLARE C1 CURSOR FOR SELECT A, B, C FROM TABLE WHERE ...
```

Then the cursor must be opened:

```
OPEN C1
```

Then the result rows can be fetched in host variables:

```
FETCH FROM C1 INTO :A, :B, :C
```

When fetching is complete, the cursor must be closed:

```
CLOSE C1
```

In dynamic SQL the SELECT statement doesn't appear as part of the DECLARE CURSOR statement but as part of the PREPARE statement:

```
PREPARE S1 FROM SELECT A, B, C FROM TABLE WHERE ...
```

Then the cursor is declared on the statement identifier:

```
DECLARE C1 CURSOR FOR S1
```

The rest is pretty much the same as the static SQL example, although in actual use the SQLDA would be used in place of the fetch into host variables, since presumably the reason the application is using dynamic SQL in the first place is because the number and types of the output columns were unknown at the time the program was written.

The major point of interest here is that the cursor must still be declared for both static and dynamic SQL and that the cursor name cannot be a host variable. That is, the number of distinct cursors that will be used at any one time in an application program must be known and declared at the time the program is written—*even if it uses dynamic SQL.* Another way of saying this is that the DECLARE CURSOR statement in dynamic SQL is declarative—just like the one in static SQL. For ad hoc query tools especially, this is a severe limitation.

Extended Dynamic SQL   To increase the flexibility of cursors, the SQL-92 standard added another cursor model: *extended dynamic cursors.* The extended dynamic cursor model allows cursors to be declared at runtime rather than at compile time. This is done through the use of the ALLOCATE cursor statement:

```
ALLOCATE cursor_name CURSOR FOR statement_name
```

where *cursor name* and *statement name* are host variables containing strings with a valid cursor name and a prepared statement name, respectively. This is shown in the following example:

```
char * sql;
char * cursor1;

sql = "select a, b, c from table where region = 'NW'";
EXEC SQL PREPARE S1 FROM :sql
cursor1 = "C1";
stmt="S1";
EXEC SQL ALLOCATE :cursor1 CURSOR FOR :stmt
```

Even after all the additions of SQL constructs meant to make cursors more flexible and specifiable at runtime, one thing is still lacking to make cursors completely dynamic under any model we've discussed. Note that it is still necessary for the application program to know what kind of statement is specified in order to know how to execute it. The PREPARE statement is general enough:

```
EXEC SQL PREPARE S1 FROM :sql;
```

But even in the dynamic SQL case, the application has to know whether the statement is a cursor in order to know whether to do

```
EXEC SQL DECLARE C1 CURSOR FOR S1;   /* :sql must contain SELECT */
OPEN C1;
```

or

```
EXEC SQL EXECUTE S1;   /* :sql must be INSERT, UPDATE, DELETE, */
                       /* CREATE, etc. It must NOT be a cursor. */
```

ODBC deviated from this model because there were real-world situations in which it was impossible to know in advance what kind of statement needed to be executed. Some specific situations for which this model would not work are the batched SQL supported by some DBMS vendors and gateway products (for example, MDI's DB2 gateway) and the stored procedure paradigm of Sybase.

Summary   In summary, embedded SQL is particularly well suited to centralized computing environments. True static SQL provides very high performance (with access plans stored in the database at compile time) combined with a nice programming model (with precompilation and the host variables providing a good interface between data from the database and the application program). However, static SQL suffers from the inability to create SQL statements on the fly and is not well suited to targeting different databases dynamically at runtime.

Dynamic SQL extends the flexibility of the embedded SQL paradigm by allowing creation of SQL statements at runtime under program control, although to be truly "dynamic" the application must use the extended dynamic form of cursors. Both static and dynamic SQL require the use of a precompiler.

As a final note, consider one thing we haven't talked about at all that is critical to client/server computing: how an application would actually specify which database it is trying to access. Up until the release of the SQL-92 standard, this was left up to the DBMS vendors to address (usually by means of special function calls), so there was no way to use SQL to specify which data source to connect to. Again, on a centralized computing system such as a mainframe, this is not an issue. However, it is of critical importance when any kind of distributed system is used. SQL-92 provides a new SQL statement called (as you might guess) CONNECT, which adds exactly this functionality. However, CONNECT has not been widely implemented, and therefore application programmers have to learn the idiosyncratic ways in which each DBMS vendor establishes connections when porting applications from one DBMS to another.

2.1.3.2 Call Level Interfaces

A *call level interface* consists of function (or subroutine) calls in a 3GL programming language such as C, COBOL, or FORTRAN. ODBC is a call level interface, as are the native APIs of many DBMSs (for example, Sybase DB-Library and Oracle OCI). At the highest level of abstraction, a call level interface does three basic things:

1. Connects to the DBMS

2. Sends SQL statements to the DBMS

3. Processes results of the SQL statements (data, status information, and errors)

A call level interface works much like the dynamic embedded SQL model except that no precompiler is involved. In one sense, every DBMS vendor supports a call level interface—the precompiler for the DBMS's embedded SQL product generates function calls, right? But as you may have noticed in Figures 2-7 and 2-8, which show the output of the IBM and Oracle precompilers, these interfaces were not intended to be used directly by programmers.[6] True call level interfaces—at least for the purposes of this book—refer to those programming interfaces specifically designed to be used by application programmers.

Many DBMS vendors provide call level interfaces in addition to their embedded SQL interfaces. The programming model for call level interfaces differs from that for embedded SQL in a number of ways:

1. Because there is no precompiler to determine data type information about the variables in the host programming language, all the information about how the data types of output columns and parameters in SQL statements relate to variables in the programming language must be specified explicitly at runtime. This adds more complexity to the programming model but also gives added flexibility and greater control. From an ease-of-programming perspective, using a call level interface is not as easy as using host variables in static SQL, but it is arguably better than forcing everything to go through the SQLDA structure in dynamic SQL.

2. There is a clean separation between the application program and SQL. With embedded SQL there is often some confusion over just which component is processing what. For example, the DECLARE CURSOR statement is declarative and often is never seen by the DBMS. So even though DECLARE CURSOR is an SQL statement, it is never processed by the DBMS. Even with dynamic SQL it can be difficult to determine which SQL statements actually flow to the DBMS. (For example, does the DBMS process the PREPARE statement itself or just the contents of the host variable specified in the statement? Usually it is the latter.) If you are trying to write and debug applications, it helps to have a clear understanding of which component processes what.

---

6. Most people I have talked to who have done a lot of programming with precompilers say they often end up fiddling around with the generated code (or the variables generated by the precompiler) for a variety of reasons. In one case a programmer was using Oracle's precompiler and liked the static SQL programming paradigm but needed the flexibility of dynamic SQL on occasion. So rather than switching to the PREPARE/EXECUTE model, he simply directly modified the variable the precompiler generated to hold the SQL statement. As long as the bindings were the same (as they were in his case), the solution worked well, but only because Oracle was doing everything dynamically under the covers. In this case, it was a real advantage for this application.

3. The process of building a program is simpler than with embedded SQL—calls to the DBMS runtime library are linked in the same way as are calls to other runtime libraries such as the C runtime library. The extra step of preprocessing each program file that contains SQL is eliminated.

4. Debugging is simpler because the code you debug is the code you wrote—not a translation into function calls generated by a precompiler.

Figure 2-10 illustrates the relationship between the call level interface and the DBMS. This figure should look familiar by now; it is the same system architecture diagram we started off with in this chapter, but with the call level interface replacing the database API. And, in fact, that is why ODBC works in this architecture; it can plug in as the call level interface component just as the native API of the DBMS vendor does.

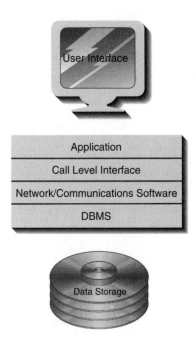

Figure 2-10.
Call level interface architecture.

Figure 2-11 on the following page compares the call level interfaces supported by Sybase (DB-Library) and Oracle (OCI) by showing how each interface would handle the same application. You can see from this example that the two programming models are much more alike than they are different. The functions and data structures have different names, and there are some interesting variances, but on the whole it is easy to see the parallels and how one interface maps to the other.

Sybase DB-Library	Oracle OCI
`#include <sqldb.h>`	`#include <ora.h>`
`main()`	`main()`
`{`	`{`
`DBPROCESS * dbproc;`	`struct csrdef lda;    /* lda area */`
`LOGINREC  *  login;`	`struct csrdef curs;  /* cursor area */`
`int cnt;`	`int cnt;`
`char   *name;`	`char    *name;`
`char   *sql;`	`char    *sql;`
`/* Log on to SQL Server  */`	`/* Log on to Oracle */`
`login = dblogin();`	`olon(&lda, "userid/password", -1, (char *)0, -1, -1);`
`DBSETLUSER(login,"userid");`	
`DBSETLPWD(login, "password");`	
`dbproc = dbopen(login, Servername);`	`oopen(&curs, &lda, (char *)0, -1, -1, (char *)0, -1);`
`/* Select number of orders for customers in Boston */`	`/* Select number of orders for customers in Boston */`

Figure 2-11.   *(continued)*
A comparison of the Sybase and Oracle call level interfaces.

Figure 2-11. *continued*

Sybase DB-Library	Oracle OCI

```
sql="select cname, count(*) from
cust c, ord o where c.id=o.custid
and c.city='Boston' group by
c.cname";

/* Define SQL statement */

dbcmd(dbproc, sql);

/* Bind output column to
variables name and cnt */

dbbind(dbproc, 1, CHARBIND,
sizeof(name), name);



dbbind(dbproc, 2, INTBIND,
sizeof(cnt), &cnt);




/* Execute SQL statement */

dbsqlexec(dbproc);

while (dbresults(dbproc) !=
NO_MORE_RESULTS)   {

/* Fetch rows -- customer name
and count will be put in the
bound variables */

while (dbnextrow(dbproc) !=
NO_MORE_ROWS)  {
    output(name, cnt);
   }
/* dbresults loop*1
dbclose(dbproc);
dbexit();
}
}
```

```
sql="select cname, count(*) from
cust c, ord o where c.id=o.custid
and c.city='Boston' group by
c.cname";

/* Define SQL statement */

osql3(&curs, sql,  -1);

/* Bind output column to
variables name and cnt */

odefin(&curs, 1, (unsigned
char *)name, sizeof(name), INT,
-1,(short *)0, (char *)0, -1,
-1,(short *)0, (short *)0);

odefin(&curs, 2, (unsigned
char *)&cnt, sizeof(cnt), INT,
-1,(short *)0, (char *)0, -1,
-1,(short *)0, (short *)0);

/* Execute SQL statement */

oexec(&curs);




/* Fetch rows -- customer name
and count will be put in the
bound variables */

while (ofetch(&curs))  {

    output(name, cnt);
   }

oclose(curs);
ologof(&lda);

}
```

In Figure 2-11 you can see, as I mentioned earlier, that the bindings between program variables (*name* and *cnt* in this figure) and SQL output columns are declared explicitly with the functions *odefin* (for OCI) and *dbbind*
(for DB-Library). This is unlike the embedded SQL examples, in which the
FETCH can be done directly into the host variables and the application does
not need to call a function to set up the binding. Equally interesting is the fact
that OCI and DB-Library allow an application to retrieve data one column at
a time rather than the entire row (as is required by embedded SQL). This
becomes very important when an application must manage a large amount of
text or binary data that typically must be manipulated in pieces rather than
all at once.

ODBC's designers recognized that all call level interfaces provide a
basic abstraction that defines three high-level elements: connecting, sending
SQL commands, and processing results. Of course, many differences exist
within this broad framework, but sticking to the framework provided ODBC
with a sufficient structure to access numerous databases effectively.

Another important aspect of the call level interface style is that it allows
programmers to use the function call paradigm coupled with dynamic library
linking in Microsoft Windows and other operating systems (for example,
shared libraries in some UNIX systems and in the Macintosh). This allows applications to have multiple implementations of the same set of function calls
executing concurrently.

2.1.3.3 Fourth-Generation Languages, RAD
Tools, or Whatever They Are Called Now

Fourth-generation languages are probably more popular today than they
have ever been, but the term itself is fading and terms such as *RAD tool* (rapid
application development tool) are being used instead. It is also difficult to
determine just what constitutes a 4GL these days, now that some traditional
3GL products have added higher-level tools (such as the Database classes in
Microsoft Visual C++) that provide much of the value of traditional 4GLs.

I use the term 4GL to mean any development tool that uses a language
at some higher level of abstraction than a 3GL (C, Pascal, COBOL, FOR-
TRAN, and so on). So I put today's popular database application development tools such as Microsoft Access, Powersoft's PowerBuilder, and Gupta's
SQL Windows in this category. A 4GL typically has great added value and simplicity when compared to a 3GL because the 4GL is focused on one particular
task. This loss of generality provides great gains in productivity, although

sometimes there can be a loss of control and performance. Often constructs in the 4GL allow programmers to integrate the data access portion of an application with the user interface, which is particularly useful because that is so hard to do in systems like Windows. (You may have noticed that none of the programming examples shown so far provide any way to interact with the screen or the keyboard.) Finally, a 4GL is almost always an interpreted language. It is not reduced to a pure executable program for the native hardware processor; instead, a language processor executes the statements dynamically at runtime.[7] This allows for extremely rapid prototyping at the expense of the highest possible performance at runtime.

Many 4GL products are now on the market. Because of the impressive productivity gains achieved with these tools, many programmers who develop database applications these days use some kind of 4GL tool.

From ODBC's perspective, 4GLs are an interesting layer that should be able to make use of the ODBC API. That is, a 4GL should be able to map its programming paradigm into calls to the ODBC API. Many 4GL tools have done so to date.[8]

Face it: programming in Windows (or in any other GUI) is extremely hard to do with a 3GL such as C. Writing a database application can be done much more quickly by using a 4GL, as long as the developer is aware of the strengths and weaknesses of the 4GL. At least that is the promise. One common scenario experienced by developers using 4GL products is known as "hitting the wall." This happens when you have a considerable amount of the application and database design working and suddenly you need some critical piece of functionality that isn't provided by the development tool or the 4GL. With some tools, you are stuck: you either have to scrap the application or redefine the problem to work around the tool's limitations. Fortunately, most tools provide a way to call through to a 3GL if necessary so that the full power of the system can be exploited. Sometimes this callthrough results in less-than-elegant final code, but it can be necessary to achieve the desired result for the application.

---

7. Microsoft Access, Visual Basic, and FoxPro are examples of products that use interpreted languages. Microsoft Visual C++ and Borland's Delphi, on the other hand, generate source code that is compiled to an executable program that doesn't require a runtime language interpreter.

8. Thumbing quickly through the October 1994 issue of *DBMS* magazine revealed the following vendors and development tools that are using ODBC: Pick Open Database, Neuron Data C/S Elements, Quadbase Systems, Popkin System Architect, Symantec SCALE, Watcom SQL—that's the first half of the issue and my thumb is tired. You get the idea.

The Inside Story
Act I, Scene I: The Beginning

ODBC began as a project whose goal was to solve the problem of accessing data in diverse databases from personal computers, especially personal computers using Microsoft applications. The primary applications in question were Microsoft Excel and what was to become Microsoft Access. In January 1988 I began researching data access issues and found that most Fortune 500 companies had large (minicomputer and mainframe) database systems but an increasing desire to use personal computers to analyze and (to a lesser extent) manipulate their corporate data. At the same time, smaller companies were using desktop database products, flat files, and even spreadsheets to manage tabular data directly on the PC.

All of these diverse sources of data were buried beneath a bewildering array of programming interfaces, data models, and network and communication technologies. Yet the data itself was almost always a collection of tables containing rows and columns that, in principle, could be manipulated by the three core relational database operations: select, project, and join. And it became clear that if Microsoft applications were ever going to be used to manipulate customer data, there had to be a way to access the data that didn't require reprogramming Microsoft Excel or Microsoft Access or other applications every time access to a new data source was needed.

In April 1988 I wrote a first draft specification that described a vision and a model for accessing diverse data sources from Microsoft Excel. The specification proposed the idea of a *database driver* and a common programming interface that effectively separated applications from the database system to be accessed. The term *database connectivity* was coined to describe the technology as a whole.

And then the fun began. As it turned out, Microsoft was not the only company thinking about database connectivity....

2.2 ISAMs

The next programming model we're going to look at is quite different from the SQL-based models described in the previous section. ODBC's mission is to access "all data," not just data in SQL databases, so let's take a high-level look at file management systems and ISAMs (index sequential access methods) and see how they relate to ODBC.

Before we discuss the ISAM architecture and programming model, we will first look at a more primitive model for data access—flat files and file I/O. Once the file I/O model has been explained, the ISAM model will be shown as a series of embellishments.

2.2.1 Flat Files and Simple File I/O

For almost all modern-day database applications, this model represents the "bad old days" of database-oriented applications. To read and write files stored on disk, developers of these types of applications typically use the functions provided with the runtime library of the programming language they are using. The model is quite simple: there are calls to open files, close files, read data, write data, and position to an offset within a file. For C runtime libraries, these calls are shown in the following table:

Functionality	MS-DOS/UNIX Function	Windows Function
Open a file	open	lopen
Close a file	close	lclose
Read bytes	read	lread
Write bytes	write	lwrite
Position to offset within a file	lseek	llseek

This model is intended to provide low-level access to files of unstructured data. There is no concept of rows or columns of data, just a stream of bytes. All of the semantic information about what is contained in the file must be encoded into the application program. For example, if a file contains customer information consisting of the customer's name, address, city, state, and zip code, a C program could be written to assume that this information is stored in a file as shown in Figure 2-12 on the following page.

Name	Address	City	State	Zip Code
Howard Snyder	2732 Baker Blvd.	Eugene	OR	97403
Yoshi Latimer	516 Main St.	Elgin	OR	97827
Jaime Yorres	87 Polk St., Suite 5	San Francisco	CA	94117
Fran Wilson	89 Chiaroscuro Rd.	Portland	OR	97219
Rene Phillips	2743 Bering St.	Anchorage	AK	99508
Paula Wilson	2817 Milton Dr.	Albuquerque	NM	87110
Jose Pavarotti	187 Suffolk Ln.	Boise	ID	83720
Art Braunschweiger	P.O. Box 555	Lander	WY	82520
Liz Nixon	89 Jefferson Way	Portland	OR	97201
Liu Wong	55 Grizzly Peak Rd.	Butte	MT	59701

Figure 2-12.
Sample customer data.

By assuming that each record is 70 bytes long, the C program can move through the records by changing the offset with *lseek* in increments of 70. Individual customer information can be read and written using a structure of the form

```
typedef struct  {
    char name[19];
    char address[26];
    char city[15];
    char state[3];
    char zipcode[5];
    char eoln[2];
} CUSTOMER;
```

and declaring a variable of type CUSTOMER:

```
CUSTOMER cust;
```

Using the primitive C functions mentioned above, it is possible to read all the records with a terse MS-DOS program:

```
main()
{
    int hFile;
    hFile = open("customer", READ);
    while(!eof(hFile))
```

```
        {
        read(hFile, cust, sizeof(CUSTOMER));
        output(cust.name, cust.address, cust.city, cust.state,
                cust.zipcode);
        }
    close(hFile);
}
```

and to position to any record in the file (again using MS-DOS code):

```
printf("\nEnter record number to display (q to quit)\n");
 for (gets(buf); buf[0] != 'q'; gets(buf) )
    {
    recnum = atoi(buf);
    lseek(h,(recnum - 1) * sizeof(CUSTOMER),0);
    cBytesRead = read(h, pcust, sizeof(CUSTOMER));
    printf("%.*s%.*s%.*s%.*s%.*s\n",
       sizeof(cust.name),    cust.name,
       sizeof(cust.address), cust.address,
       sizeof(cust.city),    cust.city,
       sizeof(cust.state),   cust.state,
       sizeof(cust.zipcode), cust.zipcode);
}
```

This is pretty crude stuff, but it shows how easy it is to move around to arbitrary positions both forward and backward within the data—something that most SQL implementations cannot do. But no one these days would seriously consider using such an approach to manage real data. The problems are many and large.

First, because the model requires the application to manage all the semantics of the data, the model doesn't lend itself to flexibility and maintainability. What if you want to make a change to the data format? Write C code. What if you have multiple applications that use this data format (for instance, an order entry application and a reporting application)? You've got a coordination nightmare. This is a graphic example of the need for *data independence* (a fundamental concept in the relational data model). That is, the structure of the physical data should be independent from the application programs that rely on it.

Second, what if you have hundreds or thousands of customers and you need to quickly find a customer by name? A simple solution would be to start at the beginning of the file and look at every record until the correct name is found, but for a large number of records that wouldn't be very efficient. The obvious answer is to keep a separate index into the data so that, given a name, the index could point to the correct record in the file. But that would add a whole new level of complexity to this scheme.

Third, what if you want to manage orders for these customers? You either have to create another file and write a lot of code to manage the relationship between customers and their orders or you have to merge the order information into each customer's data and create a much more complicated file format or repeat a lot of information.

Fourth, what if multiple applications have to access and update this information simultaneously? Nothing would prevent multiple users from overwriting each others' changes, destroying the integrity of the file altogether.

These problems are just the tip of the iceberg, yet 20 to 30 years ago this was how a lot of data management was done.

From the perspective of a standard API, could such data be accessed via the SQL programming model? The answer is yes, assuming that the file could be described as a set of rows and columns, which the preceding example clearly can.

2.2.2 The ISAM Model

Fortunately, embellishments were made to the simplistic file I/O model to solve many of its problems. Some of these were added directly to the file system of the operating system, and others were written as independent subsystems. Three major changes were made to the file I/O model to create the ISAM model:

- The ISAM model was set up specifically to be used to access data structured in rows and columns. The file I/O model was more general, but the generality made writing database applications too burdensome for the application developer.

- As its name might suggest, the ISAM model added indexes to aid performance and functionality.

- The ISAM model added locking primitives to manage files accessed concurrently by multiple programs. This meant that modifications to files could now be made in a coordinated fashion.

GLOSSARY

Locking primitive A command to lock or unlock a row in a file. Locks are typically of the type that prevent both reading and writing the row. Using locks, applications can perform a crude type of transaction processing— as long as all the applications use identical locking semantics.

In some ways the ISAM model remains quite similar to the file I/O programming model: files are opened and closed, and functions allow movement within the file—although only by row, not by an arbitrary offset. But with the addition of indexes there came the ability to easily sort rows by indexed columns, to find a row with a particular value quickly, and to find rows that match a value or expression. An ISAM runtime library usually provides a way for an application to perform updates, insertions, and deletions without having to worry about managing file growth or shrinkage directly, which was a welcome change from the way things worked with direct file I/O.

Figure 2-13 shows some of the function calls defined by the X/Open ISAM interface,[9] originally specified by Informix.

Function Name	Functionality
isopen	Opens an ISAM file
isclose	Closes an ISAM file
isread	Reads a record
iswrite	Writes a record
isdelcurr	Deletes current record
isaddindex	Adds an index to an ISAM file
isdelindex	Removes an index from an ISAM file
isstart	Selects an index
islock	Locks an ISAM file
isrelease	Unlocks a record
isunlock	Unlocks an ISAM file

Figure 2-13.
X/Open ISAM programming interface function calls.

There are two important aspects of the ISAM model to note in relation to SQL databases and ODBC. First, the operations that can be performed on ISAMs cannot be modeled in SQL very well, and sometimes they cannot be modeled at all. This is primarily due to the set orientation of SQL vs. the row- or record-at-a-time orientation of ISAMs. In the ISAM model you can position to a row in a table using a value in an index—for example, you can find the

---

9. *X/Open Developer's Specification: Indexed Sequential Access Method (ISAM).* X/Open Company Ltd., 1990.

first record that has the value *Boston* in the city column. Then you can scroll backward along the index seeing cities that collate lower—Baltimore, Ashland, and Aberdeen, for instance. In SQL, once you add the clause WHERE CITY = 'Boston', you can scroll through only the records for which that condition is true. The notion of retrieving the first record and then validly doing "fetch previous" doesn't make any sense in SQL because data is returned in a set. In the ISAM model (as with file I/O) a position in a table can be explicitly changed without relation to set membership. Note, however, that the main reason this example works is because of the single table or single file orientation of the ISAM model. What if we want to relate customers to their orders with a join, as we can in SQL? In this case, explicit position via indexes doesn't mean much, except as a means to help find records that meet a criterion that involves a column that is indexed.[10]

The second aspect of ISAMs to consider in relation to SQL and ODBC is the single-user orientation of ISAMs vs. the multiuser orientation of SQL databases. This is not to say that ISAMs are incapable of multiuser access or that SQL databases aren't suitable for stand-alone use. But the initial assumptions and target platforms for these systems determined to a great degree whether multiuser support was central (as with SQL) or a secondary embellishment (as with ISAMs). We will get into this in more detail in the next chapter in the discussion of client/server architectures, but for now it is sufficient to note that for all desktop database products the ability to handle multiple users accessing shared data is achieved with primitive network file I/O locking schemes (such as locking a range of bytes in a file).

As mentioned in Chapter 1, ODBC uses the SQL paradigm even though ISAMs (and desktop databases, which are built on the ISAM model) are a target data source type. The original design of ODBC version 2.0 called for the addition of an explicit ISAM-style programming model (called the "navigational model"), but the proposal was soundly rejected by the developers reviewing the specification, who saw the addition as a deviation from the main focus of the SQL orientation of ODBC.

---

10. This is not to say that products that support the ISAM model (such as most desktop databases) don't have any way to deal with multiple tables. For example, Xbase products (such as dBASE and FoxPro) have the SET RELATED TO and SET SKIP TO commands, which provide the ability to link records between two files and keep them synchronized.

Finally, it is important to recognize that I've greatly simplified the ISAM model here. File systems, file management systems, and ISAM-based products have gone way beyond the basic "files with indexes" description presented here. Many such systems contain features found in traditional DBMS products, including security features, integrity checking, transaction processing, and recovery. Products such as IBM's VSAM (Virtual Storage Access Method), DEC's RMS files, and the file system in Tandem's Guardian operating system are examples of systems that have very sophisticated data access facilities but that still use programming models that are more like ISAMs than like SQL.

2.3 Desktop Databases

Desktop databases such as dBASE, Paradox, and Microsoft Access have long been used to store and manage a wide variety of data for personal and shared use. These types of systems are typically maligned by proponents of traditional relational DBMSs as "toys." The desktop database crowd has often retorted that traditional relational DBMSs are complex, difficult to install and maintain, and slow, and that they don't provide the necessary functionality to build the highly interactive applications required by PC users.

From the perspective of designing a standard API for database access, such arguments were relevant only insofar as they helped guide the technical underpinnings of the technology to ensure that the data contained in both kinds of systems was readily accessible.

The first and most formidable challenge for supporting desktop databases was to determine whether the SQL set processing model would be sufficient for PC application writers desiring to use a standard API. Although a number of desktop databases now support some form of SQL, the usual method of interacting with the data is record oriented.

Desktop databases are an interesting mixture of ISAMs and the 4GL concepts discussed earlier. The Xbase language, for example, contains commands for data access in the classic ISAM paradigm, along with screen I/O commands.

The Inside Story
Act I, Scene II: Lotus "Blueprint" Is Announced

As noted in the previous installment of "The Inside Story," the first specification of Microsoft's database connectivity technology was completed early in 1988. Concurrent with the internal release of the Microsoft data access specification there appeared an announcement from Lotus that that company was also developing data access technology. Code named "Blueprint," the Lotus technology had precisely the same goals as Microsoft's, and from the announcement it was clear that Lotus was way ahead in the actual development of the technology. Here is an excerpt from some of the press coverage of that announcement:

TITLE: Lotus Blueprint architecture links PC, outside database.

AUTHOR: Briggs, George

JOURNAL: *MIS Week* VOL.: v9 ISSUE: n14 PAGINATION: p28(1)

PUBLICATION DATE: April 4, 1988

CAMBRIDGE, Mass.–Lotus Development Corp. last week introduced an architecture that features a common application interface designed to allow personal computer users access to outside databases.

As expected, Lotus said at a briefing for analysts and reporters that its new Blueprint data-access connection will enable users of Lotus software to link to such data sources as Ashton-Tate Corp.'s dBase (see March 28 *MIS Week*, page 4).

.....

Mussie Shore, senior product manager for connectivity products at Lotus, said Blueprint is a "specification" that will enable end users "to access a wide variety of data sources from within next generation Lotus applications. The specification allows users to stay within applications and selectively retrieve and arrogate data that's sitting in a very wide range and technically disparate set of data sources."

Shore said Blueprint allows connection to such data sources as personal, departmental and mainframe computers and databases stored on CD-ROM disks. Lotus said the interface is being built into all of its new spreadsheet products including 1-2-3 Release 3, the graphical 1-2-3 G, 1-2-3 for Apple Computer Inc.'s Macintosh, and 1-2-3 M (mainframe).

Shore said the architecture can be used by other vendors to connect their data sources to Lotus applications. "The user wins, the vendors win, Lotus wins," he said. "Through Blueprint, users of Lotus applications will get a competitive edge. They'll have greater efficiency in getting data. They'll have more current data to base their decisions on," said Shore.

Lotus said it will distribute a Blueprint toolkit, which will enable independent software vendors (ISVs) to build "intelligent" drivers between their data sources and Lotus applications. Oracle Corp. of Belmont, Clif., is one ISV that has announced its intent to create the drivers, said Lotus. Lotus is scheduling the toolkit for PC developers, which will include the architecture specification and related code libraries, to be released in the fourth quarter for a one-time fee of $250.

COPYRIGHT Fairchild Publications Inc. 1988

I continued work on the Microsoft specification, producing drafts that incorporated answers to the needs that were identified when we spoke with customers and database vendors. But it was not long before we had to decide whether we really wanted to compete with Lotus or work together to define a common interface.

By September 1988 the Microsoft database connectivity specification and general understanding were becoming firm. It was decided that we should see whether we could work together with Lotus in a manner that was similar to the then-current Lotus-Intel-Microsoft (LIM) specification on memory management. If our technical approaches and visions were compatible, it made more sense to work together than to compete over technology that had little direct revenue potential.

In mid-September 1988 Lotus's technical people flew to Redmond, Washington (Microsoft corporate headquarters) to present the Blueprint technology and discuss the possibility of working together. Although our high-level vision of database connectivity was the same, the technical approach differed in one fundamental way. Whereas the Microsoft plan was to use a language-based approach for applications to communicate to database drivers (using SQL), the Lotus Blueprint approach was to use data structures known as "query trees."

In the end, both companies decided that this fundamental difference would be too great to overcome, so we parted ways. At least for the moment....

The features that characterize desktop databases more than anything are their record-at-a-time orientation and their file-based table paradigm. This is exactly the same distinction we discussed earlier with ISAMs. It became clear that the SQL model could be used for desktop databases, but not without some loss of functionality, although there would be some gains as well. On the negative side, it would no longer be easy to scroll through a table, access to single tables would be slower, and positioning to a record within a single table would be slower and less flexible. On the plus side, application programmers would be able to process queries without having to write extra code, and multitable queries would be easier to process.

Aside from the set orientation and lack of direct index manipulation, the largest bone of contention for the desktop database advocates trying to use SQL-based products is probably the lack of scrolling in most SQL databases. It is unfathomable to desktop database programmers how anyone could write a real-world application that did not provide the ability to scroll. Yet none of the best-known relational database products (IBM DB2, Oracle, Sybase, Informix, Ingres, and RDB, to name a few) have any way to fetch backward through a result set. The SQL-92 standard does specify scrollable cursors, but not until the Intermediate conformance level, which might not be implemented by SQL DBMS vendors for several more years.[11]

To accommodate both traditional relational database product developers and desktop database developers, ODBC defines a very rich scrollable cursor model, but in a way that would allow cursors to be optional if the target DBMS could not support them. (ODBC's cursor model is discussed in Chapter 5.)

2.4 ODBC and Database Architectures

So far this chapter has explored various architectures and programming models for accessing data. This final section summarizes how these have influenced the design of ODBC and how well ODBC accommodates the various models.

2.4.1 Traditional Relational DBMSs and Client/Server Databases

Those who have been in the database industry for several years are likely to ask, "Why doesn't embedded SQL meet the need as the programming interface for application developers? Why is a call level interface such as ODBC needed?"

---

11. Notable exceptions to this are IBM AS/400 and Microsoft SQL Server 6, which both support scrollable cursors.

The answer really has nothing to do with technical issues and everything to do with software product distribution. Embedded SQL was and is a great solution that allows for good portability and has some other nice capabilities, such as support for static SQL. However, it achieves portability by requiring applications to use the DBMS vendor's precompiler. The precompiler generates source code in the desired programming language (COBOL, C, or whatever), and this generated code uses the function calls specific to that DBMS. (This was illustrated in Figure 2-7 for IBM and Figure 2-8 for Oracle.) To switch to another vendor's DBMS, the user must recompile the application program using that vendor's precompiler. This solution is fine when the customer has the ability to rebuild applications, but what about customers who purchase so-called "shrink-wrapped" applications—programs that the customer buys off the shelf and has no ability or desire to rebuild?

This is, of course, the case with most modern generic PC applications (spreadsheets and word processors, for example) and application development tools. The combination of Intel microprocessors and Microsoft operating systems (such as MS-DOS and Windows) has created a software market in which binary compatibility is not only possible but required by the market. The notion of having to recompile Microsoft Excel, Lotus 1-2-3, PowerBuilder, or any other "shrink-wrapped" PC application with a DBMS vendor's precompiler any time access to another DBMS is needed is clearly out of the question. Thus embedded SQL in its current form is not a potential solution.

But what if there were a way for embedded SQL implementations to access multiple backends without having to use a particular vendor's precompiler? Indeed, by standardizing the way the client sends and receives information to and from the server (the *data protocol* mentioned earlier in this chapter) and standardizing the output from a precompiler so that it uses the standard data protocol, this would be technically possible. In fact, an effort has been underway for quite some time to accomplish exactly this. The standard data protocol is called RDA (remote data access); it became an international standard in 1994. The design of RDA is very general; its SQL database access utilization is only one use and is referred to as the "SQL specialization."

So the question must be asked, "Why not use the standard data protocol (RDA) with embedded SQL to solve the database connectivity problem?" There are several reasons.

The first reason is that at the data protocol level everything has to be defined so that RDA-compliant servers can be specified. The SQL specialization of RDA was designed with the assumption that only 1989 ISO standard SQL would flow between the client and the server. This leads directly to a lowest common denominator approach that doesn't support commonly used data types such as date, time, timestamp, variable-length character data, and Blobs (binary large objects, such as documents or images). Advanced features such as stored procedures, scrollable cursors, asynchronous cancel, and a number of other vendor extensions cannot be supported by RDA. Some of these items have since been added, but at the time ODBC was being designed the RDA technical specification was too weak to handle real-world applications.

A second reason that RDA is not the solution is that the RDA approach pretty much requires every DBMS vendor either to support RDA in addition to their native data protocol or to write an RDA "server" that acts as a translator on the server from RDA to the native API or data protocol of the DBMS. DBMS vendors have not rushed to implement such a solution and, besides, most vendors already have a perfectly good data protocol and the software that worked with it (Oracle SQL*Net and Sybase's and Microsoft's Net-Library and TDS protocol, for example). So why not just implement a standard API on the client side directly on top of each DBMS vendor's existing data protocol?

A third drawback of RDA is that it raises performance concerns related to the inefficiency of the protocol itself. The RDA specification requires that every value be self-describing. For example, if a query returns 1000 rows consisting of an integer column and a character column, in every row there will be one or more bytes saying that the first column is an integer and the second a character string. So rather than having a single description at the beginning of the results that states, in effect, "For every row that follows, the first 4 bytes are an integer and the next 25 bytes are characters," RDA repeats the description of the data types for every value. This allows the client to request a conversion (for example, from a number to a string) on a row-by-row basis. This can be a nice feature, but there is no ability to turn it off; consequently, each row requested by the client brings with it a fresh description of the data type of each value. The overhead of this approach rules it out as a practical approach for high performance computing or dealing with large volumes of data.

I believe that if all these shortcomings can be overcome, RDA—or any other data protocol whose use becomes widespread, such as IBM's DRDA (Distributed Relational Database Architecture) data protocol—can become an important factor in database connectivity, although it is hard to imagine

DBMS vendors really getting behind such a protocol if it inhibits the functionality or performance of the DBMS. If RDA or DRDA becomes the data protocol of choice and is widely used, embedded SQL or a call level interface such as ODBC can be used as the programming interface.

Because the call level interface approach of ODBC seeks to provide an alternative to embedded SQL, it is natural to want to compare the approaches to see if they are functionally equivalent.

Overall, ODBC does indeed provide the same functionality as embedded SQL because ODBC does not restrict or mandate the SQL that an application can pass to the DBMS.[12] This is an extremely important point and one that we will spend more time on in Chapters 4 and 5.

However, two exceptions to the equivalence merit discussion. The first exception is the aforementioned lack of support of the singleton select statement in embedded SQL. Although support for this could be added in a later release of ODBC, the original thinking was that it wasn't much different, from the application programmer's point of view, than doing a single FETCH after executing the SELECT statement, so that is how ODBC application programmers must do singleton select. However, there can be significant performance gains in some systems with the use of singleton select. This situation is so common that any streamlining of the code would be helpful. Although singleton select support is being considered for ODBC 3.0, as of this writing no definite decision has been reached.

The second exception involves static SQL, which ODBC supports only through the stored procedure paradigm. We'll look at this in detail in Chapter 3.

For people familiar with embedded SQL, probably the most confusing part about ODBC when it is compared to embedded SQL is that ODBC cleaves the programming model into two distinct parts (function calls and executable SQL statements), whereas embedded SQL tends to blur the distinction between declarative and executable SQL statements. For example, in embedded dynamic SQL we have the PREPARE statement

```
PREPARE statement_id FROM host_variable
```

---

12. For those of you not satisfied with such a glib pronouncement of ODBC and embedded SQL equivalence, you can peruse the statement-by-statement comparison of ODBC and X/Open embedded SQL in Appendix E of the *Microsoft ODBC 2.0 Programmer's Reference* (Microsoft Press, 1994). For each ODBC function, the equivalent embedded SQL statement is given. Likewise, for each X/Open SQL statement, the equivalent ODBC function is given.

What gets sent to the DBMS at runtime? In every DBMS product I know about, only the SQL text contained in the *host variable* is sent to the DBMS, along with some form of the *statement id*. In ODBC, whenever such a distinction between declarative SQL and executable SQL is made, ODBC defines a function for the declarative part (in the example above, a function called *SQLPrepare*) and uses the executable SQL statement as an argument of the function.

ODBC and embedded dynamic SQL also differ in the way they manage cursors. Embedded SQL uses the OPEN statement to execute multiple row-returning statements (such as SELECT) and the EXECUTE statement to execute single-row non-row-returning statements (such as INSERT, UPDATE, DELETE, CREATE TABLE, and so on). In ODBC, any valid SQL statement can be executed using a single function call. This gives ODBC a distinct advantage over embedded SQL for certain types of applications. In embedded SQL the application must know whether an SQL statement is row-returning before it can execute that statement, whereas in ODBC such analysis can be performed after the statement has been executed. This difference does not matter for applications written to a fixed DBMS and a fixed table structure, but applications such as ad hoc query tools and SQL execution agents often cannot know whether an SQL statement is row-returning without parsing it. And even parsing doesn't help when the application is executing a stored procedure, which might or might not return rows depending upon several conditions controlled by the DBMS. In this case it is impossible for the client application to know in advance what will be returned.

Finally, the way data is transferred between the database and the program variables is somewhat more cumbersome in ODBC than it is in embedded SQL. Without the benefit of a precompiler to automatically supply the type conversion code at runtime, the programmer using ODBC must use function calls to declare any variable that will be bound to a column returned from the DBMS. In embedded SQL, variables are declared in the same way as normal program variables and are bound directly within the SQL statement:

```
EXEC SQL FETCH C1 INTO :NAME, :ADDRESS, :CITY, :STATE
```

In ODBC, the NAME, ADDRESS, CITY, and STATE variables would have to be explicitly bound in four separate function calls.

In summary, although ODBC and embedded SQL are largely functionally equivalent, some significant differences remain. Both use SQL, but ODBC does not support singleton select and it uses very different programming methods for static SQL–style binding. There are also differences in the way the two bind program variables to output columns, and ODBC takes a different approach to cursor handling.

2.4.2 Desktop Databases and ISAMs

Because ODBC was designed around SQL, the record-at-a-time paradigm of desktop databases and ISAMs was difficult to accommodate. But unlike most SQL products and their native programming interfaces, ODBC supports a cursor model that provides a variety of scrollable, updatable cursors so that application programmers can choose the best model for their particular situations. Beginning with ODBC version 2.0, ODBC provides a "cursor library" that supports scrolling functionality even for DBMSs that don't provide the ability to scroll at all.

The addition of the cursor library in ODBC 2.x has made ODBC much more accessible to ISAM and desktop database programmers accustomed to building applications that require scrollable cursors. But the use of explicit indexes and file I/O–like operations are not supported by ODBC and remain functionalities that ISAMs and desktop database programming models can provide and ODBC cannot. For multidatabase programming, though, it still seems better to have the unifying element of SQL across all databases rather than the ISAM model for only some.

In summary, while it is true that ODBC can be used to access all kinds of data, the programming model has a definite preference for traditional relational DBMSs using SQL rather than PC databases and ISAMs. But as I mentioned earlier, the important thing for universal data access is whether the data itself can be modeled as rows and columns, regardless of the programming model of the product that generated that data. Because the data managed by desktop databases and ISAMs can be modeled as rows and columns, ODBC's SQL model is a good choice for universal data access.

In the next chapter, we're going to explore client/server architecture in more depth so that you can see how ODBC was designed for access to client/server DBMSs.

CHAPTER THREE

Client/Server Architecture

ODBC was designed with client/server architecture in mind, but it won't do you much good to know that unless you know what I mean by client/server architecture. To lay the groundwork for what lies ahead in our discussion of ODBC architecture, this chapter provides a general description of client/server architecture as it relates to data access. After a brief introduction, we will discuss two architectures that are sometimes erroneously considered to be client/server architectures but that are actually *alternatives to* client/server architecture. Once I've cleared up the confusion about these alternatives, which I call PC file server and server/terminal architectures, we'll look at true client/server architecture.

ODBC was primarily designed to exploit client/server architectures; understanding the perspective presented here will provide insight into ODBC's design and the philosophy that continues to guide it.

3.1 Overview

The term *client/server computing* is probably the number one technical buzzword in the corporate computing culture at present (with the possible exception of *object-oriented programming*). As is the case with most new computing trends, current discussions of client/server computing seem to be generating more heat than light about what this technology is and how it works, and the confusion factor is high.

Like some of you reading this book, I have a nearly insatiable curiosity about how various businesses use computers. I almost always stick my head over the counter at a company to see what kind of software is "running the business." What I have seen tells me that use of client/server computing in large enterprises such as the health care, banking, and insurance industries is still more the exception than the rule. More often than not, when PCs are being used I find that some MS-DOS–based applications or one particular Microsoft Windows-based application is being used—and you might be surprised when I tell you what Windows-based application I see most often. Is it a Microsoft Visual Basic application? A PowerBuilder application? A custom application written in a 3GL such as C or COBOL? No. It is Windows Terminal— the terminal emulator that allows a PC to act as a "dumb terminal" to a minicomputer or mainframe.[1]

Apart from an occasional game of Solitaire when the boss isn't looking, the PC's processing power and its local hard disk resource go almost entirely untapped. This is not client/server computing; it is what I call the "server/ terminal model," which is covered later. Yet I suspect that some people believe that putting a PC on a desktop and continuing to run application software and database software on a minicomputer or mainframe have ushered them into the age of client/server computing.

I won't pretend that I can dispel all the confusion and sort out all the different uses of client/server terminology in this limited space. What I do in this chapter is give my own view of client/server architecture as it relates to DBMSs. I am deliberately restricting the material to that with which I'm most familiar: personal computers running MS-DOS, Windows, or Macintosh System 7 as clients connected to almost any other computer. I do not discuss other types of computers or operating systems as clients (for example, UNIX workstations), but these are also perfectly acceptable clients for client/server computing.

A clear picture of what client/server computing means in this context might be easier to obtain if we first look at what client/server computing is *not*. My conversations with many people about this topic over the years have led me to see that there are two primary perspectives of database architecture: the desktop database (small system) perspective and the mainframe (large system) perspective. I will describe both, but when you read my descriptions you might think that I've left out a lot of detail and in some cases oversimplified your perspective. But I'll wager that you won't have the same opinion about my description of the other perspective. When I talk to desktop database people I find that they have little awareness of how large systems really work and what their benefits are. The opposite is true with the large-system crowd when they consider desktop databases. So I hope that you will learn something about "the other guys" when you read the following two sections. Remember, neither of these perspectives describes a client/server architecture, in my opinion.

---

1. Windows Terminal is one of the applications in the Accessories program group in Windows. It is a terminal emulator that can make a PC act like a terminal to a host computer.

3.2 The PC File Server Model: Smart Client/Dumb Server

The first model we'll look at evolved from stand-alone PCs that were later net-worked so that files and print services could be shared among several users. On a stand-alone PC, the interaction with the local hard disk is managed by standard open, close, read, and write operations such as those we covered in section 2.2.1, "Flat Files and Simple File I/O." When a PC (the client) is connected to the network, it can access files on another PC (the file server) by "redirecting" one of its disk drive devices to make a logical connection to the file server. The client PC does this by using its network software to trap the file I/O operations, convert them to messages, and send them to the file server, where the actual file operations take place. To the application programmer and the end user, there is no distinction between a file I/O operation that happens locally and one that happens on the file server. This architecture is shown in Figure 3-1.

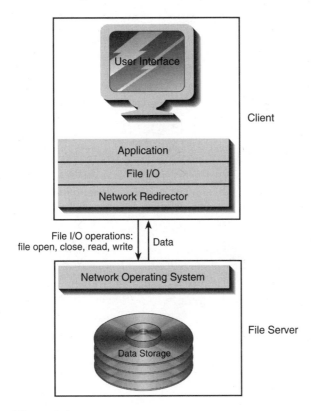

Figure 3-1.
The PC file server model.

To handle situations in which applications on multiple client PCs need to access the same file at the same time on the file server,[2] locking operations function on the network file server and client-side file I/O programming interfaces. For any kind of shared file access, such locking is critical to ensure that updates and deletions to the data happen in a consistent manner so that the integrity of the data can be preserved.

The locking functionality available to the PC application programmer using this model is called *range locking,* which allows the programmer to request a lock on a range of bytes after the program has used a seek operation to position to a certain offset in the file. (Remember offset positioning from Chapter 2?) The lock is enforced by the networking software on the file server. The only kind of lock supported in this model is an *exclusive* or *write* lock—that is, while the lock is held no other application can read or write data within the range of bytes that is locked.

This locking operation was first supported on PCs when it became part of the operating system in version 3 of MS-DOS. It was supported by the C runtime function *locking,* which was inherited from UNIX. Just like the file I/O commands *open, close, seek, read,* and *write,* the *locking* function can be redirected to a file server. In fact, in an MS-DOS–based machine in which only one application can be running at a time, a program needs to use locking operations only when it is communicating across a network to a shared file on the file server.

Desktop databases and ISAMs use range locking capabilities across a network to manage the concurrency control issues normally associated with large DBMSs. But unlike the centralized minicomputer and mainframe system, the PC file server model has all of the control of the locking being initiated by the client PC, which necessarily means that each client has to do locking without knowing what the other clients are doing. The file server has no centralized lock manager that can escalate many small range locks to one larger one. The network operating system software at the file server has no concept of a column or row of a table—a table looks just like any other file. There is no file-server–based buffering scheme other than that provided by the simple file I/O buffer management of the network file server management software. All of the lock management and file semantics are managed in each client PC.

In short, limiting the total semantic content of the interface between the client and file server to the range locking model puts a pretty severe limitation on the kinds of processing that can be done, and that is why I call this

---

2. Often the shared file on the file server is referred to as the *database* or the *database file.* I'm going to stick with the term *file* in this section to reduce the number of terms. It is certainly true, regardless of the terminology, that the file on the network server is used as a database.

model the *smart client/dumb server model*—all the intelligence is on the client PC, and the file server is not much more than a shared disk.

This is not to say that such systems are not useful or have disappeared. On the contrary, all desktop databases (including FoxPro, Microsoft Access, and Paradox) that support multiuser access still manage data this way when a data file is located on a network file server. Microsoft Access has even added some support for security and transactions within the file server model.

The good news about this architecture is that it distributes the processing power to the desktop, making easy-to-use applications that exploit the graphical user interface power of the PC a snap to build (well, at least *possible* to build). The file server is completely out of the loop when it comes to processing screen I/O requests—the client CPU, memory, and video display shoulder the burden of putting data on the screen and manipulating it once it is received. If the user wants to process the data further (to perform a calculation on the values or to store some of the data on the local hard disk, for instance), that doesn't affect the file server's ability to service other users at all. Users can switch to another task and work on something completely unrelated to the file server without placing CPU or disk I/O demands on the file server.

A second advantage of the PC file server model is that because the shared data is just a file, it is easy to provide forward and backward scrolling through data by using the *seek* primitive that is included in the repertoire of file I/O commands. Indexes maintained on the file server, when combined with ISAM programming models, provide high-speed access to the data by allowing client programs to use the index files directly (although these files also must be locked when index entries need to be modified because of an insertion or update). For Xbase products and most other desktop database products (such as R:BASE and Paradox), indexes and data are kept in separate files, although some products such as Microsoft Access keep both indexes and data in the same physical file.

A third advantage of the model is speed. If the requirements of the application are such that the data on the file server is being treated more like a file than a multiuser DBMS, the performance is usually very good.

But the PC file server model has many disadvantages as well. The low-level locking paradigm means that client applications have to hope for the best when they are trying to obtain a lock to update a record, and often programmers have to add logic to the client application to detect and handle locking conflicts. If any part of the particular section of the file that a client is trying to access is locked by another client, an error is returned to the first client and the application has to try again (and again and again, if necessary) until it is able to acquire the lock.

Because of the reduced concurrency that results when write locks are held among several client applications, many clever schemes have been invented by desktop database vendors to simulate read locks (also known as shared locks) to minimize locking conflicts in the data file. One of these schemes is to create a separate lock file; another is to lock beyond the end of the file. Both techniques allow the exclusive lock to act as a semaphore so that multiple writers can be serialized correctly. But, of course, this means that the application developer (or the writer of the runtime library of the desktop database or the ISAM) has to write even more elaborate code to manage the locking paradigm. Locking is the responsibility of the application programmer—if a mistake is made, it can cause the integrity of the file to be violated or it can lead to deadlocks.

A second drawback of the PC file server model is that this model makes it too easy for the end user to open a data file on the file server and read or write to random parts of it. For example, an end user might accidentally open the file in Windows Notepad, type a few characters, save the file, and then exit. Because the file server has no intelligence to know that Notepad (or any other application that doesn't know the file format) should not be allowed to modify that file, the file could be corrupted and could render inoperable the application using it. After all, it is just another file—a stream of bytes—from the file server's point of view. There is no provision for centralized security of access to data, nor is there the ability to detect which user did what.

Third, there is no concept of transactions and roll-forward recovery such as that provided by DBMSs on minicomputers and mainframes. Failures at the file server (disk crashes, network failures, and power outages) often result in corrupted data with little hope for returning the file to a consistent state. The only solution would be to copy the entire file from a backup file.

The fourth and most significant drawback of the PC file server model involves the amount of data that flows between the client and the file server across the network. Because users typically want to view only a subset of data at any given time, desktop databases must be able to process queries. But because all the processing apart from the simple file I/O happens on the client, each client has to locally process queries and the data to satisfy those queries. And this means that a lot of data must flow across the network. Each time a client does a read operation, the data flows from the file server to the client.

For example, let's assume that there is a customer file with 1000 records and a user makes a request to find all the customers in that file who live in Boston. The desktop database runtime library can execute the query in one of two ways.

The first way is used if there is no index on the city column of the customer file. In this scenario, the program has no choice but to open the file, read every record across the network, and do the comparison on the PC client. If every row in the customer file is 100 bytes long, that is 100,000 bytes flowing across the network (1000 records × 100 bytes per record). But if only 25 customers are in Boston, the records the user really needs occupy only 2500 bytes (25 records × 100 bytes per record), not 100,000. But in the PC file server model all records (100,000 bytes of data) must flow across the network. And when 10 users are running the same query, the entire file is being sent to every client, which means not only that there is a lot more network traffic (1,000,000 bytes total in this case) but that every PC client duplicates the effort of the other clients. (Every client looks at every record in the file, keeps the 25 records for which the city column contains "Boston," and discards the other 975 records.)

Of course, the network file server buffer management system will provide some caching of the data, but it certainly can't provide any higher-level optimization. With today's fast CPUs, networks, and hard disks, even the processing just described can be done with good performance—as long as the amount of data stays small and the number of users doesn't grow too large. But clearly, streaming entire files across a network simply doesn't scale up to more data and more users without causing serious throughput problems.

The second way to execute the query "find all customers in Boston" would be used if there is an index on the city column in the customer file. Rather than reading the whole file from the file server, the client opens the index and reads chunks of the index from the file server until the range of the index spans the value "Boston." When the correct section of the index has been found, the index will provide the information (a set of record numbers or file offsets) that specifies where the "Boston" records are located in the data file. Using the information in the index, the application can begin reading only the "Boston" records. Again, each time a read operation is requested by the client PC application, the data flows from the file server to the client. But this situation is much more efficient than that of the previous example: far less data is sent across the network because a few index pages were read first.

However, even with this improvement the situation is far from optimal, especially when a query involves multiple tables, as real-world queries often do. For example, it is just as likely that a user would want to know what products were ordered by customers in Boston, which involves at least four tables (customers, orders, line items, and products). If each customer has an average of five orders with five items in each order, and if the product file has 500 records, the amount of data required to process the query multiplies rapidly: 1000 customers × 5 orders × 5 items = 25,000 records that have a corresponding record in the products file. Now picture the network data flow and processing required to read the indexes and data in four tables across the network to each PC and add to that the writing, locking, and unlocking commands for managing multiuser modifications to the shared data, and you quickly come to the realization that a moderately sized amount of data and number of users will bring even today's fast networks to their knees.

Of course, the situation would be greatly improved if we could resolve the query on the file server and only send back to the client the data that was requested. This is exactly what the client/server model does. But before we look at the client/server model in more detail, let's look at the other (opposite) perspective: the server/terminal model.

3.3 The Server/Terminal Model: Dumb Client/Smart Server

I use the *server/terminal model* to describe the architecture of most minicomputer and mainframe systems. We looked at this architecture briefly in the previous chapter (in section 2.1.1). In contrast to the PC file server model, in which the server has no intelligence beyond simple file management, the server/terminal model is highly centralized and, in effect, all the intelligence is in the server and none is in the client. In this case the client is a terminal (or a PC running a terminal emulator), which is really nothing more than a display device. In this model the client has no ability to understand and process the data being displayed. You have probably heard the term *dumb terminal;* here I use *dumb client/smart server* to describe the architecture.

In the server/terminal model application programs run on a mainframe and the information flow to clients consists of screen I/O commands. The usual term for describing the mainframe or minicomputer is the *host,* although the term *server* could be used as well.

When a user types something at the terminal, the keystrokes (in most cases) are being processed by the host and echoed back to the terminal screen. All of the resources (CPU, disk, and memory) required to run the data management software *and* the applications for every user are located on the host. Whereas in the PC file server model the application processing of the video display is performed by the client CPU (in other words, the application logic runs on the client and performs screen I/O on the client) and keeps shared file I/O on the server, in the server/terminal model the application runs on the server (the host) and sends screen characters to the client (the terminal). Figure 3-2 shows the components of the server/terminal model.

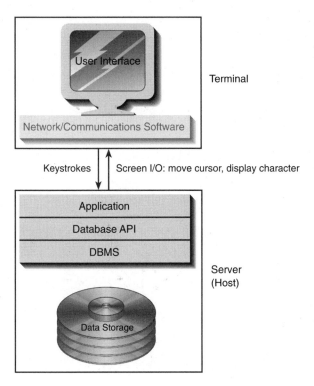

Figure 3-2.
The server/terminal model.

In terms of deploying an application across an enterprise, it greatly simplifies things to have the application in one place rather than distributed to many PCs. If the application needs to be customized, the administrator just installs the new version of the application on the host. All the users will get the update and every terminal will reflect the same consistent view and behavior in the application. If such a change were necessary in the PC file server model, ensuring that each desktop obtains the updated application could be a difficult chore.

Of course, one problem with having all the computing power centralized is that response time degrades as the number of users multiplies and the processing requirements increase. Unlike the PC file server model, in which file I/O is handled by the server and application logic is running on each client, in the server/terminal model both the application logic and the file I/O are handled by the same computer.

Recall the "find all customers from Boston" example from the preceding section. In the PC file server model, we saw that the clients did the bulk of the processing. Let's consider what happens in the server/terminal model with the same example.

First of all, when the host-based application requests that the DBMS find all customers in Boston, nothing flows from the terminal to the host—the application is already on the host. Presuming that an SQL DBMS manages the data store, the application passes the string SELECT * FROM CUSTOMERS WHERE CITY = 'BOSTON' to the DBMS. The DBMS (not the application program) processes the request by scanning all 1000 rows of the customer table (or by using an index on the city column, if one exists and the optimizer determines that this would provide the best performance). Note that the terminals don't have to make the choice about how to access the data, as the client PCs running the applications do in the PC file server model. After the DBMS has resolved the query for customers in Boston, the application fetches only 25 rows, not the entire table, from the database. Any multiuser update issues such as enforcement of locks and serialization of access are also performed within the DBMS—not within the application logic.

When it is time to display the information on the end user's terminal, the application generates the appropriate terminal protocol.[3] Some terminal protocols have various codes embedded within them to control the placement of information on the display; others have only the ability to paint an entire screen of information. In the former case, to place the customer name at row 3, column 5, on the screen, the application program generates a "position cursor" command using the appropriate terminal protocol sequence for the user's terminal type, followed by some encoding of row 3 and column 5. Then the actual customer name is displayed at the current screen cursor position. Keep in mind that the application on the host must do this level of processing for every client request, unlike in the PC file server model in which only the data flows to the client and the client takes care of the screen I/O processing. In the server/terminal model, both data and screen I/O commands flow to the client (terminal).

So even though the data management portion of the process doesn't cause excessive network traffic to flow between the server (host) and client

---

3. Actually, the application code almost never gets involved in generating the actual terminal protocol but generates a more generic output request and leaves it to some lower-level software component to deal with formatting the correct terminal protocol.

(terminal) as in the PC file server model, a whole new kind of data is flowing: screen I/O information. Combined with the fact that often every client (terminal) keystroke requires processor cycles on the host, it is clear to see that there is no distribution of processing at all. So in the case of a PC running the Terminal application that comes with Windows, there is no advantage to having a PC at all—the host is still bearing the entire burden of running the application, and the application must share the central processing power with the DBMS.

Again there are difficulties when this model must accommodate more data and more users. The demands on the host computer's resources increase and there is no hope of offloading any of the processing to the client—a PC with a 286 processor and a modem can run a host-based application using Windows Terminal just as effectively as a Pentium-based or PowerPC-based PC can.

Finally, I shouldn't have to say much about the fact that this model places some severe limitations on the types of applications that can be used. This is a serious drawback. The popularity of Windows and other graphical user interfaces is evidence enough that definite productivity gains can be realized when the resources available on the PC are exploited. The simple ability to manipulate data from a shared store in a variety of ways (in a grid, a chart, or a form, for instance) without requiring additional processing power from the host is just one of the capabilities that the server/terminal model cannot handle. This model is also unable to support sharing data between different applications, which is another (although lesser) limitation. The ability to retrieve data, do a trend analysis, chart the analysis, and place the data and chart into a word processing document streamlines the process that manages and presents the information required to make decisions for a business. Such processing capabilities are simply not feasible when a terminal is the only tool provided for the end user.

Now that we've looked at what client/server computing is *not*, it's time to look at the real thing.

3.4 The Client/Server Model: Smart Client/Smart Server

Client/server architecture addresses (among other things) many of the shortfalls of the other models by using the resources of both the client and the server to their fullest potential. As in the server/terminal model, the intelligence is in the server, and therefore centralized control and high-level semantics can be applied. But as in the PC file server model, the application logic resides on the client, not on the host, so that it can make effective use of all the resources the PC has to offer without causing a bottleneck at the server.[4]

A client/server system has three main components: the client, the server, and the data protocol that flows across the network. These components are depicted in Figure 3-3. In reality the system comprises many more components than just these, but this diagram is a useful simplification for showing the big picture. By the way, if you're curious about where ODBC fits into Figure 3-3, it would be the database API component.

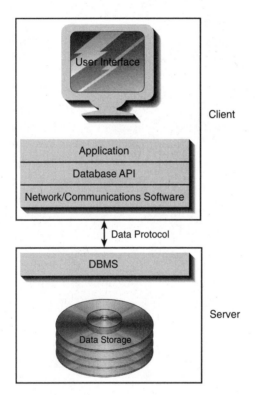

Figure 3-3.
A simplified representation of client/server architecture.

---

4. One of the more popular hybrids of this approach as of this writing is a "three-tier" architecture, in which some of the application logic is moved to an intelligent application server that is distinct from the DBMS. This scenario comprises three intelligent components: the client, the application server, and the DBMS server. This model is a good solution for enforcing business rules that are common to multiple applications. The rules can be centralized on the application server, which provides consistency across client applications and allows for the processing of complex logic that cannot always be supported in the DBMS.

3.4.1 The Role of the Client in Client/Server Architecture

As in the PC file server model, in a client/server system the application logic runs on the client. The application is responsible for managing the information displayed on the screen and interacting with the server, but the way it does this differs from the PC file server model: it does not use file I/O primitives. Instead, the application uses an entirely different programming paradigm—the database API—that provides a much higher level of abstraction than simple file I/O. Although there are some alternatives, this discussion will define this database API as a combination of SQL and some programming mechanism (such as a call level interface or embedded SQL) that sends the SQL to the DBMS.

SQL's use of tables and columns to request information and manipulate data (as opposed to the more primitive file I/O or ISAM commands) is very useful for the client-side software that interacts with the DBMS. However, the data processed in this way is still not at the level the end user needs. The end user needs the information to be transformed from tables and columns of data into objects relevant to the task at hand: an order form, a personnel form, or a product description, for example. This is the job of the application—to turn the tables and columns of data into meaningful displays and actions, and in many cases to enforce the business rules if they cannot be enforced directly by the DBMS.

Below the database API in our simplified representation of client/server architecture is the network/communications interface. The network/communications interface is yet another abstraction that hides the details of the particular layers of network software that are being used (such as NetWare, TCP/IP, or SNA). The core of the network programming interface looks remarkably like the simple file I/O (open, close, read, and write) model (without the range locking interface, however), although there are some important differences, such as the network programming interface's ability to cancel requests in progress and deal with a number of issues related to asynchronous processing. Finally, the network interface deals with the network transport layer to actually transmit and receive data to and from the server.

> ### GLOSSARY
>
> **Business rules** Rules and policies that define how a business operates. For example, a simple business rule is "Order amount cannot exceed credit limit." Here's another: "Minimum amount ordered must be greater than $10.00." The last section in this chapter describes a more complex business rule.

Figure 3-4 summarizes the client-side components and shows the functionality supplied by the programming interface of each component.

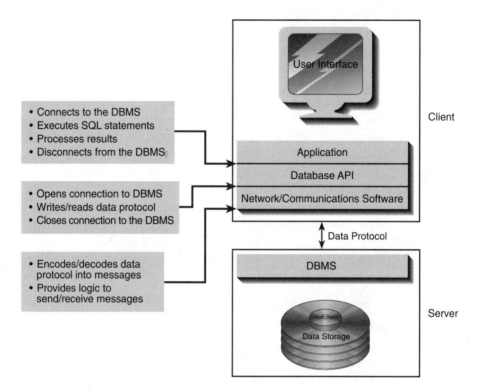

Figure 3-4.
The client components in client/server architecture.

The Inside Story
Act I, Scene III: The More the Merrier

By early 1989 the Microsoft Data Access API had been renamed Open SQL, and several companies had reviewed the specification and provided feedback. At this point, the programming interface in the specification was very much like the Sybase programming interface (DB-Library), with additions to handle other database models and removal of the functions that were specific to Sybase. The specification had been significantly influenced by Tom Haggin, a founder of Sybase; Rao Yendluri from Tandem; and Dick Hackathorn, a founder of MicroDecisionware.

Tom Haggin designed and implemented the first version of Sybase's DB-Library and was designing Sybase's Open Server technology at that time. Open Server had very interesting possibilities as a technology for supporting server-based database connectivity. Tom's practical, hands-on experience with designing programming interfaces was an enormous asset.

Rao Yendluri was championing a similar vision for database connectivity within Tandem and the rest of the database industry. Interestingly enough, Rao's specification was also called Open SQL. The Tandem solutions for solving the database connectivity problem were different from the Microsoft approach, however, in that the Tandem approach used embedded SQL and a common wire protocol to achieve interoperability. Yet Rao provided great insight into the problems to be solved and the merits of various approaches.

Dick Hackathorn taught me the basics of IBM mainframe technology—DB2, SNA, CICS, VTAM, APPC, LU2 (3270), and all those other wonderful acronyms that IBM has given us. In 1989 IBM was the dominant player in the corporate database arena. If you didn't have a good solution to connect the desktop to the IBM mainframe, you couldn't even get a corporate customer to listen to your database connectivity story.

Bob Muglia from Microsoft was also instrumental in driving the specification forward. His technical knowledge, management skills, initiative, and ability to build consensus among differing technical viewpoints provided the environment in which the specification work flourished.

Many companies were becoming interested in database connectivity issues, and it was just a matter of time before some wanted a bigger piece of the action....

3.4.2 The Role of the Server in Client/Server Architecture

The DBMS running on the server in a client/server system controls access to the data. It interacts with clients by means of a network interface and the data protocol. Although I haven't shown the server-side network interface in any of the previous diagrams, it is there in reality. The DBMS itself usually consists of several components, as shown in Figure 3-5.

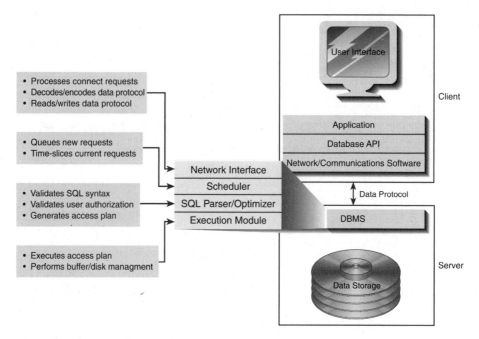

Figure 3-5.

The server components in client/server architecture.

3.4.3 Getting from Here to There and Back Again: The Data Protocol

The method that clients and servers use to communicate seems to be one of the least understood elements of client/server computing, yet it is absolutely critical to an understanding of how the overall system operates. Most people understand conceptually how mainframes "talk" to terminals and how PCs do file I/O across a network to a file server. But how does the communication work in client/server architecture? I call the information that flows between a client and a server the *data protocol*, which has a much higher semantic content than either terminal protocols or file I/O operations have. Many protocols are involved in networks; they are used from the hardware level of the network up through several layers of networking software. For example, Ethernet is a popular physical network that uses a protocol called CSMA/CD (Carrier Sense Multiple Access with Collision Detection) to avoid collisions between signals, and TCP/IP is a popular network transport layer.

The term *data protocol* describes the form of the information that the database API sends to the server by means of a programming interface that looks very much like simple file I/O (that is, it opens a connection to the server, it reads, it writes, and it closes the connection). The actual information exchanged between the client and the server includes things like SQL strings, results sets from queries, and error messages, all of which are typically encoded in a very terse format in order to reduce the actual number of bytes that need to be sent across the network. You'll see a detailed example of one data protocol format (the Microsoft SQL Server TDS data protocol format) in Chapter 6. The flow of the data protocol is made possible by all the other underlying layers of networking software and hardware, but we won't get into the lower network layers—that would take another entire book.

The two primary technologies used for data protocols are messaging and remote procedure calls (RPCs). We'll look at both next.

3.4.3.1 Messaging

Messaging refers to the flow of bytes, grouped into messages, between the database API on the client and the DBMS on the server. These messages convey the client requests to be executed by the DBMS and the result data and status information to be returned to the client. But, of course, one cannot just send any old "stream of bytes" from a client to a server and expect the server to make sense of it. The messages must have the correct format, just like the data in a spreadsheet file or in a word processing document file must be in the correct format. There is a specific definition for the ordering of different types of information. Some data protocols that use messaging are Tabular Data Stream (TDS), used by Microsoft and Sybase; Oracle's SQL*Net protocol; the ISO Remote Data Access (RDA) protocol; and IBM's Distributed Relational Database Architecture (DRDA). Most message formats follow the "tag, length, value" (TLV) paradigm, which simply means that a message begins with information about the type of message (the *tag*), then specifies the length of the value, and ends with the value itself, which must be of the length specified.

Messages are constructed by the client and server based on function calls made by the database API and the DBMS, respectively. For example, with Microsoft SQL Server, when the end user wants to execute an SQL statement the application program uses a function call in ODBC called *SQLExecDirect*. The Microsoft SQL Server ODBC driver takes the SQL string specified in *SQLExecDirect* and builds a message in the format required by Microsoft SQL Server (TDS) in order to send the request. The TDS stream is of the form:

```
message_header SQL_string
```

The message header contains a byte that declares that this is an SQL command (this corresponds to the tag mentioned above), a status byte identifying whether this packet is the last one (in TDS, packets are usually 512 bytes long), two bytes that specify the length of the SQL string, and a few other bytes not relevant for this example. Following the message header is the actual SQL string itself.

This stream of bytes is placed in a buffer, the buffer address is passed as an argument in a function call to the network interface, and the network interface writes the contents of the buffer to the network, much as if the contents were a local disk file.

The network interface module on the server reads the stream, looks at the message header type byte, and recognizes that the client wants an SQL string to be executed. It calls the scheduler to get this particular request queued and then goes back to waiting for other client requests and sending results back to clients as directed by the scheduler.

When the request is fulfilled by the server, the server instructs the network interface to send the appropriate results to the client. This information includes a general status report declaring whether the request succeeded or not and, if it succeeded, any additional status information (such as the number of rows affected by an update, insert, or delete statement). In most DBMSs, the client then sends a fetch request to the server to retrieve any rows resulting from a query. In other cases (such as Microsoft SQL Server 4.*x*) the result data is streamed to the client immediately after the query is executed, and the client does not have to send a fetch request; in still other cases (such as Microsoft SQL Server 6 and IBM's DRDA) the client and server dynamically decide whether to use the row-at-a-time model or the all-rows-at-once model based on such criteria as whether the application needs to update the data from the query.

To send the information back to the client, the server constructs the appropriate message stream (again following the TDS format) and sends it to the client when the client does a read operation to the network. The client decodes the message and places various elements of the message in the application's output argument buffers and then returns to the application.

Let's go through a real-world example using Microsoft SQL Server.[5]

Since this is a book on ODBC, this example uses the ODBC API as the programming interface used by the application. But you should keep in mind that the equivalent functions in the native database API for Microsoft SQL Server (DB-Library) would have exactly the same effect, because it is the TDS protocol, not the function call interface, that controls what the DBMS does.

---

5. If you would like to see the equivalent example for IBM's DRDA, consult section 7.5.2 of Richard Hackathorn's excellent book, *Enterprise Database Connectivity* (Wiley & Sons, 1993).

In this example we will send a simple SELECT statement through the various layers on the client and across the network, observe how the statement is executed by the server, and retrieve result rows that are returned through the layers on the client.

First of all, let's assume that the client application has already established a connection to Microsoft SQL Server by using one of the ODBC functions to make the connection. (We'll go over what happens at connection time in Chapter 6, "A Tour of the Microsoft SQL Server Driver.") The information we want from Microsoft SQL Server is the set of customers in the state of Washington who have placed more than 20 orders. To specify the SELECT statement we want to execute, we call the ODBC function *SQLExecDirect*:

```
ret = SQLExecDirect(hstmt,
    "SELECT Name, City, Count(*)
    FROM Customers C, Orders O
    WHERE O.CustID = C.CustID AND C.State = 'WA'
    GROUP BY C.Name, C.City
    HAVING (Count(*) > 20)", SQL_NTS);
```

The function call *SQLExecDirect* calls an internal function in the Microsoft SQL Server ODBC driver that takes the SQL statement from the second argument of *SQLExecDirect* and creates a buffer that contains a TDS message header, which includes the length of the SQL string (150 bytes), followed by the SQL string itself. The address of this buffer is used as an input argument to the network interface library function *ConnectionWrite*, which sends the stream to the server. After the write operation has been completed, the Microsoft SQL Server ODBC driver immediately calls the *ConnectionRead* function, which waits for information to be returned from the server. (Note that this last part is true only in the case of synchronous processing. In asynchronous processing the application program gets control again and can check periodically for completion of the request.)

On the server, the network interface has actually had a thread "sleeping" on our connection. When the write operation from the client is finished, the connection thread "wakes up" and reads the TDS stream. When it sees the "SQL command" message type in the message header, the network interface code generates a *language event*, which indicates that the client wants to execute an SQL command. The event handler schedules our SQL statement for execution. During execution, the parser verifies that the syntax is correct, that the table and column names we have requested exist, and that we have the necessary privileges to access them. Then the optimizer determines which indexes (if any) to use and generates the access plan. The access plan is passed to the execution module and immediately begins sending the rows that satisfy the query back to the client as it finds them. (Note that this last step differs from what happens in other DBMSs, although Microsoft SQL Server 6 will have a way to defer sending the data to the client until the data is requested with a fetch statement from the client.)

The TDS stream that is constructed on the server to be sent back to the client has two parts:

- A description of the returned data (name, city, and count of orders), which is often called the *metadata* (data about data)

- The data itself, divided into rows

Recall that in the client the *ConnectionRead* function has been waiting until the server sends back some data. The first thing the driver sees is the metadata: the three COLNAME tokens (tags) that let the driver know that there are three columns and what their names are, and the three COLFMT tokens that disclose the data types and lengths of the data strings (two character strings for the character data and a 4-byte integer for the count). The driver begins parsing the buffer to look for tokens. As it finds the COLNAME and COLFMT tokens, it puts the information contained within them into data structures so that the information can be returned when the application asks for it with the *SQLDescribeCol* or *SQLColAttributes* ODBC function. After it does this, the driver returns control to the application.

The application program will now retrieve all the data. To do so, it will first bind the three columns to program variables using the *SQLBindCol* function:

```
UCHAR szName[26], szCity[16];
SDWORD lOrderCount, cbName, cbCity, cbOC;

SQLBindCol(hstmt, 1, SQL_C_CHAR, szName, sizeof(szName), &cbName);
SQLBindCol(hstmt, 2, SQL_C_CHAR, szCity, sizeof(szCity), &cbCity);
SQLBindCol(hstmt, 3, SQL_C_SLONG, &lOrderCount, sizeof(SDWORD), &cbOC);
```

Nothing is sent to the server when these functions are executed; the only thing that happens is that data structures within the Microsoft SQL Server ODBC driver on the client are modified to remember the addresses of the

---

G L O S S A R Y

Bind To assign a value returned from a DBMS to a program variable in the client application.

variables in which the data and indicator information will be stored when the data is fetched.

To fetch the data, the application calls *SQLFetch* in a loop until the return code is SQL_NO_DATA_FOUND:

```
for (; (rc = SQLFetch(hstmt)) != SQL_NO_DATA_FOUND;)
    DisplayData(szName, szCity, lOrderCount);
```

Each time *SQLFetch* is called, the driver reads from the network to look for a ROW token. The ROW token is always followed by the data as described in the COLFMT token. In our example, that would be the length of the customer name, the customer name, the length of the city name, the city name, and the count of orders, in that order. As the driver reads this data, it places it into the addresses specified by the application with *SQLBindCol*.

After the last row has been returned, the server sends a DONE token so that the client knows not to read any more data. When the driver reads the DONE token, it sets the return value of the *SQLFetch* function to SQL_NO_DATA_FOUND and the application program drops out of the fetch loop.

In summary, messaging is one kind of data protocol by which clients and servers communicate. The messages have a much higher semantic content than the file I/O type of data flow in the PC file server model and the terminal emulation type of data flow in the server/terminal model because the messages deal with objects that are database oriented (such as column names, data types, data values, and SQL strings) rather than terminal or file oriented. But with this semantic richness comes more complexity: both client and server must parse the message streams to determine what request and response are desired. In the technique we'll look at next, the information flow is handled by an entirely different mechanism.

3.4.3.2 Remote Procedure Calls

A *remote procedure call* (RPC) is simply a function call that is made on a client computer but executed on a server computer. That is, rather than having the database API convert a function call to a message in some particular format that can be sent across a network, RPCs encode the function call itself directly into a data stream and send that.[6]

---

6. This is actually an oversimplified definition, but it is sufficient for this discussion. In reality, it is possible to use RPCs for *anything* that can be expressed as a function call, not just the database API calls. One interesting case that I won't discuss in depth is the use of RPCs at the next layer below the database API: the network interface layer. If an RPC system supports a wide variety of network transports, the DBMS vendor doesn't have to write a specific network interface layer for each network; the RPC system uses the appropriate network software and frees the DBMS vendor to write only one client- and server-side implementation.

The typical method used to "remote" a function call across a network is to use an RPC runtime library and some *encoding rules* (rules that designate the function name and the type and length of each argument for each function that is to be executed remotely) instead of the usual method that links a subroutine library to the application. The RPC library is usually referred to as a *stub* or *stub library*. A similar method is used on the server, although the actual implementation of the function resides there. The RPC runtime library knows how to take a function call in a 3GL and convert it into a data stream that can be sent across the network. The server side of the RPC system knows how to take the data stream that represents the function call from the network and reassemble it into a real function call.

For example, an RPC system can encode a C function into a message that consists of the function name and a list of the arguments required by the function. After the client sends the message to the server, the server part of the RPC system detects the function to be called, reconstitutes the message into the function and its argument, and calls the function on the server. When the function has been executed, the return value and output arguments (if any) are converted into a message by the RPC server. The message is sent to the client, and the client RPC system then sets the return value and output arguments of the function and returns to the application.

If you think the above description seems awfully similar to the description of messaging in the previous section, you are right—the two are functionally equivalent. Let's look at an example that is the RPC equivalent of the messaging example in the previous section. In the messaging example, when the application called *SQLExecDirect* the Microsoft SQL Server ODBC driver composed a message consisting of a message header and an SQL string and called a function (*ConnectionWrite*) in the network interface layer to send the message to the server. In the RPC equivalent the client would send an encoded form of the *SQLExecDirect* function and its arguments (including the SQL string) to the server, where it would be reconstructed into the original call to *SQLExecDirect*. The function would then actually be invoked on the server just as if it were executed locally. With both messaging and RPCs, the essential information gets from the client to the server, although the form of the information that flows across the network in the first method is very different from that which flows in the second.

Although both messaging and RPCs are equivalent *functionally*, both are not equally well suited to the database world, at least in my opinion. Here's why.

RPCs work well when the semantic content exchanged between the client and the server is known by the client and fits naturally into the function call paradigm—that is, when the data flowing to and from the server can be described by data types in the native programming language, even if the data type is complex, such as an array of structures in C. The key point is that for RPCs to be really useful, the application program must be able to provide a data structure of the correct type for output data *before* the remote function call is made. Although unstructured data can be handled if the application passes a typeless chunk of memory as an argument (in C, giving it a type of *void* *), the application must then interpret the contents of the buffer. This is not a lot different from parsing a message, except that the application, instead of the database API component, has to parse it.

Another distinctive characteristic of RPCs is their inability to pass state information across function calls. For example, it is not possible to pass a pointer to a memory location in one remote function call, store that pointer, and assume that some later function call can implicitly modify that memory. Why? Because actual memory locations on a client are meaningless in an RPC-based system. The server cannot possibly know the memory location of a variable on the client.

As it turns out, these two characteristics of RPCs make data access difficult when the application cannot program in advance the structure of the data being returned to it. The reasoning behind this is very similar to that discussed earlier (in Chapter 2) with regard to dynamic SQL and static SQL. If the application programmer knows what columns are to be returned from the server, it is easy for the programmer to pass the correct number of variables of the correct type via an RPC. But without that knowledge, it isn't possible for the programmer to declare the RPC properly. And RPCs' inability to handle state information makes it impossible to support the idea of binding as described earlier. You can't make a function call that returns the next row of information and puts the row in a buffer that you defined earlier in another function call.

Let's look at an example that demonstrates the strengths and weaknesses of RPCs. You might recognize this as the same example used in Chapter 2 to demonstrate static and dynamic SQL:

```
EXEC SQL declare C1 cursor for
    select empname, deptno from emp where deptno = :dept;
EXEC SQL open C1
while (SQLCODE == 0)
    {
    EXEC SQL FETCH c1 INTO :name, :dnum
    }
```

First, a function to execute the SELECT statement could be remoted to the server:

```
FindEmployees(dept);
```

The RPC system would pass this request to the server, where the server-side implementation might actually use the same SQL statement shown above:[7]

```
SELECT empname, deptno FROM emp WHERE deptno = :dept;
```

Then for each row returned, the application could call

```
while(FetchEmployee(name, &dnum))
    Display(name, dnum);
```

Like the FETCH command in the embedded SQL example discussed previously, each call to *FetchEmployee* would go to the server to fetch the next row and return the two columns of data in the variables provided. This is very elegant and seems more natural to developers than intermixing regular programming syntax with SQL.[8]

In cases such as this, in which the output can be predicted at the time the application is written, the RPC model works extremely well. The programmer can simply declare an array of structures for the desired number of rows to fetch and pass the array as the argument to the fetch function, and the server would return multiple rows in one trip across the network. Each call would return the desired number of rows until the result set was exhausted.

However, consider the case in which the structure of the output is not known in advance by the client application. (This is very similar to the embedded static SQL vs. dynamic SQL discussion we had in Chapter 2.) How would an RPC system handle the fact that the number and types of output arguments are not known? One method is to simply pass a large typeless buffer and build the logic into the application to decode the results. But then why bother with RPC in the first place? This is exactly the same as the messaging model, except that now each application must decode the contents of the buffer. It seems better to let some lower-level module decode and encode the data stream and present it in logical units to the application—which is, in fact, the messaging approach.

"But hold on a minute," you say. "Why can't RPCs be designed to return smaller, more logical units of data to the application?" Good question. They

---

7. In order to make all this actually work, the developer needs to install the *FindEmployees* function on the server, register it with the server-side RPC service, compile the client-side definition of the *FindEmployees* function into a stub library, and link the stub library with the client-side application.

8. Because the SQL model and the programming language model are quite different, intermixing the two has sometimes been referred to as an "impedance mismatch."

can. But when a system uses RPCs to return one column at a time for every row, the amount of network traffic skyrockets. Returning a single value per function call with an RPC means that for every value in every row you make a round trip across the network. This makes about as much sense as writing a 100-byte file in 100 separate 1-byte write statements. Obviously, some level of buffering would improve performance dramatically.

The only balanced approach is to use highly encoded data structures and reduce the strongly typed nature of most 3GL, at which point it becomes just a matter of personal preference whether to use RPCs or messaging.

RPCs and Stored Procedures *Stored procedures* were introduced by Sybase[9] in the 1980s as a means of allowing business rules and logic to be distributed between clients and servers in a very flexible way. For example, here is a pretty realistic business rule: "The quantity of a product ordered cannot exceed the amount in inventory. If the quantity is not sufficient to fill an order or if the inventory quantity falls below 10 percent of nominal stock on hand, generate a reorder request." Clearly an application could write the necessary SQL statements and conditional logic to enforce such a rule. Assuming that the application does the business rule enforcement, it might include code similar to the example below. (We'll use a product ID of *widget 1* and a quantity of *27* for clarity here; in practice both of these values would be replaced by program variables.)

```
SQLExecDirect(hstmt, "SELECT QtyOnHand, StockQty FROM products WHERE
            productID = 'widget 1'", SQL_NTS);
SQLFetch(hstmt);
/* Enforce business rule: determine whether quantity of order */
/* can be filled by current inventory. (QtyOnHand and StockQty */
/* are program variables bound to columns of the same name in */
/* the results of the above query.) */
if (QtyOnHand < 27 || (QtyOnHand - 27) < (StockQty/10))
    {
    /* First determine whether order can be filled at all */
    if (QtyOnHand < 27)
        /* Tell user there is not enough stock to fill order */
        OrderCannotBeFilled()
    /* In either case, submit reorder request */
    SQLExecDirect(hstmt, "INSERT into REORDER values('widget 1')",
                SQL_NTS);
    }
```

---

9. Many other vendors now have or will soon have support for stored procedures in their DBMSs. Oracle now supports stored procedures in version 7 of the Oracle DBMS. The ANSI and ISO SQL standards committees are also working on adding stored procedures to the SQL standard, although the standard uses the term *persistent stored module* (PSM) instead of *stored procedure.*

I think everyone would agree that such rules should be enforced centrally in the DBMS whenever possible. That way, even if many different kinds of applications access this data, the rule will always be enforced consistently. The stored procedure approach would move the logic for our example business rule to the stored procedure on the server, and the only way any application could process an order would be to call the stored procedure. Assuming that the stored procedure on the server was called *ValidateOrderQty*, the application logic would become

```
SQLExecDirect(hstmt, "{?=call ValidateOrderQty('widget 1', 27)}",
              SQL_NTS);
if (ret == CANNOT_FILL_ORDER)
    /* Inform user that order cannot be filled */
    OrderCannotBeFilled()
```

Note how all the interaction with the underlying tables is hidden from the application. In fact, the invocation of the stored procedure looks an awful lot like a regular function call: it has a name, some arguments, and a return value. The key point is that when an application uses a function call approach with stored procedures, such an approach has exactly the same expressive power as the "pure" RPC approach but still uses the messaging model under the covers. In other words, an RPC is just another kind of message.

In short, RPCs can either be used directly or with the messaging approach. The fundamental point is that a system needs to have a way to get a function name and its arguments from the client to the server and a way to get any output arguments and a return value back to the client. That's it. Either "pure" RPC or the messaging approach using the stored procedure paradigm will work.

3.5 Summary

This chapter discussed three architectures for data access: the PC file server model, the server/terminal model, and the client/server model. It explained how the three main parts of client/server systems (the client, the server, and the data protocol) work, although a great many details were omitted. In summary, the client connects and sends requests to the server, the server responds with status and results, and the data protocol carries the information between client and server across the network. The data protocol's role is the same regardless of whether the messaging approach or the RPC approach is used: both work as data protocols and are functionally equivalent.

This concludes the background information portion of this book. In Chapter 4 we're going to start getting into the specifics of ODBC.

CHAPTER FOUR

ODBC Architecture

Chapters 2 and 3 provided a lot of background material about DBMSs, programming models, and computing architectures to help you understand ODBC. Now it's time to look at ODBC itself. This chapter presents a basic introduction to ODBC architecture, describes its major components, and discusses some of the motivations that led to certain design decisions.

4.1 ODBC Is Built on the Client/Server Model

Chapter 3 presented a simplified view of client/server architecture consisting of a client, a server, and a data protocol that allows the client and server to communicate with each other. Although this model is ideally suited to a traditional relational DBMS, in which a physical network connects the client PC to the DBMS on another machine, it is general enough to accommodate a wide variety of topologies, including local desktop databases such as dBASE, in which no network is involved at all. ODBC was designed to be used with systems that can fit into the client/server architecture model. Specifically, if it had not been built to work with this architectural framework, ODBC could not have met the following requirements for traditional relational DBMSs:

- Provide a standard API
- Exploit all the functionality of any given DBMS
- Provide performance equivalent to any DBMS's native API

All three requirements could be met only if ODBC was based on client/server architecture. Why? The answer can be found in Figure 3-4 from Chapter 3, which showed the components of the client in client/server architecture. That figure is repeated on the following page as Figure 4-1, with added emphasis on the database API component.

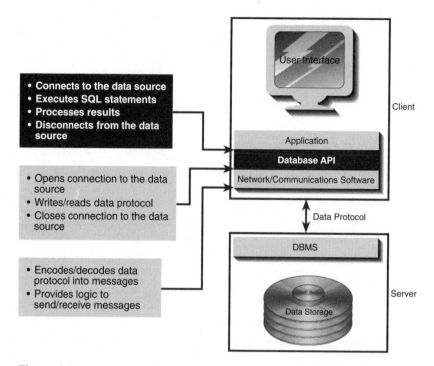

Figure 4-1.

Client components of client/server architecture.

ODBC exploits the fact that it doesn't really matter what the database API component is, because *the real measure of the functionality and performance of the DBMS is determined by the data protocol and SQL capabilities of the DBMS.* That is, as long as the database API component can emit and receive the same data protocol in the same manner as the DBMS's native programming interface, the server won't know the difference. The server's only input from the client is the data protocol—it knows nothing of the client-side programming interface. The database API module in the diagram could be the native DBMS API or some other API; it has no effect on functionality or performance as long as the data protocol is the same.

> NOTE: The astute reader will realize that it isn't quite this simple. What if the data protocol uses RPCs rather than messages? Then, in fact, the data protocol *is* the native programming interface. However, no products (to my knowledge) actually work this way because of the model mismatch and subsequent performance difficulties explained in the previous chapter. But even if RPCs are

used as the data protocol, a standard API can still be used if it is mapped to the native API, which in this case would be remoted to the server. However, in this case an extra layer is required for the standard API, whereas the extra layer would not be needed if both the standard API and the native API emit and receive the message-based data protocol directly.

Thus the design of ODBC rests on the client/server architecture model and the assumption that any programming interface that can emit and receive the data protocol of any SQL DBMS will function and perform just like the native API for the DBMS.

But ODBC is not limited to client/server DBMSs; it also works with desktop databases and file-oriented data stores such as spreadsheets and text files. ODBC's overall architecture is flexible enough to accommodate these types of data sources, although the terminology gets stretched a bit.

Let's take a look at the components of ODBC architecture to see how they all fit together.

4.2 Components of ODBC Architecture

As mentioned above, the architecture of ODBC is based on the client/server model, yet it is flexible enough to handle non-client/server DBMSs. ODBC's architecture has four components:

- **Applications**   Applications are responsible for interacting with the user via the user-interface and for calling ODBC functions to submit SQL statements and retrieve results.

- **The Driver Manager**   The Driver Manager loads and calls drivers on behalf of applications.

- **Drivers**   Drivers process ODBC function calls, submit SQL requests to specific data sources, and return results to applications. Drivers are also responsible for interacting with any software layers necessary to access data sources. Such layers include software that interfaces to underlying networks or file systems.

- **Data sources**   Data sources consist of sets of data and their associated environments, which include operating systems, DBMSs, and networks (if any). The term *data source* is used rather loosely to describe any software component that is not one of the three described above.

Figure 4-2 shows the four components of ODBC architecture and how the term *data source* describes both file-oriented data stores and client/server DBMSs. Note that in the ODBC architecture the database API component in Figure 4-1 has been divided into two components, the ODBC Driver Manager and the ODBC driver.

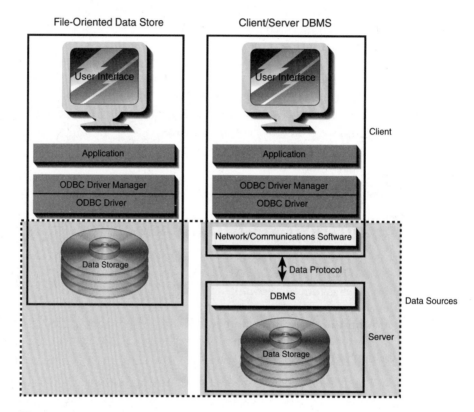

Figure 4-2.
The components of ODBC architecture.

The next sections look at these components in depth.

4.2.1 Applications

Applications do all the work external to the ODBC interface. For example, a spreadsheet is an application; it uses ODBC to access data in a database and then presents that data to the user for manipulation. Applications use ODBC to connect to data sources, send SQL requests to those data sources, and retrieve results.

4.2.2 The Driver Manager

The ODBC Driver Manager, as its name suggests, manages interactions between application programs and drivers. Although Figure 4-2 does not show it, multiple applications and multiple drivers can be managed simultaneously by the Driver Manager.

4.2.2.1 Overview

An application calls an ODBC function in the Driver Manager, and the Driver Manager routes the call to the correct driver. When an application first uses ODBC to connect to some source of data, the Driver Manager determines which driver is required and loads that driver into memory. From that moment forward, the Driver Manager simply takes any incoming function call from the application and calls the function of the same name in the driver (unless it is a function call that the Driver Manager itself processes, as is the case when the application asks for the name of a driver). When the application calls the ODBC function that disconnects, the Driver Manager unloads the driver from memory. (However, if more than one application is using the driver, the driver is not unloaded from memory until the last application is finished with it.)

The Driver Manager also performs some rudimentary error checking to ensure that functions are being called in the right order and that arguments contain valid values. This error checking relieves driver developers from a burdensome task because many of the usual robustness checks that drivers have traditionally been responsible for are enforced by the Driver Manager.

A driver is responsible for receiving requests from the Driver Manager, for interacting with the DBMS, and also for using any communications software (such as network or dial-up software) that is required to access the server. At a minimum a driver must establish and maintain a connection to the server, send SQL commands, and retrieve results.

It would be reasonable to think that applications could interact with drivers directly without using the Driver Manager, and, in fact, ODBC could have been designed that way. But it would have meant that every application developer would have had to do more work to manage the mechanics of handling drivers. In particular, an application would have to

- Manage driver loading and unloading
- Build and manage arrays of pointers to functions and use indirect function calls
- Present to the end user some meaningful way to map from a driver to real-world sources of data (customers, sales, order tracking, and inventory, for example)

If the dream of allowing multiple applications to access the same data was to be realized, a single, consistent user interface for connecting to diverse sources of data had to be employed. Otherwise, each end user would have to learn each application's interface for managing the drivers and the connections to the DBMS. Even though connecting to the data source is the same operation (from the end user's point of view) regardless of whether the application is a spreadsheet, a report writer, or a form, in the real world each application tends to have its own unique model and presentation scheme. Thus, leaving the driver management and end-user interface for connecting to the data source up to each application was counter to the goal of consistency. So the Driver Manager provides the user interface necessary to help applications connect to the appropriate source of data by prompting the user for a data source name and then mapping that name to the correct driver.

4.2.2.2 Windows Dynamic-Link Libraries

One goal of ODBC is to provide access not just to multiple sources of data but to multiple sources of data *at the same time.* This immediately raises a technical difficulty: how can an application call the same function but have it execute different code? Any developer knows that if you define a function twice, the linker will generate an error saying something like, "Duplicate symbol defined: *function name.*"

To solve this problem, we looked to a part of the Windows architecture that allows for the dynamic linking of libraries (hence the name dynamic-link library, or DLL). A program that uses dynamic linking while it is running can load and use another program. Windows itself relies heavily on dynamic linking. Windows-based applications call functions to perform screen painting, disk I/O, message processing, and all of the other services provided by the system. But, of course, no Windows-based application includes the complete set of Windows runtime libraries. Rather, when a function is called by an application, Windows determines which dynamic-link library contains the call, loads the library from the disk into memory, and calls the function in the library.

Other operating systems use the same concept. For instance, UNIX and the Macintosh use what they call "shared libraries," and VAX/VMS uses "shared images." Although the details and functionality of these concepts differ, the effect of their implementation is the same: programs can be divided into components that can be linked together at runtime. (Dynamic loading, on the other hand, is not quite as universally supported.)

In the design of ODBC, we exploited this idea to allow multiple implementations of the ODBC API to be loaded at the same time. We've seen that ODBC provides the Driver Manager to allow applications to avoid having to manage the loading and unloading of drivers. But how does the Driver Manager handle multiple applications and multiple drivers that all support the same entry points? The Driver Manager does this by calling functions indirectly and by using DLLs.

In Windows there are actually two ways in which the linker links a DLL to an application. The first method is to link an application to an *import library* that defines all the entry points in the DLL. When the application is linked, the import library defines all the entry points for the DLL, but none of the code from the DLL is actually included in the program's EXE file. When the application is executed, Windows automatically looks for the DLL on disk and loads it into memory. If the DLL is not present, the application itself will not run. From the application's point of view, this kind of DLL linking is the same as linking the library statically into the application, except that the link doesn't happen until runtime.

The second way to link a DLL to an application is to explicitly load the DLL at runtime. In this case the application has to manage everything itself. It must explicitly load the DLL by name using the Windows *LoadLibrary* function. Once the library is loaded, the application must determine each entry point in the DLL by calling another Windows function, *GetProcAddress*. Each entry point can be loaded either by the function name (the slow way) or by the function's ordinal number within the DLL (the fast way). Every entry point into the DLL must be stored in memory so that it can be called later via indirect calling. That is, whereas a normal C function call is made by simply including the function's name in the application program, an indirect function call is made by referencing a pointer to a variable that contains the address of the function you want to call.

For example, a C application using a direct call might call a function named *foo* in this way:

```
result = foo(arg1, arg2);
```

But if *foo* was one of many functions in a DLL and was called indirectly, the code would look more like this:

```
GetProcAddress(hLib, pfFunctionList[i], "foo");
result = *(pfFunctionList[i])(arg1, arg2);
```

Managing several entry points in an array and doing indirect calls is messy. But it gets downright ugly if multiple DLLs are involved, because each DLL requires a separate array. However, this method does provide the ability to load multiple drivers with the same function names and to manage them separately.

Relieving application developers of this burden is one of the main purposes of the Driver Manager. The Driver Manager loads a driver, gets all of its entry points, and makes the association via a *connection handle* that is passed back to the application. Every time the application uses the handle, the Driver Manager knows which driver to call and has the address for each function in an array that it manages.

Applications typically use the import library for the Driver Manager DLL so that they can obtain the benefits of direct calling. The Driver Manager must then use indirect calling to call drivers. Although the Driver Manager can load driver entry points either by name or by ordinal, driver writers should take advantage of the faster loading of DLL entry points by ordinal. To do so, a driver writer must define the driver's entry points in the order defined by ODBC's SQLEXT.H and set a special ordinal value (199) within the driver DLL. The Driver Manager checks for the special ordinal value when it loads the driver and, if the value is present, loads the entry points in the driver by ordinal.

The Inside Story
Act I, Scene IV: The Gang of Three

By the summer of 1989, the Open SQL specification had been renamed "SQL Connectivity" (SQLC, pronounced *sequel see*) in deference to Tandem's project, and although many more companies had reviewed and commented on the specification, Microsoft, Sybase, and Lotus emerged as the key technical contributors to the specification. Yes, Lotus was now actively interested and participating in SQLC. Although Lotus was still pursuing its own database connectivity strategy (now named "DataLens" instead of "Blueprint"), it seemed clear to all of us that an SQL-based interface had the best chance of becoming an industry standard, so Lotus added its considerable expertise to the SQLC effort, mostly with the participation of Don Nadel.

Don had a thorough understanding of database connectivity issues, and, along with Tom McGary, Peter Wilkins, and Peter O'Kelly from Lotus's technical staff, Don provided an enormous boost to the technical viability and completeness of SQLC. Tom Haggin from Sybase continued to provide valuable insights on the server side as well as comparisons to DB-Library. Later on, Ed Archibald from Sybase joined in the design meetings, also providing major input.

> We thought we would all ride off into the sunset together, happily helping the client/server revolution get off the ground with our little database connectivity API.
>
> But it was not to be quite so simple, as the events of the next few months revealed....

4.2.3 Drivers

Although ODBC's goal is to make accessing data from diverse data sources as seamless as possible, the differences between DBMSs cannot and should not be glossed over. To address these fundamental differences, ODBC defines three kinds of drivers, each geared toward the general topology of one kind of DBMS. Although the functionalities of these three kinds of DBMSs differ, the differences in topology are hidden from the application by ODBC. The application doesn't need to know whether the data being accessed is on a local machine, on a LAN server, or on a mainframe on the other side of the world.

4.2.3.1 One-Tier Drivers

In ODBC, the term *one-tier driver* refers to a driver that accesses a desktop database file, an ISAM, or a flat file. For the purposes of this section, I will refer to both desktop databases and ISAMs as ISAMs because the two native programming interfaces are nearly identical. The usual configuration of such a system has the database located on the same machine as the driver; hence only one machine, or "tier," is in the picture. The major characteristic that distinguishes a one-tier driver from another type of driver is that the one-tier driver itself does all the SQL processing because the data source in such a system is not an SQL database engine or a server in the client/server sense. The native programming interface to such a data source consists of file I/O or ISAM function calls, so the driver itself becomes the SQL database engine. In other words, the driver parses, optimizes, and executes SQL statements. Figure 4-3 on the following page shows this architecture with two types of one-tier drivers: the file I/O type (such as the Text and Microsoft Excel drivers included on the sample CD) and the ISAM type (such as the Microsoft Access, FoxPro, Paradox, and dBASE drivers included on the sample CD).

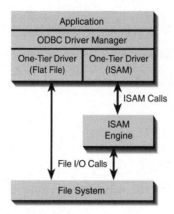

Figure 4-3.
One-tier architecture.

Because the capabilities of one-tier drivers are usually limited to file-oriented operations, it is common for one-tier drivers to have fewer features than other kinds of drivers. For example, as a rule, one-tier drivers do not support robust multiuser access and transaction processing. Writing a one-tier driver that could support these functionalities would be overwhelming in terms of size and complexity and, frankly, would not be necessary for almost all uses of such drivers.

But, like the traditional relational DBMS model shown in Figure 3-5 of Chapter 3, a one-tier driver has most of the same internal modules: an SQL parser, an optimizer, and an execution module. And, although I did not show this in Figure 3-5, the DBMS usually has an internal ISAM-like interface that manipulates indexes directly. In short, a one-tier driver is the DBMS.

Examples of one-tier drivers that use ISAM programming interfaces include drivers for dBASE, Paradox, and Microsoft Access files. Drivers that use file I/O operations directly on data files include drivers for text files and spreadsheet files.

When processing SQL statements from applications, file I/O drivers do not perform any of the optimizations that are typically found in SQL DBMSs because there are no indexes. These drivers must always search an entire file when looking for data.

ISAM drivers, on the other hand, can perform very good optimizations because, as the term implies, ISAM systems have indexes, which can dramatically improve performance over the file I/O system.

4.2.3.2 Two-Tier Drivers

Two-tier systems are the classic client/server systems. The driver (client) sends and receives the DBMS's data protocol or maps to the native database API but doesn't directly access the data. The DBMS (server) receives SQL requests from the client, executes them, and sends the results back to the client.

In a two-tier system, a driver that directly uses the data protocol is merely acting as a conduit of information to and from the DBMS, just like the native database API runtime library. A driver that maps between ODBC and the native database API acts as a translator between APIs.

Figure 4-4 shows the architectures of two kinds of two-tier systems. I have simplified the description considerably—it appears that the driver doesn't do much beyond map to the data protocol or native database API. That is certainly not the case, but the details will have to wait until Chapter 5.

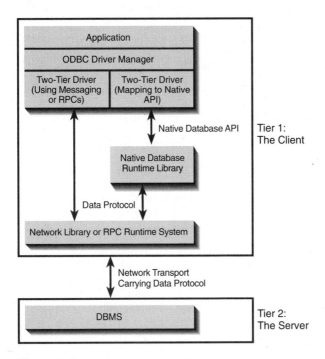

Figure 4-4.
Two-tier architecture.

Examples of two-tier drivers are Microsoft SQL Server (which directly manipulates the data protocol) and Oracle (which maps to Oracle's native database API, OCI).

An interesting variation on the two-tier theme is found in the architecture used by IBI EDA/SQL, OpenLink Software, Gnosis, and others. In this variation, which is sometimes referred to as *middleware,* the DBMS-specific data protocol does not flow from the client directly to the DBMS on the server at all. Instead, the middleware vendor's client driver communicates with the middleware vendor's server application using the middleware's own network libraries and data protocol. The server application then talks to the DBMS on the same machine, typically using the native database API runtime library.[1] This architecture is depicted in Figure 4-5.

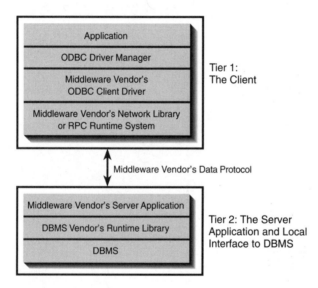

Figure 4-5.
A variation of two-tier architecture.

This architecture has the benefit of simplifying the path between the client and server because all the software (except the Driver Manager) between the application and the DBMS is provided by the middleware vendor. Two potential drawbacks are that the middleware vendor might not provide support for the particular network stack being used and that in some ways this

---

1. The term *middleware* is somewhat descriptive because a single collection of software from one vendor provides all the software in the "middle" (between the application and the DBMS) except the Driver Manager. However, the term is thrown around so loosely that it is not strictly correct to call only such architectures "middleware."

architecture isolates the clients from the DBMS. You really have to trust the middleware vendor's data protocol to be as functional and high-performance as the equivalent components from the DBMS vendor.

Figure 4-6 uses a concrete example to show the difference between the two-tier architecture discussed first in this section and the variation discussed immediately above. On the right is the OpenLink architecture for accessing an Oracle DBMS; on the left is the architecture for the Oracle driver provided by Oracle Corporation. Note the lack of a server-side software component on the left, and note the location of the OCI library (on the client on the left and on the server on the right).

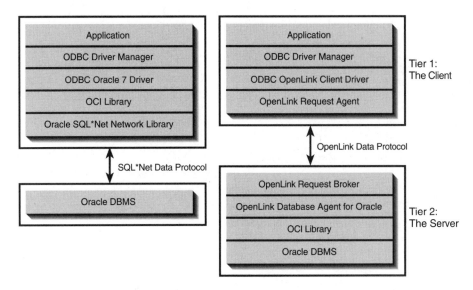

Figure 4-6.
A comparison of alternative two-tier ODBC architectures.

Either architecture is a fine choice for ODBC—there is no clear best alternative from an overall architectural design standpoint. I'm not going to get into making product comparisons and recommendations in this book, although the benchmark program provided on the CD included with this book will help you evaluate some basic performance characteristics of ODBC drivers and architectures.

4.2.3.3 Three-Tier Drivers and Beyond

Three-tier drivers are not much different from two-tier drivers from the client's perspective. The difference is that the client in three-tier systems, instead of connecting directly to the DBMS, connects to a server that acts as a gateway to the target DBMS. In fact, the gateway can and usually does actually connect to multiple DBMSs.

In systems that deploy ODBC-based applications to access multiple data sources, three-tier architecture moves a lot of the complexity from the client to the server, which can be of tremendous help in simplifying the installation, configuration, and administration of drivers. All clients use a single driver to connect to the gateway, and the gateway routes requests to the appropriate driver on the server. Figure 4-7 shows three-tier architecture.

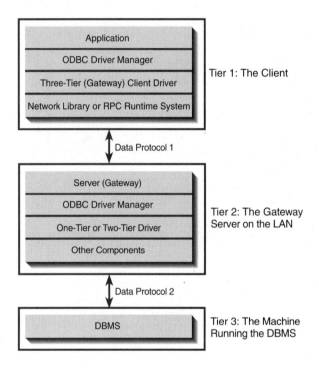

Figure 4-7.
Three-tier architecture.

You'll notice that tiers 1 and 2 are very similar. The nature of this architecture makes it easy to create any number of tiers. That is, there's no particular reason that the tier 2 machine couldn't talk to another gateway rather than to the target DBMS, effectively making the system a four-tier configuration. This is not common, however, because most of the performance gains are achieved by offloading clients to a network server, which can usually be boosted in capacity to meet the needs of more clients without adding another machine.

It is not necessary to have ODBC on the server in the three-tier case. The component directly below the server (the gateway) in Figure 4-7 could just as easily be a native database API or anything else that accesses the target data source.

4.2.3.4 A Caveat

Although the one-tier, two-tier, and three-tier models provide a good framework for understanding the different types of drivers, some drivers do not fit neatly into any of these categories.

For example, consider a driver for dBASE that accesses dBASE files on a network file server. Two machines are involved here, not one, but because the interface between the driver and the data source is file I/O, we still think of this as a one-tier driver. But if multiple users will be using this system for shared file access, the driver and the application developer need to know when the data is to be accessed concurrently by multiple users on a file server. The driver can't assume that it will be processing only local file I/O. This consideration makes the driver not purely one-tier, although it is certainly not two-tier as described above.

Another case that does not fit perfectly into the model is a client/server DBMS that is configured to run on one machine. In this case the client software and the server software are running on the same physical hardware but in logically separate processes. For example, Watcom SQL can run as a local database engine accessible only by the applications on the local machine or as a true server on a network. But because the data access is separated into another program or DLL apart from the driver itself, we still call this a two-tier architecture even though it is all running on one machine. Similarly, Microsoft SQL Server on a Windows NT–based machine can be accessed on the same machine by the Windows NT Microsoft SQL Server driver. But this is still a two-tier configuration as far as ODBC is concerned.

4.2.3.5 What Does a Driver Do?

Now that we've looked at the different types of drivers, it's time to look a little more closely at exactly what drivers do. In a previous section I said that a one-tier driver is in itself the SQL database engine, which makes it entirely different than a two-tier or three-tier driver. This section will show some of the tasks that drivers must perform in order to provide applications with a uniform programming interface and yet still exploit many features of each DBMS.

Connection Management   After the Driver Manager loads a driver, the first interesting thing that the driver must do is connect to the machine on which the data is located. In the case of one-tier drivers, by definition no network connection needs to be made, since the data is local. However, most one-tier drivers have several configuration options that are used during the connection process, which can be thought of as initializing or connecting to the driver instead of to a remote DBMS. For example, consider the options provided by Q+E's dBASE driver, as shown in Figure 4-8.

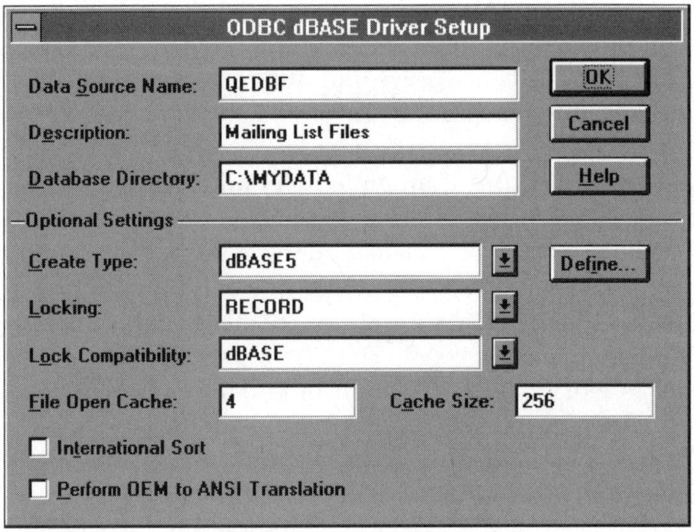

Figure 4-8.
Q+E Intersolv dBASE driver setup options.

The Locking combo box is used to tell the driver what kind of locking is to be used, if any. In the figure, this option is set to RECORD, which is used for multiuser access. A NONE setting is used for single-user access.

At connection time, the driver reads these configuration options and initializes data structures so that when the file is actually opened the correct options (for example, exclusive access or shared access) will be used.

A two-tier driver has considerably more work to do at connection time. It must establish an actual network connection to the DBMS. If the application uses the *SQLDriverConnect* function, which is almost always the case, the driver is responsible for displaying a dialog box in which the user types his or her name and password for logging in to the DBMS. Once this security information has been obtained from the user, the driver loads the appropriate network library (unless the library is directly linked into the driver). The library that is used is determined by how the driver was configured and is typically based on the type of network transport used on the computer. Then the network library functions use entries for the server name or network address provided at setup time to connect to the server. The driver gets the connection information from the ODBC initialization file (ODBC.INI) if Windows 3.x is being used, from the registry if Windows NT or Windows 95 is being used, or in some cases from its own initialization file. If the application specified a time-out value for the connection, the driver must also use a timing loop during the connection process so that control can be returned to the application if the time-out expires before a successful connection is made.

Finally, some drivers send requests to the DBMS after making the connection but before returning control to the application. For example, the Microsoft SQL Server driver sends a request to switch the context to a named database if the user specified a nondefault database during setup. Also, to streamline the return of metadata later on, the driver retrieves the definitions of all user-defined data types and sets the maximum size of text and image columns that can be read during the connection. It is worth noting that this process caused some developers to notice that connecting to Microsoft SQL Server via ODBC is slower than connecting via DB-Library. For developers who don't need the information, the overhead is inconvenient, so versions 2.x of the Microsoft SQL Server driver provide a connection option that disables this extra information retrieval, bringing the connection time for the Microsoft SQL Server driver to nearly the same level as that of DB-Library.[2]

Three-tier drivers might perform one additional step in the connection process. For example, access to the gateway might require security information, and access to the target database might require separate security information when the gateway connects to it. It is quite possible that the user will need to supply two sets of user ID and password information—one to connect to the gateway and one to connect to the target DBMS. The driver might display multiple dialog boxes to the user before the connection can be completed.

---

2. ODBC doesn't load drivers until connection time. Driver loading involves obtaining all the entry points and loading at least one code segment from the driver DLL from disk into memory. On the first connection to a particular driver, ODBC will always be slower than a native runtime library if the native runtime library has been statically linked to the application and is resident in memory. Fortunately, the overhead of loading a driver is measured in milliseconds and typically increases the overall connection time by an insignificant amount.

Error Handling   ODBC requires drivers to provide standard error codes in addition to DBMS-specific error codes to give applications a standard way of dealing with error conditions. Although DBMSs return similar kinds of errors, each does so in a different manner, using different error numbers, message types, programming styles, and so forth.

ODBC simplifies dealing with error information by providing

- A simple return code mechanism that reports success or failure for each function.

- A single standard error function (*SQLError*) that applications call every time an ODBC function fails or reports a warning.

- Standard error codes for more than 85 error conditions. A standard error code is returned in the form of an SQLSTATE, a five-character sequence defined by the ISO SQL-92 standard.

- All error information from the driver or the DBMS in addition to the standard error codes. The native error code and error message text are returned to the application via the error function.

- A tagging scheme for identifying the component that reported the error. This includes text that identifies the vendor that provided the component, the name of the component, and any other information that helps pin down the location or type of problem. For example, the tag for the Microsoft Access 2.0 driver is "[Microsoft] [ODBC Microsoft Access 2.0 Driver]," whereas the Intersolv text file driver's tag is "[INTERSOLV] [ODBC Text driver]." If other software components (such as network libraries) have identifiable errors, those are given a separate tag, as in this example, in which the error came from the Microsoft SQL Server network library for named pipes (DBNMP3): "[Microsoft] [ODBC SQL Server Driver] [DBNMP3]."

- A provision for returning multiple errors that occur from a single ODBC function call. An application retrieves multiple errors by repeatedly calling the error function. Multiple errors can occur because some DBMSs send errors in multiple parts. For example, a DBMS might report a syntax error and then follow that message with a message reporting the specific syntax violation, such as "Unexpected end of statement encountered after keyword FROM."

For an interactive application that simply displays the error message from the DBMS to the end user, the only advantage to standard error handling is the common programming style. But when an application itself takes action based on an error from the DBMS, the application developer can write much simpler code if the error codes from different DBMS vendors do not have to be checked.

Consider a somewhat obscure but important case called "serialization failure" involving an online transaction processing (OLTP) type of application. Any DBMS capable of transaction processing has a built-in method for detecting deadlocks between two transactions.[3] When the deadlock occurs, the application that initiated the transaction that was automatically rolled back will receive an error code from the DBMS informing it that the current transaction has been rolled back. The best thing for the application to do in this case is to simply restart the transaction. How would an application programmer know how to code for this situation? Each DBMS has its own error code, but with ODBC the driver translates the native error code from the DBMS to the SQL-92 standard error code for serialization failure, which happens to be "40001."

So rather than the programmer having to code something like

```
if (DBMS == SQL_SERVER && errorcode == errorcode1) ||
   (DBMS == ORACLE && errorcode == errorcode2) ||
   (DBMS == INFORMIX && errorcode == errorcode3) ...
       /* Restart transaction... */
```

in ODBC the programmer can simply write

```
if (!strcmp(SQLSTATE, "40001"))
   /* Restart transaction... */
```

and the code will work for any DBMS.

In summary, a driver must

- Map all native DBMS error codes to standard ODBC error codes (which are the error codes from the SQL-92 standard whenever possible)

---

3. A deadlock occurs, for example, when two transactions both need to update row 100 and row 10,000 in the same table. One transaction acquires a lock on row 100 and the other transaction acquires a lock on row 10,000. To complete the transaction, the first transaction now needs to read and update row 10,000, and the second transaction needs to read and update row 100 (the row that the other transaction has locked). Clearly both transactions will wait forever for the locks to be released. The DBMS will detect this "deadly embrace" (as deadlock is sometimes called) and will choose to terminate (roll back) one of the transactions and inform the client of the action taken.

■ Tag all error messages with the names of the software component and the component's manufacturer

■ Return the native error code and message text in the function argument provided for this purpose in *SQLError*

SQL Transformation   If a driver supports any of the escape clauses that ODBC defines for SQL statements (see Chapter 5), the driver must transform the escape clause so that it appears in the syntax required by the DBMS. The driver must also translate the SQL to conform to ANSI/ISO SQL if the DBMS supports a different syntax for the same functionality and if no information function in ODBC allows an application to determine how to generate the correct syntax. Of course the driver doesn't have to *add* functionality found in the standard but not in the DBMS, but if the syntax of the DBMS provides exactly the same functionality as the standard but simply does it differently, the driver must translate the standard SQL to the syntax supported by the DBMS.

Fortunately, this situation hardly occurs anymore. But it would be useful to look at two situations in the Microsoft SQL Server driver in which such translation had to occur, just by way of example.

The first situation was pretty trivial. Versions of Microsoft SQL Server prior to 4.0 used nonstandard syntax for the "does not equal" operator. The SQL standard specified <>, but Microsoft SQL Server accepted only !=. Later versions of Microsoft SQL Server supported the <> syntax, but for a while drivers had to look for the string <> in SQL statements and translate it to !=. Doing this in the driver was not too difficult or time consuming, just annoying. Of course, applications could directly use the != syntax, but then that SQL statement wouldn't work against any other DBMS.

The second situation is much trickier. Versions of Microsoft SQL Server prior to version 6.0 create columns as "not null" (not allowing null values) by default. The SQL standard says that the default is to allow nulls and to specify "not null" on a column definition when nulls are to be prohibited. For example, consider the SQL statement

```
CREATE TABLE T1 (temperature float)
```

In Microsoft SQL Server, the statement

```
INSERT INTO T1 VALUES (NULL)
```

for the table created above would fail because the column was created (by default) with nulls prohibited. A DBMS that complies with SQL standards would succeed with this same INSERT statement.

So the Microsoft SQL Server ODBC driver is required to scan all CRE-ATE TABLE statements and add the keyword NULL at the end of all column specifications that do not already have a null specification. In the preceding example, if an application generated

```
CREATE TABLE T1 (temperature float)
```

the Microsoft SQL Server ODBC driver would send the following to Microsoft SQL Server:

```
CREATE TABLE T1 (temperature float null)
```

In Microsoft SQL Server 6, the situation has improved. In this version the driver simply sends a command to the server at connection time that enables ISO SQL semantics for null column creation, and Microsoft SQL Server does the rest.

Catalog Functions One of the most important tasks of a driver is to provide information about the tables, columns, and other objects (collectively known as the *catalog*) in a DBMS in a standard way so that interactive applications and development tools can allow users to choose the items of interest. This is another case in which DBMSs have roughly the same functionality, but all provide it differently to applications. The SQL-92 standard provides a solution to this called the *schema information tables,* which are typically views that provide the information, but the schema information tables have not been widely implemented in DBMS products yet.

ODBC's approach is to provide a set of catalog functions that provide applications with the basic information they need from the DBMS's catalog. Each driver must generate an SQL query that returns the necessary information to the application in the most efficient manner possible. The SQL query the driver generates can vary considerably because each DBMS has its own system table names, column names, and indexes on its system tables, and therefore its own way to optimize the query. Sometimes the queries get pretty exotic. For example, consider the query used to return the tables that are accessible to the current user in Microsoft SQL Server. (The query itself is actually compiled in a stored procedure in the server, but the code shown in the next figure is sufficient to illustrate the point.) Figure 4-9 on the next page shows the major elements of the query.

Even if you don't read SQL, you can see that this is a very complicated query. But it is well tuned and will return the necessary information with high performance, and that is the whole point. Application programmers shouldn't have to become experts in accessing the system tables for every DBMS with maximum performance—that's the driver's job.

```
select
    table_qualifier = db_name,
    table_owner = user_name(o.uid),
    table_name = o.name,
    table_type = rtrim(
        substring('SYSTEM TABLE             TABLE       VIEW     ',
            /* 'S'=0, 'U'=2, 'V'=3 */
            (ascii(o.type) - 83) * 12 + 1, 12)),
    remarks = convert(varchar(254), null)  /* Remarks are NULL */
from sysusers u, sysobjects o
where
    o.name like @table_name
    and user_name(o.uid) like @table_owner
    /* Limit to desired types */
    and charindex(substring(o.type, 1, 1), @type1) != 0
    /* Constrain sysusers uid for use in subquery */
    and u.uid = user_id
    and (
        suser_id = 1  /* User is the system administrator */
        or o.uid = user_id  /* User created the object */
        /* Here's the magic: select the highest precedence of */
        /* permissions in the order (user, group, public) */
        or ((select max(((sign(uid) * abs(uid - 16383)) * 2) +
                (protecttype & 1))
            from sysprotects p
            /* Create outer join to correlate */
            /* with all rows in sysobjects */
            where p.id =* o.id
                /* Get rows for public, user, user's group */
                and (p.uid = 0 or p.uid = user_id
                  or p.uid =* u.gid)
                /* Check for SELECT, EXECUTE privilege */
                /* and--more magic--normalize GRANT */
                and (action in (193,224))) & 1
            ) = 1  /* Here's the final magic: compare GRANTs */
    )
order by table_type, table_qualifier, table_owner, table_name
```

Figure 4-9.
Query to retrieve Microsoft SQL Server table names.

The catalog functions defined in ODBC include

- *SQLTables*, which returns information about the tables the user can access

■ *SQLColumns*, which returns information about the columns in a table or tables

■ *SQLStatistics*, which returns information about a table, such as the number of rows it has and the indexes (if any) that are defined for it

■ *SQLSpecialColumns*, which returns the column or columns that are most efficient for positioning to a particular row and the columns that are automatically updated by the DBMS when any value in the row is updated

Additional catalog functions are available for retrieving referential integrity information (primary and foreign keys), stored procedures and their arguments, and information about the privileges granted and revoked for tables and columns.

For all these functions, the driver must generate the most efficient SQL query for the particular DBMS and retrieve the results for the information requested.

Information and Option Functions Drivers must provide information and option functions that report the various capabilities of the driver and the DBMS. The principal function here is *SQLGetInfo*. *SQLGetInfo* informs the application of the driver's conformance level, version, functionality capabilities (such as support of transactions), and many other capabilities that the application can use to adjust its behavior accordingly.

Another ODBC function, *SQLGetTypeInfo*, returns all the information about the native data types of the DBMS to the application. A driver must build a results set in which each row describes one data type. If the DBMS does not support user-defined types or some other method of adding data types to the system, the driver usually just keeps the data type information in a data structure and returns it without querying the server. However, if the DBMS supports an extensible data type system, the driver must query the server to get the built-in and user-defined types to return to the application. We'll look at the *SQLGetTypeInfo* function in detail in Chapter 5.

ODBC provides three functions for inquiring about drivers in general. These functions—*SQLDataSources*, *SQLDrivers*, and *SQLGetFunctions*—allow applications to enumerate all the installed data sources, all the drivers, and all the functions supported in a given driver.

ODBC provides two kinds of option functions: one for connections and one for statements. The options provide a way for applications to configure drivers and determine some driver capabilities. The connection options are used for transaction and miscellaneous connection-oriented purposes.

Connection options include

- An option to set the desired transaction isolation level for the current connection. The transaction isolation level determines the effect of other transactions on your transactions. The transaction isolation levels defined in ODBC were taken from the ISO SQL-92 standard. At one end of the spectrum is the SERIALIZABLE option, which ensures that other concurrent transactions have no effect on your transactions. At the other end is the READ_UNCOMMITTED option, which specifies no isolation from the effects of other transactions at all. There are five options altogether. (These options are described in detail in Chapter 5.) Different DBMSs support different capabilities for transaction isolation level, and each has a different means of setting the isolation level. For example, in Microsoft SQL Server 4.*x*, the only way to achieve the isolation level of SERIALIZABLE is to add the keyword HOLDLOCK after each table listed in the FROM clause of a SELECT statement. When an application using the Microsoft SQL Server driver sets the transaction isolation level to SERIALIZABLE, the driver automatically inserts the word HOLDLOCK after all tables in the FROM clause. Other DBMSs use statements like SET TRANSACTION to set the desired isolation level. Oracle, on the other hand, achieves true serializable isolation by means of the LOCK TABLE statement.

- An option to automatically commit every statement after it has been sent to the DBMS.

- An option to tell the driver how many seconds to wait to establish a connection before returning to the application.

- An option to force the Driver Manager to log all function calls made to it. This is a very handy debugging feature that is built into the Driver Manager.

Statement options include

- An option to enable or disable asynchronous execution of SQL statements. When asynchronous execution is enabled, an SQL statement is sent to the DBMS for processing but the driver does not wait for it to complete. Control is returned immediately to the application, and the application must check periodically to see if the request has been completed.

■ An option to tell the driver how many seconds to wait for a query to complete before returning to the application.

■ Options for fetching multiple rows with one function call.

Many of these options could have been handled by having ODBC define SQL syntax that the driver or DBMS would process. However, this is not as efficient as processing options as function calls.

Data Type Conversions   One goal of ODBC is to provide data in a form that is most usable to applications. Highly interactive applications that display data to the user typically want all data types to be converted to character strings. OLTP-style applications might want to retrieve and send data without any conversions to maximize performance. Applications that transfer data from one data source to another might want some types converted but not others.

ODBC allows applications to specify any data type conversion that makes sense. The driver is required to do the specified conversion. Alternatively, if the driver and DBMS support the standard ODBC scalar function CONVERT, the conversions can be done on the server if the client uses the CONVERT function on the desired columns in the SELECT list. The difference is that client-side conversions can be done on a row-by-row basis, whereas not all DBMSs support server-side conversions when fetching rows.

All an application has to do is indicate the data type of the C variable into which it wants to put the data, and the driver will convert the data from the server into that type or return an error if it is not possible.

4.2.4 Data Sources

Part of the ODBC mission is to hide a lot of the complexity of the underlying communications software that is usually present on client/server systems. It is important not to expose end users or even application programmers to concepts such as drivers, DBMSs, networks, server addresses, and so on. Instead, for each data source to be accessed, ODBC uses an abstraction that maps a single name (called the *data source name* or *DSN*) to all the necessary underlying software components required to access the data. The data source name is chosen by an end user or a system administrator and should be a name that makes clear to the user what kind of data it represents.

For example, an end user should be able to connect to a data source named "Payroll" without having to know the details about the DBMS, network, and client-side ODBC driver that are required to get there. In one end user's environment, for instance, the "Payroll" data could be managed by an

IBM mainframe running DB2, with the connectivity from the PC to the mainframe managed by a gateway on a LAN. A particular driver running on the PC would talk to the gateway, and an IBM SNA network would connect to the mainframe. For another user, the "Payroll" data might be managed by an Oracle system running on a Sun workstation accessed via TCP/IP directly from the PC by an Oracle driver. The point is, why would end users or even application developers need to know about all that? They don't. They just want to access the data that is important to them.

The Inside Story
Act I, Scene V: The Fateful Phone Call

In September 1989 I received a phone call from Kerry Chesbro from Teradata. (Teradata was later acquired by NCR, which was acquired by AT&T. And, in 1992, Kerry was acquired by the ODBC group at Microsoft!) Kerry had been a key reviewer of the SQLC technology and, in fact, had written an entire chapter of the specification about supporting DDE (Dynamic Data Exchange, the precursor to OLE) within SQLC. When the phone rang that Friday afternoon, the conversation went something like this:

"Hi Kerry, what's up?"

"Kyle, what do you think of this new industry consortium that is going to specify a standard interface for database connectivity?"

"*What* 'industry consortium'?"

"It's a bunch of database vendors trying to figure out how to make their products interoperate. They're doing embedded SQL, a standard protocol, and now they're talking about doing a function call interface."

"Wow, I better get some more information on these guys. Sounds like SQLC to me. Do you know when the next meeting is?"

"Yeah, it says here they're meeting Monday."

"As in Monday three days from now?"

"Yep."

"Where's the meeting?"

"At DEC in Nashua, New Hampshire."

"Oh boy. OK, thanks Kerry, I better go make travel arrangements. Thanks for the tip. Bye!"

N O T E :   Ideally, these abstract data source names would be registered and managed by some central name service. Then all clients within a corporation could hook into the name service and the Driver Manager could request the necessary information to allow the user's particular client machine to connect to the desired DBMS. Unfortunately, a standard name service that could perform such a task has yet to appear on the market and is unlikely to appear anytime soon. So for ODBC we used what was available: local initialization (INI) files that are supported by Windows versions 3.x and the registry for Windows NT and Windows 95. If and when such a global name service becomes available, the ODBC Driver Manager (and the installation components of ODBC that we haven't talked about yet) will probably be modified to use such a service as an alternative way to register, maintain, and configure drivers within the enterprise.

Specifically, the term *data source* is used in ODBC for two purposes:

1. As a conceptual term that defines the kind of data that the end user wants to access (for example, "Payroll," "Sales," or "Personnel"). In practice, the data source includes the DBMS software running on a physical machine with some operating system on some hardware platform, and the networking software required to access the machine (if appropriate) from the client. When ODBC refers to "connecting to a data source," the data source could be any of the following examples, to name just a few:

   ❑ An Oracle DBMS running on a Sun Solaris machine that is accessed via a network using TCP/IP.

   ❑ An Xbase file or files on the user's PC, in which case the network and remote hardware and operating system are not part of the communication path. In this case, the ODBC driver itself acts as the DBMS, because Xbase files are simply files—no inherent SQL engine is built into the Xbase product the way it is in Microsoft SQL Server and Oracle.

   ❑ A Tandem NonStop SQL DBMS running on the Guardian 90 operating system that is accessed via a gateway on a NetWare LAN using SPX/IPX.

2. As the actual name an end user or a system administrator assigns via an ODBC utility to describe a particular collection of software components (such as an ODBC driver and possibly other software components such as a network library, a server name or address, a DBMS, and so forth). For example, when an ODBC driver is installed on an end user's machine, the ODBC installation routine guides the user through the process of creating a data source name for the driver and the target location that contains the data that the driver will manipulate (the network address of the server name or the directory on the local machine in which data files reside).

It is the data source name that the end user sees when he or she interacts with an application that uses ODBC. The data source name is also used for configuration and administration purposes. When an application makes a connection, it typically supplies the name of a data source (not the name of a driver or a server).[4] The Driver Manager then maps the data source name to the appropriate driver, and that driver manages the rest of the connection process.

A few examples should help illustrate the relationship between drivers and data sources. Figure 4-10 shows the driver setup dialog box for the Oracle driver, Figure 4-11 shows the driver setup dialog box for the FoxPro driver, and Figure 4-12 shows this dialog box for the Microsoft SQL Server driver.

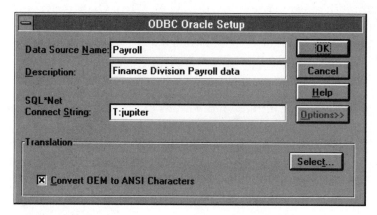

Figure 4-10.
Oracle driver setup dialog box.

---

4. ODBC also supports the ability to circumvent the data source abstraction, which is useful primarily for one-tier drivers. The *SQLDrivers* function and the DRIVER keyword used in conjunction with *SQLDriverConnect* provide the ability to make what ODBC calls a "DSN-less connection."

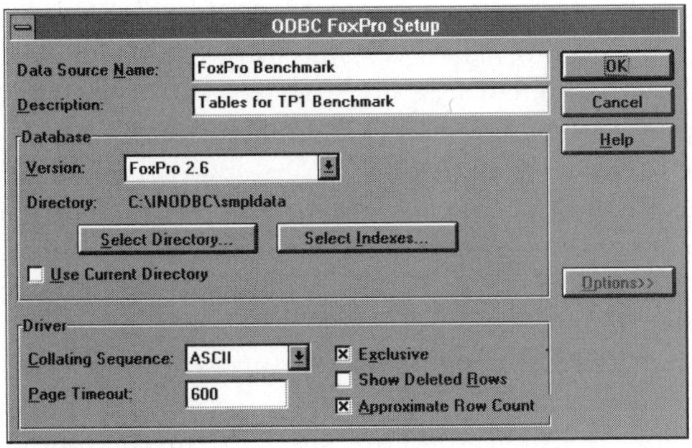

Figure 4-11.
FoxPro driver setup dialog box.

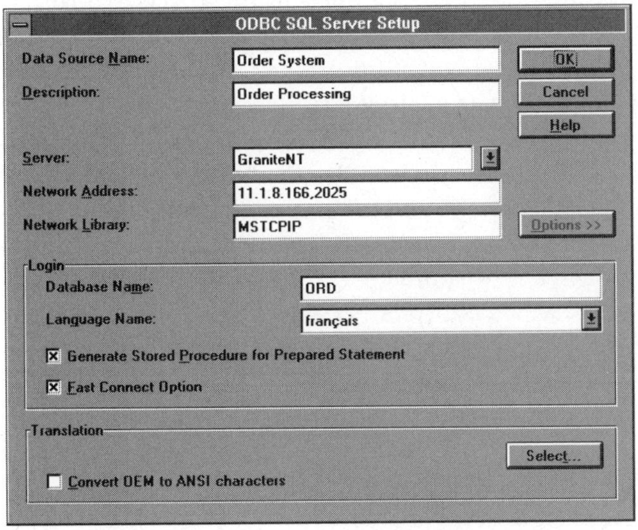

Figure 4-12.
Microsoft SQL Server driver setup dialog box.

Note that the edit controls for the data source name and the description are the same for all drivers but the controls that follow vary.

In the Oracle example, the network information is captured in the form of an SQL*Net connection string that denotes the kind of network that is involved (T: for TCP/IP in this example) and an alias name for the particular server.

The FoxPro driver example has nothing at all about networking or servers but includes a lot of information specific to directories, indexes, and other items specifically related to accessing FoxPro files.

In the Microsoft SQL Server driver example, the relevant pieces of information include the network address of the server, which will vary depending upon the type of network being used. Named pipes, the default, uses the name of the server machine itself as the network address. However, for TCP/IP, as shown in Figure 4-12, the IP address and socket number are required. You can also see that the Microsoft SQL Server driver has its own unique characteristics: unlike most DBMSs, Microsoft SQL Server uses the concept of multiple named "databases" per server. The default database to connect to is usually established by the system administrator, but if the end user regularly uses multiple databases, two ODBC data sources can be used to simplify connecting to the appropriate database.

It should be clear from the examples that drivers and DBMSs are diverse. But once all the details are supplied in these dialog boxes, the data source names hide all the complexity from application programmers and end users while still giving drivers and system administrators the ability to configure drivers for their particular needs.

If you use applications that use ODBC, you probably have noticed the dialog box shown in Figure 4-13. From the end user's viewpoint, this is the only dialog box that the user should need to connect to a particular server. (Of course, there are situations for which security information such as a user ID and a password need to be supplied by the end user. Such requests would follow this dialog box, which is displayed by the ODBC Driver Manager.) And because a single driver/DBMS combination can be configured in many different ways, the user can have many data sources that use the same driver but different options.

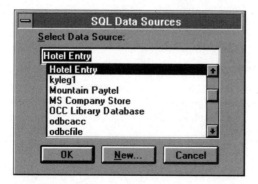

Figure 4-13.
ODBC (version 2.10) SQL Data Sources dialog box.

In retrospect, it isn't clear that this abstraction of drivers and the underlying communications software into data sources was as beneficial as we first believed it would be. Some application developers are confused by the model and would prefer to explicitly load drivers. This is especially true for applications that use drivers to access desktop databases and flat files on the end user's machine. For these the most natural paradigm is the File Open model used by most Windows-based applications using their own file types. The data source abstraction doesn't help in this case and actually causes a lot of confusion. This was the main reason that we added the ability to explicitly load drivers in ODBC 2.0. For certain classes of applications (primarily those wanting to deal exclusively with local desktop databases), this makes dealing with ODBC a lot easier.

For client/server DBMSs, however, the simplification of multiple driver configurations into easy-to-understand names has proven to be very useful, although many people still ask, "How do I load driver X?" and it takes some explaining to help them understand the data source idea.

4.3   A Walkthrough of a Simple Request

So far we've looked at fairly high-level descriptions of how applications interact with the ODBC Driver Manager, which in turn interacts with drivers, which in turn interact with DBMSs. To finish this chapter, let's see what happens when an actual application uses ODBC. We looked at a high-level example in the last chapter, and now we're going to go one step deeper. We're still going to overlook a lot of the bells and whistles of ODBC and concentrate on the basic mechanics of each component, but we'll look inside each component in more detail than before.

Before we begin the walkthrough, a brief discussion of how applications use DLLs is in order. When an application that uses ODBC is linked, it usually links with the Driver Manager's import library (ODBC.LIB or ODBC32.LIB, the latter for 32-bit operating systems such as Windows NT and Windows 95). The Driver Manager contains the entry points for every ODBC function, as do ODBC drivers. When an application that uses ODBC is installed on the end user's machine, ODBC.DLL (the actual Driver Manager code referenced by the ODBC.LIB import library) and one or more drivers are usually installed with it. When the user runs the application, ODBC.DLL is loaded into memory. If another application using ODBC is already running, Windows does not load the DLL from disk again but instead just increases the *instance count* for ODBC.DLL. The instance count is the mechanism used by Windows to keep track of the number of applications that are using a DLL at any given time. When the last application using a DLL unloads it, Windows removes the DLL from memory. But if an application unloads the DLL and one or more applications are still using the DLL, the DLL will remain in memory.

Now we are ready for the six steps of our walkthrough.

Step 1: The Environment and Connection Handles Are Allocated   When the application is ready to use ODBC, it first allocates two handles, the *environment handle* and the *connection handle,* by using two ODBC function calls, *SQLAllocEnv* and *SQLAllocConnect.* We won't bother with the environment handle until later. But the connection handle is especially important and is used often by the Driver Manager. When these two functions are called, Windows knows that the functions are contained in ODBC.DLL because of the import library the application was linked with. Typically the application calls these functions during initialization, before anything has been displayed on the screen.

What actually happens in the Driver Manager when *SQLAllocConnect* is called? Not a lot. Some memory is allocated for the connection handle, and the handle is returned to the application. Note that no driver has been involved up to this point—the only interaction has been between the application and the Driver Manager.

This is a good time to mention that there are always two sets of handles in ODBC: one set in the Driver Manager that is passed between the application and Driver Manager and another set that is passed between the Driver Manager and the driver. With this setup each driver can have a different data structure on its own handle and does not have to worry about interfering with the information that the Driver Manager needs to store for each handle. At this point in the walkthrough, only the application/Driver Manager handles have been allocated. The driver's environment and connection handles will be allocated in step 2.

Figure 4-14 shows the interaction between the application code and the Driver Manager when the application calls *SQLAllocEnv* and *SQLAllocConnect.*

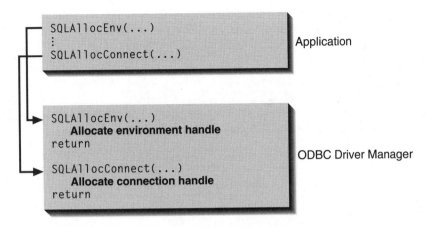

Figure 4-14.
*Walkthrough step 1: interaction between the application and the Driver
Manager during handle allocation.*

Step 2: The Application Calls a Connection Function   Next the application makes
a connection to a data source. ODBC has three different functions for making connections, but we'll look at just the simplest one: *SQLConnect.*[5] The
SQLConnect function takes as its arguments the connection handle, a data
source name, and a user ID and password.

When *SQLConnect* is called in the Driver Manager, the Driver Manager
uses the data source name specified as the second argument of *SQLConnect* to
find the ODBC driver associated with the data source. The mapping is contained in the ODBC.INI file in Windows versions 3.*x* or in the registry in Windows NT and Windows 95. Figure 4-15 on the following page shows an
example of a data source called "Company Store" in ODBC.INI that is being
mapped to the Microsoft SQL Server driver. (This example is for an application that does online ordering and inventory checking.)

---

5. Almost all ODBC applications use a different function, *SQLDriverConnect,* which handles a lot of
the details of connecting that an application would have to handle itself using *SQLConnect.*
However, for the purposes of showing how the various components interact, this walkthrough uses
the simpler function, *SQLConnect.*

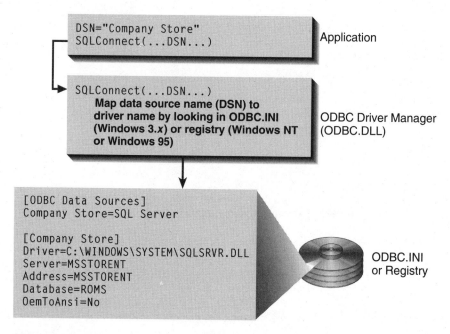

Figure 4-15.
Walkthrough step 2: the Driver Manager mapping the data source name to the driver.

Step 3: The Driver Manager Loads the Driver   The Driver Manager now calls the Windows function *LoadLibrary* using the right side of the Driver entry in ODBC.INI—C:\WINDOWS\SYSTEM\SQLSRVR.DLL in this example. The Driver Manager obtains a library handle for the SQLSRVR.DLL driver when it calls *LoadLibrary,* and using the handle, it then calls the Windows function *GetProcAddress* for each function in the driver. Each function address is stored in an array associated with the connection handle. Figure 4-16 depicts the process.

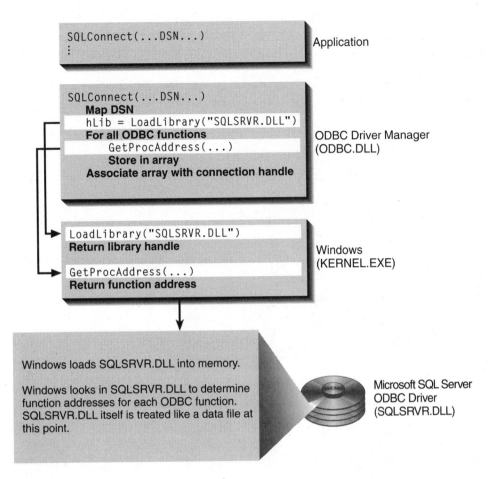

Figure 4-16.
Walkthrough step 3: the Driver Manager loading the driver.

Step 4: The Driver Manager Calls the Driver's Handle Allocation Functions   The
Driver Manager calls the functions *SQLAllocEnv* and *SQLAllocConnect* in the
driver. Remember that the driver wasn't loaded when the application called
these functions in the Driver Manager, so now they must be called in the
driver. Also, if the application used the function *SQLSetConnectOption* to set
some options for the connection (such as how long to wait for a connection
before returning to the application), the Driver Manager calls the driver's
SQLSetConnection function at this time. Figure 4-17 shows the process assuming that no connection options were set.

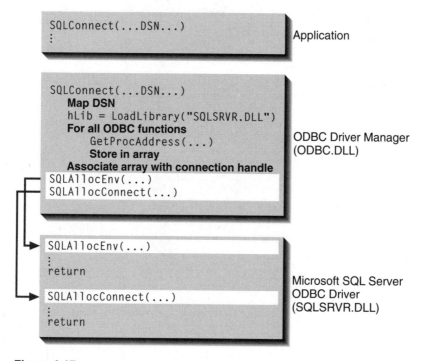

Figure 4-17.
*Walkthrough step 4: the Driver Manager calling allocation functions in
the driver.*

Step 5: The Connection to the Server Is Made   The Driver Manager (finally) calls
the *SQLConnect* function in the driver. Remember, this was the function that
the application called in the first place. It is worth digressing a bit here to
note that the loading of the driver DLL is the main reason why some developers say that making connections with ODBC sometimes takes longer than

making connections with the native API, especially when the native API, rather than a DLL, is statically linked to the application. Loading DLLs and calling the allocation functions in a driver are not things a native API would do, but they are required by the ODBC architecture. However, we have found that the actual connection to the server is usually the most time consuming part of the connection process—so much so that the overhead involved in loading the DLL is negligible (measured in milliseconds on an Intel 486 processor). Because connection time is almost never a performance-critical part of an application, it didn't worry us too much in the design.

Now the driver must process the *SQLConnect* function call. For a one-tier driver, such as one that accesses dBASE files, there is nothing to do because there is no network connection to make. For a client/server driver, such as the Microsoft SQL Server driver in our example, processing the *SQLConnect* call involves using the network interface software installed in the client machine to make a connection to the physical server specified as a part of the data source name. To accomplish this, the driver uses configuration information that it stored earlier in ODBC.INI when the data source name was created. (This is something we didn't discuss specifically in the context of this example, although it is described in the previous section. As part of the configuration process for a driver, the user is prompted for the server name, the network address, or both, as appropriate. The driver then stores this information in ODBC.INI.)

After the connection to the server has been established, a client/server driver usually sends the user ID and password to the server for the DBMS's security subsystem to validate. Recall that the user ID and password were passed as arguments to *SQLConnect*. If the user ID and password are not valid, the server returns an error to the client driver, which maps the error code to the standard required by ODBC (in this case "28000 - Invalid authorization specification"). The driver returns control to the Driver Manager, which returns control to the application with the standard error (and the native error code and message text returned by the server).

If the user ID and password are valid, the server returns an indication of success and the driver returns the standard SQL_SUCCESS return code to the Driver Manager, which returns the value to the application. We're connected at last! Throughout this process, the application has simply been waiting for the function call to *SQLConnect* to return. Figure 4-18 on the next page shows the connection process.

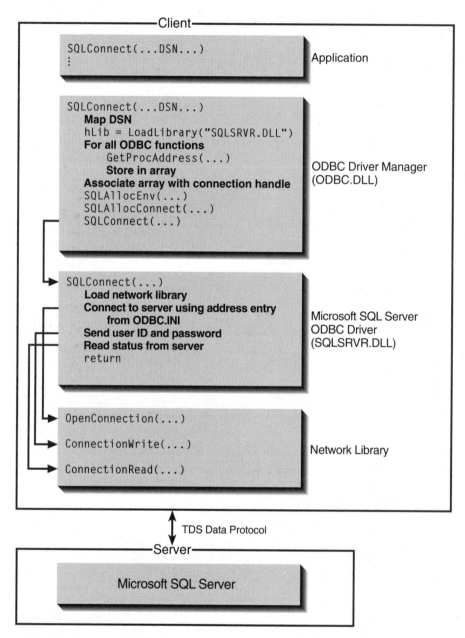

Figure 4-18.
Walkthrough step 5: making the connection.

Step 6: An SQL Statement Is Executed   If you followed all that, you'll be relieved to know that the worst is over, at least in terms of complexity on the client side. Now that we are connected, the rest of the interactions among the application, the Driver Manager, the driver, and the DBMS are pretty straightforward. To send an SQL command to the server, first the application needs to allocate a statement handle. To do this the application calls *SQLAllocStmt*, which causes the Driver Manager to allocate its own statement handle and then call *SQLAllocStmt* in the driver. The driver then allocates its own statement handle and returns control to the Driver Manager, which returns control to the application.

The statement handle is the real workhorse in any ODBC application because it is used to send all SQL commands to the server and to retrieve all results. Once allocated, the statement handle can be used for any number of SQL statements, provided that the statement handle isn't in use (fetching rows resulting from a SELECT statement, for instance). Some programmers have made the mistake of thinking that statement handles cannot be reused and end up allocating a new one every time something needs to be sent to the server. Not only is this unnecessary, it's inefficient to frequently allocate and deallocate handles.

Now let's see what happens when we try to execute an SQL statement. The simplest way to execute SQL statements in ODBC is to call *SQLExecDirect*. *SQLExecDirect* takes an SQL string and sends it to the server. It doesn't matter what kind of SQL statement the string is; in fact, it doesn't even have to be SQL. So it would really be more accurate to say that *SQLExecDirect* delivers to the server whatever text the application supplies. For our example, we'll assume that the following query is used for the SQL statement:

```
SELECT PRODUCT, COUNT(*) AS Ordered
FROM ORDERS
WHERE CUSTOMER='kyleg'
GROUP BY PRODUCT
HAVING COUNT(*) > 1
```

For those not fluent in SQL, the English language equivalent of this query is, "Which products have I ordered more than once?"

The application might generate the SQL string in response to the user clicking a button or some other event. Or the application might be a very simple ad hoc query application in which the SQL string is entered directly, such as the example shown in Figure 4-19 on the next page, which is taken from the VBODBC sample program on the CD included with this book. Figure 4-20 on page 139 shows the steps that are taken to get the SQL statement from the application to the server.

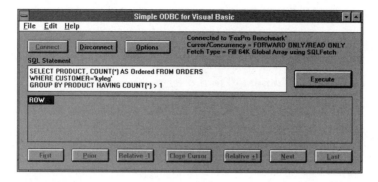

Figure 4-19.
The application ready to execute the SQL statement.

The server receives the request to execute the query, processes it, and when the query execution is finished, returns the results to the client. Note that most DBMSs, unlike Microsoft SQL Server, would simply return a message reporting the success or failure of the query and wait for a subsequent fetch command from the client before returning any actual results of the query. In Microsoft SQL Server's case, however, all the results are sent to the client without the client having to send anything to the server to request them.[6]

Note in Figure 4-20 that after the driver calls *ConnectionWrite*, the driver immediately calls *ConnectionRead*, which waits for a response from the server. In ODBC we call this *synchronous mode*, which is the counterpart to asynchronous mode, described earlier. We'll talk more about these modes in the next chapter, but for now we'll assume that our example uses synchronous mode—it makes the explanation simpler.

As soon as the server sends a response to the client, the *ConnectionRead* function in the network library reads the data from the network and returns it to the driver. What does the server send? If you think back to Chapter 3, you'll remember that in Microsoft SQL Server's case the data protocol is TDS (Tabular Data Stream). So the results from the server are messages encoded according to the TDS specification.

---

6. This is true except in Microsoft SQL Server 6, in which applications can choose to have the data sent in one continuous stream or in one or more rows at a time.

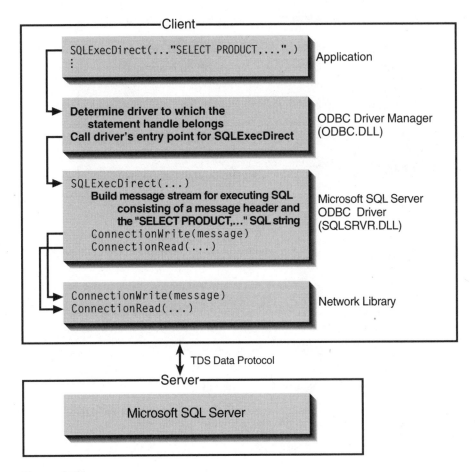

Figure 4-20.
Walkthrough step 6: executing an SQL statement.

The example in the previous chapter described how the data protocol is decoded and passed back to the application, so I won't repeat it here. In this example the application fetches the data with *SQLFetch*, reading the rows of data from the network until a DONE message is received from the server. For our example query showing the count of products, two columns (the product name and the count of products) would be returned for every row, as shown in Figure 4-21 on the following page.

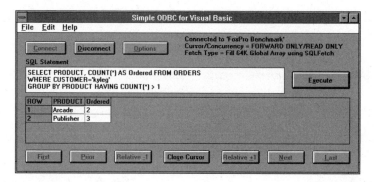

Figure 4-21.
Result data from the walkthrough.

4.4 Summary

In this chapter we've looked at the ODBC architecture. In summary, this chapter discussed

- How ODBC was designed and optimized for client/server architectures

- What the components of ODBC are: applications, the Driver Manager, drivers, and data sources

- How ODBC handles the wide differences in network topologies and frameworks by introducing the concept of a "data source"

- How the dynamic loading of libraries in Windows (and other architectures) allows for polymorphism (multiple concurrent implementations of the same API)

- How a simple request is processed and what happens in each of the various layers of software

By now you have a good enough grasp of the basic technical workings of ODBC to dive into the next chapter, where many aspects of ODBC are described in detail.

C H A P T E R   F I V E

ODBC in Depth

In this chapter we cover the major features of ODBC that we haven't already covered. This chapter gives you the "whys"—the reasoning behind the design decisions—for each technical feature of ODBC. If you are a developer, you'll find many of the details (the "hows") missing. The sample programs included in Part II of this book, along with the *Microsoft ODBC 2.0 Programmer's Reference* (Microsoft Corporation, 1994) will help fill in the gaps.

The topics are not presented in any particular order, so you don't need to read the sections sequentially. About one third of this chapter (section 5.5) deals with the ODBC cursor model and is the most technically challenging material to read, so I'd suggest tackling that at a separate sitting.

5.1 ODBC Handles

A *handle* is nothing more than an application variable in which the system can store context information about an application and some object used by the application. For example, in a C program for Windows the main handle used is the window handle, but other handles are used as well: device context handles, memory handles, and instance handles, to name a few. ODBC uses three kinds of handles: environment handles, connection handles, and statement handles. Within Windows, a handle is used to access a data structure for which only Windows knows the details. The same is true with ODBC: applications never look "inside" a handle and cannot directly manipulate the contents referenced by the handle. This concept, known as *information hiding,* is a sound software engineering principle.

One of the fundamental issues ODBC had to address was how to allow applications to use multiple drivers simultaneously and let each driver have its own data structure so that the driver can maintain context with the application. The solution was to use and embellish the handle concept that is used by Windows.

ODBC uses handles in the same way a Windows-based C program does but takes them one step further. In Windows, the various handles are always managed by Windows itself; consequently, the data structure underlying each handle is defined and managed by Windows and is always the same. But in ODBC, we wanted to provide a way for driver developers to define their own data structures and yet still use the handle scheme to keep their data structures private. On the one hand, application developers need to have a standard way to reference the handles required to use ODBC functions, but on the other hand, we didn't want to force driver writers to accept our idea of what the contents of the data structures should look like. To further complicate matters, the Driver Manager has its own information to manage on each handle, and that information cannot be accessed by either the applications or the drivers.

To solve the problem, we defined allocation functions for each handle, to be processed by each driver. The allocation functions allow a driver to attach its own private data structure to each handle even though the application always uses the same kind of handle. This also allows the Driver Manager to keep its own set of handles to manage the drivers and provide the necessary mappings between applications and drivers. The three kinds of handles used in ODBC—environment handles, connection handles, and statement handles—are associated in a hierarchical fashion, as shown in Figure 5-1.

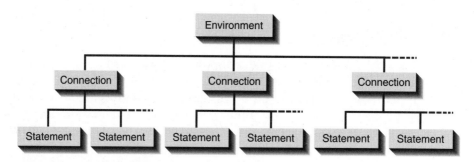

Figure 5-1.
The hierarchy of ODBC handles.

ODBC also uses the handle concept to ensure robust error handling and to make it easier for application developers to write multithreaded applications. These two advantages explain why every ODBC function takes a handle as its first argument. Without this use of handles, it would be very difficult to report errors that occur when a function is called. ODBC would either have to return all the error information from the function as the return value or as output arguments, or it would have to keep the error information in a global memory area accessible by the application.

The problem with the first approach is that error information is complex: it usually includes an error number, a message, and—in ODBC's case—a standardized error. That effectively rules out returning a simple scalar value as the result of every ODBC function. Adding three arguments to every ODBC function would overly complicate the API. Another problem is that some DBMSs return multiple errors, so some mechanism is needed to enumerate the errors. I suppose one could cram all the errors together and let the application programmers write the code to decipher the compound error, but that would run counter to our goal of trying to keep it simple.

The problem with using a global memory area for error information is that this approach is difficult to manage, especially when the system is coordinating multiple applications accessing global data. And that's in a non-preemptive multitasking system such as Windows. It is flat out wrong to use unprotected globals for error information in a multithreaded environment such as Windows NT, OS/2, or Windows 95. Why? If a function is called without a handle and it generates an error that is posted to a global area, what is to keep another thread from reading it? Something, somewhere, has to keep some context so that the error information can be returned to the correct application. Posting it to a global memory area would require the use of semaphores or some other concurrent processing control mechanism to serialize access, and then the Driver Manager would still have to figure out a way to tag each error with the identities of the application and the correct thread within the application. A solution to the latter problem would require the application to register each thread ID with the Driver Manager or come up with some other way to let the Driver Manager coordinate error information. The complications of this approach get pretty overwhelming, so the far simpler solution is to require a handle on every ODBC function call.

The handle approach in a multithreaded environment always makes it clear to both the application and the Driver Manager where context and error information should be kept. When an error occurs, there is never a question about what the application is supposed to do: it should pass the handle that was used in the function that generated the error to the ODBC error function, *SQLError*.

The context information kept in the handle can also be used to facilitate additional features in a driver, such as *synchronous cancel*. Synchronous cancel allows an application to start executing an SQL statement on one thread and then cancel the execution of it on another thread. This is possible only because of handles—the handle used to execute the statement can be used in another thread to cancel that statement because the handle lets the Driver Manager know it is the same request.

I'd like to make one final point before we discuss the handle types in greater depth. There are always two sets of handles: one set is allocated within the Driver Manager and is used between an application and the Driver Manager, and the other set is allocated by a driver and is used between the Driver Manager and the driver. This allows each driver to have its own data structure for each handle without requiring that the Driver Manager and application understand the contents of the handle. Whenever an application passes a handle to the Driver Manager, the Driver Manager doesn't pass it along to the driver but instead passes the handle allocated by the driver.

That's the basic background on handles. Now we'll look a bit more in depth at each of the three types of handles used in ODBC.

5.1.1 The Environment Handle

The environment handle is the global context handle in ODBC. Every program that uses ODBC starts off with the function that allocates the environment handle (*SQLAllocEnv*) and finishes with the function that frees the environment handle (*SQLFreeEnv*). All other handles (all connection and statement handles for this application) are managed within the context of the environment handle. For example, the environment handle is used within the Driver Manager to keep track of the number of connections and their state (connected or disconnected). Only one environment handle can be allocated for each application. Following the usual Windows naming scheme, an environment handle is usually referred to as an *henv* (handle to an environment).

In addition to being the global placeholder for the other handles and for context information, the *henv* is used for only four other purposes in the ODBC API:

- To pass to *SQLError* any errors that occur at the environment level, such as an attempt to free the environment handle while connections are still active or an attempt to pass an invalid *henv* during connection handle allocation.

- As the context handle for *SQLDataSources*, the function that enumerates the data sources currently installed.

- As the context handle for *SQLDrivers*, the function that enumerates the drivers currently installed.

- To manage transactions when the *SQLTransact* function is used to commit or roll back all open transactions on all connections. That is, rather than having an application commit or roll back each outstanding transaction on a connection handle with a separate call to *SQLTransact*, the *henv* can be used to force the Driver Manager to do the commit or rollback on all connections. It is important to point out that the Driver Manager is *not* providing a global transaction service in which all transactions on all connections would be treated as a single transaction. This would, of course, be a useful service to provide, and, in truth, the use of the *henv* within *SQLTransact* was designed to hook up to a global transaction monitor in the future. But until there is a universally supported way to allow different DBMSs to participate in a single global transaction, there isn't much point in even attempting to provide this directly from the Driver Manager.[1] It is also almost never appropriate, in my opinion, to let client PCs act as global transaction monitors; this should be a server-oriented task.

5.1.2 The Connection Handle

A connection handle manages all information about a connection. From a driver writer's perspective, this means that a connection handle is used to keep track of a network connection to a server or alternatively to keep track of directory and file information if the local file system is the source of data. From the Driver Manager's perspective, a connection handle is used to identify the driver used in the connection and for all routing of function calls. Using the Windows naming scheme, a connection handle is referred to as an *hdbc* (handle to a database connection).

An *hdbc* is allocated with a function call that associates it with the environment handle: *SQLAllocConnect(henv, &hdbc)*. It is deallocated with the *SQLFreeConnect* function. The Driver Manager stores the *hdbc* inside the data structure referenced by the *henv*. In fact, because multiple connection handles can be allocated, the Driver Manager actually keeps a list of connection handles associated with the environment handle.

After the *hdbc* is allocated, it can be used to make a connection. We saw in Chapter 4 (section 4.3) what happens when the connection function *SQLConnect* is called. It is the connection handle that stores the array of function pointers for a specific driver.

---

1. There seems to be growing acceptance of X/Open's XA programming interface for transaction processing. If transaction-processing monitor vendors and DBMS vendors support the XA interface, it would pave the way for ODBC to support global transactions.

After the connection function has successfully completed, the driver is loaded into memory. Now the driver has a connection to the database server and is ready to process SQL statements. At this point we say the *hdbc* is in an *active* or a *connected* state, to distinguish it from an *hdbc* that is in an *allocated* state.

Keep in mind that the connection process causes the Driver Manager to pass to the driver the requests to allocate an environment handle and a connection handle, so allocation of the driver's environment and connection handles does not happen at the same time that it happens in the application but when the application calls *SQLConnect* or another connection function. For every ODBC function that is called, the Driver Manager will look up the corresponding entry point in the array of function pointers stored in the connection handle and make an indirect call to the driver.

In addition to storing the overall connection context information, a connection handle is used for the following purposes in the ODBC API:

- To establish a connection using *SQLConnect*, *SQLDriverConnect*, or *SQLBrowseConnect*, and to break the connection using *SQLDisconnect*.

- To pass to *SQLError* any errors that occur at the connection level, such as the failure to load a driver, the failure to connect to the server across the network, all communication errors (for example, network or wide area network connection drops), the expiration of a connection time-out, the attempt to use a connection already in use, and so forth.

- To set connection options such as time-outs, transaction isolation levels, and other options that are set using the *SQLSetConnectOption* function.

- As the main transaction management handle. The context of a transaction is determined by the *hdbc*. That is, the set of all the statements associated with an *hdbc* constitutes the scope of the transaction. Although the *SQLTransact* function can be used with an environment handle, as discussed in the previous section, it is most often used with a connection handle.

- As an argument of the informational functions *SQLGetInfo* and *SQLGetFunctions*, which return information about the driver, data source, and connection associated with the *hdbc*. A third informational function, *SQLNativeSQL*, uses the *hdbc* to return SQL strings to an application, translating escape clauses (see section 5.8.2.3) to DBMS-specific syntax and performing other transformations.

5.1.3 **The Statement Handle**

The statement handle is the real workhorse of the ODBC API. It is used for all processing of SQL statements and catalog functions. Each statement handle is associated with only one connection. When the Driver Manager receives a function call from an application and the call contains a statement handle, the Driver Manager uses the connection handle stored within the statement handle to route the function call to the correct driver.

A statement handle is created by an allocation function (*SQLAllocStmt*) and is destroyed by a deallocation function (*SQLFreeStmt*). Just as the function *SQLAllocConnect* associates a connection handle with an environment, so the first argument to *SQLAllocStmt* (a connection handle) associates a statement handle with a particular connection. The shorthand name for a statement handle is *hstmt*. An *hstmt* is used to maintain state information to ensure that functions are called in the right order by the application. For example, it doesn't make sense to allow an application to fetch the next row of data if no SQL statement has been executed. The Driver Manager keeps track of what has happened and stores the information in its statement handle.

Drivers use statement handles for all their data structures related to executing SQL statements and processing results. For example, all drivers have some way of representing the names, types, and lengths of columns returned from a SELECT statement, and this information is associated with an *hstmt*.

One of the more controversial aspects of ODBC has been its use of statement handles for processing all SQL statements, in contrast to embedded SQL, which makes an explicit distinction between multiple-row–returning statements (cursors) and all other statements. Indeed, early versions of ODBC had "cursor handles" in addition to statement handles, but in the end there was a slight advantage to having the statement do all the SQL. The advantage is apparent for situations in which an application might not know whether rows will be returned. This is possible if an application allows users to enter SQL directly, if one application acts as an execution agent for another application, if some row-returning statements are intermixed with other statements, or if a Microsoft SQL Server or Sybase stored procedure that returns rows was invoked.

5.2 **The ODBC Connection Model**

In this section we'll look at how an application uses ODBC to establish a logical connection to a data source.

In ODBC the term *connection* is used to describe the process of establishing the necessary context so that an application can send information to and

147

receive information from a data source. This process includes loading the appropriate ODBC driver, establishing a logical network connection to a server on a local or wide area network and authenticating the user, and providing any other contextual information necessary to allow the application to begin executing SQL statements. If the data source is a local desktop database or a flat file, the connection process might consist of simply loading an ODBC driver. In either case, establishing a connection in ODBC requires the Driver Manager and the driver to do whatever it takes to establish the necessary context so that an application can execute an SQL statement or one of the catalog functions (such as *SQLTables*, which gets the list of tables accessible by the current user).

5.2.1 Background

The goal of making the connection process interoperable was a technical challenge. The diverse types of drivers, data sources, network topologies (such as local files, servers on a local area network [LAN], or LAN gateways to other systems), security systems, and the idiosyncratic behaviors of each DBMS made designing a standard API for connections quite difficult. The diversity in the connection models for the different DBMSs shown in these examples will give you some idea of what we were up against:

- Microsoft SQL Server uses the concept of multiple named "databases" on a physical server. When a user connects to a server, the DBMS establishes a current context that determines which collection of tables, stored procedures, rules, and other objects the user can access by default. Every user with an account on that server is assigned a default database, but the user can change the database context dynamically at runtime. To provide the maximum flexibility for connecting to Microsoft SQL Server, ODBC had to provide a way for the user to establish the desired database context and do it in a way that relieved application programmers from having to write code specifically for Microsoft SQL Server.

- Connecting to an IBM DB2 DBMS on a mainframe via a LAN gateway (such as the Micro Decisionware Database Gateway product) sometimes requires multiple logins. The client first connects to a gateway server on a LAN, and then the gateway server connects to the mainframe. In some cases, the user name and password required to connect to the gateway server on the LAN are not the same as the user name and password required to connect to the mainframe, so the user might have to supply two sets of login information.

■ Accessing local dBASE files doesn't require any "connection" in the sense of doing anything with a network, so loading the driver is all that is necessary.

Not all these differences must be revealed to the end user, however. Some differences can be addressed by options that are specified when a driver is installed and configured. For example, the Microsoft SQL Server case could be handled by having the user configure the driver via the ODBC control panel device to connect to a specific database. Or the Microsoft SQL Server system administrator could assign the default database on the server end. But neither solution helps the end user who wants to be able to connect to different databases quickly and easily at runtime.

Some differences should not be hidden from the end user, most notably when security information is involved. It would be tempting to try to force all connection scenarios to specify the data source name, user ID, and password. But recall the example of the LAN gateway and mainframe above that requires two separate logins. From ODBC's perspective, it is not acceptable to force the gateway to store the mainframe user ID and password so that the LAN user ID and password can be automatically mapped to the correct mainframe user ID and password. ODBC followed the tried-and-true adage, "The only place a user ID and password should be stored is in the user's head."

5.2.2 **The ODBC Solution**

ODBC's approach is to ensure maximum flexibility by allowing connection options to be set either by a separate configuration process or dynamically at runtime, while at the same time shielding applications from the characteristics of each target DBMS. To solve the problem of diverse connection models, ODBC exposes three connection functions: *SQLConnect, SQLDriverConnect,* and *SQLBrowseConnect.*

5.2.2.1 *SQLConnect*

The simplest function, *SQLConnect,* assumes that the desired connection can be made by supplying a data source name, user ID, and password. For the majority of direct connections from a PC to a target DBMS, this is sufficient. This function presumes either that the application will prompt the end user for security information or that the security information is hard-coded into the application. The *SQLConnect* function is the only connection function found in the ISO standard CLI.

5.2.2.2 *SQLDriverConnect*

The most commonly used connection function is the *SQLDriverConnect* function. *SQLDriverConnect* handles the entire connection process for an application, prompting the end user for any necessary information to complete the connection. *SQLDriverConnect* makes use of standard user interface paradigms such as Windows, Macintosh, and OS/2 so that even when a driver displays a dialog box, the end user will not notice that a new application is running. This, of course, causes difficulties when ODBC is used on any operating system that does not have a standard user interface (such as MS-DOS, UNIX, and mainframe operating systems). With these systems it is safer to stick with *SQLConnect* or *SQLBrowseConnect.*

SQLDriverConnect allows the application programmer to specify as much or as little about the connection as he or she wants to. The application can let ODBC do everything, it can supply the name of the data source to connect to and let ODBC prompt the user for any additional required information, or it can supply everything required to make a connection without using ODBC to prompt the user for anything. In the simplest case, the application doesn't specify any information at all about the connection. It simply supplies the connection handle returned from *SQLAllocConnect,* a window handle, an option specification of *SQL_DRIVER_COMPLETE,* and zeros or NULLs for the rest of the arguments:

```
rc = SQLDriverConnect(hdbc, hwnd, NULL, 0, NULL, 0, 0,
                 SQL_DRIVER_COMPLETE);
```

An application that calls *SQLDriverConnect* in this fashion requires the Driver Manager and driver to do all the work required to establish the connection. These components are responsible for all interactions with the end user.

Let's take a closer look at what happens in such a case. First, when the Driver Manager detects that the application has supplied no data source (when the third argument of *SQLDriverConnect* is NULL or an empty string), it displays the data sources dialog box to prompt the end user to select the data source. Figure 5-2 shows the data sources dialog box. Note that the New button can be used to add a new data source "on the fly" if necessary.

After the end user has selected a data source, the Driver Manager loads the appropriate driver and then calls the driver's *SQLDriverConnect* function using the data source name as one of the arguments.

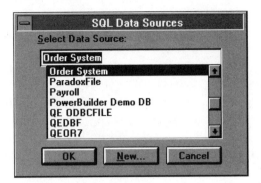

Figure 5-2.
The ODBC data sources dialog box displayed by the Driver Manager.

The driver must now obtain from the user all the information it needs to complete the connection. In some cases (dBASE systems, for example), there is nothing more to do because nothing more is needed to establish the context for executing SQL statements. In other cases (client/server database systems, for example), the driver must prompt the user for all required information and for any optional connection information. Figure 5-3 shows an example of the login dialog box presented by the Microsoft SQL Server driver.

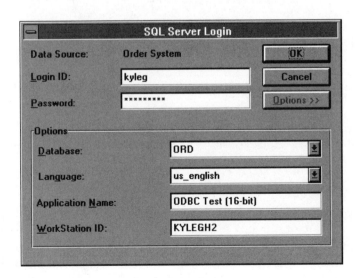

Figure 5-3.
The Microsoft SQL Server driver login dialog box.

In addition to the usual Login ID and Password edit controls, the dialog box presents some options unique to Microsoft SQL Server, including the database name discussed earlier.

Once the user has successfully logged in to the server, control returns to the application. The application can now begin executing SQL statements. Note that the application programmer did not have to write any code to manage the connection process, yet the connection process can still exploit the various features of each target DBMS. This is because the driver, which can present the DBMS-specific connection attributes to the user, is controlling the process. If required, the driver can present multiple dialog boxes to guide the user through the connection process for network and security topologies of any level of complexity.

Figure 5-4 shows the login dialog box presented by Intersolv's NetWare SQL driver. Although the information requested is very different from that requested for the Microsoft SQL Server driver, the application uses the same *SQLDriverConnect* call it uses for the Microsoft SQL Server driver.

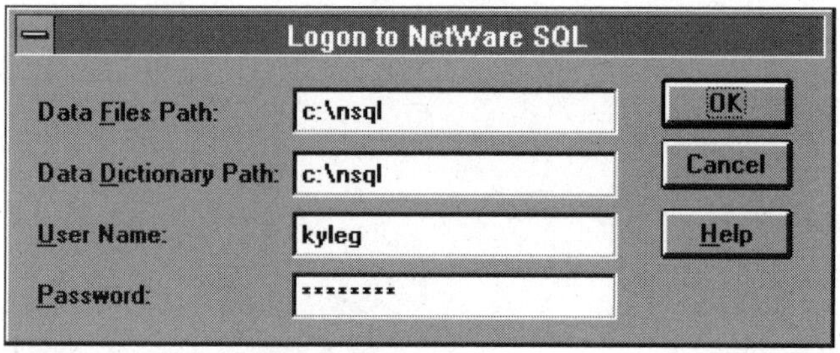

Figure 5-4.
The NetWare SQL driver login dialog box.

SQLDriverConnect is the easiest way to connect to a data source, and that's why most application developers prefer it.

5.2.2.3 *SQLBrowseConnect*

SQLBrowseConnect has the same flexibility as *SQLDriverConnect* but allows applications to control the look and feel of everything the end user sees in the connection process. So instead of having the Driver Manager and driver display dialog boxes, the application calls *SQLBrowseConnect* to get a string that contains all the connection attributes for which the driver would normally prompt the user. The application can then build its own dialog box dynamically using the information specified by *SQLBrowseConnect*.

SQLBrowseConnect returns the information in attribute-value pairs. For example, the Microsoft SQL Server driver returns the following string when it is called by *SQLBrowseConnect*:

```
SERVER:Server={GraniteNT};UID:Login ID=?;PWD:Password=?
```

The meaning of this string is as follows: The words in all caps are the keywords that the driver needs in order to complete the connection. The mixed-case word following each keyword is the "user-friendly" name that the application should use when building a dialog box to prompt the end user. The user-friendly name is also used for localized versions of these names so that dialog boxes built for specific locales can be managed dynamically. On the right side of each equal sign (=) is either a list of items, enclosed in curly braces ({}), that can be placed in a list box for the user to select or a question mark, which signifies that the application should prompt for a single value in an edit control. An attribute can also be preceded by an asterisk (*), which indicates that the attribute is optional.

After the application has retrieved the information requested from the user, it supplies that information in the connection string and again calls *SQLBrowseConnect*. After receiving the information, the driver can either complete the connection or return to the application with another string of information to be filled in. The process repeats until the driver and application have negotiated all the attributes necessary to complete the connection.

5.2.2.4 Summary

ODBC provides a rich set of functions for connection management. For simple requirements, the *SQLConnect* function will do. For more advanced situations or for situations in which the maximum capability of a DBMS must be exploited, *SQLDriverConnect* or *SQLBrowseConnect* is more useful. Almost all drivers and applications use *SQLDriverConnect* because it provides a powerful way to establish a connection while requiring the least amount of work on the part of the application programmer.

5.3   ODBC SQL Execution Models

Now that we've seen what it takes to connect an application to the desired data source, it's time to look at how an application uses the data stored in the data source. In ODBC, that means examining how SQL statements are executed, which is the subject of this section.

ODBC supports three different execution models for SQL statements. The first is the simplest to program because everything happens in one function call (from the application programmer's perspective). The second model separates the specification of the SQL statement from its execution, although both occur at runtime. The third model also separates specification from execution, but with the key distinction that the specification can (and typically does) happen prior to runtime.

Each model has its own strengths and weaknesses. The model chosen by an application programmer depends on whether he or she is more interested in ease of programming, performance, or the ability to repeatedly execute SQL statements.

To understand the differences, you first need to understand what actually happens when an SQL statement is executed. Here is the sequence of events:

1. The SQL statement itself must be formulated by an application or a user.

2. The SQL statement must be sent to the DBMS.

3. The SQL statement must be parsed and optimized, yielding an access plan that the DBMS will use to actually execute the query. The access plan indicates which index or indexes to use (if any), the order in which to retrieve data from tables and then join them, how and when sorting will be done, and many other considerations.

4. The access plan is actually executed. In most implementations, authorization checks (ensuring that the user has appropriate permissions to use the tables and columns specified in the SQL statement, for instance) are made in this step, although this can also be done in the third step.

5. The client and the server interact to send status information and data to the client as requested by the client.

The three execution models in ODBC each accomplish the same end, but each one differs with regard to when and where (on the client or on the server) each step is performed.

5.3.1 ExecDirect

The ExecDirect model combines all the steps in a single function call to *SQLExecDirect*. The SQL statement is specified, sent to the server, and executed, all in one step. The ExecDirect model is best suited for ad hoc SQL statements or SQL statements that will be executed only once. Parameters can be used, but they act merely as placeholders that the driver replaces with the parameter values before it sends the SQL statement to the server.

The DBMS discards the optimization information used to execute the SQL statement after execution is complete. If the same statement is specified again with *SQLExecDirect*, the entire process of parsing and optimizing happens again.

To use this model, the application programmer simply specifies:

```
SQLExecDirect(hstmt, sql_statement, SQL_NTS);
```

5.3.2 Prepare/Execute

The Prepare/Execute model allows the application programmer to separate steps 1, 2, and 3 from steps 4 and 5. That is, the SQL statement is "prepared" (sent to the server, parsed, and optimized) first and executed later. When the statement is executed, what flows to the server is not the SQL statement itself, but merely some way of referencing the statement so that the access plan can be executed immediately. Parameters are often used in these SQL statements, so the only items that flow to the server are the reference to the access plan and the parameter values, not the entire SQL statement.

The Prepare/Execute model should be used when repeated execution of the same SQL statement is needed and when the SQL statement must be constructed dynamically during runtime. The access plan is deleted from the DBMS after the program ends (or in some cases at the end of a transaction).

Performance of the execution portion will be faster than with the ExecDirect model because parsing and optimizing is not done at that point.

To use this model, the application programmer specifies the preparation part first

```
SQLPrepare(hstmt, sql_statement, SQL_NTS);
```

and then later (presumably in a loop) calls

```
SQLExecute(hstmt);
```

5.3.3 Stored Procedures

The stored procedures model is like the Prepare/Execute model except that with stored procedures, the preparation step can be done independently from the application and the stored procedure persists beyond the runtime of the application. That is, in the Prepare/Execute model both preparation and execution must be executed within the same program; a stored procedure can be specified once and stored in the DBMS, and application programs never need to perform the preparation phase at all.

Stored procedures are the closest equivalent to static SQL, which was discussed in Chapter 2. Recall that with true static SQL, the only items passed between the client and the server when the application executes are the identifier for the appropriate section of the access plan and the parameter values, if any. So it is with stored procedures, although in this case the "identifier" is the stored procedure name.

Another key difference is worth noting. Usually access privileges for static SQL applications can be granted to the *application* itself, rather than to the user running the application. With stored procedures, however, access privileges are based only on the identity of the user. This can lead to administrative difficulties if the same user can access different elements of the database depending on which application he or she is using. To my knowledge, no implementation of stored procedures allows application-based privileges to be defined and maintained.

To use stored procedures in ODBC, the application programmer uses the ExecDirect model but uses the SQL statement to specify the stored procedure name:

```
SQLExecDirect(hstmt, "{? = call proc1(?,?,?)}", SQL_NTS);
```

5.3.4 Asynchronous Execution

Regardless of which of the three execution models is used, ODBC allows applications to submit SQL statements for execution in two modes: synchronous and asynchronous. When *synchronous execution* (the default) is used, ODBC functions will not return control to the calling application until the function has finished executing. When *asynchronous execution* is specified, the application gets control before the function has finished executing and must periodically check to see whether the function has finished (or cancel the execution of the function).

Asynchronous execution was designed to allow applications to submit time consuming SQL statements to the DBMS and still be able to continue processing while waiting for the result from the DBMS. For example, a complex SELECT statement that involves many large tables and that was submitted via *SQLExecDirect* might take several minutes for the DBMS to process. On operating systems that do not support preemptive multitasking, such as Windows 3.*x*, asynchronous processing allows the user to perform some other task instead of staring at the hourglass until the DBMS finishes processing the SQL request. On operating systems that do support preemptive multitasking, such as Windows NT, Windows 95, OS/2, and UNIX systems, the operating system itself provides the capability for applications to do asynchronous processing. All the application needs to do is allocate a separate thread or process that executes the time-consuming SQL statement.

ODBC allows several functions to operate asynchronously. The primary functions that benefit from asynchronous execution are those that are used to execute SQL requests: *SQLExecDirect*, *SQLPrepare*, and *SQLExecute*. However, any ODBC function that might cause network traffic or that might be subject to waiting for another user's lock to be freed can operate asynchronously. The *Microsoft ODBC 2.0 Programmer's Reference* contains a complete list of the functions that operate asynchronously.

When an ODBC function executes asynchronously, it returns a special value (SQL_STILL_EXECUTING) to indicate that its execution is not finished. The application can perform other work for some period of time and then call the ODBC function again. To return control to Windows, an application typically either calls the Windows *Yield* function or posts a user-defined message to itself and drops out of the message processing loop in the normal fashion. In the latter case, when the application processes the user-defined message, it calls the ODBC function again and, if SQL_STILL_EXECUTING is returned, posts the user-defined message again. When the asynchronous function completes, it returns the appropriate return code based on the outcome of the function (SQL_SUCCESS, SQL_SUCCESS_WITH_INFO, or SQL_ERROR) instead of SQL_STILL_EXECUTING. If the application wants to cancel the operation before it completes, it can do so by calling *SQLCancel.*

Not every driver and DBMS can support asynchronous execution and asynchronous cancel. If an application attempts to enable asynchronous processing when the driver does not support it, the error "Driver not capable" will be returned.

An application can enable asynchronous mode by calling either the *SQLSetConnectOption* function or the *SQLSetStmtOption* function with the SQL_ASYNC_ENABLE flag. Note that once the asynchronous function has been called and has returned the SQL_STILL_EXECUTING return code, very few ODBC functions can be called on that *hstmt* (and the *hdbc* associated with it) until the original function has finished. The only other ODBC functions that can be called are *SQLCancel*, *SQLAllocStmt*, *SQLGetFunctions*, and the original function.

5.4 Retrieving Data from the Data Source

Now that we've seen how SQL statements are executed in ODBC, it's time to look at how data is retrieved from the data source. When an SQL SELECT statement returns rows to the application, the application can use one of three methods provided by ODBC to get the data. Before we look at those, I'd like to point out that the INSERT, UPDATE, and DELETE statements also return information to the application. But in this case the information that is returned is not the actual rows or data but rather an indication of how many rows were modified by the INSERT, UPDATE, or DELETE statement. In other words, these are *non-row-returning statements*, in contrast to SELECT statements, which are *row-returning statements*. After one of these statements is executed, the ODBC function *SQLRowCount* is used to return the number of rows in the data source that were affected.

For row-returning statements such as SELECT statements or stored procedures that return rows, ODBC provides three ways to retrieve data. Using a single function call, an application can retrieve a single value, an entire row of values, or multiple rows of values.

5.4.1 Retrieving One Value Directly

One way an application can retrieve data is by using a function call (*SQLGetData*) for every column in every row. The application supplies function arguments that specify the column number and a variable in which to receive the data, and after the function call has been successfully executed the value for the given column is returned in the variable. The application uses two loops to retrieve an entire results set, as in this example:

```
/* For all rows */
for (rc = SQLFetch(hstmt); rc == SQL_SUCCESS; rc = SQLFetch(hstmt))
    /* For all columns in current results set */
    for (colnum = 1; i <= columns; colnum++)
        SQLGetData(hstmt, colnum, ..., &value, ...)
```

SQLGetData is also used for another very important purpose: the piece-meal retrieval of large text and binary data (such as images). It is often difficult or impossible for an application to allocate a single piece of memory big enough to hold a large data object, such as a 50-page document or a high-density bitmap that might exceed 1 million bytes in size. Memory allocation concerns are particularly well-founded in 16-bit environments like Windows, in which dealing with single chunks of memory larger than 64 KB is difficult. If such large items are stored in the database, the application must retrieve them in smaller pieces, and that is what *SQLGetData* does. To accomplish this piece-by-piece retrieval, the application calls *SQLGetData* using the same value for the column number argument again and again. Each time *SQLGetData* returns, it informs the application how much data is left to be retrieved. The application can then adjust the amount of data to be read at one time to fit the available memory, make use of the local hard disk, paint the screen in a piece-by-piece fashion, or do whatever else is necessary to manage the large data value.

5.4.2 Retrieving an Entire Row or Multiple Rows

An application retrieves an entire row of values or multiple rows of values using a technique called binding. *Binding* is a term that is used in many different ways, but in this context it means associating the data from the data source with variables in the application program. In contrast to *SQLGetData*, which directly returns values in variables, the binding of a variable to a column of a results set persists beyond the scope of one function call. When we say that a column in a results set is *bound* to a variable, we mean that the variable receives the values from the column without requiring the application to supply the variable as an argument to an ODBC function.

NOTE: The analogous situation applies to parameters in an SQL statement: the parameters are bound to variables, which will supply the actual values for the parameters later in the application. Bound columns and parameters work in similar ways in ODBC, but for now we'll restrict our discussion to bound columns to keep things simple.

5.4.2.1 Binding Columns for a Single Row

In contrast to the *SQLGetData* programming model shown in the previous section, when an application uses binding there is no need for the inner loop to span all the columns for every row. Instead, the bindings for each column are set up in advance, and when the application fetches a row, the values from each column are automatically stored in the bound variables:

```
/* For all columns in current results set */
for (i = 0; i < columns; i++)
    SQLBindCol(hstmt, ..., &value[i], ...)

for (rc = SQLFetch(hstmt); rc == SQL_SUCCESS; rc = SQLFetch(hstmt))
    /* value[i..n] contains data for current row */
```

In this example, the driver stores the address of the variable when *SQLBindCol* is called, and later when *SQLFetch* is called the driver uses that address as the location in which to store the value from the database. Each time *SQLFetch* returns, the bound variable contains a new set of values.

ODBC supports the binding of some or all columns of one row or of multiple rows. If an application is binding only one row, it can use a combination of binding and direct retrieval with *SQLGetData*. In fact, this combination is necessary when large text or image data is involved because only *SQLGetData* can be used to retrieve data in pieces.

5.4.2.2 Binding Columns for Multiple Rows

ODBC's support of multiple-row binding was designed with several goals in mind:

■ To provide high-bandwidth data transfer between the driver and the application. With a single ODBC function call, an application can retrieve as many rows and columns as desired.

■ To support DBMSs that expose array capabilities across the network. Although most client/server DBMSs send one fetch command to the server for each row returned, some DBMSs (such as Oracle) allow one fetch operation to specify several rows to be returned. This capability greatly reduces network traffic and enhances performance.

■ To provide a *virtual window* for interactive applications that need to display several rows and columns of data and scroll them in response to user input. By fetching the same number of rows that can be displayed on the screen, the application can rely on ODBC to synchronize data in the DBMS with data in the application's variables. The application simply needs to call the *SQLExtendedFetch* function with the appropriate option to allow the application to scroll up or down the required number of rows based on the user's input. The user's input could be the use of the arrow keys to scroll up or down one row, the use of PgUp or PgDn to scroll one screen, or the use of scroll bars to move a relative distance from the current row, for example.

The virtual window concept requires a bit more explanation. From the application's point of view, the results set is like a big array. The display screen is capable of displaying a subset of the array at any one time, so the first and last rows displayed on the screen correspond to a "first row displayed" and a "last row displayed" in the big array. Whenever the data is scrolled, the "first row displayed" and the "last row displayed" change. For example, in a downward scroll, the first and last display rows in the array must advance by one; in an upward scroll they must decrease by one. If the screen is resized, the relative distance between the first and last display rows changes.

Figure 5-5 depicts a results set and virtual window movements over it. Each scrolling operation moves the virtual window up or down over the results set, causing different rows of the results set to be placed in the application's memory.

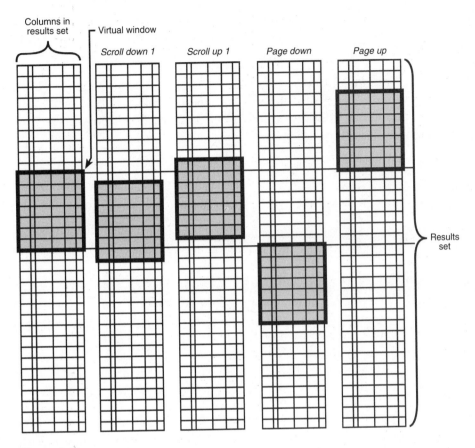

Figure 5-5.
Virtual window movements.

ODBC provides multiple-row binding so that applications can define a data structure that corresponds to a virtual window. ODBC uses the term *rowset* to describe the set of rows most recently fetched into application variables. The application binds the data structure to the columns in the results set, and then the driver ensures that the data structure is populated with the correct rows of the results set as scrolling occurs.

If you are thinking that this resembles the simple file I/O model presented back in Chapter 2, you're right. However, there is one huge difference: the results sets here are not necessarily bound to a single table but can be the results of any query. Updating becomes more of a challenge, of course, when multiple tables are involved in a results set because the semantics of the update can be ambiguous. But the ability to map the results of literally any query to this virtual window concept is a powerful one.

To provide the maximum flexibility for application programmers who want to use the virtual window metaphor, ODBC supports two ways in which an application can bind multiple rows: *row-wise binding* and *column-wise binding*.

Row-Wise Binding   Row-wise binding was designed to provide direct mapping between an array of structures in C and the columns in a specific results set. For example, consider a simple customer list consisting of name, address, city, state, and zip code:

```
typedef struct {
    short sCustID;
    char szName[19];
    char szAddress[26];
    char szCity[15];
    char szState[2];
    char szZipcode[5];
} CUSTOMER;
CUSTOMER aCust[10];
```

The variable *aCust* (array of customers) has space for information about 10 customers; each element of the array contains the information for one customer, and each field of the structure contains one attribute of the customer. For example, the name of the fifth customer is referenced by *aCust[4].szName*. (C arrays are zero-based, so the array element 4 is actually the fifth item in the array.) Figure 5-6 shows how this structure is laid out in memory. (The width of the structure elements is not exact.)

Row-wise binding in ODBC allows structures like that shown in Figure 5-6 to be the virtual window for a query, exactly like the virtual window shown in Figure 5-5. In this example, the query could be:

```
SELECT custID, name, address, city, state, zipcode
FROM cust WHERE state in ('WA', 'OR')
```

The application would bind each element of the structure to a column of the results set, specify how many rows to fetch at one time (in this example, 10), and then begin fetching the results with *SQLExtendedFetch*. Each call to *SQLExtendedFetch* fills the 10 elements of the array with the columns of the result. As the user scrolls forward or backward, the driver adjusts the data in the array. Scrolling down one row requires the driver to move the second through the tenth elements of the array to the first through the ninth positions and fetch the next row from the database and insert it in the tenth element's position in the array, as shown in the "Scroll down 1" diagram in Figure 5-5.

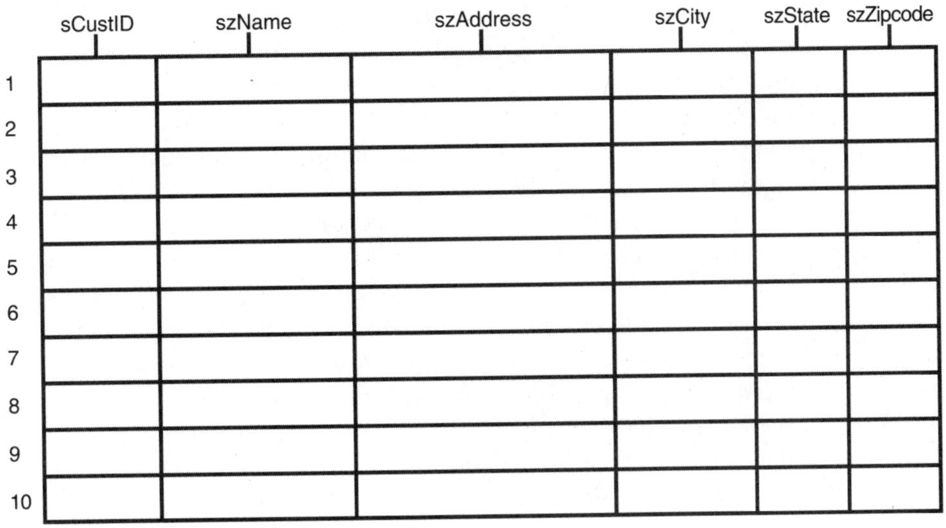

	sCustID	szName	szAddress	szCity	szState	szZipcode
1						
2						
3						
4						
5						
6						
7						
8						
9						
10						

Figure 5-6.
An array of structures for customer data.

Now these 10 rows of the results set can be referenced just like an array of structures in a normal program. The array acts as the virtual window on the results set.

That's conceptually how it works. In reality it's a little more complicated. The first complication involves dealing with NULL (unspecified) values from the database. Because NULLs cannot be represented with normal values, a separate variable (called the *indicator* in embedded SQL) must be used. ODBC uses the same variable to hold the length of the actual data or NULL, whichever applies. So, in fact, the preceding example isn't quite right for ODBC's use. A length element must be supplied for each element of the structure, and this must be passed as an argument to the driver during the binding process. So the structure really needs to look more like this:

```
typedef struct  {
    short sCustID;       long  cbCustID;
    char szName[19];     long  cbName;
    char szAddress[26];  long  cbAddress;
    char szCity[15];     long  cbCity;
    char szState[2];     long  cbState;
    char szZipcode[5];   long  cbZipcode;
} CUSTOMER;
CUSTOMER aCust[10];
```

A second complication is how to handle truncation for variable-length data such as character and binary data. The application needs to know whether data is too long to fit in the declared variable and, if so, how much data has been truncated. To provide this information, ODBC requires the driver to use the output length variable in the structure to return the total length of the data available. If the variable supplied to hold the actual data isn't long enough, the driver places only what will fit, sets the output length to the total amount available, and returns a warning from *SQLExtendedFetch*. If *SQLExtendedFetch* returns the truncation warning, the application must look at all the variable-length columns to see which ones have an output length greater than the variable length. This should never happen with fixed-length data types, but if, for example, the database administrator decides to switch to 9-digit zip codes, an application written to handle truncation properly will not crash but will continue running until the zip code field can be lengthened.

A third complication arises from the fact that as soon as the application has some rows from the results set in the array, those rows are no longer guaranteed to be the same as the actual, changeable data in the database corresponding to them. If the transaction isolation level is less than repeatable read (see section 5.5.3), rows in the array might in fact have been updated or deleted in the database by someone else. Also, if a keyset-driven cursor (see section 5.5.2.2) is being used, any deleted rows will still appear in the array when scrolling operations occur. How can an application determine the status of rows in an array? ODBC provides a status array in *SQLExtendedFetch* for exactly this purpose. The status array has the same number of elements as the array for the data. When the driver detects that a row has been changed or deleted, it sets the appropriate element of the array to a special value that denotes its status: updated, deleted, inserted, or unchanged.

A fourth complication arises when the user updates, inserts, or deletes a row. Typically the user changes one row on the screen, which corresponds to an element in the array. How can the driver discover which row was updated or deleted so that it can update the database correctly? ODBC provides another function that is used in conjunction with *SQLExtendedFetch* to achieve this end. The function, *SQLSetPos*, allows the application to set the "current row" within the rowset and perform updates, deletions, and insertions. And if the application wants to update or delete every row in the rowset with a single operation, *SQLSetPos* allows that too. The TYPEGEN and VBFETCH samples described in Part II show how row-wise binding is used.

Column-Wise Binding   Column-wise binding binds contiguous memory for an individual column rather than for rows. This allows applications to use a separate array for each column of the result. Everything else is the same as in the description for row-wise binding. Column-wise binding is more useful than row-wise binding when the form of the results set is not known in advance and therefore a C structure to bind the results set cannot be known at the time the program is written. Column-wise binding allows the application to use the multirow fetch model by constructing the type and number of bound variables (arrays) dynamically after the results set has been described.

From the application programmer's point of view, column-wise binding makes it impossible to treat a row of the rowset as an offset into the array of structures: the convenience of referencing a column in a row (using something like *aCust[5].sCustID*, for example) is not available. Rather, the application programmer uses the array variable for the column directly (for example, *sCustID[5]*). It is more likely that the variable name would not reflect the name of the column, however, since the primary reason for using column-wise binding in the first place is that the structure of the results set is not known ahead of time.

The Inside Story
Act I, Scene VI: Road Warriors

The industry consortium meeting was one of the first meetings of what was to become the SQL Access Group. The attendees represented nearly every major DBMS vendor. Although the members agreed to proceed with the technical design for an interoperable version of SQL based on ANSI SQL and a standard wire protocol based on RDA, there was a major bone of contention as to whether the group should seek to develop a subroutine style or a "call level" interface in addition to embedded SQL. I was carrying version 1.5 of the SQLC specification in my briefcase. What should I do? Tell the group about the work? Wait until the group decided whether they even wanted a CLI?

I decided on the latter, but at private conversations at the break I found out that it was DEC that was most interested in pursuing this technology. An ensuing conversation with Jeff Balboni from DEC made it clear that DEC could provide some expertise to broaden our understanding of the DBMS vendor's perspective, and so DEC, as represented by Jeff Balboni and Larry Barnes, began to attend the SQLC design meetings.

The "gang of three" had become the "gang of four": DEC, Lotus, Microsoft, and Sybase. We continued to work on the specification, meeting every month for two or three days, hopping around between

(continued)

continued

Washington, New Hampshire, Massachusetts, and California from October 1989 until June 1990. The time between meetings was spent writing detailed change proposals, implementing all the editing changes, prototyping, and, for some of us, attending the meetings of the emerging SQL Access Group.

It was a time of intense intellectual challenge, a time that those of us who worked so hard on the specification (Don Nadel and Tom McGary from Lotus, Tom Haggin and Ed Archibald from Sybase, Jeff Balboni and Larry Barnes from DEC, and Bob Muglia and I from Microsoft) remember fondly. With Lotus and Microsoft championing the cause of application programmers and DEC and Sybase providing the DBMS vendors' viewpoint, we were fairly confident that we were covering a broad scope of needs.

It was during this period that the SQLC specification began to lose its resemblance to Sybase's DB-Library and become more like ANSI SQL with respect to cursors and other key technologies. Betsy Burton, then a Sybase product manager, recalls the day during these formative times that Ed Archibald appeared in her office during a break from a grueling SQLC design meeting.

"This isn't DB-Library anymore," she remembers Ed saying. It was true. And it was to become even more so in the months ahead, as the amount of input to the specification was about to increase by leaps and bounds....

5.5   The ODBC Cursor Model

Early in the development of ODBC (in fact, before the term ODBC was invented), Rick Vicik of Microsoft took the collection of ideas and proposals for cursor management and pioneered the design of a general cursor model for client/server architectures. This model became the basis of cursors in ODBC and several other products. I am indebted to Rick for allowing me to use his "Microsoft Scrollable Cursor API" paper, much of which is included in this section.

Before we get into the ODBC cursor model itself, let's look at how cursors exist in the world today and what implementation problems they face.

5.5.1   Background

As defined in Chapter 2, a *cursor* is a mechanism that allows the individual rows resulting from a query to a DBMS to be processed one at a time, in a fashion similar to processing records in an ordinary disk file. The mechanism is called a cursor because it indicates the current position in a results set, just as the cursor on a computer screen indicates the current position in, for example, a document.

The cursor model in ODBC attempts to reconcile two aspects of DBMSs and applications: the way most DBMSs actually work and the way most interactive application programs would *like* DBMSs to work.

Most DBMSs provide a simple model for retrieving data after a query has been submitted to them. Rows are returned to the application one at a time in the order specified by the query until the end of the set is reached. There is no provision for going back to a previous row—the only way this can be done is by reexecuting the query and starting from the beginning. Updating (or deleting) the last row fetched with the SQL statement

```
UPDATE table SET (column = value, ...) WHERE CURRENT OF cursor
```

might or might not be supported by the DBMS. For example, Microsoft SQL Server and Oracle do not support this syntax directly on the server but can simulate its effect in their embedded SQL products and through other methods in their native 3GL APIs. IBM database products do support the UPDATE ... WHERE CURRENT OF statement.

Interactive applications, especially those written for personal computers, often need to allow the user to scroll through returned data forward or backward using the arrow keys, the PgUp or PgDn key, or the scroll bar and a mouse. A cursor that provides the ability to move forward and backward within a results set is called a *scrollable cursor*. A cursor that allows a user to change or delete data in addition to scrolling is referred to as a *scrollable, updatable cursor.*

In addition to the scrollability and updatability of cursors, there is one more element to consider: the effects of multiple users reading or writing the same data at the same time. Managing concurrent access to shared data is enormously complex and involves a blend of technologies from the worlds of database management and transaction processing, which in turn have borrowed heavily from operating system research and implementation. The term *transaction isolation* (meaning the management of concurrent access) refers broadly to this topic and is the term used in the SQL-92 standard, but the subject is known by other names too. To quote from the experts, "This topic is variously called *consistency* (the static property), *concurrency control* (the problem), *serializability* (the theory), or *locking* (the technique)." [2]

---

2. J. N. Gray and Andreas Reuter, *Transaction Processing: Concepts and Techniques*, Morgan Kaufmann Publishers, 1993, p. 375.

Without a solid understanding of transaction isolation, you cannot really understand all the issues surrounding cursors. But presenting all that information here is well beyond the scope of this book, and other references[3] already do an excellent job of explaining it. I'll provide high-level definitions for some terms, but most of the time I'm going to assume that you are familiar with the concepts and problems related to transaction isolation.

One transaction processing term that must at least be mentioned here is *serializability*. The informal definition of *serializable transactions* is "a set of transactions for which the overall effect on the database is the same as with any given serial execution of the transactions." In other words, any outcome that can be obtained by running the transactions individually, but completely, in any order is deemed correct. Any concurrent, interleaved execution of the transactions that does not produce one of the outcomes of serialized execution is incorrect. The trick is to achieve the *effect* of running transactions sequentially but in fact to interleave executions so that higher concurrency is possible.

For now, it is sufficient to mention that when and how changes are made in the database by your own and by other transactions always involves trade-offs in *consistency* (the degree to which one user's transactions are visible to other users) and *concurrency* (the number of transactions that a DBMS allows to proceed at the same time). You cannot have complete isolation from other transactions and high concurrent use of the data at the same time. Although high concurrency is always desirable, isolation is not. For example, a report writer application that makes two complete scans of a set of data must ensure that no other transaction changes the data while the two scans are being made; otherwise the detail information might not add up to the totals. The report writer application needs a completely consistent view of the data— complete isolation from other transactions. An airline reservation system, on the other hand, always needs to have the latest information regarding seat availability, so the system requires updates to the database to be reflected immediately to everyone who is using the same data to assign seats.

ODBC provides a wide range of options for controlling the trade-off between consistency and concurrency. A driver works in conjunction with the transaction processing facilities in a DBMS to provide some or all of the options defined by ODBC.

---

3. J. N. Gray and Andreas Reuter, *Transaction Processing: Concepts and Techniques,* Morgan Kaufmann Publishers, 1993; Jim Melton and Alan R. Simon, *Understanding the New SQL: A Complete Guide,* Morgan Kaufmann Publishers, 1993; Richard D. Hackathorn, *Enterprise Database Connectivity,* Wiley & Sons, 1993. In my opinion, the best general reference for transaction processing is the Gray and Reuter volume, in which Chapter 7 covers transaction isolation and provides a thorough treatment of concurrency vs. consistency issues.

5.5.2 Cursor Types in ODBC

ODBC defines three types of cursors: static, keyset-driven, and dynamic. We'll look at each type and how it relates to scrollability, updatability, and transaction isolation. But first we'll see how ODBC cursors relate to the cursors defined in SQL-92 and how most DBMSs support cursors.

5.5.2.1 SQL-92 and Conventional Cursors

Although recent definitions of cursor behavior[4] specify that a cursor results set cannot change after it has been materialized at cursor open time, earlier interpretations were more dynamic. In his Turing Award Lecture, E. F. Codd stated that a DBMS can decide whether a cursor is to be "materialized *en bloc* prior to the cursor-controlled scan or materialized during the scan."[5] In IBM's System R (the first relational DBMS), cursors were intended to be sensitive to changes in the underlying data if the results set could be materialized incrementally. If incremental materialization is used, an update to the base relation "immediately becomes visible via the cursor."[6] If incremental materialization is not possible, changes to the underlying data are not visible via the cursor (and all subsequent retrievals return warnings indicating that the data might not be current). To get current data, the application must close and reopen the cursor. Because of this limitation, incremental materialization was considered to be more desirable and anything else was a fallback. With incremental materialization, a cursor's sensitivity to change can be classified as *dynamic;* without incremental materialization, its sensitivity is *static.*

With conventional cursors (including those defined in SQL-92), an application that needs to reflect an update back to the database must construct an UPDATE statement that duplicates much of the information in the cursor definition. Either all columns must be blindly updated (whether they were actually changed or not) or the UPDATE statement must be constructed dynamically by the application each time an update occurs.

SQL-92 added backward, relative, and absolute scrolling to its cursor behavior. On the face of it, this appears to satisfy the needs of interactive client/server applications, which typically scroll around in the results set,

4. American National Standards Institute (ANSI), "Database Language SQL," ANSI X3. 135-1989 (October 1989); American National Standards Institute (ANSI), "Database Language SQL," ANSI X3. 135-1992 (January 1993); C. J. Date, *A Guide to the SQL Standard,* third ed., Addison-Wesley, 1993, pp. 16 and 110.

5. E. F. Codd, "Relational Database: A Practical Foundation for Productivity" (Turing Award Lecture), *CACM*, February 1982.

6. M. M. Astrahan et al., "System R: A Relational Approach to Data," *ACM TODS* 1 (2), 1976.

making occasional updates. However, since updates are disallowed if SCROLL is specified,[7] SQL-92 scrollable cursors are actually of limited use.

The SQL-92 standard added to cursor definitions another interesting option that was not in previous versions of the SQL standard: the option SENSITIVE/INSENSITIVE.

The SENSITIVE/INSENSITIVE option controls the visibility of changes made by the cursor owner (via another cursor or via noncursor operations). Selection of the INSENSITIVE option effectively creates a copy of the results set. If INSENSITIVE is specified, the cursor is not updatable, not even by the cursor owner.[8] If INSENSITIVE is not specified, the effects of changes made by the cursor owner and by other users are *implementation-dependent*. Because any user who wants to be insulated from his or her own updates as well as the updates of others can just make a snapshot copy of the results set, the INSENSITIVE option does not seem to be very useful. The really important issues such as the effects of changes made by others or by the cursor owner are not addressed specifically for cursors.

The following statements drawn from various sources referring to the standard provide some insight into the capabilities of scrollable cursors in SQL-92:

- Cursor open "conceptually causes the select to be executed, and hence identifies the corresponding set of rows."[9]

- "The collection of rows resulting from the evaluation of [the WHERE clause] then becomes associated with the cursor, and remains so until the cursor is closed again."[10]

- "If INSENSITIVE is specified, OPEN will effectively cause a separate copy of [the table(s) specified in the FROM clause] to be created and the cursor will access that copy…. Update and delete current operations are not allowed on a cursor for which INSENSITIVE is specified."[11]

- "Changes that your application makes in a transaction cannot be affected by other transactions that may be updating the database."[12]

7. Jim Melton and Alan R. Simon, *Understanding the New SQL: A Complete Guide,* Morgan Kaufmann Publishers, 1993, p. 268.

8. C. J. Date, *A Guide to the SQL Standard,* third ed., Addison-Wesley, 1993, p. 112.

9. C. J. Date, *A Guide to the SQL Standard,* third ed., Addison-Wesley, 1993, p. 16.

10. C. J. Date, *A Guide to the SQL Standard,* third ed., Addison-Wesley, 1993, p. 110.

11. C. J. Date, *A Guide to the SQL Standard,* third ed., Addison-Wesley, 1993, p. 112.

12. Jim Melton and Alan R. Simon, *Understanding the New SQL: A Complete Guide,* Morgan Kaufmann Publishers, 1993, p. 265.

5.5.2.2 The ODBC Cursor Types: Static, Keyset-Driven, and Dynamic

ODBC cursors, in contrast to conventional cursors, support most of the features desired by the developers of interactive client/server applications: forward and backward scrolling, direct access by position in the results set, and positioned updates (even if the results set was defined with ORDER BY). Multiple rows can be returned by a single fetch operation to improve network efficiency and to support the virtual window model described in section 5.4. As described earlier, when multiple-row fetch is used by an application, the term *rowset* describes the rows returned by the most recent fetch operation. With ODBC cursors, an entire screenful of rows can be protected against *lost updates* (one transaction unknowingly overwriting another transaction's changes) without unnecessary concurrency reduction, and changes can be reflected back to the database in a single operation. Updates can be committed without losing position in the results set.

Another element in ODBC cursors is their ability to accommodate client/server systems, in which both client and server play a role in the correctness (accuracy or timeliness) of data. That is, you can retrieve data from a database to a local data store, in which case the data will be quite consistent and the data, once read, cannot be affected by other transactions. But, of course, over time that data will become more and more "stale" as other transactions modify the data on the server and those changes are not reflected in the local copy.

ODBC provides a cursor model that allows drivers to simulate scrollable, updatable cursors, even if the underlying DBMS does not. A discussion of these models requires the introduction of some terminology that describes a wide variety of data manipulations.

With a *static cursor,* changes made to the underlying tables are not visible until the cursor is closed and reopened; with a *dynamic cursor,* changes are visible immediately. Most actual implementations fall somewhere between these two extremes. A common characteristic of many of the "in-between" implementations is the concept of the *keyset.*

The *keyset* is the set of unique row identifiers of a results set. (More precisely, it is the set of identifiers of the rows that made up the results set at the time the cursor was opened. That is, the membership and ordering of the cursor remain fixed as long as the cursor is open.) If any changes are made to the underlying data after the cursor is opened, the keyset provides a way to identify those rows that comprised the results set at the time the cursor was opened. The keyset concept is of little use with nonscrollable cursors because rows cannot be revisited without closing and reopening the cursor, but it becomes very important when backward scrolling is allowed. For example, many existing cursor implementations continue to show rows that no longer qualify under the WHERE clause when those rows are revisited. The keyset identifies those rows that comprised the results set when the cursor was opened so that the rows can be reaccessed. The keyset is a subset of the results set as it existed at the time the cursor was opened, which might differ from the current results set because of updates made by other users.

A variation on the keyset type of cursor is a cursor for which keys are retrieved for only part of the results set and refetched whenever the application scrolls outside the range of the keys currently stored at the client. A keyset cursor that does not contain all the keys for the entire results set is called a *mixed cursor* because it exhibits the characteristics of a keyset cursor within the keyset but the characteristics of a dynamic cursor outside the keyset.

The four cursor models in ODBC and their relative trade-offs when the DBMS uses its lowest transaction isolation level are shown in Figure 5-7. These types are specified with the SQL_CURSOR_TYPE option in *SQLSetStmtOption* (except for the mixed cursor type, which is implicitly specified by a keyset size that is smaller than the size of the entire results set when the query is executed).

	Accuracy	Consistency	Concurrency	Performance
Static (snapshot)	Poor	Excellent	Good	Varies
Keyset-driven	Good	Good	Good	Good
Dynamic	Excellent	Poor	Excellent	Varies
Mixed	Varies	Fair	Good	Good

Figure 5-7.
Cursor models and their trade-offs.

Static (Snapshot) Cursors   In a static cursor, the membership, ordering, and values of the results set are fixed at cursor open time. Changes made by the cursor owner (or by any other user) are not visible while a static cursor is open. Values, membership, and ordering remain fixed until the cursor is closed. This type of cursor is most useful for read-only applications that do not need the most up-to-date data or for applications for which multiple users never need to modify data concurrently. In SQL-92, the INSENSITIVE option of the cursor declaration provides this behavior with respect to changes made by the cursor owner's transaction.[13] To completely exclude the effects of other transactions, the cursor owner's transaction would have to be executing at the SERIALIZABLE transaction isolation level. (See section 5.5.3.)

One way to implement static cursors (also known as snapshot cursors) is to make a local copy of the data that results from a query. Each time a row is fetched, it is stored by the driver (or, in ODBC 2.*x*, by the cursor library), typically in memory, and then spooled to a local file if necessary. When the last of the results are retrieved by the client, no further interaction with the DBMS is needed. As the application scrolls backward, the data returned is from the local copy of the data. No changes made to the data in the database from other transactions are reflected on the client; consequently, any changes the client makes to data in the database must be done carefully to ensure that the update is performed on valid data. For example, if someone else has changed values in the row or deleted the row, the update might not be valid.

Static cursors provide a very consistent view of the data—nothing changes, because the data has been copied. And because the DBMS isn't involved after the last row is fetched, this type of cursor also offers good concurrency once all the data has been read. Before the last row is fetched, however, the DBMS will typically hold a lock on each row (or each set of rows, if page-level locking is used), so if the application retrieves data based on user demand and the user decides to take a break or go out to lunch while in the midst of perusing rows before the last row, locks might continue to be held, keeping other users from updating those records.

The biggest drawback of this model is that the user doesn't see changes from any other transaction, so static cursors score low on the accuracy scale. Also, allowing the user to change selected data presents some special challenges. For example, should the user be able to change the data buffered locally and have it reflected in the database? If so, what if the data the user is trying to change based on the locally stored version has changed in the database? In ODBC, there are ways to handle updates on static cursors. Those techniques will be described in section 5.5.4.

An alternative to copying the entire results set to the client is for the DBMS to support static cursors on the server by using a temporary table to hold the results set on the server. A third alternative is for the DBMS to support static cursors using the same locking techniques it uses for transaction

---

13. Jim Melton and Alan R. Simon, *Understanding the New SQL: A Complete Guide,* Morgan Kaufmann Publishers, 1993, p. 265; C. J. Date, *A Guide to the SQL Standard,* third ed., Addison-Wesley, 1993, p. 112.

isolation. The most common technique is for the DBMS to lock every row returned to prevent updates by other users. A static cursor using this method has several alternatives. One extreme is to apply shared locks as rows are visited or, worse, to apply a shared lock to the entire table or set of tables. A shared lock (S-lock) notifies other users that an item is being read. Any number of users can S-lock the same item. The other extreme is to exclusively lock the entire results set at cursor open time. An exclusive lock (X-lock) can be acquired on a particular item by only one user at a time and only if there are no S-locks on the item. X-locking the entire results set usually reduces concurrency to an unacceptable level, but S-locking as rows are visited might require users to try several times before they can successfully update an item. In both cases, high consistency will be achieved if the locks are held until the end of the transaction; however, any strategy other than locking the entire results set at cursor open time could result in blocking (waiting for a lock to be released) or even in a deadlock as rows are fetched. Even locking at open time can result in a deadlock or blocking if the transaction holds other locks at the time the cursor is opened.

When the locking approach is used, the DBMS should lock all rows examined while the results set is being produced, not just those rows that are returned.[14] For example, a WHERE clause containing a subselection with an aggregate on another table should lock the rows examined in that other table. Insertions that intrude on the definition of the results set (*phantoms*) should also be prohibited. The method typically used is to lock an index range. If the DBMS cannot prevent phantom inserts at the row level, the entire table must be locked.

Multiversioning techniques must be considered static because the updates of others are not visible and updates to a previous version by the cursor owner cannot be permitted. (You cannot change the past.)

GLOSSARY

Multiversioning A nonlocking concurrency control technique in which copies, or *versions,* of changed rows are managed by the DBMS and the client is given only the versions of rows that are consistent with the client's transaction.

---

14. K. P. Eswaran et al., "The Notions of Consistency and Predicate Locks in a Database System," *CACM,* November 1976.

Keyset-Driven Cursors   In a keyset-driven cursor, the membership and ordering of the results set are fixed at open time but values can change. If a change causes a row to fail to qualify for membership in the results set, the row remains visible until the cursor is reopened. If a change affects where a row should appear in the results set, the row does not move until the cursor is reopened. If a row is deleted, the key acts as a *placeholder* in the results set to permit a fetch by absolute position within the results set. Insertions by others are not visible. Insertions by the cursor owner should appear at the end of the results set. The advantage of this type of cursor is its ability to access the most up-to-date values and yet be able to fetch rows based on absolute position within the results set.

Implementation of keyset-driven cursors can be achieved by saving only the unique row identifiers of the results set (the *keyset*). A row identifier can be a row ID (if available), a unique index, a unique key, or the entire row. The keyset can be maintained on the server (in a temporary table) or on the client. The keyset can be built as the rows are visited or it can be built by a background task. Later selections against the results set are performed using the keyset rather than the original criteria that defined the results set. Some implementations[15] allow the keyset to be named and saved, which makes it similar to a view except that it is defined by row enumeration instead of by selection criteria. Figure 5-8 on the following page depicts the various parts of a keyset-driven cursor.

Changes to values are visible because a unique row identifier is used to refetch the actual data. (Only the committed changes of other users are visible.) If the refetch fails because the row has been deleted, a special form of "not found" is returned. In some implementations, the row ID mechanism is also the record versioning mechanism. If a row is changed, that row becomes "not found" when revisited, even if it still meets the selection criteria. The proper approach is to use a unique identifier and versioning information to distinguish between rows that have changed since they were last visited and rows that no longer exist.

There is a more dynamic variation of keyset-driven cursors in which the "holes" left by deleted rows are not exposed. Whenever a "hole" is encountered, the keyset is scanned in the same direction for the first "non-hole." This makes fetching by absolute position impossible. Rows that no longer meet the selection criteria could also be filtered out, but moving them around to meet the static ordering criteria would be too costly (and not significantly more useful than the functionality provided by a fully dynamic cursor).

---

15. Gupta Technologies, Inc., *SQLBase Technical Reference Manual* (version 3.4), April 1988.

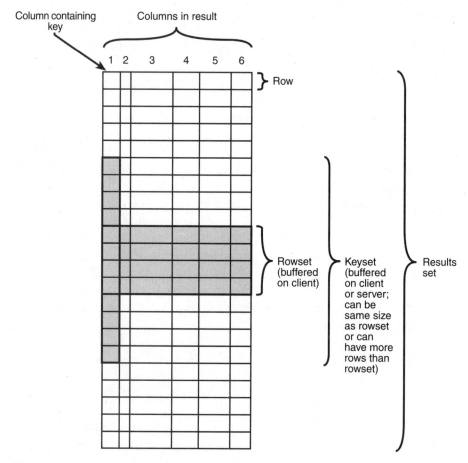

Figure 5-8.
Components of a keyset-driven cursor.

Dynamic Cursors In dynamic cursors, all committed changes (including insertions) made by anyone and all uncommitted changes made by the cursor
owner are visible to the cursor owner. Deletions are not flagged as missing;
the row simply no longer appears. Updates made by anyone can affect membership and ordering of the results set. This includes updates that do not directly affect results set values (such as a change to another table referenced in
a subselection). Fetching by relative position within the results set is possible,
but fetching by absolute position is not possible because placeholding
"holes" are not left to indicate deleted rows. This type of cursor is required by
applications that deal with highly dynamic data and require up-to-the-minute

information with regard to the existence of rows as well as the values within them. (A good example of this is a list of unassigned customer problem reports in a problem-tracking application.)

The technically correct way to implement dynamic cursors is for the underlying DBMS to create a selective index that defines the membership and ordering of the results set. Since an index is updated when other users make changes, a cursor based on such an index would be sensitive to changes made by anyone. Additional selection within the results set is possible by processing along the selective index. Results sets can be named and saved by making the selective index persistent.

Dynamic cursors can also be implemented without selective indexes by taking advantage of explicit ordering (using ORDER BY or GROUP BY) or implicit ordering (using an index or the keys of all tables involved). If the explicit ordering is not unique, keys should be used to define the order of the duplicates. Performance will be adequate if the optimizer evaluates the results set along suitable indexes. This approach will be difficult for complex joins, especially if views (or unions) are involved. Performance will be unacceptable if the optimizer does not process along an index.

Dynamic cursors should be sensitive to the effects of indirect changes made by the cursor owner or by other users. For example, a cursor definition might contain a WHERE clause with a subselection that contains an aggregate on a different table. If a change were made to the table in the subselection, the results set of a dynamic cursor could be affected even though no data retrieved by the cursor has changed.

Mixed Cursors   In a mixed cursor, the keyset is defined to be larger than the rowset but smaller than the results set. Its behavior is a cross between that of a keyset-driven cursor and that of a dynamic cursor. As long as the cursor moves within the keyset, its behavior is the same as that of a keyset-driven cursor. When the cursor moves to a row outside the keyset, its behavior is the same as that of a dynamic cursor. Note that when the cursor moves outside the keyset, a new keyset must be generated that includes the row to be fetched. For example, fetching the previous row when the current row is the first row in the current keyset would require retrieving the key values for the number of rows in the keyset and then filling the rowset based on those key values.

5.5.3 Cursor Types and Transaction Isolation Levels

SQL-92 defines four transaction isolation levels, and it is useful to see how the cursors in ODBC work in conjunction with these definitions. Here are simplified definitions of each transaction isolation level in SQL-92, in order from least to most isolated:

- **READ UNCOMMITTED (also known as dirty read)**   A transaction is not isolated. Writes from other transactions can be read before the end of the transaction.

- **READ COMMITTED (also known as cursor stability)**[16]   A transaction is isolated from the effects of other transactions for the current row but not necessarily for any other rows. For example, after the cursor has moved off a row, another transaction can modify or delete that row, so subsequent executions of the same SELECT statement will see the changes.

- **REPEATABLE READ**   A transaction is isolated from the effects of other transactions except in the case of phantom inserts. That is, if another transaction inserts a row that matches the WHERE clause of the cursor and the cursor in the first transaction is reopened, the new row inserted by the other transaction will be visible. In all other respects, REPEATABLE READ is the same as SERIALIZABLE.

- **SERIALIZABLE**   A transaction is isolated from the effects of other transactions.[17]

ODBC uses these same terms when an application wants to set a transaction at a given isolation level. ODBC also defines a fifth isolation level called VERSIONING, which was added to accommodate transaction isolation levels that don't precisely fit the ISO SQL-92 definitions, such as Oracle's READ CONSISTENCY transaction isolation level. The ISO definitions are generally explained by different types and levels of locking, but VERSIONING doesn't use locking. For example, in Oracle's case, the READ CONSISTENCY transaction isolation level is really a superset of READ COMMITTED. Unlike the ISO SQL-92 READ COMMITTED level, Oracle's READ CONSISTENCY guarantees that all the data read by a single query is from the same database

---

16. See Gray and Reuter, 1993, p. 399, for an example that shows the subtle differences between cursor stability and what Gray and Reuter call "2 degree isolation."

17. This does not mean that the *only* way to achieve serializability is through this transaction isolation level. Application programs and DBMSs can provide serializable transactions by using other techniques. For example, if locking is used to control concurrent access to shared data, serializable transactions are guaranteed if the transaction sets read (or share) locks on everything it reads, sets write (or exclusive) locks on everything it writes, never releases a lock before all locks have been acquired, and holds write locks until the end of the transaction.

version; however, successive queries see the latest database version unless the transaction is read-only.[18]

Figures 5-9, 5-10, and 5-11 on pages 180 to 182 summarize the behavior of keyset-driven, dynamic, and static cursors with regard to changes made by the cursor owner and by other users. Changes made by other users can be either *direct*, which means that the changes affect the value of an item retrieved, or *indirect*, which means that the changes affect only the ordering and membership of the cursor. An example of the latter is when another table is used in a subselection and a user changes a row in the table referenced in the subselection, which subsequently changes the rows or ordering of the rows in the cursor.

Keyset-driven cursors and dynamic cursors can be either serializable or nonserializable. If S-locks are held until commit time, a cursor is serializable, regardless of whether the rows were read via a keyset or dynamically.

In serializable keyset-driven or dynamic cursors, it is possible to apply locks either at cursor open time or as the rows are visited. If the locks are applied at open time, updates by other users will be disallowed and the behavior of the cursor becomes similar to that of a static cursor except that the cursor owner can make updates. Static cursors are a special case because they are always serializable.

The behavior of the most common isolation levels used (READ COMMITTED and SERIALIZABLE) are shown in the following figures for comparison. Uncommitted changes made by other users ("dirty data") are not visible. Figure 5-9 shows that serializable keyset-driven cursors behave the same as the SERIALIZABLE isolation level and that nonserializable keyset-driven cursors are very similar to the READ COMMITTED level (except that the user has no way to see his or her own updates in conventional cursors because updates are prohibited if SCROLL is specified).[19] The ANSI SQL standard is unclear on cursor behavior with regard to changes made while the cursor is open, and implementations vary.[20]

---

18. Unfortunately, the *Microsoft ODBC 2.0 Programmer's Reference* states that VERSIONING has the same isolation characteristics as SERIALIZABLE. That is not correct. In Oracle's case, to achieve true serializability applications must use the LOCK TABLE statement.

19. Jim Melton and Alan R. Simon, *Understanding the New SQL: A Complete Guide,* Morgan Kaufmann Publishers, 1993.

20. C. J. Date, "A Critique of the SQL Database Language," in *Relational Database: Selected Writings,* Addison-Wesley, 1986.

	Keyset-Driven Serializable	SERIALIZABLE Isolation Level	Keyset-Driven Nonserializable	READ COMMITTED Isolation Level
Changes Visible				
User's Updates	Yes	Yes[*]	Yes	Yes[*]
User's Deletions	Yes[†]	Yes[*]	Yes	Yes[*]
User's Insertions	Yes[‡]	Yes[*]	Yes	Yes[*]
Others' Updates	No	No[§]	Yes	Yes[*]
Others' Deletions	No[†]	No[§]	Yes	Yes[*]
Others' Insertions	No	No[§]	No	Yes[*]
Ordering and Membership Affected				
User's Direct Updates	No	No[#]	No	No[#]
User's Indirect Updates	No	No[#]	No	No[#]
Others' Direct Updates	No	No[§]	No	No[#]
Others' Indirect Updates	No	No[§]	No	No[#]
Absolute Fetch Supported	Yes	No[**]	Yes	No
Locking Behavior	[††]	[††]	[‡‡]	[§§]

* User cannot actually see changes without scrolling backward or closing and reopening.

† Deletions leave "holes" to maintain absolute position.

‡ User's insertions appear at the end.

§ No update or deletion made by other users is visible. (Snapshot copy or results set is locked, and phantoms are prohibited.)

\# No change can cause a row to be processed twice.

** If deletions are permitted (even user's own deletions), absolute fetch is impossible.

†† Results set locked at cursor open time, or each row locked as visited.

‡‡ U-lock (update lock) on current rows or optimistic concurrency control (compare values or row versioning column value). U-locks are compatible with S-locks but not with X-locks. Only one U-lock at a time is permitted on an item.

§§ Current row U-locked (if opened for update).

Figure 5-9.
Comparison of keyset-driven cursors and SERIALIZABLE and READ COMMITTED isolation levels.

	Dynamic Serializable	SERIALIZABLE Isolation Level	Dynamic Nonserializable	READ COMMITTED Isolation Level
Changes Visible				
User's Updates	Yes	Yes*	Yes	Yes*
User's Deletions	Yes	Yes*	Yes	Yes*
User's Insertions	Yes	Yes*	Yes	Yes*
Others' Updates	No	No†	Yes	Yes*
Others' Deletions	No	No†	Yes	Yes*
Others' Insertions	No	No†	Yes	Yes*
Ordering and Membership Affected				
User's Direct Updates	Yes	No‡	Yes	No‡
User's Indirect Updates	Yes	No‡	Yes	No‡
Others' Direct Updates	No	No†	Yes	No‡
Others' Indirect Updates	No	No†	Yes	No‡
Absolute Fetch Supported	No§	No§	No	No
Locking Behavior	#	#	**	††

* User cannot actually see changes without scrolling backward or closing and reopening.

† No update or deletion made by other users is visible. (Snapshot copy or results set is locked, and phantoms are prohibited.)

‡ No change can cause a row to be processed twice.

§ If deletions are permitted (even user's own deletions), absolute fetch is impossible.

Results set locked at cursor open time, or each row locked as visited.

** U-lock (update lock) on current rows or optimistic concurrency control (compare values or row versioning column value). U-locks are compatible with S-locks but not with X-locks. Only one U-lock at a time is permitted on an item.

†† Current row U-locked (if opened for update).

Figure 5-10.
Comparison of dynamic cursors and SERIALIZABLE and READ COMMITTED isolation levels.

	Static Serializable	SERIALIZABLE Isolation Level
Changes Visible		
User's Updates	No*	Yes†
User's Deletions	No*	Yes†
User's Insertions	No*	Yes†
Others' Updates	No‡	No‡
Others' Deletions	No‡	No‡
Others' Insertions	No‡	No‡
Ordering and Membership Affected		
User's Direct Updates	No*	No§
User's Indirect Updates	No*	No§
Others' Direct Updates	No‡	No‡
Others' Indirect Updates	No‡	No‡
Absolute Fetch Supported	Yes	No#
Locking Behavior	**	**

*   Cursor owner does no updates.

†   User cannot actually see changes without scrolling backward or closing and reopening.

‡   No update or deletion made by other users is visible. (Snapshot copy or results set is locked, and phantoms are prohibited.)

§   No change can cause a row to be processed twice.

If deletions are permitted (even user's own deletions), absolute fetch is impossible.

**   Results set locked at open time, or each row locked as visited.

Figure 5-11.
Comparison of static cursors and SERIALIZABLE isolation level.

5.5.4 Concurrency Control

The primary concurrency control alternatives for achieving different levels of transaction isolation are locking and optimistic concurrency control.[21]

---

21. This description assumes that the client-side software, not the DBMS, is performing the optimistic concurrency control. Other forms of concurrency control are optimistic (in other words, they do not use locks), but they are performed within the DBMS. An example of such a technique is Oracle's READ CONSISTENCY transaction isolation level.

Optimistic concurrency control is used when an application is "optimistic" that no other transactions will update the data before the application has had a chance to. This is in contrast to *locking*, or "pessimistic" concurrency control. With optimistic concurrency control, a row is checked before it is updated or deleted to ensure that no other transactions have modified the row since it was originally fetched. The check can be based on a special row versioning column or on the values of all the columns in the table. If the latter method is used, any Blob (binary large object) is generally excluded due to its size and the assumption that it is not the only differentiating column for a row.

5.5.4.1 Concurrency Control in ODBC

In ODBC, the application specifies the type of concurrency control to be used by passing one of the following options to *SQLSetStmtOption:*

- ■ **SQL_CONCUR_READ_ONLY** This option indicates that no updates will be attempted. (Some optimizations might be possible with this read-only access.)

- ■ **SQL_CONCUR_LOCK** This option indicates that data is to be locked as it is fetched so that another transaction cannot modify the row. An update lock (U-lock) is preferred, since it doesn't prevent other readers but does prevent other writers. Because some DBMSs do not expose such a lock to applications, an application can perform a "dummy update" (setting one column equal to itself) on the rows before they are fetched to acquire an exclusive lock on the row (or on the page containing the row).

- ■ **SQL_CONCUR_ROWVER and SQL_CONCUR_VALUES** These options indicate that optimistic concurrency control is to be used instead of locking. When optimistic concurrency control is used, data is not locked between the time it is read for display and the time it is updated. If no protection is provided, lost updates can occur if another user updates the same data during that interval.

GLOSSARY

Row versioning column A column whose value is updated by the DBMS whenever any column in the row is updated.

Optimistic concurrency control protects against lost updates by rejecting any updates that are based on data that has changed. It provides more concurrency than locking but is more expensive in terms of performance than locking if a collision occurs. It is called "optimistic" because it works best when collisions are infrequent. SQL_CONCUR_ROWVER indicates that a special row versioning column (determined when the application calls *SQLSpecialColumns*) can be used to detect changes. SQL_CONCUR_VALUES indicates that only comparison of values is to be used to detect changes. If SQL_CONCUR_ROWVER is specified, the row versioning column of the rows must be saved. If such a column is not available, the driver can substitute SQL_CONCUR_VALUES instead.

5.5.4.2 Cursors and Ending Transactions

In order to conform to SQL-92 and FIPS 127, all open cursors must be automatically closed upon commitment. This is a hindrance for interactive applications that typically scroll through results, making occasional updates. After a commitment, the application must reopen all cursors and "spin down" each to get back to where it was. This unhelpful behavior is actually required by test number 60 in the NIST SQL Test Suite[22] and has been included in each version of the ANSI SQL standard since 1986.

Note, however, that not all cursors enforce this behavior, especially cursors in single-tier systems, since these are not based on ANSI-compliant DBMSs. In ODBC, an application can use the *SQLGetInfo* function with the SQL_CURSOR_COMMIT_BEHAVIOR option to query the behavior of a cursor on a commit or rollback operation.

> ## GLOSSARY
>
> **FIPS 127** A document, published by the National Institute of Standards and Technology, that defines a test suite to determine conformance of SQL DBMSs to the ANSI/ISO SQL standard.

---

22. National Institute of Standards and Technology, "NIST SQL Test Suite for FIPS 127-1 Adoption of ANSI X3.135-1989 and ANSI X3.168-1989" (version 2.0), December 1989.

5.5.4.3 The Relationship of Concurrency Control to Isolation Levels

It is important to point out that although ODBC provides a way for an application to specify both the desired transaction isolation level and explicit concurrency control options, it isn't clear which options make sense and which don't.

For example, if a DBMS supports the SERIALIZABLE isolation level and the application sets that level via *SQLSetConnectOption*, it would be silly for the application to also use any concurrency control options other than SQL_CONCUR_READ_ONLY. Why? Because when the application tells the DBMS that it wants to be completely isolated from other transactions, there is no reason to do further specification of either locking or optimistic concurrency control on the client; the DBMS will do all the work.

Application programmers should follow similar reasoning when using the other options. Does setting the isolation level to REPEATABLE READ and then using the locking or the optimistic concurrency control option described above make sense? Yes, but only if the application will be re-executing the same query and will need to be aware of new rows that appear in the results set.

The concurrency control options specified in ODBC are most often used by an application that specifies a low transaction isolation level such as READ COMMITTED or READ UNCOMMITTED. In effect, an application that combines the options and levels in this manner is saying that it wants to have the benefit of (probably) higher concurrency in exchange for doing more programming to check for inconsistent updates. ODBC's intention was to let the application programmer make the choice. Depending on the semantics, an application that performs integrity checking on the client with explicit locking or optimistic concurrency control instead of letting the DBMS do all the work via transaction isolation levels could achieve much higher concurrency levels. But keep in mind that the responsibility for ensuring correctness would belong to the application instead of the DBMS.[23]

---

23. I know of one case in which application programmers at a large corporation used a low transaction isolation level and thought that they had correct behavior in the application. But when the application was tested with many users, they experienced the classical "lost update" problem and thought that the DBMS was to blame. You can't have it both ways!

The Inside Story
Act II, Scene I: The SQL Access Group

In the last episode, the "gang of four" (DEC, Lotus, Microsoft, and Sybase) was hard at work defining the SQL Connectivity API. In June 1990, we put the final touches on version 1.12 of the SQL Connectivity specification and submitted it to the SQL Access Group (SAG). Microsoft and Sybase at that time formally joined the SQL Access Group, although Lotus didn't join until almost a year later.

In the true democratic spirit of committees, SAG declared "open season" for call level interfaces, and anyone who wanted to could bring a CLI specification and defend it before the technical subcommittee. By September 1990, several companies had presented CLI specifications, and the pros and cons of these specifications were vigorously debated.

We had to perform major surgery on SQLC when the committee imposed the requirement that the CLI could not expose any more functionality than that which was in the current SQL standard (ANSI 89). Out went scrollable cursors, catalog functions, stored procedure support, driver-prompted connections, extensible data type support, and much more. The SQLC specification went from 120 pages to about 50 but held together pretty well, considering the requirement. It sure was painful to delete all those functions we had worked so hard on, though. In the end, when the final vote was cast, it was the SQLC specification that carried the day and thus became the "base document" for the SQL Access Group's CLI.

The strongest competing proposal by far was from Oracle. The proposal from Gary Hallmark at Oracle was so elegant, in fact, that we at Microsoft came very close to dumping SQLC and calling Oracle to inquire about working with them on their specification. Had Gary's work not been so closely tied to the RDA protocol, who knows what might have happened. As it turned out, the Oracle guys were able to influence the SQLC-based CLI significantly with their work and their excellent technical knowledge of programming interfaces and portability. In particular, Gary Hallmark, Andy Mendelsohn, Richard Lim, and Sanjeep Jain all made significant contributions to the specification both within SAG and, later, when working directly with Microsoft.

A new technical subcommittee of SAG was formed in October 1990 to work specifically on the CLI, and I was elected chairman. Technical committees were already working on embedded SQL and the standard wire protocol, the latter known as the FAP (Formats and Protocols) committee. Thus SQLC was no longer a product of four companies but was now an open specification that could be influenced by anyone who attended the SAG meetings.

The CLI got the attention of other committees too. Jim Melton, the editor of the ANSI SQL and ISO SQL documents, sent out via email a long critique of the CLI near the end of 1990. I replied with an equally long email responding to many of his concerns. Jim attended the next SAG technical meeting in January 1991, and once we explained how the technology differed from embedded SQL, he was quite satisfied that the CLI had something to offer. Jim's assistance in interpreting the SQL standard was invaluable in ensuring that the CLI didn't stray too far from embedded SQL unless absolutely necessary.

5.5.5 Scrolling

ODBC provides two functions for fetching rows from a results set. The first, *SQLFetch,* is used to retrieve rows from forward-only cursors, one row at a time. The second, *SQLExtendedFetch,* is designed to fetch rows from scrollable cursors and provides the ability to fetch multiple rows with one call.

For scrolling operations, *SQLExtendedFetch* provides the following options, which match the FETCH options in SQL-92:

- SQL_FETCH_NEXT fetches the next rowset.

- SQL_FETCH_PRIOR fetches the prior rowset.

- SQL_FETCH_FIRST fetches the first rowset.

- SQL_FETCH_LAST fetches the last rowset.

- SQL_FETCH_RELATIVE fetches the rowset n rows from the start of the current rowset. The value n can be positive or negative.

- SQL_FETCH_ABSOLUTE fetches the rowset beginning at the nth row in the results set.

However, unlike the SQL-92 options, the *SQLExtendedFetch* options allow an application to fetch either a single row or multiple rows. The application must use a statement option to specify how many rows are to be retrieved by a single call to *SQLExtendedFetch.*

One of the new features in ODBC 2.0 is support for bookmarks. A *bookmark* is a value that can be used to quickly and easily reposition a cursor to a particular row in a results set. Each bookmark is a 32-bit value that the application requests from the ODBC driver for a particular row. The application repositions the cursor to that row by calling *SQLExtendedFetch* with the special fetch type of SQL_FETCH_BOOKMARK. In interactive applications, a bookmark is often used when the user clicks on a particular displayed row to update it but then, before doing the update, scrolls down or up so that the row with the focus scrolls off the screen or possibly out of the rowset. When the user types something, the focus is still on the row that he or she clicked on, and that row must be displayed again.

There are many ways to implement bookmarks. For example, an application could use a fully keyset-driven cursor and store the key value for the row that was clicked on. When it needs to return to the row, the application could search the keyset for the key value previously stored. Or it could keep an array of logical row numbers (one for each row), store the row number and the key of the row clicked on, and use the row number for a relative offset from the current row. Either case involves a fair amount of bookkeeping for the application that could and should be handled by the driver. Also, this approach works only with fully keyset-driven and static cursors—dynamic cursors are much harder to manage because their membership is not fixed.

Bookmarks were designed to allow applications to store a specific row and return to that row with a minimum of effort on the application programmer's part. They are independent of the cursor model used (static, keyset-driven, or dynamic). Not all drivers support bookmarks, so the application needs to check for this capability before assuming it can be used.

5.5.6 Positioned Update and Delete Statements

A positioned update or delete statement takes the form:

```
UPDATE ... WHERE CURRENT OF cursor
```

or

```
DELETE ... WHERE CURRENT OF cursor
```

These are very useful for screen-based applications that allow users to scroll through the results set, updating and deleting rows as they go. In such applications, the application positions the cursor on a row and then calls a positioned statement to either update the row with the data entered by the user or delete the row. Unfortunately, many DBMSs today do not support positioned update and delete statements, and, as we saw earlier, SQL-92 does not even allow scrollable cursors to be updated. Fortunately, ODBC supports positioned update and delete statements in the ODBC cursor library, which we will cover next. Positioned statements can also be simulated by the application.

5.5.7 The Cursor Library in ODBC 2.0

In ODBC 1.0 we defined the cursor model but left it up to driver writers to implement it. Unfortunately, almost no one did so because it was a daunting task. Many application programmers were forced to write their own scrollable cursor implementations using the techniques described in sections 5.5.2.2 and 5.5.8.

In ODBC 2.0 we decided that we could provide a simple scrollable cursor model that would work with most drivers. Application programmers would get the benefit of guaranteed scrollable cursors and wouldn't have to write their own cursor code. The implementation of scrollable cursors is called the *cursor library*. It fits into the ODBC architecture as a peer software component to the Driver Manager. The Driver Manager calls the cursor library, and the cursor library calls the driver and in some cases calls back to the Driver Manager.

We provided the simplest of the scrollable cursor models: static cursors. However, the model is implemented in such a way that keyset-driven cursors can be simulated with only a little added effort on the application programmer's part (by binding the key columns and retrieving the actual data with *SQLGetData*). Full support for multiple-row cursors[24] is provided so that an application can fetch as many or as few rows as needed at one time.

Positioned updates and deletions are also supported to allow programmers to build applications that can scroll and update data.

An application enables the cursor library by calling *SQLSetConnectOption* with the SQL_ODBC_CURSORS option. Once this is done, the application can use the scrollable cursor functions that are defined in ODBC Conformance Level 2 (*SQLExtendedFetch, SQLSetPos,* and the options for cursors in *SQLSetStmtOption*).

The sample application CRSRDEMO.C in the ODBC 2.0 SDK shows how scrollable, updatable cursors can be used by applications. Keep in mind that

---

24. The *Microsoft ODBC 2.0 Programmer's Reference* uses the term *block cursors* to refer to multiple-row cursors.

the cursor library doesn't support the ability to change the rowset size dynamically, so the virtual window concept described earlier can't be fully implemented (unless, of course, the application restricts the user from resizing the window and always displays the same number of rows).

5.5.8 Simulating Cursors

Because many existing DBMSs do not support scrollable cursors and the ODBC cursor library supports only static cursors, some applications and drivers might find it necessary to simulate cursors on their own. The following sections briefly discuss how scrollable cursors can be implemented by applications.

5.5.8.1 Keyset-Driven Cursors

Keyset-driven scrolling requires the use of unique row identifiers to ensure unambiguous reaccess to rows. If a persistent, unique row ID is supported by the DBMS, the application should use it. If the DBMS's row ID is not guaranteed to be persistent or unique, a unique index must be used instead. If a unique index is not available, a primary key can be used (if one can be identified). In the worst case, the entire row can be used as a key (unless there are duplicate rows). In the following discussion, the term *key* means the appropriate unique row identifier.

When a user opens a cursor, the application must determine the best key to use for the table (or view). To preserve interoperability, the application should use one of the ODBC standard catalog functions, *SQLSpecialColumns* or *SQLStatistics*, rather than issuing select statements against the native system catalog tables. It then must add the key columns to the selection list if they are not already present. The number of key values that will be buffered (the keyset size) is specified in the *SQLSetStmtOption* function. The application uses *SQLExecDirect* or *SQLExecute* to buffer the keys at cursor open time. The application can provide relative and absolute scrolling within the keyset by indexing into the saved keys and accessing the original tables with a WHERE clause that contains the values of the saved keys. It can scroll forward beyond the keyset by selecting all rows greater than the last key (or ORDER BY) columns. It can scroll backward beyond the keyset by selecting all rows less than the last key (or ORDER BY) columns.

Ordering is determined by the order in which the keys were saved. The application does not have to reexecute subqueries that defined the results set because the keyset encapsulates that information. For maximum performance, multiple rows can be fetched with a single select statement as long as the total number of ANDs and ORs in the WHERE clause does not exceed what the DBMS can optimize. Beyond that, separate select statements must be used for each multiple of the maximum WHERE clause items.

For a refresh, the specified row is refetched into the same buffer using a SELECT statement with a WHERE clause constructed from the saved key values. A flag is set in the returned status array of *SQLExtendedFetch* if the row is not found or if it has changed.

5.5.8.2 Dynamic Cursors

Scrolling with dynamic cursors requires explicit ordering (using ORDER BY or GROUP BY) or implicit ordering (using a unique index). If there is a unique index or if the ORDER BY or GROUP BY is performed by following an index instead of sorting, performance will be adequate. (If the above criteria are not met, performance will be unacceptable for large results sets.) To scroll forward, an application selects the rows that have key values greater than the current key fetched, as in this example:

```
SELECT * FROM t1 WHERE key > lastkey ORDER BY key ASCENDING
```

To scroll backward, the application selects rows that have key values less than the current key value, as in this example:

```
SELECT * FROM t1 WHERE key < lastkey ORDER BY key DESCENDING
```

Things get more complex with composite keys, but fortunately composite keys are not frequently used. (In general, a database designer will often invent a single column surrogate key rather than deal with the many complexities of multipart keys.) For example, a two-part key would require a much more complex WHERE clause:

```
SELECT * FROM t1
WHERE key1 > lastkey1 or (key1 = lastkey1 and key2 > lastkey2)
```

If the ordering column is not the primary key, the application should use the ordering column. In either case, if the column that is used is indexed, forward scrolling performance will be adequate. Scrolling backward will not be efficient unless the optimizer chooses to materialize the results set incrementally via an index.

5.5.8.3 Mixed Cursors

Mixed-mode scrolling is a workaround solution designed to handle those cases for which it is undesirable to buffer the keys for the entire results set, but for which efficient forward and backward scrolling are also desired (although only within a limited range). If the keyset cannot hold the keys from the entire results set, the cursor must switch from keyset-driven to dynamic scrolling when the end of the keyset is reached. If the ORDER BY columns are different from the key columns, the driver must save the ORDER BY column values in addition to the key column values at the boundaries of the keyset.

5.5.8.4 Dynamic Scrolling of Complex Selections

When a cursor uses the dynamic scrolling technique described in section 5.5.8.2, if the DBMS evaluates the results set by any method other than incremental materialization along an index, poor performance will result. On the other hand, the technique can handle almost any kind of select statement.

Primary key and foreign key joins, arbitrary non-key joins, and self-joins can be handled by the dynamic scrolling technique. The application might have to add columns to the selection list for uniqueness or ordering, which could result in the duplication of column names. In such a case, the select statement must then be reformatted with table alias prefixes. Performance on arbitrary non-key joins will be unacceptably slow if many rows must be scanned.

A subquery introduced with = is not a problem because it returns only a single value. A subquery introduced with IN can return many values, but each value in the outer SELECT statement should appear in the final result only once. A correlated subquery is not a problem because the inner part is reevaluated for each occurrence of the outer part. Subqueries in the selection list (which are permitted in SQL-92) are handled in the same way as ordinary subqueries (including correlated subqueries in the selection list). An application does not need to delve into the subquery when processing the outer query for tables and keys. Performance might suffer with a noncorrelated subquery because the subquery will be reevaluated for each scroll operation.

5.5.8.5 Scrolling of Aggregates

A selection with scalar aggregates produces only a single row and does not have to be scrolled. A selection with vector aggregates (those with the GROUP BY clause) produce multiple rows. When GROUP BY is used, there is no need to add columns to the selection list to produce uniqueness. The duplicates will be compressed into a single unique row; therefore, the GROUP BY clause can be considered to be the key. If there is an ORDER BY in addition to the GROUP BY, consider the ORDER BY major and the GROUP BY minor and handle the ORDER BY and GROUP BY columns as though they were one large key.

The aggregates themselves must be recomputed when the cursor is scrolled, but that is consistent with keyset-driven and fully dynamic behavior. (Values can change for either, but membership and ordering are fixed at cursor open time for keyset-driven cursors.)

5.5.8.6 Positioned Update and Delete Statements

Unique row identifiers are required for positioned update and delete statements. (See the discussion of simulated keyset-driven cursors in section 5.5.8.1 for information about how to determine these identifiers.) Positioned operations are limited to buffered rows, which must be contained within the keyset. The actual update or delete operation is performed using a searched update or delete. The WHERE clause is constructed from the saved keys for the specified row and either the row versioning column or the remaining column values, depending on the concurrency option specified on the fetch. If the buffered rowset consists of more than one row, the function *SQLSetPos* must be used to position to an individual row within the rowset before the positioned update or positioned delete statement is issued.

For a positioned delete, a searched delete statement must be constructed with a WHERE clause containing the key columns. If the rows were not fetched with SQL_CONCUR_LOCK, either the row versioning column or the remaining selected columns must be added to the WHERE clause. The values of these columns are buffered during the *SQLExtendedFetch* operation as specified by the concurrency control option in *SQLSetStmtOption*.

For a positioned update, the WHERE clause is constructed in the same way. If the values parameter is non-NULL, it is inserted into the update statement being constructed. If the values parameter is NULL, a SET clause is constructed from the data in the bound buffers. If no buffers are bound and no values parameter is provided, an error is returned. If SQL_CONCUR_VALUES was specified in the cursor definition and the values parameter is NULL, the present value of each buffer is compared with the original value that was saved during the fetch for concurrency control, and the column will be added to the clause only if there is a difference.

GLOSSARY

Searched update and searched delete These are the counterpoints to positioned update and positioned delete. Rather than telling the DBMS which row to update or delete, the program tells the DBMS to find the desired row.

5.5.8.7 Other Options

SQLSetPos is used with the SQL_ADDON option to insert new rows in a cursor. The INSERT statement to add the new row is constructed from the data in the bound buffers. If the cursor is keyset-driven, the inserted rows are also added to the keyset.

To explicitly lock a row, the application reselects the row using FOR UPDATE if the underlying DBMS has such a capability. Otherwise, the application performs a dummy update on the specified row in order to obtain an exclusive lock. In most DBMSs, it is sufficient to set any non-key column to itself (for example, *SET city = city*).

If the cursor definition involves a join (or a view that contains a join), the semantics of deleting and updating are not obvious from the cursor definition. One solution could be to use the list of columns in the FOR UPDATE clause of a standard cursor definition. If all columns listed are from a single table, only that table needs to be updated or deleted. The DBMS will handle referential integrity. (Deleting a master row will orphan the detail rows unless there is a cascade delete constraint or a cascade delete trigger in the DBMS.)

Changing the primary key of a detail row will either reassign the row to a new master row or create dangling detail rows. The effect of changing the primary key of the master row is similar. If the FOR UPDATE clause lists columns from more than one table, the updatable view problem (semantically ambiguous updates) arises. One solution is to assume that the "most many" table (the table that has no references to its primary key from another table) is the only one affected, but finding that table is not easy without the required primary key/foreign key information in the system catalog.

5.6 Data Types

The design of ODBC had two ambitious goals with regard to data types:

- Define a standard set of data types rich enough to retrieve data from all DBMSs without losing the semantic properties of the data.

- Provide a way to return all the native data types of a database (including user-defined types) so that applications can dynamically construct CREATE TABLE statements that can exploit every data type supported by the DBMS.

To accomplish the first goal, we researched the SQL standard and the top 10 database products (in terms of market share) and compiled a list of their data types, including the type names, length limits, and all behavioral characteristics. From this list we created a list of data types to which every data type on the initial list could be mapped without loss of information.

To accomplish the second goal, we defined the function *SQL GetTypeInfo,* which returns all the information about each data type in a given DBMS. The type information is returned in a way that allows an application to prompt the end user through the creation of a table, using the native data type names and characteristics of the DBMS, without the application having to know the specifics about the target DBMS.

5.6.1 The ODBC Data Types

The data types in ODBC had to be defined so that no information would be lost between a DBMS and an application, and yet applications had to have an interoperable way to deal with data types so that DBMS-specific knowledge wouldn't have to be encoded in application logic. Specifically, ODBC had to provide a precise definition of the data placed into an application's memory buffers; otherwise the data wouldn't have any meaning. For example, the form of data returned by a DBMS for date and time data varies considerably among DBMSs. Some systems return the date and time in the form of an 8-byte integer, others return it in the form of a floating-point number, and still others return it as a character string. Clearly an application must know what kind of variable to use when retrieving data from a statement such as this:

```
SELECT ship_date FROM orders
```

Other characteristics of the data, however, do not have to be defined so precisely. For example, the maximum length of character data types varies widely. But there is no reason to enforce a limit in ODBC as long as applications can determine the limits from the driver. However, this does mean that if an application copies data from one database to another, it can't assume that the length limits of the two databases are the same. For example, if an application fetches a 1000-byte character buffer from a column of one DBMS and the other DBMS has a limit of 255 characters to its character data type, the second DBMS will act accordingly (inform the end user, disallow the request, truncate the data, or take some other such action).

The application programmer must have a way to describe three things in an application program:

- the type of the column or expression in a table
- the type of the variables in which data from a DBMS is stored
- the actual C type declaration of the variable itself

For example, if an application retrieves an integer column from a DBMS but wants to put the actual data values in a character string, it needs to be able to tell ODBC that the column is an integer and that the type of the variable being used to store the value is a character string, and it needs to be able to declare the variable itself in the program. (We could have decided that ODBC would dictate which C data type must be used to store each SQL data type and let the application programmer worry about conversions, but that didn't seem very helpful.)

In order to build robustness and reliability into ODBC, we felt that it was better to be explicit and declare the types of data in a buffer rather than inferring them from the SQL types. ODBC supports the SQL type/C type distinction by providing a set of SQL type names that begin with the prefix *SQL* and a similar set of descriptions for C types that begin with the prefix *SQL_C.*

The ODBC SQL types are simply an enumerated list of symbolic constants (*#define* directives in C). Note that these SQL types are found in SQL DBMSs but not necessarily in the C language or in any other programming language. Each SQL type corresponds to a number. Numbers are used so that applications and ODBC can communicate the SQL type of a column or parameter. For example, in the *pfSQLType* argument of the *SQLDescribeCol* function, a driver tells an application what the type of a result column is. The type must be one of the SQL_ types (SQL_INTEGER, SQL_VARCHAR, SQL_DATE, and so on). Wherever possible we used SQL data type names and semantics defined in the ANSI/ISO SQL-92 standard. Not only does this avoid "reinventing the wheel," it also means that as DBMS vendors implement the standard, the data types in ODBC and the database products will converge and interoperability will be improved.

The SQL_C types are also an enumerated list of symbolic constants, but these relate to types in the C programming language, not in SQL. The SQL_C types are used when an application needs to tell ODBC about the type of a variable being used to send data to or receive data from the driver. You might wonder why we didn't just use the C types themselves. But remember, the application needs to pass the type as a function argument, and it is not legal in C syntax for a function call to use an actual type name. For example,

```
foo(long);  /* You can't do this */
```

is not a valid function call, but

```
foo(SQL_C_INTEGER);  /* This is OK */
```

where SQL_C_INTEGER is just a numeric constant is valid. So for functions such as *SQLBindCol* that accept pointers to variables of any type (integer, character string, floating point, and so on), there must be a way for the application to tell ODBC that a variable is of a particular C type. It is for this purpose that ODBC provides the SQL_C types such as SQL_C_SHORT, SQL_C_CHAR, and SQL_C_LONG, which correspond to the C types *short*, *char*, and *long*.

The actual C type definition names (known as *typedefs*) that correspond to the SQL_C types follow the Microsoft standard C naming convention known as *Hungarian notation* in honor of Microsoft software developer Charles Simonyi, who invented it. For example, the ODBC C typedefs include SWORD (a signed word, literally *signed short int*), UCHAR (an unsigned character or byte, literally *unsigned char*), and SFLOAT (a signed single-precision floating-point number, literally *float*).

Now that you've digested all that, here's an example that shows how the ODBC data types are used to satisfy the three needs of application programmers defined at the beginning of this section. Let's say that an application is accessing IBM's DB2 DBMS and it selects a column of type DECIMAL(12, 5). If the application calls *SQLDescribeCol*, the ODBC SQL type in the *pfSQLType* output argument will be returned as SQL_DECIMAL. The precision (12) and scale (5) are returned too, but we won't bother with them in this example. C does not have a DECIMAL data type (although PL/I does), so ODBC uses the SQL_C type as a way to do the mapping and specify any conversions between the SQL type and an appropriate C type. The *SQLBindCol* or *SQLGetData* function can be used to specify the type of the variable in which to return this data, so the application would use SQL_C_CHAR to convert the DECIMAL value to a character string or SQL_C_DOUBLE to convert it to a floating-point number. If SQL_C_CHAR is used, the C variable specified to actually receive the data should be declared as a character string (using the ODBC typedef UCHAR or something equivalent). If SQL_C_DOUBLE is used, the C variable should be the ODBC typedef SDOUBLE or something equivalent. In summary, a column of SQL type DECIMAL is described in an

ODBC application as SQL_DECIMAL and is stored in a C variable described as SQL_C_CHAR or SQL_C_DOUBLE in the ODBC function. The C variable itself is declared as UCHAR or SDOUBLE using ODBC's typedefs.

Here are the ODBC data types, divided by category:

■ **Character (text) data types**   ODBC defines three character types: a fixed-length character type (SQL_CHAR), a variable-length character type (SQL_VARCHAR), and a type for long character data such as a document (SQL_LONGVARCHAR). The first two types were taken directly from the CHAR and VARCHAR types of the SQL-92 standard. Every DBMS has one or both of these types. It would be reasonable to assume that the SQL_LONGVARCHAR type should just be SQL_VARCHAR with a longer maximum length, but it turns out that several DBMSs have additional semantics and restrictions on their long character data types that don't apply to the regular SQL_VARCHAR type. For example, Microsoft SQL Server and Oracle do not allow any comparison operators (=, <, >, and so forth) other than LIKE on their long character types (called "text" and "long" respectively), whereas their VARCHAR types allow all comparisons.

■ **Numeric data types**   ODBC defines 10 numeric types: 7 *exact numeric* (fixed-point decimal and integer) types, for which there are exact representations, and 3 *approximate numeric* (floating-point) types, which are used to represent numbers with exponents and are subject to some imprecision. The exact numeric types are described in the following table:

Exact Numeric Data Types

Type	Used For
SQL_BIT	Truth (Boolean) values; can contain only the value 0 or 1
SQL_TINYINT	Integers that fit into a single byte (8 bits)
SQL_SMALLINT	Integers that fit into 2 bytes (16 bits)
SQL_INTEGER	Integers that fit into 4 bytes (32 bits)
SQL_BIGINT	Integers that fit into 8 bytes (64 bits)
SQL_DECIMAL, SQL_NUMERIC	Fixed-point decimals

You'll notice that there are two fixed-point types, SQL_DECIMAL and SQL_NUMERIC, both taken directly from the SQL-92 standard. Why are there two fixed-point types in the SQL standard? SQL expert Jim Melton explains that this has to do with the subtle differences between fixed-point type definitions in PL/I and COBOL—two of the languages for which there are bindings for embedded SQL in the standard. (I am indebted to Jim for much of the discussion that follows, including the example.)

If you read the standard carefully, you'll see that the description of the fixed-point data type contains specific semantics for PL/I and COBOL (the DECIMAL type for PL/I and the NUMERIC type for COBOL). Neither type can be used with any other language directly as a host variable in embedded SQL, although within SQL both types can be defined and used. FLOAT, REAL, and DOUBLE PRECISION were included in the SQL standard for several languages and cannot be used with COBOL at all. If the standard had limited itself only to those types that could be used with all languages, it would have included SMALLINT, INT, CHAR, and nothing else!

The detailed semantics of NUMERIC and DECIMAL will make their differences apparent. The semantics of NUMERIC are

```
NUMERIC(p, s)
```

where precision is exactly equal to p and scale is exactly equal to s, and the semantics of DECIMAL are

```
DECIMAL(p, s)
```

where precision is no less than p and scale is exactly equal to s.

Therefore, you should use NUMERIC to get an exception any time your results exceed p digits of precision. DECIMAL is a little more forgiving, but the precision is implementation-defined, so you don't always know just *how much* more forgiving it is.

It is not unreasonable to define the "...no less than..." specification for DECIMAL semantics because of the way PL/I works. In COBOL, packed-decimal data is specified with an *exact* picture and the compiler generates compulsive code to ensure that the data has *exactly* the given precision. PL/I, on the other hand, recognizes that decimal data will often be implemented by integer hardware or other hardware that has a rigid number of digits of precision; therefore, the PL/I DECIMAL type needs to support no less than the requested precision, but it can allow more precision. The presumption in the SQL binding to PL/I (which is really the only place that DECIMAL can be used except inside the database itself) is that the DECIMAL columns would use the same hardware data type, and there is thus no chance of "blowing" the host data variable.

Therefore, in embedded COBOL you must use NUMERIC, not DECIMAL. You can use DECIMAL only when invoking SQL from PL/I. PL/I will handle the "at least" semantics, so it's not a problem in that case.

An example will make this more clear. Consider the following:

```
CREATE TABLE t1 (
  d1   DECIMAL(10, 2),
  n1   NUMERIC(10, 2)
) ;
```

Assume that I first execute this statement:

```
INSERT INTO t1 (d1, n1)
  --     1,000,000.00  2,000,000.00
  VALUES ( 1000000.00, 2000000.00 ) ;
```

I know for a fact that the following statement will succeed

```
UPDATE t1
  SET d1 = d1 * 10,   -- 10,000,000.00
      n1 = n1 * 10 ;  -- 20,000,000.00
```

because the resulting values are within the specified precision. And I know for a fact that the next statement will fail

```
UPDATE t1
  SET n1 = n1 * 10 ;  -- 200,000,000.00
```

because we have now caused the NUMERIC column to exceed the specified precision. But I cannot tell whether this statement will succeed or fail

```
UPDATE t1
  SET d1 = d1 * 100 ;  -- 1,000,000,000.00
```

because the DECIMAL column might offer extra digits of precision, or it might not.

I hope that clears up some of the confusion regarding DECIMAL and NUMERIC. In ODBC, the default C type for DECIMAL and NUMERIC is a character string because C has no way to directly represent fixed decimal numbers. You can always convert to other numeric types (such as DOUBLE and INTEGER) too, as long as the values will fit in the specified type and you are aware of exact vs. approximate numeric representations if a floating-point type is used.

The following table describes the approximate numeric data types:

Approximate Numeric Data Types

Type	Used For
SQL_REAL	Single-precision floating-point numbers
SQL_DOUBLE, SQL_FLOAT	Double-precision floating-point numbers

You'll notice that there are two types for double-precision floating-point numbers. There are two reasons for this: the first is because the ISO SQL standard has both FLOAT and DOUBLE data types; the second is because we messed up. The FLOAT data type is supposed to take an optional argument that defines the minimum number of bits required in the mantissa of the floating-point number (called the *precision*). Depending on that number, the DBMS will use either REAL or DOUBLE. In ODBC we didn't define the precision for FLOAT, so we gave it the same semantics as DOUBLE.

■ **Binary data types** ODBC defines three binary types that exactly parallel the character types: a fixed-length binary type (SQL_BINARY), a variable-length binary type (SQL_VARBINARY), and a type for long binary data such as bitmaps and images (SQL_LONGVARBINARY). The first two binary data types were taken directly from the BIT and BIT VARYING types of the SQL-92 standard, although the standard uses the number of bits to describe the length of the column, whereas ODBC uses the number of bytes, reflecting the usage in existing database products. Although character data can usually be printed directly on the screen, binary data generally requires some interpretation before it can be displayed, if it is displayable at all. For example, a bitmap or an image could be in any one of several formats commonly used by applications today, such as BMP, ICO, PCX, TIFF, and so forth. Audio and video data would be stored in binary columns as well.

■ **Date and time data types** ODBC defines three date and time types taken from the SQL-92 standard: DATE, TIME, and TIMESTAMP. DATE and TIME are what you'd expect: year, month, and day for DATE and hour, minute, and second for TIME. TIMESTAMP is a combination of the two and includes fractions of a second.

Some data types don't fit well into these categories because they are, well, weird. Weird data types are based on other data types, but they have additional behaviors or semantics that require special treatment. For example, some DBMSs have a type that is used as an automatic primary key. It is generated by the DBMS itself and is usually called a *pseudocolumn;* it cannot be part of any CREATE TABLE statement. It can be selected but not inserted or updated by application programs. Oracle's pseudocolumn is called a ROWID, Ingres's is called a TID (for tuple ID), and RDB's is called a DBKEY. A slight variant of this is what we refer to in ODBC as an *auto-increment* data type, which is typically an integer value that is automatically incremented by 1 and inserted into every new row created. Unlike pseudocolumns, auto-increment columns are created by users in CREATE TABLE statements. Microsoft Access, Microsoft SQL Server 6, and Informix each support an auto-increment type (called COUNTER, IDENTITY, and SERIAL, respectively).

Another example of a weird data type is one that the DBMS updates whenever a transaction commits a change. An application can check the value to see whether anyone has changed the record since the application last read it. Microsoft SQL Server's and Sybase's TIMESTAMP and Gupta's ROWID are examples of this.

ODBC deals with weird data types in two ways. If the type can be used by an application in a CREATE TABLE statement, the type is described by the *SQLGetTypeInfo* function. If the type is a pseudocolumn that is generated and maintained by the database or if it is a column that can uniquely identify a row in a particular table, the function *SQLSpecialColumns* is used. (We didn't have the guts to call the function *SQLDoesThisTableHaveAnyWeirdDataTypes*, but we were tempted.)

So the data type information available from ODBC spans a wide range of data types found on most DBMSs and also includes some types with interesting, or weird, behavior.

The Inside Story
Act II, Scene II: Meanwhile, Back at the Ranch...

Back at Microsoft, we were still implementing the SQLC specification like mad and decided that, although we needed to follow what the SAG committee ultimately specified, we also needed the additional features that the original SQLC specification contained.

So we split the specification into Core functions (the SAG functions) and two levels of extensions: Level 1 for the features most commonly needed by applications and the features that could be implemented relatively quickly by driver writers, and Level 2 for everything else.

In December 1991 Microsoft hosted the first design preview of the SQLC specification for the ISV community. More than 50 vendors attended, listened to the technical presentation, and reviewed the specification, and many gave excellent feedback suggesting how to improve it. By winter 1992 the SAG specification was looking pretty solid, as were the Microsoft extensions. The name of the technology was changed again, and this time the name stuck: Open Database Connectivity (ODBC).

In March 1992 Microsoft hosted the first formal developer's conference for ODBC and released the beta version of the ODBC 1.0 Software Development Kit. Incorporating all the feedback from the conference took longer than we expected; consequently, the official ODBC 1.0 release did not occur until September 1992.

Interestingly enough, after the March 1992 beta release of ODBC 1.0 Lotus again emerged with some proposed changes to the specification. Although we were hard-pressed to make our September ship date, we were able to accommodate Lotus's request to have a connection function that provided the same functionality as the driver-prompted connection function (*SQLDriverConnect*) but that allowed the application instead of the driver to control the prompting of the end user. So give the people at Lotus credit for the *SQLBrowseConnect* function in ODBC; it's there because of them.

5.6.2 *SQLGetTypeInfo* and Dynamic Table Creation

The *SQLGetTypeInfo* function is used by applications that need to learn everything there is to know about the data types for a particular data source. It also returns information about the mapping that will be performed between the native data types in the database and the ODBC types described previously.

Part of the philosophy of *SQLGetTypeInfo* is to show the types that the user is familiar with on his or her DBMS instead of a set of standardized names. ODBC assumes that the user already knows the data types on the target DBMS, so presenting one set of type names for all DBMSs and hoping that the drivers would do the right mapping was not acceptable. However, providing database-specific data type names and characteristics tended to fly in the face of interoperability, so we needed to ensure that applications could present and use the type information without having to know the detailed semantics behind it.

SQLGetTypeInfo requires the driver to accomplish two things. One is to accurately reflect the data types of a backend in a way that allows an application to issue a CREATE TABLE statement for all the data types on any DBMS, including user-defined types if they are supported by the DBMS. The other is to tell an application how each data type in the DBMS will be mapped to variables in the C programming language and provide information about other attributes to help the application display and manipulate the data appropriately. *SQLGetTypeInfo* returns a results set that has 15 columns and that can be processed like any other results set. Each row of the results set describes one data type. The columns of the results are described below.

TYPE_NAME   The TYPE_NAME column contains the native data type name as defined by the DBMS. This seems pretty straightforward; you'd expect names such as CHAR, VARCHAR, FLOAT, and INTEGER to be returned here. That is the case most of the time. But for a data type that is made up of more than one word and that has a length specified in the middle of its name, empty parentheses are embedded in the type name in the position for the length specification. If no length is specified or the length is specified after the type name, no parentheses are returned as part of the type name.

This somewhat convoluted rule is necessary because some data types for IBM databases (and possibly others) do specify the length in the middle of the type name. For example, the data type for variable-length binary data of length 150 in IBM's DB2 and DB2/2 products is declared like this:

```
VARCHAR (150) FOR BIT DATA
```

So the type name returned in *SQLGetTypeInfo* in this case would be

VARCHAR () FOR BIT DATA

Were it not for the embedded length specification, we could have just assumed that all length specifications followed the type name and let the applications add the parentheses on their own. But because of the embedded length specification problem, applications have to scan returned type names for parentheses and insert the length in the appropriate position or put it at the end. Kind of nasty, but we couldn't think of a better solution other than getting IBM to rename its types!

Unfortunately, the *Microsoft ODBC 2.0 Programmer's Reference* does not do a very good job of explaining all these intricacies, so this point has caused a fair amount of confusion.

DATA_TYPE The DATA_TYPE column contains the ODBC type number to which the native database type will be mapped. For example, the Watcom SQL driver returns a type name "long binary" and maps it to the ODBC data type SQL_LONGVARBINARY, whereas the Microsoft SQL Server driver returns a type name "image" that is also mapped to the SQL_LONGVARBINARY data type.

PRECISION The PRECISION column contains the maximum length specification of the data type. In ODBC we were a bit loose with terminology and departed slightly from the usage of this term in the SQL-92 standard. In ODBC the PRECISION attribute is one of three attributes dealing with length (the other two are LENGTH and DISPLAY_SIZE), but all data types have a defined use for the term *PRECISION*. In the SQL-92 standard, the term by itself is used only when describing exact numeric data types (DECIMAL, NUMERIC, and the integer types). The term *PRECISION* is used in the SQL-92 standard in conjunction with a qualifier in the catalog tables (also known as the information schema) for use in other data types (such as DATETIME_PRECISION and NUMERIC_PRECISION). Sometimes a different word is used altogether (as in CHARACTER_MAXIMUM_LENGTH and CHARACTER_OCTET_LENGTH).

But in ODBC every type uses the term *PRECISION* as follows:

■ For character and binary types, PRECISION is the number of characters of the defined type. For example, CHAR(10) or VARBINARY(10) have a PRECISION of 10. The maximum length of the type is returned by *SQLGetTypeInfo*, so if a DBMS supports a maximum length of 255 for its CHAR type, 255 is returned for PRECISION.

■ For numeric types, PRECISION is the maximum number of decimal digits the type can hold. For example, a DECIMAL (10, 2) type has a PRECISION of 10. The maximum precision is returned by *SQLGetTypeInfo*, so if the database supports a maximum precision of 15, the value 15 is returned for type DECIMAL. For the SMALLINT type (a 2-byte integer), PRECISION is 5, because a signed 2-byte integer can hold at most five digits (the value 32,767). For the DOUBLE type (an IEEE 8-byte floating-point number) PRECISION is 15, because that is the maximum number of digits that the mantissa of such a floating-point number can hold.

■ For date and time types, PRECISION is the number of characters the type has when it is in standard ODBC format: 10 for SQL_DATE (*yyyy-mm-dd*) and 8 for SQL_TIME (*hh:mm:ss*). The situation for SQL_TIMESTAMP is a bit more complicated. First of all there are optional fractions of a second, so the length of the data will vary based on the precision. If this were the only issue, PRECISION would always equal 19 (*yyyy-mm-dd hh:mm:ss*) plus the number of digits supported for fractions of a second (if any) plus 1 for the decimal point. So IBM's DB2 TIMESTAMP type has a PRECISION of 26 (*yyyy-mm-dd hh:mm:ss.ffffff*) because it supports fractional seconds down to the microsecond.

However, we also provided slightly more generality with this type by allowing PRECISION to specify any subset of the SQL_TIMESTAMP data type. For instance, a value of 16 for PRECISION would mean that SQL_TIMESTAMP didn't support seconds at all and would always have the form *yyyy-mm-dd hh:mm*. I'm not sure whether any DBMS actually uses this "feature," but the feature does map to a subset of the INTERVAL type defined in SQL-92. Unfortunately, SQL_TIMESTAMP is not rich enough to accommodate all the variants of INTERVAL. Starting with ODBC 2.10, support for INTERVAL has been improved by the addition of extended data types in ODBC for all the INTERVAL subtypes defined in SQL-92 (for example, YEAR, MONTH, YEAR_TO_MONTH, DAY, HOUR, and so forth). Support was also added for double-byte Unicode characters. Not all drivers are required to support these data types, of course, but drivers that support INTERVAL or UNICODE data types should use the defined values and follow the described behavior as specified in the RELNOTE2.WRI supplied with the ODBC 2.10 Software Development Kit.

Appendix D of the *Microsoft ODBC 2.0 Programmer's Reference* contains the values for PRECISION for all ODBC data types.

The main reason we chose to use PRECISION in this way was that it seemed easier to put all the length specifications in one location rather than include separate columns for each kind of length and use nulls when PRECISION doesn't apply, which is the way it works in the standard. That is, in the information schema in SQL-92, you have to know that when the data type is CHAR or VARCHAR, you look for the length specification in the CHARACTER_MAXIMUM_LENGTH column; when the type is NUMERIC, you look in the NUMERIC_PRECISION column; and when the type is TIMESTAMP, you look in the DATETIME_PRECISION column. In ODBC you always look in the same location: the DISPLAY_SIZE, PRECISION, or LENGTH column, depending on whether you are looking for the display size, the logical length, or the physical length.

LITERAL_PREFIX The LITERAL_PREFIX column is used to describe the character or characters with which to begin a literal in an SQL string for the given data type. For example, in the SQL statement,

```
INSERT INTO T1(name, amount) VALUES ('Joe', 123.45)
```

the literal prefix for the name column is a single quote ('), and for the amount column no prefix is needed. Most DBMSs support this usage. But for the other data types, such as date and time and binary, there isn't much consistency among products. The table below provides a brief look at the literal prefixes for just one data type for a few different products.

Literal Prefixes for the BINARY Data Type

DBMS	Native Type Name	Literal Prefix
SQL-92 standard	BIT	B ' or X '
Microsoft SQL Server	BINARY	0x
Watcom SQL	BINARY	'
Oracle	RAW	'
IBM DB2/2	CHAR () FOR BIT DATA	x

You can see that there is not a lot of consistency in the literal prefix used, so ODBC requires a driver to return the correct characters so that an application can generate SQL statements appropriate to the backend. An alternative would have been to define the literals in ODBC and require all drivers to parse SQL statements and do the required translation. However, that would have put a large burden on the driver writers, whereas the work for application programmers in this case was not very difficult: get a value from

SQLGetTypeInfo, put it into a variable, and use the variable when generating SQL strings.

For data types that don't have a literal prefix, such as numeric types, the value NULL is returned in this column. However, there is at least one case in which a numeric type can have a prefix: the Microsoft SQL Server MONEY type, which uses a dollar sign ($). For example,

```
INSERT INTO T1(name, amount) VALUES ('Joe', $123.45)
```

is legal. In fact, the dollar sign is required to express the maximum value that MONEY columns are capable of storing because without the dollar sign the literal value is treated as a conversion from a floating-point or integer type, neither of which contains as high a precision as that allowed by MONEY.

LITERAL_SUFFIX   The LITERAL_SUFFIX column is used to describe the characters that terminate the literal of a given type. The character used to terminate a literal is not always the same as the prefix. In most cases, when the suffix is different, it is simply not there. For example, in Microsoft SQL Server, Oracle, and IBM DB2/2, no literal suffix is needed for the binary data type, so *SQLGetTypeInfo* returns NULL.

CREATE_PARAMS   The CREATE_PARAMS column describes the kind of information that should be supplied with the data type name when it is used in a CREATE TABLE statement. For variable-length data types such as character and binary types, the column contains the string *max length*. For the exact numeric types DECIMAL and NUMERIC, the column contains the string *precision, scale*. These terms are not rigorously defined in the *Microsoft ODBC 2.0 Programmer's Reference* because the original intent was that the CREATE_PARAMS information would be presented to the end user so that the application need not understand it. Unfortunately, this is too simplistic. For example, some applications will want to put the precision and scale in two different edit controls and so will have to know to parse the CREATE_PARAMS information to some degree.

The CREATE_PARAMS column is typically used by applications that provide an interactive table-building capability that tells the end user the kind of information to fill in for the length of the data type. For example, Figure 5-12 shows the dialog box used to create a table in Microsoft Query. The Length and Decimal edit controls are enabled or disabled depending on the value found in CREATE_PARAMS. Note that Microsoft Query uses the terms *Length* and *Decimal* to equate to *precision* and *scale* in ODBC. If

CREATE_PARAMS is NULL, both options are disabled, as shown in Figure 5-12. If the term *max length* is returned, the Length control is enabled, as shown in Figure 5-13, and if *precision, scale* is returned, both the Length and the Decimal controls are enabled, as shown in Figure 5-14 on the next page.

Figure 5-12.
The effect of CREATE_PARAMS = NULL *in Microsoft Query.*

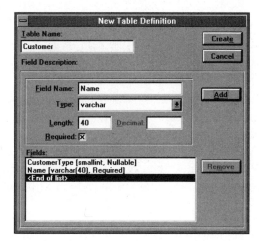

Figure 5-13.
The effect of CREATE_PARAMS = max length *in Microsoft Query.*

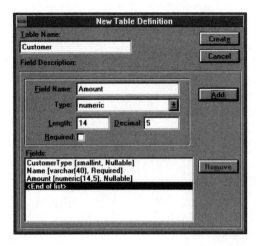

Figure 5-14.
The effect of CREATE_PARAMS = precision, scale *in Microsoft Query.*

NULLABLE   The NULLABLE column returns a value that specifies whether the data type can contain null values. At first glance this might seem like a strange thing to inquire about: doesn't every data type allow nulls? No, as it turns out. Some DBMSs have Boolean types that can contain only true or false values. The Microsoft SQL Server "bit" data type is one such type that does not allow nulls. In contrast, dBASE supports a Boolean data type called "logical" that does support nulls.

The value in this column is used to let an application know whether it can add the clause "not null" after the data type name. For example,

```
create table table1 (b bit null)
```

is not legal in Microsoft SQL Server and would fail, returning a syntax error. The NULLABLE column can contain one other value, which is used when the driver cannot determine whether or not a type is nullable: SQL_NULLABLE_UNKNOWN. This value is included in the ODBC specification because there can be user-defined data types that inherit nullability (or non-nullability) from some underlying type but that do not directly contain this information.

CASE_SENSITIVE   The CASE_SENSITIVE column is used to inform an application of whether the data type contains data that is case sensitive. For example, a CHAR column that is case sensitive and contains the value *Smith* will not be found by the following SELECT statement:

```
SELECT * FROM customer WHERE name = 'SMITH' or name = 'smith'
```

This information can be used to ensure that searches will be successful. Alternatively, an application can choose to use one of the standard ODBC string functions to uppercase a column, as in this statement:

```
SELECT * FROM customer WHERE {fn ucase(name)} = 'SMITH'
```

SEARCHABLE   Some data types have specific search characteristics, such as the kinds of operators (if any) that can be used in a WHERE clause. For example, columns of Oracle's LONG and LONG RAW types cannot be used in a WHERE clause at all. Columns of Microsoft SQL Server's TEXT type can be used in a WHERE clause, but only with the LIKE operator. Other data types can be used with all comparison operators (=, <, >, and so on).

The SEARCHABLE attribute is useful for interactive query applications or development tools that need to validate the types of operations that can be performed on columns of certain data types.

UNSIGNED_ATTRIBUTE   Although the SQL-92 standard presumes that all numeric types are signed, some products (such as Microsoft SQL Server) contain unsigned numeric data types, and others (such as Tandem) have both signed and unsigned variants of their numeric types. The UNSIGNED_ATTRIBUTE column provides the necessary information for applications to validate numbers on the client so that the user can be warned if a sign is entered for an unsigned quantity.

MONEY   The MONEY column returns a value that specifies whether the data type is used for currency values. Because several DBMSs (Ingres, Informix, and Microsoft SQL Server, to name a few) use such a data type but have different characteristics and map to different ODBC types, it was necessary to provide a simple way for applications to identify such currency types.

AUTO_INCREMENT   One of the "weird" data types I mentioned earlier was the type that auto-increments. The AUTO_INCREMENT column returns a value that identifies whether the type will automatically be incremented by 1 every time a new row is inserted. This is a nice feature that database designers can use to make automatic primary keys that are guaranteed to be unique.

One possible goal for future versions of ODBC is to provide a way to return the value that is generated from AUTO_INCREMENT columns when an INSERT statement is executed. Currently some DBMSs have a way to return this information, but ODBC has no way to expose it through the API.

LOCAL_TYPE_NAME   The LOCAL_TYPE_NAME column is used to return non-English-language forms of type names so that localized versions of application programs can use the local language form of a type name for display purposes. For example, the French-language version of a driver would return a LOCAL_TYPE_NAME of *DECIMALE* for the SQL_DECIMAL data type.

Application programmers whose programs display type names from *SQLGetTypeInfo* should always use LOCAL_TYPE_NAME rather than TYPE_NAME if they plan to distribute their applications in non-English-speaking countries. However, an application should still use TYPE_NAME in the actual CREATE TABLE statement—the SQL standard and DBMS products do not support localized type names in the SQL language. The LOCAL_TYPE_NAME value is used only for display purposes in ODBC.

MINIMUM_SCALE and MAXIMUM_SCALE   The MINIMUM_SCALE column and the MAXIMUM_SCALE column return information about data types that have scale but don't quite conform to the standard usage of scale defined for the DECIMAL and NUMERIC types, which allows the scale to be any value less than or equal to the precision. For example, both Microsoft SQL Server and Microsoft Access have currency data types that are exact numeric types but support only a scale of 4. The types behave like DECIMAL in all other respects, but they do not allow the scale to be anything other than the value 4.

As you can see, the *SQLGetTypeInfo* function returns a lot of information about data types. The purpose of this function is to inform applications about all the characteristics of data types so that applications can get an accurate picture of the behavior of each column and can handle the columns as expected by the user.

5.7   Levels of Interoperability

We've looked at most of the elements of ODBC and how they work together. Now it is time to look at a higher-level ODBC issue, one that has caused a fair amount of confusion. The issue is *interoperability,* which in the case of ODBC means how well the programming interface (and more importantly, how well the applications that use it) can handle accessing data from diverse DBMSs.

There are many solutions to this problem, some of which have been discussed in previous chapters of this book (using a standard data protocol such as RDA, for example). Here we are going to look at a few more approaches to this problem and then specifically at how ODBC handles the issue.

5.7.1 The Least Common Denominator Approach

The first solution developers come up with when they are trying to solve the interoperability problem is to support only the functionality that is common to all DBMSs. This is called the *least common denominator* approach. This solution requires the identification of the SQL dialect, semantics, and set of data types that are supported for all DBMSs and the assurance that applications will use only those features. Then, by definition, all applications will be able to use all the different DBMSs because any functionalities that differ are simply not available to applications.

Of course, the big questions are what such a subset of SQL and data types would look like and whether it would be powerful enough for real-world applications. The answer to the second question is yes, but only for a very small set of applications. If the set of data sources is large enough, the differing functionalities of the DBMSs eventually make the common subset very small. For example, when we researched many different DBMSs, we found that the common subset of data types was reduced to one: character strings. However, for simple applications this approach can work.

It should be clear from earlier chapters that although ODBC can work within the context of the least common denominator framework, it isn't constrained to do so.

5.7.2 Hardwiring to a Particular DBMS

At the other end of the spectrum of solutions, the application developer can write code to specifically target each DBMS that he or she wants the application to be able to work with. (Here I am using the term *application* in the generic sense, meaning either an application for end users or a development tool used to generate an application for end users. It is the latter type that most often needs to target multiple DBMSs. That is, most end-user applications will target only one DBMS in production, whereas development tools generally must have the ability to generate applications for many different DBMSs.) Because such an application will have built-in knowledge of the capabilities of each DBMS, the application is free to use as many or as few of a DBMS's features as necessary, thus overcoming the limitations of the least common denominator solution.

One way an application can implement this is to include code that directly addresses the native API of each DBMS. This approach requires that the developer write a lot of conditional code specific to each DBMS. In the resulting application, all the knowledge about the capabilities of each DBMS is encoded into the application's logic.

For each DBMS the application wants to target, the programmer must write code specifically for that DBMS. If you look back at Figure 2-11 in Chapter 2, which shows the Oracle and Sybase programming interfaces, you'll notice that the APIs are similar in structure but vary in detail. That is, the models are roughly the same, but coding to both is still coding to two entirely different APIs. The sheer complexity and size of code within an application that codes directly to multiple native APIs quickly becomes prohibitive, so most applications develop a standard API layer to shield the application logic from having to change every time a new DBMS is targeted.

To satisfy the need to use the full functionality of each DBMS to build powerful applications, the layer must provide some method for exposing the functional capabilities of each system. (For instance, an application must be able to find out whether a particular DBMS is capable of performing an outer join.) Then the developer must consider the problem that arises from the fact that every DBMS has its own set of system tables or its own catalog (the tables in a DBMS that describe the tables and columns of the end user's data). To address this, an API layer typically defines a standard way to access a catalog and puts the DBMS-specific functionality into the lower layer of software so that the application doesn't have to bother with it. And so the list goes on; each difference among the various DBMSs is dealt with in the lower layer of software to separate the core of the application from the messy details of the DBMSs. But this is exactly the same architecture used for ODBC!

Figure 5-15 depicts the layers employed by an application that uses its own standard API to access Microsoft SQL Server and Oracle, as compared to the same layers employed by ODBC. The components are the same for any client/server DBMS.

It is perfectly reasonable for application developers to use their own standard APIs rather than ODBC. Their APIs will be tuned to exactly what their applications need—there is no reason to be more general than that. However, the costs and benefits of this solution must be analyzed. Inventing a standard database API is not a trivial task, especially if the full power of each DBMS is to be exploited. Writing the special translators for each DBMS is also not trivial.

Perhaps an analogy will be helpful. Not many applications ship with their own video drivers (one for each kind of monitor and video card supported) and printer drivers (one for each kind of printer supported) anymore. They used to, because some application vendors believed that they could provide better performance or more functionality than the standard drivers built into Windows. In fact, some vendors even tried to market this as a competitive advantage.

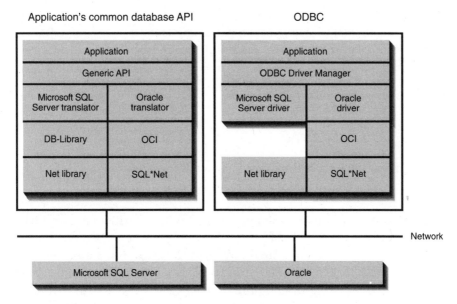

Figure 5-15.
The architecture of a hardwired application compared with ODBC.

But while their developers were busy writing the next set of video and printer drivers, their competitors were busy putting new features into the products themselves to make the products more attractive to the customers. In the end, the marginal performance gains from writing native video and printer drivers were negated by the arrival of better drivers on the market, and these developers were left behind because they tried to compete in areas that were not essential to the application's reason for being.

The parallels in the database access arena should be clear. In the end, the benefits of a standard database API allow application developers to focus on their central concern—building development tools and/or business applications—without having to spend a lot of time on noncore technology such as that involved in writing to every vendor's native API.

215

5.7.3 The Middle Ground: Adaptive Programming

So if least common denominator technology is not powerful enough for general-purpose applications, and if coding to each DBMS vendor's native API is too difficult, what is the best solution? With ODBC we took the approach that we call *adaptive programming.*

With adaptive programming the application programmer can call functions to inquire about the capabilities of a driver. An application can then modify its own behavior based on what the driver and DBMS can do. So rather than the application developer writing code such as

```
if (DBMS == ORACLE) {
    ... }
else if (DBMS == SQLSERVER) {
    ... }
else if (DBMS == DB2) {
    ... }
....
```

the developer tests for capabilities without regard to the target DBMS. An application can test for 115 such capabilities using ODBC version 2.0.

For example, one capability ODBC can test for is whether a particular DBMS supports outer joins. In ODBC, the application programmer would call the *SQLGetInfo* function with the SQL_OUTER_JOINS option to inquire about the current driver. If the driver supports outer joins, it returns a positive response; otherwise, it returns a negative response. In the particular case of outer joins, the response is not a simple "yes" or "no" because a "yes" response must also indicate the type of outer joins supported—partial (two tables only) or full.

How would an application use such information? In the case of outer joins, an ad hoc query tool or interactive query builder in a development tool would use this information to prompt the user for the desired type of join. If outer joins are supported by the DBMS, the "outer join" option will be active; if not, it will be disabled or not displayed at all.

By using the capabilities exposed by the driver and the DBMS, the application can be adaptive. It can exploit the full power of a DBMS as needed by testing to determine the DBMS's capabilities. When the DBMS doesn't support a piece of functionality, that feature of the application isn't available to the user.

Enabling an application to fully exploit all the capabilities of a DBMS is a difficult task, but it is vastly easier than coding to multiple native database APIs, and it allows the application developer to decide how much of the DBMS's power to use. There is a direct trade-off between the power of the application and the ease with which it is programmed. That is, it is possible to

216

use the least common denominator approach with ODBC if such an approach is appropriate for the application. In such a case, the application doesn't have to check for capabilities at all; it just uses least common denominator SQL and the basic core-level functions of ODBC. It is easy to write such an application, relatively speaking.

But programmers who opt for ease of programming sacrifice some of the power to exploit DBMS features and remain interoperable. For example, it would be foolish for a development tool that supports the building of applications for multiple DBMSs to assume outer join support for every DBMS. Users of the tool would not be pleased when it generated SQL that could not be executed by some DBMSs.

At the other end of the spectrum, a programmer can test for every possible capability and adapt the functionality of the application accordingly. This requires that the programmer write a lot of conditional code in the application, but the code will adapt to a new DBMS *even if the application wasn't written with that particular DBMS in mind.* The important point here is that it is the application or tool developer who chooses whether to use the full features of a DBMS.

This description should make clear one of the fundamental design goals of ODBC: to let application programmers choose how interoperable they want their applications to be. Interoperability should not be forced on them by the ODBC API or by the overall architecture. Rather, ODBC should help developers when they need it and get out of the way when they want to exploit DBMSs as they see fit.

You'll see that many of the samples described in Part II use the adaptive programming technique to modify their behavior according to the capabilities available in the driver and the data source.

5.8 Conformance Levels

Another aspect of the interoperability issue has to do with conformance levels. Conformance levels make up the highest category of capability partitioning in ODBC. Following are several reasons why we introduced conformance levels in ODBC:

■ To provide a way for applications and drivers to implement portions of the API specific to their needs without having to implement unnecessary functionality. Not only does this reduce the development time and therefore the time-to-market for the drivers, it results in simpler, smaller drivers. It also provides a clear migration path for obtaining greater levels of functionality in later releases of drivers and applications.

■ To align ODBC with concurrent work in standards bodies so that the distinction between truly standard and extension portions of the API would be readily apparent. The SQL standard itself has maintained conformance levels since its first release in 1986. There were two levels then; with SQL-92 (the current standard) there are three.

■ To help achieve interoperability. At lower conformance levels, an application has less work to do to interoperate, but lower levels also have less functionality. At higher conformance levels, an application has greater power, but higher levels require greater complexity.

ODBC defines two sets of conformance levels: one for the function calls (API conformance) and one for the level of SQL (SQL conformance) supported. Each kind of conformance has three levels. These will be covered in more detail, but first some higher-level explanation is in order.

One of the most confusing issues regarding ODBC is the SQL conformance levels. Many people believe that because ODBC defines these SQL levels, only the SQL defined in each level can be passed to the DBMS. Not so. The main purpose for including the SQL conformance levels was merely to provide a guideline for interoperability, not a constraint on what applications can use or on what drivers must restrict from flowing to the server. A second purpose was to encourage driver writers for ISAM data sources who were writing their own SQL parsers to use the grammar defined in ODBC because it was based on the SQL defined by X/Open, which in turn is based on the SQL ISO standard. A third purpose was to provide some level of assurance that if a driver indicated that a level was supported, developers could indeed count on *everything* in that level to be available for use. Finally, we needed a place to put our "escape clause" SQL extensions (see section 5.8.2.3) and thought a separate conformance level was the best way to accommodate that.

5.8.1　API Conformance

API conformance is used to categorize the sets of function calls supported by a driver. An application can ask a driver which conformance level it supports and then use the functions within that conformance level. The rule is that if a driver indicates that it supports a conformance level, it must support everything in that level. It is also acceptable for a driver to support some functions in the next level. To accommodate such cases, ODBC allows applications to test for individual functions (using *SQLGetFunctions*) so that the maximum functionality of a driver can be used.

As mentioned earlier, there are three API conformance levels: Core, Level 1, and Level 2.

5.8.1.1 Core

The Core conformance level was taken directly from the X/Open SQL Access Group CLI specification as it existed in May 1992. At the time, we believed that the specification was extremely stable, and, in fact, the first official publication of the CLI by X/Open in October 1992 was very close to the May specification.

The goal for ODBC was to provide this conformance level so that implementors who wanted to use only the standard API would have a clearly defined subset of the ODBC API that would accomplish just that. A secondary goal was to have a clear way for developers to use the least common denominator style of interoperability in alignment with the goals of the standards bodies.

Technically, the Core API does all the basic stuff a database application needs to do:

- Performs simple connection management

- Executes SQL statements using the dynamic SQL model of the SQL standard (preparing and executing a statement, optionally supplying parameter values at runtime) and sends SQL statements directly to DBMSs in one call

- Retrieves data from SQL SELECT statements into variables with simple cursor management routines (binding with fetch forward one row at a time)

- Performs transaction management functions to commit or roll back transactions

- Provides a standard way to handle error information

5.8.1.2 Level 1

The first set of extensions for the API is Level 1. Level 1 adds functionality that allows developers to build a wider variety of full-featured applications than is possible with the Core-level functions. Level 1 exposes the functionality that most DBMSs contain, so driver writers do not have to do a lot of additional work to simulate features found in Level 2 that the DBMS doesn't support. However, driver writers supporting Level 1 are required to provide some added value to help applications with connection management, Blob (binary large object) support, and the adaptive programming model. The latter elements make writing the driver more challenging but result in a product that is much more full featured. Level 1 is the minimum level that Microsoft recommends for driver writers because most applications require Level 1 conformance.

In addition to all the Core-level functions, ODBC Level 1 API conformance contains the following:

- Additional connection management functionality so that an application can use the user interface provided by the driver for connecting to the data source.

- Functions for retrieving and sending large data values (Blobs) from and to the server. The main advantage of this is the ability to retrieve and send a single value for a column in a table in chunks rather than all at once, as is required by the binding model in the Core conformance level.

- Adaptive programming functions that allow an application to inquire about the capabilities of the driver and the DBMS.

- A function (*SQLGetTypeInfo*) that determines all the data types of the target DBMS and how each would be mapped to its equivalent ODBC type on the client.

- Catalog functions, which are used to obtain information about the objects stored in a DBMS. These objects include tables, columns (including pseudocolumns and other columnlike objects with special behavior or semantics associated with them, such as Oracle ROWIDs or Microsoft SQL Server TIMESTAMP columns), and statistics (indexes and other information).

5.8.1.3 Level 2

Level 2 contains every function we could think of to provide a rich, robust data access API. In addition to Level 1 functions, Level 2 provides the following:

- Scrollable cursors. Since most DBMSs do not contain support for scrolling forward and backward, scrollable cursors often have to be simulated by the client. As described in section 5.5, ODBC defines a very extensive cursor model to accommodate the varying needs of applications and DBMSs. The cursor library supplied with ODBC version 2.0 allows applications to use scrollable cursors for drivers that are only Level 1–compliant.

- Additional connection management, which allows an application to dynamically build its own user interface for handling any connection scenario.

■ Additional catalog functions for returning referential integrity information (primary and foreign keys for tables), privilege information (which tables and columns are accessible to the user), and information about stored procedures and the arguments for each one.

■ Miscellaneous other goodies, such as functions that return an SQL statement after transformations are done on it by the driver (see section 5.8.2.3), that allow drivers to use "translation DLL" technology for character set translations, and that provide additional information about parameters for use in SQL statements.

5.8.2 SQL Conformance

There are three SQL conformance levels. As mentioned previously, these are guidelines rather than restrictions. Applications are free to send any SQL statement to a DBMS even if the statement is not described within the ODBC SQL conformance levels. Drivers must support all the SQL statements for a conformance level if they report (via *SQLGetInfo*) that they support that level.

5.8.2.1 Minimum SQL

The minimum SQL conformance level contains the barest essentials needed to write ODBC applications. The purpose of minimum SQL was twofold:

1. To provide a least common denominator subset of SQL so that applications can interoperate with a minimum amount of effort as long as the limitations on SQL functionality are not too constraining

2. To provide a target SQL grammar for driver writers who want to create drivers to access flat files and ISAMs

Consequently, the minimum grammar contains only simple SQL constructs:

■ Simple CREATE and DROP TABLE statements (no ALTER TABLE statement)

■ Simple SELECT, INSERT, searched UPDATE, and DELETE statements

■ Simple expressions

■ Character data types (CHAR, VARCHAR, and LONG VARCHAR)

5.8.2.2 Core SQL

The intent behind the core SQL level of conformance was to provide exactly the same functionality defined by the X/Open SQL specification. Since X/Open's stated intention was to allow the creation of portable applications using SQL, it was assumed that any DBMS vendors who didn't already support the full SQL specified by X/Open would soon do so. Most of the SQL functionality in the X/Open specification is taken directly from the ISO standard for SQL. The only differences are some limits and restrictions specified by X/Open to facilitate the creation of portable applications and some extensions not covered by the standard (such as index creation).

Most SQL DBMS vendors supported core SQL when ODBC 1.0 shipped in fall 1992. However, it was a bit surprising that most flat file and ISAM driver writers also tried to support core SQL. By the time the ODBC 2.0 developer's conference occurred in September 1993, we had received strong feedback that driver writers could conform to core SQL for everything but the positioned UPDATE, positioned DELETE, and SELECT FOR UPDATE statements and the UNION clause. The consensus from the driver developer community was that these constructs should be moved to the next conformance level so that more drivers could report that they conformed to core SQL.

Core SQL adds these features to minimum SQL:

- More DDL (data definition language) functionality (ALTER TABLE, CREATE/DROP INDEX, CREATE/DROP VIEW, and GRANT/REVOKE)

- Full SELECT statement functionality, including subqueries and set functions (SUM, MAX, MIN, AVG, and COUNT)

- More data types (DECIMAL, NUMERIC, SMALLINT, INTEGER, REAL, FLOAT, and DOUBLE PRECISION)

5.8.2.3 Extended SQL

Extended SQL describes the SQL extensions unique to ODBC and provides a convenient category for advanced SQL features and data types that many DBMSs support but for which there is no equivalent in the SQL standard.

The ODBC SQL extensions provide essential interoperability functionality for application writers. Four types of functionality are widely implemented in DBMSs, but each DBMS uses its own syntax. These functionalities are the representation of date and time literals, the syntax for outer joins, the syntax for scalar functions, and the invocation of stored procedures. ODBC defines SQL syntax that leverages the SQL-92 standard but requires drivers to translate ODBC's syntax into the syntax required by the DBMS. However, to avoid requiring driver writers to build a complete SQL parser, ODBC provides some "syntactic sugar" to allow the translations to be done with simple string scanning routines. We call this syntactic sugar the *escape clause*. The escape clause is nothing more than a pair of curly braces ({ }) surrounding the standard form of the SQL syntax and a one-character or two-character token that specifies the type of the clause. It is unfortunate that this escape clause business is necessary at all. It would be much simpler if all DBMS vendors supported the SQL-92 syntax for those areas it defines. That will happen someday, but until all DBMS products comply, the escape clause or something like it will have to be used.

The next few pages describe the specific areas for which the escape clause is used.

Date and Time Literals   Many DBMSs support some or all of the data types DATE, TIME, and a combined form called TIMESTAMP (sometimes called DATETIME). However, the literal format used with SQL statements varies. For example, the format required in Oracle 6 is *mmm dd, yyyy,* whereas for DB2 it is *yyyy-mm-dd.* In fact, no two systems seem to represent date and time literals the same way! The ISO SQL standard representation for DATE data is *yyyy-mm-dd,* so that is what ODBC uses. If a driver indicates that it supports the DATE data type, the application programmer should always use the date escape clause, which is *{d 'yyyy-mm-dd'}.* For example, to select orders placed on August 12 or August 19, 1995, the application should generate the following:

```
SELECT OrderNum, OrderDate
FROM Orders
WHERE OrderDate = {d '1995-08-12'}
OR  OrderDate = {d '1995-08-19'}
```

The Oracle driver would translate this query as:

```
SELECT OrderNum, OrderDate
FROM Orders
WHERE OrderDate = 'Aug 12, 1995'
OR  OrderDate = 'Aug 19, 1995'
```

The Microsoft SQL Server driver would translate it as:

```
SELECT OrderNum, OrderDate
FROM Orders
WHERE OrderDate = '08-12-1995'
OR  OrderDate = '08-19-1995'
```

There are similar escape clauses for TIME and TIMESTAMP. All of them use the ISO standard format for the syntax of the literals, and the driver must translate the syntax to a form acceptable to the DBMS.

Outer Joins   Like the date and time literals syntax, outer join syntax varies among the DBMSs that support outer joins. Outer joins are very handy for what I call "if any" queries, such as the query, "Show all customers in Boston and their orders, if any." For customers having no current orders, the inner join would not show the customer at all, whereas the outer join would simply return a null for the order information and still return the name of the customer.

We originally intended that ODBC use the outer join syntax from the SQL-92 standard, but we found that no DBMS actually supported all the variants of outer joins specified by the standard. So we used a subset of the outer join grammar from SQL-92 that covered the current implementations, and we left a provision for the more full-featured SQL-92 format as an option. The main limitation of most DBMSs was their inability to support the nesting and precedence necessary to accommodate multiple outer joins. Here is the ODBC outer join syntax:

> *outer_join* ::= *table_name* [*correlation_name*] LEFT OUTER JOIN
> {*table_name* [*correlation_name*] | *outer_join*} ON *search_condition*

For example, for the "Show all customers in Boston and their orders, if any" query, the ODBC syntax would be:

```
SELECT cust.custname, ord.ordernum
FROM {oj cust LEFT OUTER JOIN ord ON cust.custid = ord.custid}
WHERE cust.city = 'Boston'
```

The Oracle driver would translate this query as:

```
SELECT cust.custname, ord.ordernum
FROM cust, ord
WHERE cust.custid = ord.custid (+) AND cust.city = 'Boston'
```

The Microsoft SQL Server driver would translate this query as:

```
SELECT cust.custname, ord.ordernum
FROM cust, ord
WHERE cust.custid *= ord.custid AND cust.city = 'Boston'
```

Eventually, DBMSs will come to use the SQL-92 standard for outer join syntax so that such translations will not have to be performed in ODBC drivers; the SQL-92 syntax will be supported in the DBMS itself.

Scalar Functions   A scalar function is a function that operates on a single value, such as the functions that compute absolute values or extract substrings. Scalar functions differ from set functions (sometimes called aggregate functions), which operate on a set of values, such as the SUM, MAX, MIN, and AVG functions.

Like the other functionalities that use escape clauses, the scalar functions are widely implemented but vary in syntax among DBMSs. ODBC supports more than 60 scalar functions. Wherever possible, we took the syntax definition of the scalar functions from the SQL-92 standard, and for scalar functions that are not part of the standard, we looked at other programming language standards (C, FORTRAN, and COBOL). Finally, we tried to ensure that all remaining scalar functions that existed in two or more commercial DBMS products were specified, usually choosing the syntax used by the product with the largest market share.

ODBC supports five categories of scalar functions: numeric, string, time and date, system, and conversion. A few examples are given below. The complete list is described in Appendix F of the *Microsoft ODBC 2.0 Programmer's Reference*.

Numeric Functions   Numeric functions include those functions that determine square roots, sine and cosine, and logarithms, to name a few. Here's an example showing the use of an absolute value function:

```
SELECT {fn abs(temperature)}
FROM table1
```

Like the syntax in other types of escape clauses, this syntax will be translated into the syntax of the absolute value function supported by the DBMS.

String Functions   String functions include the functions that extract substrings, perform case conversion, and determine string length, to name a few. Here's an example showing the concatenation of two strings:

```
SELECT {fn concat(LastName, {fn concat(", ", FirstName)})} FROM table1
```

This example shows that the ODBC scalar functions can be nested.

Time and Date Functions   Time and date functions include the functions that extract time and date elements from a column and do time-based calculations. Here's an example using the current date function:

```
SELECT ordnum
FROM orders
WHERE orddate < {fn curdate()} - 7
```

This query shows that an ODBC scalar function can be used in a WHERE clause. In general, an ODBC scalar function can be used anywhere that an expression can be used. This example also shows that an ODBC scalar function can be part of an expression. This particular query returns the orders that were entered more than one week before the current date.

System Functions   System functions include the function that returns the current user, as shown here:

```
SELECT ordnum
FROM orders
WHERE employee = {fn user()}
```

This example returns all the orders entered by the current user.

Conversion Function   The data type conversion function converts a data type to a different data type on the server, as shown here:

```
SELECT ordnum
FROM orders
WHERE {fn convert(orddate, SQL_CHAR)} like '199%'
```

This example shows the simple conversion of a date column to a character string. It also shows how powerful the use of scalar functions in expressions can be. In this case, the query returns all orders made in the 1990s.

Stored Procedure Invocation   A key element of high-performance client/server computing is the use of stored procedures to centralize business logic on the server rather than in client applications. ODBC supports the invocation of stored procedures independent of the DBMS. However, ODBC does *not* provide a way to define the contents of a stored procedure. This is one case in which DBMSs differ so widely that defining a standard language and asking drivers to translate from it to a DBMS's native stored procedure syntax would be too onerous.

Stored procedures operate much like procedure calls in standard 3GLs. A stored procedure has a name and can have arguments and a return value. The arguments can be the equivalent of call-by-value arguments (arguments that can't be modified by the called procedure) or call-by-reference arguments (arguments that can be modified by the called routine). However, unlike 3GL procedure calls, stored procedures in some implementations (notably Microsoft SQL Server) can have side effects such as the return of results and status and error messages.

The ODBC syntax for stored procedure invocation is

{[? =] call *procedure_name*[(*arg1, arg2, ...*)]}

A parameter (question mark) must be used for the return value (if any) and any output arguments because it is bound to a program variable. Input arguments can be either literals or parameters.

Below is a code fragment that calls a stored procedure and binds the arguments. It takes one input argument and returns a value. This stored procedure computes a sales tax rate given an input zip code.

```
/*
The stored procedure we're going to call is of the form
    TaxRate = GetTaxRate(ZipCode);

First bind the return value to the floating-point variable TaxRate.
After execution, the variable TaxRate will contain the return value of
the stored procedure.
*/
rc = SQLBindParameter(hstmt1, 1, SQL_PARAM_OUTPUT, SQL_C_FLOAT,
    SQL_FLOAT, 0, 0, &TaxRate, 0, 0);
/*
Next set and bind the zip code argument to the stored procedure. The
variable ZipCode sends the value to the stored procedure.
*/
ZipCode = 98053;
rc = SQLBindParameter(hstmt1, 2, SQL_PARAM_INPUT,  SQL_C_LONG,
    SQL_INTEGER, 0, 0, &ZipCode, 0, 0);
/*
Call the stored procedure using the ODBC standard syntax
*/
rc = SQLExecDirect (hstmt1, "{? = call GetTaxRate(?)}", SQL_NTS);
/*
Build message for display
*/
sprintf (szBuf, "The tax rate is: %f", TaxRate);
```

5.9 Driver Installation, Setup, and Configuration

Another design goal for ODBC was to simplify the installation and configuration of drivers but to do so in a way that was consistent for a variety of drivers. This required us to provide a number of different capabilities, including:

- The necessary tools and templates for driver writers to make it easy for them to distribute their drivers. In addition to eliminating the redundancy of requiring each driver writer to write an installation program, ODBC enforces consistency in the installation user interface and, more importantly, in the locations in which drivers are installed and how they are configured. At the same time, it is important for driver writers to have the necessary flexibility to set up their components and prompt the user directly for any additional setup or configuration information.

- A completely programmatic way for applications to automatically install ODBC components using all, some, or none of the user interface provided by ODBC. For example, some application programmers bundle one or more ODBC drivers with their applications but want them to be installed "silently" (without any user interaction at all).

- A configuration tool so that drivers can be added, configured, and maintained independently from either an application or a driver writer's setup program.

To accomplish the first goal, the ODBC SDK includes a sample setup program in source code form so that driver writers can "fill in the blanks" and have a ready-to-use setup program for their drivers.

The second goal was satisfied by providing a setup and installation programming interface so that applications can use all, some, or none of the standard ODBC user interface for installation.

The third goal was satisfied by automatically installing the ODBC control panel device in the Windows Control Panel. This way, even if applications install ODBC components silently, the user can still configure the drivers and data sources via the Control Panel.

To best understand how ODBC accomplishes the seemingly conflicting goals of having a standardized setup while at the same time allowing driver writers to have the freedom to customize their installation, we must look at how the overall installation architecture works. Here's the sequence of events during normal driver installation:

1. When the setup program (SETUP.EXE on the ODBC driver installation disk) is run, the first thing it does is display the welcome dialog box shown in Figure 5-16.

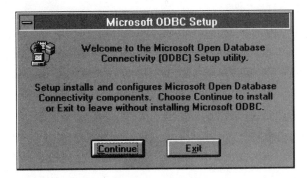

Figure 5-16.
The welcome dialog box.

2. The setup program calls the function *SQLInstallODBC*, which is part of the installer API of ODBC. Like all installer functions, it is included in the ODBCINST.DLL library, which is part of the ODBC SDK and can be freely redistributed by driver writers and applications.

3. The *SQLInstallODBC* function displays the driver installation dialog box (shown in Figure 5-17 on the following page). The setup program builds this dialog box dynamically by reading entries in another file, ODBC.INF. The ODBC.INF file determines what drivers and related files are to be installed and provides a lot of other information. The Advanced button allows the user to set installation options such as those that disable the built-in version checking the installer uses to ensure that older versions of drivers are not copied over newer ones and those that control whether the Driver Manager and data translators are installed. The user can also check the version numbers of all the components to be installed.

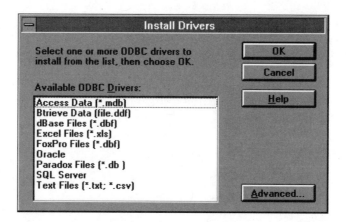

Figure 5-17.
The driver installation dialog box.

4. After the driver files have been copied to the proper location and information in various initialization files (ODBC.INI, ODBCINST.INI, or the registry) has been added or updated, control returns from ODBCINST.DLL to the main setup application. Assuming that no errors have occurred, the setup application next calls the function *SQLManageDataSources,* another function in the installer API.

5. The *SQLManageDataSources* function displays the Data Sources dialog box (Figure 5-18), which is the key to mapping drivers to data source names. (The motivation behind the data sources concept is explained in Chapter 4.) This dialog box is the focal point for all configuration and management of ODBC drivers and data sources. Anything that can be done with ODBC configuration can be done from this dialog box. This dialog box is also displayed when users run the ODBC Administrator tool or use the ODBC tool in the Windows Control Panel. Chapter 24 of the *Microsoft ODBC 2.0 Programmer's Reference* does a good job of explaining the various capabilities accessible from this dialog box, so I won't explain all the buttons and their actions here.

6. The user clicks the Setup button after selecting a data source name to indicate that he or she wants to configure an individual driver. Up to this point, all of the software has been provided by the

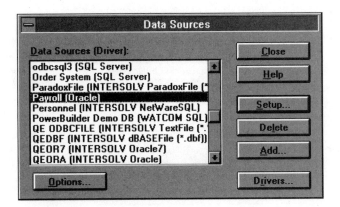

Figure 5-18.
The Data Sources dialog box.

ODBC SDK, albeit with customizations that might have been added by driver writers. But now things change: this is where the driver writer gets control over the configuration process. The writer of an ODBC-compliant driver must provide a setup library (usually referred to as the *setup DLL*) as either a separate DLL or part of the driver DLL. The one requirement is that the driver writer must expose an entry point called *ConfigDSN*. When the user clicks the Setup button, the ODBC installer ODBCINST.DLL looks at the initialization file ODBCINST.INI and determines where to find the driver's setup routine. The driver's setup DLL is loaded, and the entry point *ConfigDSN* is called.

7. The *ConfigDSN* function displays the dialog box appropriate for that particular driver. (The dialog box for the Oracle driver is shown in Figure 5-19 on the following page.) The driver writer is free to prompt the user for whatever interactions are appropriate for the driver. Note that because this dialog box is for one particular driver, its appearance will differ depending on the driver. The user sets the desired options, and the setup DLL then records these for future use, usually in the ODBC.INI initialization file. However, rather than requiring setup DLLs to modify the initialization files directly, the installer provides several function calls so that these files are managed carefully and in a consistent manner.

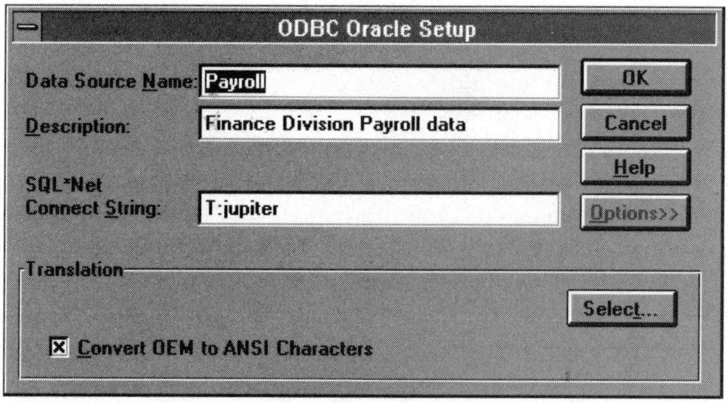

Figure 5-19.
The dialog box for the Oracle driver.

That's enough detail for now, although the installer includes more features and function calls than those described here, such as installation and configuration of translation DLLs for character set translation. These other features are described in the *Microsoft ODBC 2.0 Programmer's Reference*.

One other item does merit discussion, however. One of the needs expressed by corporate customers was to avoid having to go through the same setup procedure on each individual client PC. To accommodate this request, ODBC was designed so that the ODBC installer can be run in *auto mode*. Auto mode installation requires only a network server to be set up with the appropriate drivers and configuration options, and each client can simply run the setup program with the /AUTO switch and a specification of the network file server. Instead of prompting the user through the process of selecting drivers and configuring data sources, the program "clones" the network file server's setup on the client. In a large enterprise, this reduces the setup procedure to simply connecting to the network drive and running the ODBC SETUP.EXE program with the /AUTO switch. The ODBC installer takes care of copying all the correct files from the network server to the client.

Another twist on this is running ODBC directly from the file server—that is, with no components installed on the client PC at all. This assumes that Windows itself is running on the network file server and that all ODBC software will be loaded into the client PC's memory across the network. In ODBC 2.1, the necessary code was added to the Driver Manager to allow this configuration to work. Previous versions assumed the existence of an ODBC.INI file on the client and prevented the use of a completely networked version of ODBC.

5.10 Qualifiers in Table Names

A table is the most fundamental element of a relational database. All DBMSs support the simplified method of referring to a table by specifying its name. For example,

```
SELECT * FROM customer WHERE state IN ('WA', 'OR')
```

specifies the table named *customer.* But this is an oversimplification because in the DBMS a table name implies a lot of context that can also be specified explicitly in an SQL statement, such as the table's owner, the container for the table name, and sometimes the location of the table in a distributed DBMS. Specifying the table name alone assumes the defaults for the other elements of the table name. But table names can also be *qualified* by prefixing or suffixing other names to the table name to explicitly specify the defaults or override the defaults altogether. For example, most DBMSs assume that a table name by itself means the table owned by the current user. So if a user named Fred is currently connected to the DBMS, the above SQL statement is equivalent to:

```
SELECT * FROM fred.customer WHERE state IN ('WA', 'OR')
```

If a user named Mary wants access to the customer table (and if Fred has defined the necessary privileges to allow that), she must specify the qualified name *fred.customer*; using *customer* alone would return an error because the DBMS would try to access the name *mary.customer.* As it turns out, qualifying table names with owner names is just the tip of the iceberg.

Each DBMS has chosen a different means to qualify table names to specify a particular context. For example, in SQL-92 a table name can be qualified by a *catalog* and a *schema owner.* In Oracle, a table is identified by the table owner and the table name, but a *location name* can also be appended to the table name to indicate that the table actually resides on a different system from the one to which the application is currently connected. For example,

```
SELECT * FROM fred.customer@Denver WHERE state IN ('WA', 'OR')
```

accesses the customer table that is owned by Fred and that is located on the Denver system.

In Microsoft SQL Server, tables are identified by a database name, a table owner, and a table name. For example,

```
SELECT * FROM dbx.fred.customer WHERE state IN ('WA', 'OR')
```

accesses the customer table owned by Fred in the database dbx.

dBASE tables, which are actually files on a PC, are identified by a directory name and a filename. For example,

```
SELECT * FROM c:\mydata\customer.dbf WHERE state IN ('WA', 'OR')
```

accesses the customer table in drive C in the MYDATA directory.

ODBC needed to address all these different naming schemes in one model so that applications would know how to specify table names appropriately without having to understand the naming rules for each DBMS. This was necessary both to specify correct SQL syntax and to provide users of ad hoc query tools the ability to choose tables in a manner most natural for the particular DBMS. (For example, a user connected to Oracle should be presented with table names and owner names, but a user of dBASE files should be presented with filenames and directories.)

ODBC started with the assumption that any table name could have an optional owner name associated with it. If an owner name is specified, a period separates the owner name from the table name. This assumption is valid in client/server DBMSs but not in desktop databases, which typically have no security and therefore no owner names associated with them. However, the owner name was optional in any case, so even the desktop database case could be handled. All other elements of table names are specified in a qualifier in ODBC. A qualifier can be as diverse as a directory name (for dBASE) or a location identifier (for Oracle).

In addition to specifying correct SQL syntax, the ODBC qualifiers are used primarily in the catalog functions, which are the functions that return information about the tables, columns, indexes, and other elements in a particular DBMS. When an application calls *SQLTables,* for example, the table name, owner, and qualifier are returned.

Figures 5-20, 5-21, and 5-22 show how different DBMSs return information about tables. Figure 5-20 shows the return values from *SQLTables* for the Watcom SQL ODBC driver, Figure 5-21 shows the return values from *SQLTables* for the dBASE ODBC driver, and Figure 5-22 shows the return values from *SQLTables* for the Microsoft SQL Server ODBC driver.

Qualifier	Owner	Name	Type	Remarks
NULL	DBA	contact	TABLE	NULL
NULL	DBA	cust_order	TABLE	NULL
NULL	DBA	customer	TABLE	NULL

Figure 5-20.
Example return values from SQLTables *for the Watcom SQL ODBC driver.*

Qualifier	Owner	Name	Type	Remarks
C:\MYDATA	NULL	CUSTOMER	TABLE	NULL
C:\MYDATA	NULL	ORDDTAIL	TABLE	NULL
C:\MYDATA	NULL	ORDERS	TABLE	NULL

Figure 5-21.
Example return values from SQLTables *for the dBASE ODBC driver.*

Qualifier	Owner	Name	Type	Remarks
PUBS	DBO	authors	TABLE	NULL
PUBS	DBO	title_view	VIEW	NULL
PUBS	DBO	titles	TABLE	NULL

Figure 5-22.
Example return values from SQLTables *for the Microsoft SQL Server ODBC driver.*

As you can see, there is quite a lot of diversity in representation for tables. An ODBC application can use all three parts of a name when it is constructing table names in SQL statements to specify precisely which table is being accessed. An application also must use a few other options to be fully interoperable. These include the identification of the character that separates the qualifier from the rest of the table name (a period for most client/server databases, but a backslash for dBASE), the location of the qualifier (before or after the table name), and how qualifiers can be used in SQL statements (that is, in which DML and DDL statements they can be used). The application can discover all of these characteristics of tables by calling *SQLGetInfo* with one of the SQL_QUALIFIER options.

5.11 Summary

We've covered a lot of material in this chapter. By now, you've seen many aspects of ODBC at a conceptual level. In the next chapter, the final chapter of Part I, we switch from looking at how applications use ODBC to an inside look at an ODBC driver.

The Inside Story
Act II, Scene III:
ODBC, ISO, CLI, and the Grand Unification Theory

At about the same time that ODBC 1.0 was released, the SAG CLI specification was released as a preliminary specification by X/Open. The core functions of ODBC were almost identical to those in the SAG CLI specification. The SAG CLI specification had changed somewhat due to the addition of COBOL support. The changes were necessary to keep the C and COBOL versions of the CLI as closely aligned as possible.

In October 1992 the specification was reviewed and accepted by the ANSI SQL committee as the base document for a new binding style for SQL. The specification was reviewed and accepted by the ISO DBL (Database Language) committee in November 1992.

Although three separate standards bodies (SAG-X/Open, ANSI, and ISO) have the specification and thus have the potential to diverge, everyone has worked together with amazing cooperation from the beginning. The SAG-X/Open technical committee did almost all the actual technical work on the specification, but the specification was converted at major milestones from X/Open style to ANSI/ISO style and subsequently reviewed by ANSI and ISO.

In 1993 the technical committee began to embellish the specification, in part to make it align better with some of the newer constructs in the SQL-92 standard for embedded SQL. This caused some concern with regard to ODBC, because no one wanted two standards: a de facto standard (ODBC) and a de jure standard (the ANSI, ISO, and SAG-X/Open specification). Fortunately, by the end of 1993 the SAG-X/Open specification had converged on ODBC's conformance Level 1 as a technical goal and had cleanly partitioned the new features from SQL-92 to avoid incompatibilities.

Because of the excellent technical work of the SAG-X/Open committee members as well as their ability to work cooperatively with ANSI and ISO, the next version of ODBC, version 3.0, will probably add all the features in the "true" standard CLI. This will allow ODBC 3.0 to be a pure superset of the international CLI standard, enabling developers to write to only the ISO standard if they want or to use the extensions in ODBC. As long as ODBC and the standards bodies continue to work cooperatively, developers will be able to concentrate on writing productive software instead of learning APIs.

CHAPTER SIX

A Tour of the Microsoft SQL Server ODBC Driver

This book would be incomplete without a look behind the scenes at an actual ODBC driver. This chapter describes how the ODBC driver for Microsoft SQL Server was designed and implemented. This discussion should give you enough detail to allow you to form a more concrete view of some of the theoretical aspects of the ODBC API. Most of the chapter focuses on the driver supplied with Microsoft SQL Server version 4.21, but a section is included that describes the features of the driver supplied with the latest release, Microsoft SQL Server 6.

This description of the driver is by no means exhaustive. We cover the major features of the driver, including how it works within the overall architecture and how it handles connections, statement execution, cursors, stored procedures, and data types.

6.1 Special Considerations

In some ways, the Microsoft SQL Server ODBC driver does not really represent a typical ODBC driver. Microsoft SQL Server contains many advanced features that are found in few other products (stored procedures, triggers, and user-defined data types, to name a few), and it also differs substantially from most other DBMSs in some fundamental ways, most notably in its lack of true cursors.[1]

However, despite these characteristics, the Microsoft SQL Server ODBC driver is a good example of a well-implemented driver that provides performance that is equal to or greater than that of the "native" API, DB-Library.

---

1. Microsoft SQL Server 6, however, offers the most comprehensive support for ODBC cursors of any DBMS currently available.

This is because the Microsoft SQL Server ODBC driver is not another layer of software on top of DB-Library. Instead, like DB-Library, the driver uses the TDS data protocol from the transport-independent network libraries (*netlibs*) provided by Microsoft SQL Server. The functionality of the driver is nearly on par with that of DB-Library; the omission of some features from the ODBC driver is mostly due to time-to-market pressures rather than any limitations of the ODBC API.[2]

The Microsoft SQL Server ODBC driver fully exploits client/server architecture in the way we originally envisioned for all client/server DBMS drivers. Any driver for a client/server DBMS can and should use this model to achieve the best performance and functionality.

6.2 Microsoft SQL Server System Architecture

The architecture of a system using ODBC and Microsoft SQL Server is similar to the standard architecture for any client/server configuration that was described in Chapter 3. Figure 6-1 shows the various client and server software components for the Microsoft SQL Server ODBC driver and Microsoft SQL Server.

By now you should understand the general scope and purpose of the user interface, the application, the ODBC Driver Manager, and the driver. The other components require a bit more explanation.

The network library has two components: one on the client and one on the server. This architecture shields the DBMS interface software from the details of the specific network being used—a highly desirable situation because interfaces to the lower-level network software vary depending on the type of network transport and protocol used (TCP/IP, SPX/IPX, named pipes, SNA LU 6.2, and so forth). For example, naming schemes to identify the server are different on different types of networks. With named pipes the server is identified by a name like \\server1\pipe\sql; with a direct TCP/IP

---

2. The two main features that are missing from the driver are BCP (bulk copy) and two-phase commit. ODBC can support something similar to BCP if the driver provides the *SQLParamOptions* function and maps arrays of input parameters for INSERT statements to the BCP commands or batched SQL supported in TDS. However, a workaround for the second omission is not so easy. Although the ODBC API suggests that the *SQLTransact* function could support two-phase commit by passing the environment handle to the driver, the current implementation of the Driver Manager (version 2.10) does not pass the environment handle to the driver, making support of two-phase commit within a single driver impossible. At the time of this writing, a more comprehensive approach to two-phase commit is being considered for ODBC 3.0.

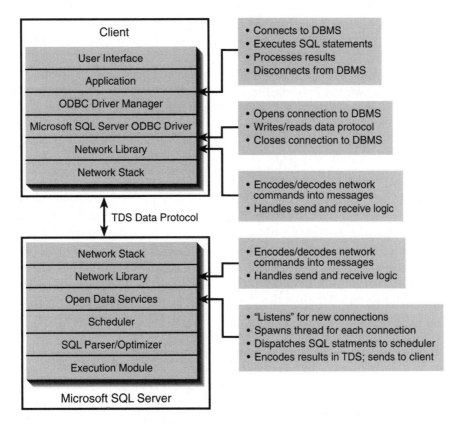

Figure 6-1.

*Architecture of a system that uses the Microsoft SQL Server ODBC driver and
Microsoft SQL Server.*

connection an IP address and socket number such as 11.1.8.166,2025 are required; and so on. But from the client database API's perspective, the differences are not germane to the task at hand (connecting to a database server),
so it makes more sense to abstract the interface into a more generic "open
the connection" function and let some lower-level piece of software determine whether a pipe name or an IP address and socket number should be used.

If you're thinking that the concept of network libraries is a lot like the
concept of ODBC drivers, you're right. The named pipes netlib can be replaced by the one for TCP/IP without requiring any reprogramming in
the ODBC driver (or in DB-Library, for that matter). Of course, when the
network changes, the available capabilities might change. (For example,

some networks support asynchronous I/O and others don't.) But that is far easier to deal with than having to release a separate driver (or a new version of DB-Library) for each type of network.

The programming interface to the network library is quite simple. There are nine function calls in all, the most important being the ones that make and drop a connection, send and receive data, and handle asynchronous communications.

The data that flows "on the wire" between the client and the server is called the Tabular Data Stream (TDS) protocol. As described in the example in section 3.4.3.1 (Chapter 3), the ODBC driver generates TDS to send data to Microsoft SQL Server and decodes the TDS stream after reading data from the server. When the driver sends data to the server using the *ConnectionWrite* function in the network library, it sends TDS; when it reads data from the server using the *ConnectionRead* function, the data is always encoded in TDS.

On the server, the Open Data Services (ODS) component provides the foundation for the rest of the Microsoft SQL Server DBMS (and other server applications). ODS provides a simple event-driven programming model that manages events such as incoming connections, SQL requests, and the sending of data back to clients. On Windows NT, every client connection causes ODS to create a new thread that will service that connection.

ODS transforms the TDS protocol into an API. That is, when a request is received from the client, ODS decodes the TDS tokens and calls the appropriate event handler for the request. Requests include connection requests, SQL requests, RPC[3] requests, and disconnection requests. Each event handler calls a function within Microsoft SQL Server and passes the appropriate elements of the TDS data stream as arguments to the function. Similarly, when Microsoft SQL Server needs to send status information or data to the client, it calls an ODS function that in turn transforms the function call arguments into TDS data stream elements and calls the server-side network library to send the TDS stream to the client.

The rest of the server components make up the core of the Microsoft SQL Server DBMS itself, and Figure 6-1 on page 239 shows a few of the major components. Some elements are not shown, such as the security subsystem, the transaction manager, and the recovery manager. But you don't need to understand these details of Microsoft SQL Server to understand ODBC, so we'll move on.

---

3. These are not the same kind of RPCs discussed in section 3.4.3.2. The RPCs discussed here refer to an efficient encoding of stored procedures.

6.3 Connecting to Microsoft SQL Server

Connecting to Microsoft SQL Server requires that the driver do three things:

1. Establish the network connection to the server.

2. Send the *login record* to Microsoft SQL Server. This record contains the user ID, the password,[4] and many other client-side configuration parameters.

3. Query the DBMS for configuration information such as case sensitivity options and user-defined data types, and set options to support ODBC's use of text and image columns.

In the first step, the driver establishes the network connection to the server. To do so, it must determine the server name or network address from the data source name. The data source name is either passed from the application to the Driver Manager or the Driver Manager prompts the user to choose the data source name. After the Driver Manager loads the driver, the data source name is passed to the driver as an argument of one of the ODBC connection functions (*SQLConnect*, *SQLDriverConnect*, or *SQLBrowseConnect*). Similarly, either the application passes the user ID and password in the arguments of the connection function or the driver prompts the user for them, depending on what options the application has designated.

The Microsoft SQL Server ODBC driver also supports an option that allows the application programmer to specify a time-out value for the connection process. If the application specifies that it will not wait more than a certain amount of time to establish a connection, the driver will return control to the application when the time-out interval has expired. Time-outs are useful if a system has an extremely busy server or large amounts of network traffic. The login time-out is set by using *SQLSetConnectOption* with the SQL_LOGIN_TIMEOUT option.

In the second step, the driver sends the login record to Microsoft SQL Server. The user ID and password are sent in the login record unless Windows NT integrated security is enabled. Most applications typically use the *SQLDriverConnect* function in the Microsoft SQL Server ODBC driver to prompt the user for the user ID and password. *SQLDriverConnect* displays a

---

4. The user ID and password will not be sent if Microsoft SQL Server is running with Windows NT integrated security. In that case, Windows NT will automatically use the ID and password that were entered by the user when the computer was started.

dialog box that prompts the user for this information as well as other optional information that is specified with the login record, such as the application's name or the language in which to return error messages.

Figure 6-2 shows the login dialog box that is displayed by the Microsoft SQL Server ODBC driver when *SQLDriverConnect* is called.

The Database combo box requires a bit of explanation. Unlike most other DBMSs, Microsoft SQL Server supports multiple named databases on a single server, each of which has a separate name space for tables. (In other words, the same table name can be created by the same user in two different databases.) A client can establish a context to a named database on Microsoft SQL Server. By default, each user is assigned to a particular database, but the assignment can be changed while an application is running, although this is not typical. The ODBC driver allows the user to enter a database name and switch to that database context during the connection process.[5] In addition, once a valid user name and password have been specified, the driver's login dialog box can enumerate the database names if the user needs additional prompting.

The third and final step the driver performs to complete the connection involves processing some additional queries to gather various pieces of information that will optimize performance later on. For example, the driver

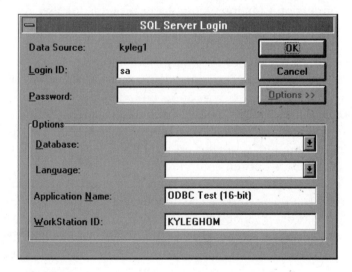

Figure 6-2.
The login dialog box from the Microsoft SQL Server ODBC driver.

---

5. What actually happens is that the login record is sent to the server, and then a command ("use *database_name*") is sent to the server to switch the context to another database.

queries Microsoft SQL Server for the user-defined type names at connection time so that it will be able to return the data type names of user-defined data types to the application. The querying is done ahead of time because data type information is very expensive to retrieve when it is most needed—while processing the results of a query. However, not all applications need the user-defined data type names, so the driver provides a *fast connect* option that doesn't execute this query.

The other queries that are executed (if the fast connect option is not set)[6] include checks that determine what case sensitivity option is installed at the server, which version is in use for the stored procedures installed at the server for the ODBC catalog functions, and how to set the default return size for text and image (large character and binary data) columns.[7]

6.4 Statement Processing

Microsoft SQL Server does not support the PREPARE concept exposed by dynamic SQL. As described in previous chapters, the dynamic SQL PREPARE command sends an SQL statement to the DBMS, which compiles and optimizes it and returns a reference (the *statement identifier*) to the compiled SQL, also known as the access plan. Then the application can use the dynamic SQL EXECUTE command one or more times simply by specifying the *statement identifier* returned by the PREPARE command. The only information that flows to the DBMS when EXECUTE is called is the statement identifier (or some encoded form of it), which refers to the access plan, and any parameters. The entire SQL statement is not sent to the DBMS.

With Microsoft SQL Server, even though the true PREPARE command is not supported, stored procedures can be used to achieve exactly the same effect. When an application calls the ODBC function *SQLPrepare*, the Microsoft SQL Server driver generates a stored procedure that contains the SQL statement. Microsoft SQL Server then compiles and optimizes the stored procedure. When *SQLExecute* is called, only the stored procedure (and associated parameters, if any) is sent to the server. When Microsoft SQL Server executes the stored procedure, it uses the compiled form of the stored procedure.[8]

---

6. In the ODBC driver for Microsoft SQL Server 6, the informational queries have been optimized enough to remove the need for the fast connect option.

7. By default, Microsoft SQL Server will send only the first 4096 bytes of a text or image column to the client. ODBC's default is to retrieve all the data, so an option must be set to tell Microsoft SQL Server to do the same.

8. To be precise, the first time the stored procedure is executed, further optimization is done and the resulting access plan is stored in Microsoft SQL Server's procedure cache. For subsequent executions, the fully optimized plan is used directly from the procedure cache.

6.5 An Example Using *SQLDriverConnect* and *SQLPrepare*

I've found that I never really understand something until I can see how it works. So at the risk of overwhelming you with detail, in this section I make an actual trace of a simple connection and statement preparation using the Microsoft SQL Server ODBC driver. This example uses the ODBC Test program included with the ODBC version 2.0 SDK and an internal Microsoft SQL Server tool to show the contents of the TDS that flows between the client and the server.

To begin this example, I use the menus in ODBC Test to allocate handles and to call *SQLDriverConnect.* Then I use *SQLPrepare* with this statement:

```
select * from sysusers where uid < ?
```

The sysusers table contains one row for each user who has an account on Microsoft SQL Server. In this example, the entire sysusers table looks like this:

suid	uid	gid	name	environ
-2	0	0	public	NULL
-1	2	0	guest	NULL
1	1	0	dbo	NULL
2	3	0	probe	NULL
3	4	0	kyleg	NULL

After ODBC Test calls *SQLPrepare,* I specify one parameter and set it to the value 5 using *SQLBindParameter.* Then I call *SQLExecute* to run the query. You'll see that only the stored procedure name and the parameter value are sent to the server. A parameter value of 5 returns all rows from the table because the largest value in the uid column is 4. The results set is retrieved with *SQLFetch* and *SQLGetData.* (I've removed most of the details of this process from the trace.) Then *SQLExecute* is called again with a new parameter value of 3 and the data is retrieved as before. This time, only the first three rows are returned.

The next several pages show the trace of what happens. First, ODBC Test makes the following ODBC calls:

```
SQLAllocEnv
SQLAllocConnect
SQLDriverConnect
```

I specify no connection information in the arguments to *SQLDriverConnect*, so the Driver Manager and the driver prompt me for the data source name, user ID, and password.

Note that nothing happens between the driver and the server until *SQLDriverConnect* is called. Then the TDS data stream that is shown below is generated by the Microsoft SQL Server ODBC driver. The driver's *SQLDriverConnect* function maps the data source name kyleg1 to the network server name, which is also called kyleg1. Then the driver connects to the data source *kyleg1* and sends the login record containing the name of the client machine (*KYLEGHOM*), the user ID (*sa*), the name of the application (*ODBC Test (16-bit)*), and other pieces of information. All this is done with the netlib functions *ConnectionOpen* and *ConnectionWrite*.

```
Connection Succeeded, pipe # = 6
ConnectionWrite    : wrote 512 bytes
0000: 02 00 02 00 00 00 01 00 4B 59 4C 45 47 48 4F 4D    ........KYLEGHOM
0010: 00 00 00 00 00 00 00 00 00 00 00 00 00 00 00 00    ...............
0020: 00 00 00 00 00 00 08 73 61 00 00 00 00 00 00 00    .......sa.......
0030: 00 00 00 00 00 00 00 00 00 00 00 00 00 00 00 00    ...............
0040: 00 00 00 00 00 02 00 00 00 00 00 00 00 00 00 00    ...............
0050: 00 00 00 00 00 00 00 00 00 00 00 00 00 00 00 00    ...............
0060: 00 00 00 00 00 32 33 37 30 33 00 00 00 00 00 00    .....23703......
0070: 00 00 00 00 00 00 00 00 00 00 00 00 00 00 00 00    ...............
0080: 00 00 00 05 03 01 06 0A 09 01 01 00 00 00 00 00    ...............
0090: 00 00 00 00 4F 44 42 43 20 54 65 73 74 20 28 31    ....ODBC Test (1
00A0: 36 2D 62 69 74 29 00 00 00 00 00 00 00 00 00 00    6-bit)..........
00B0: 00 00 12 6B 79 6C 65 67 31 00 00 00 00 00 00 00    ...kyleg1.......
```

After the call to *ConnectionWrite* sends the data, a call to *ConnectionRead* is made to retrieve any data that is sent from Microsoft SQL Server. Two informational messages flow back from the server: one about the default database context (*master*) and the other about the default language context (*us_english*). The TDS stream is shown on the following page.

```
ConnectionRead (peek)    : peek bytes 190 bytes
ConnectionRead (read)    : read attempt 512 bytes Maximum
ConnectionRead : read 190 bytes
0000: 04 01 00 BE 00 00 00 00 E3 0F 00 01 06 6D 61 73    .............mas
0010: 74 65 72 06 6D 61 73 74 65 72 AB 37 00 45 16 00    ter.master.7.E..
0020: 00 02 00 25 00 43 68 61 6E 67 65 64 20 64 61 74    ...%.Changed dat
0030: 61 62 61 73 65 20 63 6F 6E 74 65 78 74 20 74 6F    abase context to
0040: 20 27 6D 61 73 74 65 72 27 2E 06 4B 59 4C 45 47     'master'..KYLEG
0050: 31 00 00 00 E3 0D 00 02 0A 75 73 5F 65 6E 67 6C    1........us_engl
0060: 69 73 68 00 AB 3B 00 47 16 00 00 01 00 29 00 43    ish..;.G.....).C
0070: 68 61 6E 67 65 64 20 6C 61 6E 67 75 61 67 65 20    hanged language
0080: 73 65 74 74 69 6E 67 20 74 6F 20 27 75 73 5F 65    setting to 'us_e
0090: 6E 67 6C 69 73 68 27 2E 06 4B 59 4C 45 47 31 00    nglish'..KYLEG1.
00A0: 00 00 AD 10 00 01 04 02 00 00 06 53 65 72 76 65    ...........Serve
00B0: 72 04 02 00 00 FD 00 00 00 00 00 00 00 00          r............
```

Now that we are successfully logged in to Microsoft SQL Server, the driver needs to obtain some information that it will use later and sends several commands as a single batch to Microsoft SQL Server. (Note that these are not sent if the application requests the fast connect option with *SQLSetConnectOption*.)

The commands include *select usertype* ..., which selects all user-defined data type information (not applicable in this example); *exec sp_server_info 500*, which runs a stored procedure on the server that checks the version numbers of some stored procedures to ensure that the versions of the driver and those of the stored procedures are compatible; *select 501*, ..., which checks to determine whether the server was installed with the case-sensitive option; and *set textsize* ..., which tells the server to send back complete Blob data, not just the first 2 KB (the server default). The TDS stream sent by the driver is shown here:

```
ConnectionTransact    : writing 147 bytes
0000: 01 01 00 93 00 00 01 00 73 65 6C 65 63 74 20 75    ........select u
0010: 73 65 72 74 79 70 65 2C 74 79 70 65 2C 6E 61 6D    sertype,type,nam
0020: 65 20 66 72 6F 6D 20 73 79 73 74 79 70 65 73 20    e from systypes
0030: 77 68 65 72 65 20 75 73 65 72 74 79 70 65 3E 3D    where usertype>=
0040: 31 30 30 20 65 78 65 63 20 73 70 5F 73 65 72 76    100 exec sp_serv
0050: 65 72 5F 69 6E 66 6F 20 35 30 30 20 73 65 6C 65    er_info 500 sele
0060: 63 74 20 35 30 31 2C 4E 55 4C 4C 2C 31 20 77 68    ct 501,NULL,1 wh
0070: 65 72 65 20 27 61 27 3D 27 41 27 20 73 65 74 20    ere 'a'='A' set
0080: 74 65 78 74 73 69 7A 65 20 32 31 34 37 34 38 33    textsize 2147483
0090: 36 34 37                                           647
```

Finally, the results of the queries are read from the server, as shown below. Control does not return to the application from the *SQLDriverConnect* call until all of this has taken place.

```
ConnectionTransact    : read 270 bytes
0000: 04 01 01 0E 00 00 00 00 A0 13 00 08 75 73 65 72    ...........user
0010: 74 79 70 65 04 74 79 70 65 04 6E 61 6D 65 A1 10    type.type.name..
0020: 00 06 00 00 00 34 05 00 00 00 30 12 00 00 00 27    .....4....0....'
0030: 1E AE 03 00 00 00 00 FD 11 00 00 00 00 00 00 00    ................
0040: FF 41 00 00 00 00 00 00 00 7C A5 0A 45 2F 00 00    .A.......|..E/..
0050: 00 00 A0 2C 00 0C 61 74 74 72 69 62 75 74 65 5F    ...,..attribute_
0060: 69 64 0E 61 74 74 72 69 62 75 74 65 5F 6E 61 6D    id.attribute_nam
0070: 65 0F 61 74 74 72 69 62 75 74 65 5F 76 61 6C 75    e.attribute_valu
0080: 65 A1 11 00 07 00 00 00 38 02 00 00 00 27 3C 02    e.......8....'<.
0090: 00 00 00 27 FF AE 03 00 00 00 00 D1 F4 01 00 00    ...'............
00A0: 11 53 59 53 5F 53 50 52 4F 43 5F 56 45 52 53 49    .SYS_SPROC_VERSI
00B0: 4F 4E 0A 30 32 2E 30 30 2E 34 31 32 37 FF 51 00    ON.02.00.4127.Q.
00C0: 00 00 01 00 00 00 FF 41 00 00 00 01 00 00 00 79    .......A.......y
00D0: 00 00 00 00 FE 09 00 00 00 01 00 00 00 A0 03 00    ................
00E0: 00 00 00 A1 10 00 07 00 00 00 38 0D 00 00 00 26    ..........8....&
00F0: 04 07 00 00 00 38 AE 03 00 00 00 00 FD 11 00 00    .....8..........
0100: 00 00 00 00 00 FD 00 00 00 00 00 00 00 00          .............
```

Note that the netlib function call *ConnectionTransact* is used instead of calls to *ConnectionWrite* and *ConnectionRead. ConnectionTransact* is a more efficient form of writing and reading in which only one round trip to the server is needed. *SQLDriverConnect* returns SQL_SUCCESS_WITH_INFO, so the *SQLError* function is called to retrieve the informational messages about the database name and language as described above. There were two messages; *SQLError* is called until no more messages are returned. The return values from *SQLError,* shown below, are the standardized error code (SQLSTATE), the native error code sent by Microsoft SQL Server, and the message with the ODBC error message tag prefix.

```
SQLError
    01000
    5701
    [Microsoft][ODBC SQL Server Driver][SQL Server]
    Changed database context to 'master'
SQLError
    01000
    5703
    [Microsoft][ODBC SQL Server Driver][SQL Server]
    Changed language setting to 'us_english'
```

The application then calls *SQLGetInfo* with the SQL_USER_NAME option, which causes the driver to send a query to the server to get the current user name.

The server returns the following TDS stream. In Microsoft SQL Server, the user name is not necessarily the same as the login name, hence the return value here of *dbo*:

```
ConnectionTransact    : writing 26 bytes
0000: 01 01 00 1A 00 00 01 00 73 65 6C 65 63 74 20 55  ........select U
0010: 53 45 52 5F 4E 41 4D 45 28 29                    SER_NAME()

ConnectionTransact    : read 39 bytes
0000: 04 01 00 27 00 00 00 00 A0 01 00 00 A1 06 00 02  ...'............
0010: 00 00 00 27 1E AE 01 00 00 D1 03 64 62 6F FD 10  ...'.......dbo..
0020: 00 00 00 01 00 00 00                             .......
```

Now a statement handle is allocated, the parameter is bound, and *SQLPrepare* is called:

```
SQLAllocStmt
SQLBindParameter
SQLPrepare
    select * from sysusers where uid < ?
```

When *SQLPrepare* is called, a stored procedure is generated on Microsoft SQL Server. The procedure name is generated using *odbc#*, the login name (*sa*), and a unique number. Parameter names are generated with a *P* followed by the parameter number. Here is the TDS stream generated by the driver, followed by the result from Microsoft SQL Server indicating successful creation of the stored procedure:

```
ConnectionTransact    : writing 89 bytes
0000: 01 01 00 59 00 00 01 00 63 72 65 61 74 65 20 70  ...Y....create p
0010: 72 6F 63 20 6F 64 62 63 23 73 61 34 35 31 36 32  roc odbc#sa45162
0020: 36 33 20 40 50 30 20 73 6D 61 6C 6C 69 6E 74 20  63 @P0 smallint
0030: 61 73 20 73 65 6C 65 63 74 20 2A 20 66 72 6F 6D  as select * from
0040: 20 73 79 73 75 73 65 72 73 20 77 68 65 72 65 20  sysusers where
0050: 75 69 64 20 3C 20 40 50 30                       uid < @P0

ConnectionTransact    : read 17 bytes
0000: 04 01 00 11 00 00 00 00 FD 00 00 00 00 00 00 00  ................
0010: 00                                               .
```

Next *SQLExecute* is called, and the only items that are sent to the server are the stored procedure name and the parameter value (5) in its native data type (a 2-byte integer, in this case). The value in TDS is highlighted at the end of the second line in the hex dump below. The bytes are swapped because of the Intel architecture.

```
ConnectionTransact    : writing 32 bytes
0000: 03 01 00 20 00 00 01 00 0E 6F 64 62 63 23 73 61  ... .....odbc#sa
0010: 34 35 31 36 32 36 33 00 00 00 00 26 02 02 05 00  4516263....&....
```

The results, including the metadata and data, are returned from the server in the following TDS stream:

```
ConnectionTransact    : read 176 bytes
0000: 04 01 00 B0 00 00 00 00 7C C2 BF 09 34 00 00 00  ........|...4...
0010: 00 A0 1A 00 04 73 75 69 64 03 75 69 64 03 67 69  .....suid.uid.gi
0020: 64 04 6E 61 6D 65 07 65 6E 76 69 72 6F 6E A1 1B  d.name.environ..
0030: 00 06 00 00 00 34 06 00 00 00 34 06 00 00 00 34  .....4....4....4
0040: 12 00 00 00 27 1E 02 00 00 00 27 FF AE 05 00 00  ....'.....'.....
0050: 00 00 00 00 D1 FE FF 00 00 00 00 06 70 75 62 6C  ............publ
0060: 69 63 00 D1 FF FF 02 00 00 00 05 67 75 65 73 74  ic.........guest
0070: 00 D1 01 00 01 00 00 00 03 64 62 6F 00 D1 02 00  .........dbo....
0080: 03 00 00 00 05 70 72 6F 62 65 00 D1 03 00 04 00  .....probe......
0090: 00 00 05 6B 79 6C 65 67 00 FF 51 00 00 00 05 00  ...kyleg..Q.....
00A0: 00 00 79 00 00 00 00 FD 00 00 00 00 05 00 00 00  ..y............
```

Next I use the GetDataAll tool in ODBC Test, which calls the following functions to determine the number of result columns (five), to determine the data type and name of each column, and to retrieve the results.

```
SQLNumResultCols
SQLDescribeCol ... cols 1-5
SQLFetch ...SQLGetData rows 1-5
SQLFreeStmt
    SQL_CLOSE
```

Note that nothing flows to the server on any call to *SQLDescribeCol* or *SQLFetch*. The next section discusses why that is true.

When the statement is executed again, only the *SQLExecute* function (not the *SQLPrepare* function) is called again. In this case, I have set the parameter value to 3.

As before, only the stored procedure name and parameter value, not the original SQL statement, flow to the server. This time the parameter value of 3 is highlighted at the end of the second row in the TDS stream below. Again the results of the query are returned. This time, as you can see, only three users are returned, reflecting the effect of the new parameter value.

```
ConnectionTransact    : writing 32 bytes
0000: 03 01 00 20 00 00 01 00 0E 6F 64 62 63 23 73 61  ... .....odbc#sa
0010: 34 35 31 36 32 36 33 00 00 00 00 26 02 02 03 00  4516263....&....

ConnectionTransact    : read 148 bytes
0000: 04 01 00 94 00 00 00 00 7C C2 BF 09 34 00 00 00  ........|...4...
0010: 00 A0 1A 00 04 73 75 69 64 03 75 69 64 03 67 69  .....suid.uid.gi
0020: 64 04 6E 61 6D 65 07 65 6E 76 69 72 6F 6E A1 1B  d.name.environ..
0030: 00 06 00 00 00 34 06 00 00 00 34 06 00 00 00 34  .....4....4....4
0040: 12 00 00 00 27 1E 02 00 00 00 27 FF AE 05 00 00  ....'.....'.....
0050: 00 00 00 00 D1 FE FF 00 00 00 00 06 70 75 62 6C  ............publ
0060: 69 63 00 D1 FF FF 02 00 00 00 05 67 75 65 73 74  ic.........guest
0070: 00 D1 01 00 01 00 00 00 03 64 62 6F 00 FF 51 00  .........dbo..Q.
0080: 00 00 03 00 00 00 79 00 00 00 00 FD 00 00 00 00  ......y.........
0090: 03 00 00 00                                      ....
```

Now we drop the statement handle:

```
SQLFreeStmt
    SQL_DROP
```

The stored procedure created with *SQLPrepare* is deleted from the server.

```
ConnectionTransact    : writing 32 bytes
0000: 01 01 00 20 00 00 01 00 64 72 6F 70 20 70 72 6F  ... ....drop pro
0010: 63 20 6F 64 62 63 23 73 61 34 35 31 36 32 36 33  c odbc#sa4516263

ConnectionTransact    : read 17 bytes
0000: 04 01 00 11 00 00 00 00 FD 00 00 00 00 00 00 00  ...............
0010: 00                                               .
```

The application drops the connection to the server using *SQLDisconnect*, which causes the driver to call the *ConnectionClose* function in the netlib, which ends the network connection to the server.

The server is now out of the picture, and the application completes the disconnection process:

```
SQLFreeConnect
SQLFreeEnv
```

I hope that this example has given you some idea of what really goes on under the covers of the Microsoft SQL Server driver. A few tips are relevant here. One thing that should be obvious is that *SQLPrepare* and *SQLExecute* should be used only when repeated executions of an SQL statement are necessary. For a single execution (or, if the statement is simple enough, for a small number of executions) of a statement, the overhead of creating and dropping the stored procedure will equal or exceed the execution time for the statement, so using *SQLPrepare* and *SQLExecute* will actually be slower than just sending the SQL string to *SQLExecDirect*. More complex SQL statements (especially those that include numeric parameters) stand to gain the most from the use of *SQLPrepare* and *SQLExecute*. Numeric parameters aid performance because they are sent in their native data formats so the server does not have to convert them from text as it would in a nonparameterized SQL statement. That is, when the statement

```
insert into table1(amt1, amt2) values (399, 45.454)
```

is sent to the server, the values 399 and 45.454 must be converted from text to their respective data types (in this case, integer and floating-point).

The conversion issue can be significant, especially with floating-point numbers, for which conversions are time consuming. I have heard of a developer who discovered this when sending eight floating-point values to Microsoft SQL Server as part of an automated process monitoring system. The values were collected by the client and sent directly to the server for computation and storage. The developer reported close to a 20-percent increase in speed by using *SQLPrepare* and *SQLExecute* with SQL_C_DOUBLE parameters instead of using *SQLExecDirect*.

Application programmers using the Microsoft SQL Server ODBC driver might also want to consider defining a stored procedure explicitly and then just invoking it from the application, instead of using the implicit method described above. This allows the application to avoid creating and dropping the stored procedure each time the application is run, but it also severely limits the application's interoperability with DBMSs that do not support stored procedures. Because *SQLPrepare* and *SQLExecute* are ODBC core functions, they are guaranteed to work with all drivers. So the application programmer can choose the option that best fits his or her need. For development tools, the most generic solution (using *SQLPrepare* and *SQLExecute*) makes sense; for a C order-entry application written to access only Microsoft SQL Server or Oracle 7, using explicit stored procedure calls is the way to go.

6.6 Cursors in Microsoft SQL Server

Before Microsoft SQL Server 6 was released, the previous versions did not support true cursors as defined by ANSI SQL. The usual cursor implementation has the client send a fetch request across the network to the server for every row that has resulted from a SELECT statement. The server in turn sends the row of data back to the client across the network. This is what I call the "badminton" model: the client and the server are the two players; each time the client needs a row it sends a fetch request to the server. (The client hits the birdie to the server.) The server then sends a row back to the client. (The server hits the birdie to the client.) The volley continues as long as the client sends fetch requests and there are more rows to return.

In the badminton model, the DBMS and the client application are closely aligned with respect to the position of the cursor on the client and on the server. When the client application wishes to update or delete the last row fetched, the DBMS can easily comply because it knows exactly which row was last sent to the client.

Microsoft SQL Server versions prior to version 6, on the other hand, use what is sometimes called the "firehose" model. Once a SELECT statement is sent to the server, there is no volley of fetch requests and row returns between client and server. Instead, the server simply sends all the rows to the client without any further prompting by the client. As the client calls FETCH, the rows are read off the network.

The firehose approach has obvious benefits for read-only processing: reduced network traffic and, therefore, higher performance. The disadvantage is that the client and the server are not synchronized with respect to the cursor position, and therefore positioned updates and deletes cannot be supported. The server sends rows to the client until the network buffers on both the client and the server are full or until there are no more rows to send. As the client reads rows from the buffer, the server sends more rows. The server has no idea what rows, if any, have actually been read by the client and therefore has no idea what the client considers to be the "current row." Figure 6-3 depicts the badminton and the firehose approaches to cursors.

The ODBC driver for Microsoft SQL Server did not support positioned updates and deletes in its first release precisely because of this problem. But now that you have read Chapter 5, you should recognize that Microsoft SQL Server's lack of support of the traditional (badminton) cursor model doesn't mean that the traditional model can't be simulated on the client. And as long as the primary key for a table in the results set can be identified, the client can simulate positioned updates and deletes by using searched update and delete with the primary key value for the current row. The cursor library in ODBC 2.0 provides such a simulation.

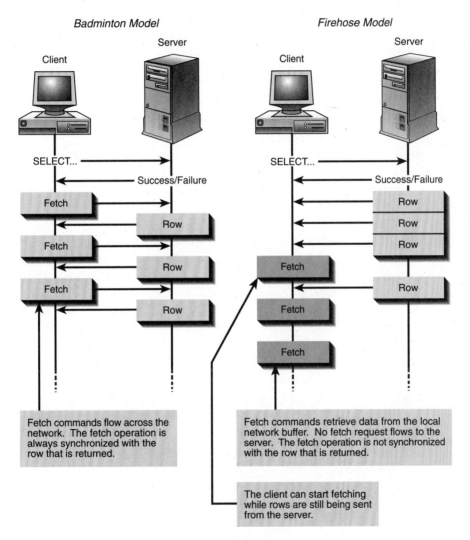

Figure 6-3.

A comparison of two cursor models.

6.6.1 The ODBC Cursor Library and the Microsoft SQL Server 4.21 ODBC Driver

The cursor library in ODBC 2.0 adds scrollable, updatable cursor functionality to any Level 1 ODBC driver that does not already provide scrolling. Since the ODBC driver for Microsoft SQL Server 4.21 is a Level 1–compliant driver, the cursor library can be used to achieve this end.

6.6.1.1 Support for "Fat" Cursors

Since the cursor library provides support only for static cursors, implementing the multirow or "fat" cursor model is simply a matter of mapping the application's calls to *SQLExtendedFetch* with multiple calls to *SQLFetch* and caching the results as they are read. For each call to *SQLExtendedFetch*, the driver calls the *SQLFetch* function for the number of rows specified in the SQL_ROWSET_SIZE option of the *SQLSetStmtOption* function. The cursor library keeps 64 KB of data in memory; if more data beyond 64 KB is retrieved, the library writes the rows that have been read into a temporary file on the local hard disk.

The binding of multiple rows to the application's array must be managed entirely within the cursor library. Both column-wise and row-wise binding are supported by the cursor library, but row-wise binding has a special optimization built in for the best possible performance. When the application binds an array of structures so that the memory is contiguous, the cursor library fills the entire rowset from the disk cache with almost no additional manipulation. In the typical case, the data is retrieved in one block transfer with a single disk read from the local cache directly into the bound buffers. With column-wise binding or noncontiguous row-wise bindings, the cursor library must place each value into the correct bound address for each column and for each row in the rowset.

To position the cursor within the rowset and perform updates and deletes within the fat cursor, the cursor library itself must implement *SQLSetPos* and the positioned update and delete (UPDATE ... WHERE CURRENT OF and DELETE ... WHERE CURRENT OF) SQL statements.

One negative aspect of this cursor library implementation for the Microsoft SQL Server 4.21 ODBC driver is that read locks are held on the data pages of tables while Microsoft SQL Server reads and sends the pages to the client. If the application stops calling *SQLExtendedFetch* before all the results are read (because, for example, the user stops scrolling through the result data), other applications will be prevented from updating rows on the locked page. A possible enhancement to the cursor library under consideration for Windows 95 is to use threading to read ahead and fill the local cache in the background. However, this must be done carefully to avoid excessive network traffic. For Microsoft SQL Server 6, using server-side cursors eliminates the locking problem (see section 6.6.2).

6.6.1.2 Support for Positioned Updates and Deletes

The central issue for positioned updates and deletes is how to identify the row to be changed. The cursor library does not require the results set to have a unique key, so positioned operations can affect more than one row. Consequently, the cursor library reports SQL_SC_NON_UNIQUE for the SQL_SIMULATE_CURSOR option in *SQLSetStmtOption*.

The cursor library constructs a searched update or delete for the positioned update or delete statement generated by the application when the SQL statement UPDATE ... WHERE CURRENT OF or DELETE ... WHERE CURRENT OF is specified by the application. The cursor uses all the values in the row; if a column that contains unique values has been selected, only one row will be updated.

Like all simulations, with this approach there is the added overhead required to manage keys on the client and perform all the necessary checks for concurrent updates by other users that again have to be managed on the client. The DBMS has all the information necessary to do this type of processing directly on the server. It would be far better if the DBMS itself could directly support cursors.

Microsoft SQL Server 6 provides this support, and it supports the true cursors in both the badminton model and the firehose model described previously. The ODBC driver for Microsoft SQL Server 6, in conjunction with the cursor library, can support either server-side or client-side cursors. And that is a great segue into the next topic.

6.6.2 Cursors in Microsoft SQL Server 6

Instead of simply sending all the data back to the client immediately upon executing a SELECT statement, Microsoft SQL Server 6 will open a real badminton-style cursor if the client requests anything other than a read-only, one-row-per-fetch, forward-scrolling cursor. One important difference between the basic badminton model and Microsoft SQL Server 6's implementation, however, is that the server also supports fat cursors within the badminton model. That is, Microsoft SQL Server 6 will actually send back multiple rows with a single fetch call. This feature is the key to high performance and reduced network traffic.

The use of server-side cursors is actually initiated on the client; the driver determines whether the statement passed in *SQLExecDirect* is a SELECT statement or a stored procedure. If it is one of these, instead of sending the SQL string directly to Microsoft SQL Server as in previous versions, the driver invokes an extended stored procedure called *sp_cursoropen* and uses the SQL statement and other options as its arguments. The specific syntax is

```
sp_cursoropen(cursor, stmt, scrollopt, ccopt, rows)
```

In this syntax,

- *cursor* is a handle that is returned by the procedure and mapped to the current *hstmt* in the driver.

- *stmt* is the SQL statement itself, which is either a SELECT statement or a stored procedure invocation. The stored procedure must contain a single SELECT statement; if it does not, an error will be returned by the server.

- *scrollopt* is one of the cursor types (as discussed in Chapter 5) that is specified in *SQLSetStmtOption(... SQL_CURSOR_TYPE)*: KEYSET, STATIC, DYNAMIC, or FORWARD_ONLY.

- *ccopt* is one of the concurrency control options (also as discussed in Chapter 5) specified in *SQLSetStmtOption(... SQL_CONCURRENCY)*: READ_ONLY, LOCK, ROWVER, or VALUES.

- *rows* is a return value that contains the number of rows in the result, if that number is available when the cursor is opened (for example, if the server must sort the data to satisfy an ORDER BY clause in the SELECT statement).

The *sp_cursoropen* stored procedure causes the SQL statement to be executed and the metadata of the results to be returned. To retrieve more rows, the driver issues another stored procedure, *sp_cursorfetch*, which retrieves the next rowset. As you might imagine, the syntax for *sp_cursorfetch* looks quite a bit like that for *SQLExtendedFetch*:

```
sp_cursorfetch(cursor, fetchtype, rownumber, nrows, values, ...)
```

In this syntax,

- *cursor* is the handle that is returned by *sp_cursoropen*.

■ *fetchtype* is NEXT, PREV, FIRST, LAST, ABSOLUTE, RELATIVE, BY_VALUE, REFRESH, or INFO. ABSOLUTE can be used only if the cursor was declared to be keyset-driven or static. BY_VALUE requires the optional *values* parameters (see the last item in this list). FORWARD_ONLY cursors can use only the parameters INFO, FIRST, NEXT, and REFRESH. The positions for NEXT, PREV, and RELATIVE are determined with respect to the cursor position, which is considered to be the first row in the previous fetch operation. If the current fetch is the first fetch, the cursor position is considered to be before the start of the results set. If a fetch operation fails because the requested cursor position is beyond or before the results set, the cursor position will be set to beyond the last row or before the first row, respectively.

■ *rownumber* is the absolute or relative number of the row to fetch. It is used only when *fetchtype* is ABSOLUTE or RELATIVE.

■ *nrows* is the number of rows to fetch. This value corresponds to the rowset size.

■ *values* is an optional series of data value parameters used only with BY_VALUE fetches. This option allows the application to position to a specific row in the results set by value.

With Microsoft SQL Server 6, the ODBC driver no longer has to manage all the keys for keyset-driven cursors on the client and process SELECT statements using key values to accomplish scroll fetching. Now all the driver has to do is issue the stored procedure invocations, and Microsoft SQL Server does the rest.

For the operations allowed by *SQLSetPos*, such as the update, insertion, explicit locking, and deletion of rows, there is yet another stored procedure: *sp_cursor* effectively performs the operations specified by *SQLSetPos*.

Let's walk through another example to see how all this really works. Let's assume that we want to implement a 10-row virtual window as described in Chapter 5. As the user scrolls using the keyboard and the mouse, we'll have to retrieve the appropriate set of rows. When the user wants to make an update, we'll have to make sure that the row we're looking at is locked and then issue the update.

6.6.2.1 Scrolling the Data

First we need to tell the driver that we want to have a rowset size of 10, so we call *SQLSetStmtOption* with the SQL_ROWSET_SIZE option set to 10. We want a dynamic cursor, so we'll call *SQLSetStmtOption* again and set

SQL_CURSOR_TYPE to SQL_CURSOR_DYNAMIC. Finally, because we are going to do an update, we'll need to specify how changes between the client and the server will be detected, and for this example we'll ask the driver to compare values. That is, when the application is ready to perform the update, the driver will get the current values of the row to be updated and compare them to the current contents of the row that is stored locally to ensure that no other transactions have updated the row since the application read it. Once again, we use *SQLSetStmtOption*, this time with the SQL_CONCURRENCY option set to SQL_CONCUR_VALUES. Nothing flows to the server when these options are specified—the driver just remembers them until execution time.

Now we are ready to execute the SQL statement, so we call the *SQLExecDirect* function. The driver checks to see whether this is a SELECT statement and then generates the stored procedure call:

```
sp_cursoropen(cursor, "SELECT ...", SQL_CURSOR_DYNAMIC,
              SQL_CONCUR_VALUES)
```

The stored procedure is sent to the server, the SQL statement is parsed and optimized, and the cursor handle is returned to the client, along with the metadata for the SELECT statement. The cursor handle is associated with the current *hstmt*. The first exchange between client and server is shown in Figure 6-4.

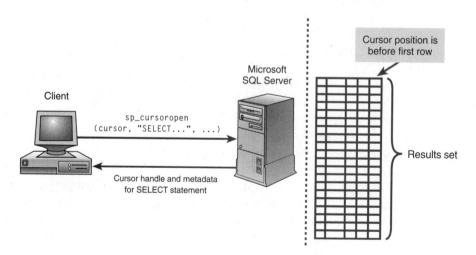

Figure 6-4.
Opening the cursor.

We are ready to get the first set of rows now, so the application calls *SQLBindCol* to specify the variables that will hold each column of data. The most natural data structure for the virtual window model is an array of structures. A structure has one data field and one output length field for each column in the result. The array must consist of at least 10 elements so that it will have enough room to hold one rowset. Once the columns are bound, we call *SQLExtendedFetch* to fill the rowset with the first 10 rows.

When *SQLExtendedFetch* is called with the SQL_FETCH_NEXT argument, the driver sends another stored procedure call to the server:

```
sp_cursorfetch(cursor, SQL_FETCH_NEXT, 0, 10)
```

The server then sends the first 10 rows from the SELECT statement to the client. In turn, the driver stores the data in the bound buffers specified in *SQLBindCol*. The interaction between the client and the server is shown in Figure 6-5.

If the user presses the PgDn key, the application again calls the *SQLExtendedFetch* function with the SQL_FETCH_NEXT argument and the same process occurs:

```
sp_cursorfetch(cursor, SQL_FETCH_NEXT, 0, 10)
```

And we move down 10 rows in the results set, as shown in Figure 6-6 at the top of the following page.

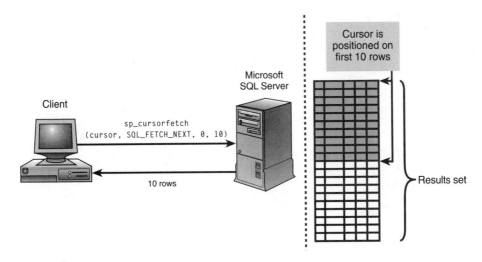

Figure 6-5.
Fetching a rowset.

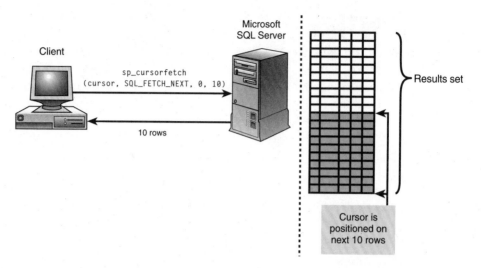

Figure 6-6.
Fetching the next "page" of results with the PgDn key.

If the user presses the PgUp key at this point, the application calls *SQLExtendedFetch* with the **SQL_FETCH_PRIOR** argument and the driver generates:

```
sp_cursorfetch(cursor, SQL_FETCH_PRIOR, 0, 10)
```

Now we're back where we started, as shown in Figure 6-7.

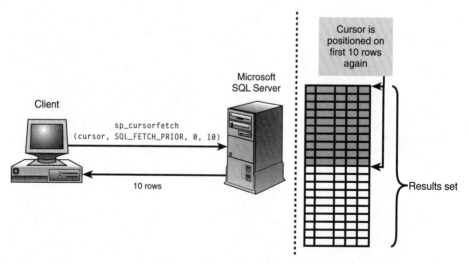

Figure 6-7.
Fetching the previous "page" of results with the PgUp key.

Keep in mind, however, that because this is a dynamic cursor the rows retrieved might not be the same 10 rows we started with. If the transaction isolation level for the current transaction is less than SERIALIZABLE, other applications could have performed updates, insertions, and deletions that would have an effect on which rows are returned. In fact, even while the cursor is positioned on a set of rows, changes can occur to those rows if the CONCURRENCY option is not LOCKCC. We'll see the effects of some of these options when we perform the update. For now, let's finish our scrolling discussion by looking at another common operation: scrolling by a single row, usually in response to the user pressing the up or down arrow or performing an equivalent mouse operation.

To scroll down one row when the user is positioned on the last row displayed on the screen (and in the rowset), the application uses relative fetching by issuing the *SQLExtendedFetch(hstmt, SQL_FETCH_RELATIVE, +1)* function call. The corresponding stored procedure call is

```
sp_cursorfetch(cursor, SQL_FETCH_RELATIVE, 1, 10)
```

The effect is shown in Figure 6-8.

Note that this refreshes the entire rowset with all 10 rows, even though only 1 row is needed to position the cursor correctly. Although this seems inefficient, keep in mind that unless the transaction is SERIALIZABLE or LOCKCC concurrency has been specified, changes could have been made to

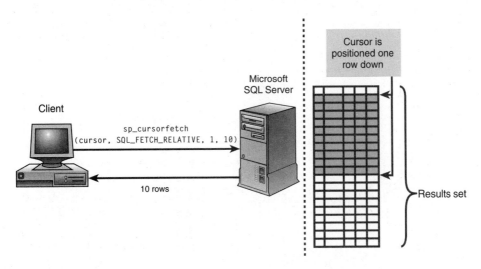

Figure 6-8.
Scrolling down a single row.

the rows by other transactions. Fetching all 10 rows ensures that the most current data is sent to the client.

One potential optimization could be to have the driver retrieve only 1 row and fill in the 10-row cache locally by executing

```
sp_cursorfetch(cursor, SQL_FETCH_NEXT, 0, 1)
```

instead of using the SQL_FETCH_RELATIVE argument.

This will send only 1 row across the network, but it requires the driver to shift the contents of the rowset buffers to eliminate the first row, copy the second and following rows "up," and finally store the new row at the end of the results set. When this is done, the server is no longer synchronized with the rowset on the client. Because the server thinks that the client now wants concurrency control on only 1 row, not on all 10, the server will free the locks on the other 9 rows in the rowset. Depending upon the client application, this might or might not be acceptable. If the application is using LOCKCC concurrency and expects the server to ensure that no other transactions can affect the current rows, this is clearly not acceptable because only 1 row would be locked. However, if the application can tolerate the server being out of sync and displaying potentially "old" data and is willing to refresh the entire rowset when necessary, it would be acceptable.

The first release of the Microsoft SQL Server 6 ODBC driver (version 2.5 of the driver) does not perform the optimization that sends only one row in response to a relative fetch of one row. This spares applications from having to deal with the complexities of managing locks correctly for transactions and avoids leaving applications open to the problems that result from inconsistent results.

6.6.2.2 Updating or Deleting Data

When scrollable cursors are used, updates or deletes of fetched rows are usually initiated by some action of the end user. Typically, the user presses an arrow key or clicks the mouse to select a particular row and then types in the new values for the row. In our application, we're assuming that the memory addresses that are bound to the columns are the same memory addresses that the application is using to get the input from the user. Because the driver also knows the memory addresses of the bound buffers, it automatically gets the new values entered by the user when it is called by the application. The application can perform an update or a delete with *SQLSetPos* and have considerable flexibility over how to handle concurrency control issues. In our example, we'll look at two approaches for handling concurrency: a "hope for no conflicts" approach using optimistic concurrency control and a more conservative, guaranteed approach.

We'll assume that the fifth row in the 10-row rowset is to be updated. In the "hope for no conflicts" approach, the application simply issues the following call:

```
SQLSetPos(hstmt, 5, SQL_UPDATE, SQL_LOCK_NO_CHANGE);
```

What does this mean and what does it cause to happen? A lot, as it turns out. First, the driver issues a corresponding stored procedure call to tell the server to update row 5:

```
sp_cursor(cursor, UPDATE, 5, values...)
```

The *values* argument is the set of column values in row 5 of the current rowset. All values in the rowset are included because the driver doesn't know which values have been changed in the rowset by the application. (We'll see a way to send just the updated columns to the server shortly.) The driver could check the values if it kept a duplicate copy of the rowset, but that would be inefficient.

What happens if another transaction had altered one or more of the values in the row we just updated? In the "hope for no conflicts" approach, our application would get an error like this:

```
SQLSTATE = "37000", NativeError = 16934, ErrorMsg="[Microsoft][ODBC SQL
Server Driver][SQL Server] Optimistic concurrency check failed, the row
was modified outside of this cursor"
```

Then the application would have to reselect the row to get the new value and try again. And maybe the same thing would happen. Wouldn't it be better to know that the update is going to work the first time by ensuring that no other transaction can modify the row?

Ensuring the update's success is the essence of the second approach. In this case, before it issues the update, the application first positions to the row to be updated and explicitly locks it. To accomplish this, the application calls *SQLSetPos* with slightly different arguments:

```
SQLSetPos(hstmt, 5, SQL_POSITION, SQL_LOCK_EXCLUSIVE);
```

As the **SQL_LOCK_EXCLUSIVE** argument implies, this will place an exclusive lock on the row to be updated. The driver issues the equivalent stored procedure call:

```
sp_cursor(cursor, LOCK, 5)
```

Once *SQLSetPos* returns, we can issue the update as before:

```
SQLSetPos(hstmt, 5, SQL_UPDATE, SQL_LOCK_NO_CHANGE);
```

If the application uses the default commit mode of AUTO_COMMIT, the lock will be released on the server as soon as the update is completed. Otherwise, the lock will be held until the application calls *SQLTransact.*

The "hope for no conflicts" approach is safe to use in scenarios in which there is only one updater in the set of applications accessing the server or when the likelihood of experiencing update collisions is known to be small. For all other situations, it is better to use the more conservative, guaranteed approach.

One final issue on concurrency control must be discussed: what happens if another transaction is holding a shared or exclusive lock on the row the application wants to update? In short, the application has no alternative but to wait. If an exclusive lock affects one or more rows, even the call to *SQLExtendedFetch* will wait; for a shared lock, the rows can be fetched but not updated. If the application is using the ODBC asynchronous option, control will be returned to the application on a periodic basis as long as the lock is held by the other transaction. If this option is not being used when the update is issued, the application will simply "hang" on the call to *SQLSetPos* until the other transaction releases the locks or, if a time-out value has been set, when the time-out expires.

6.6.2.3 Other New Features of the Microsoft SQL Server 6 ODBC Driver

In addition to the excellent cursor support in the Microsoft SQL Server 6 ODBC driver, a number of other new features are also worth mentioning:

- The driver is fully ODBC Level 2–compliant. That is, it supports every function in the ODBC API, providing a very rich feature set for application developers.

- The driver supports multiple *hstmt*s on a single connection. Prior to the release of Microsoft SQL Server 6 and its ODBC driver, the firehose cursor model described earlier prevented ODBC applications from using a connection to the server until all the rows were fetched from a SELECT statement. This led to an often frustrating situation for application writers who wanted to use multiple statement handles on a single connection but were prevented from doing so. With Microsoft SQL Server 6, as long as server-side cursors are used, multiple statement handles can be used as in other DBMSs.

- Microsoft SQL Server 6 supports temporary stored procedures that are automatically deleted when a connection to the server is ended.

In prior versions of the server and the driver, if a client application used *SQLPrepare* and terminated abnormally, the stored procedure that was created would remain on the server and had to be manually deleted. With Microsoft SQL Server 6 these stored procedures will automatically be deleted when the connection to the server is terminated.

■ The driver allows keyset-driven cursors to have the keyset asynchronously generated on the server. When a keyset-driven cursor is specified by the client, Microsoft SQL Server stores the keys in a temporary table on the server. As an option, the client can specify that the keyset should be generated using a separate thread. Not only does this allow for the full functionality of keyset-driven cursors, it also makes maximum use of idle time on the server, provides better responsiveness to clients, and saves the client from having to manage the fetching, caching, and deletion of the keys on the client.

■ The Microsoft SQL Server 6 ODBC driver supports an option to keep cursors opened and positioned across transaction boundaries. Applications can update or delete rows in a cursor, commit the changes permanently to Microsoft SQL Server, and then continue fetching.

6.7 Stored Procedures

We've already seen how the *SQLPrepare* function implicitly generates a stored procedure, but how can an application call stored procedures directly? And how are the more advanced functions of stored procedures in Microsoft SQL Server, such as return values and output parameters, handled in ODBC? In this section we answer these questions.[9]

6.7.1 Executing Stored Procedures in ODBC and DB-Library

We've already touched on the standard syntax for stored procedures:

{[? =] call *procedure_name* [(*param*, ...)]}

Used in conjunction with *SQLBindParameter*, stored procedure parameters are passed in their native format (that is, integers are passed as binary

---

9. The VBSPROCS example in Part II shows how many varieties of stored procedures are called from Microsoft Visual Basic.

integers, not as character strings). This point is a bit confusing, especially for those familiar with DB-Library, which can invoke stored procedures either purely as text, as in

```
dbcmd(dbproc, "exec proc1 23.4, 'fred', '11/18/95'")
```

or by using the more efficient method of passing parameters in their native data types:

```
dbrpcinit(dbproc, "proc1");
dbrpcparam(dbproc, 1, FLOAT, &p1);
dbrpcparam(dbproc, 2, CHAR, p2);
dbrpcparam(dbproc, 3, DATETIME, &p3);
dbrpcsend(dbproc);
```

Whereas the first method sends to the server one string that must be parsed and the parameters converted to their native data types (FLOAT, CHAR, and DATETIME), the *dbrpcsend* function encodes a message that consists of the procedure name (*proc1*) and each parameter of the stored procedure in the data type specified (an 8-byte IEEE floating-point number for parameter *p1*, a 4-byte character string for parameter *p2*, and an 8-byte DATETIME structure for parameter *p3*). On the server, the procedure can be executed directly without having to parse and convert each argument.

The latter method uses what are referred to as *remote procedure calls* (RPCs), but I find that usage to be confusing because it is not the same as the RPC technologies discussed in Chapter 3 (section 3.4.3.2) that are used for third-generation programming languages. The two are very similar conceptually, but real RPCs are more general and static (defined when the program is written), whereas the Microsoft SQL Server RPCs are very database specific and are defined dynamically. DB-Library provides a separate set of function calls to invoke the kind of RPCs shown above, and these generate a different TDS stream than stored procedures passed as text.

In ODBC there is no such distinction. If parameters are specified for the stored procedure, as in

```
SQLBindParameter(hstmt, 1, FLOAT, &p1);
SQLBindParameter(hstmt, 2, CHAR, &p2);
SQLBindParameter(hstmt, 3, DATETIME, &p3);
SQLExecDirect(hstmt, "{call proc1 (?, ?, ?)}");
```

the procedure is executed using the RPC form of the TDS stream. If literals are used for parameters, as in

```
SQLExecDirect(hstmt, "{call proc1 (23.4, 'fred', '11/18/95')}");
```

the statement is sent as a standard text command. The application programmer using ODBC does not have to use a different set of function calls based on the invocation method.

6.7.2 Enumerating Stored Procedures on the Server

ODBC has two catalog functions for enumerating stored procedures and their parameters. These functions are useful for writers of development tools who want to help application developers select and use stored procedures.

The *SQLProcedures* ODBC function lists all the stored procedures; *SQLProcedureColumns* lists the parameters for a stored procedure, including each parameter's data type, its length, and whether the parameter is input, output, or both.

6.8 Data Type Handling

Microsoft SQL Server represented a special challenge for ODBC designers because it supports user-defined data types. A user-defined data type is based on one of the Microsoft SQL Server base types but has additional semantics associated with it, such as constraints. For example, a type called ZIPCODE could be created as *char(5)*. Then, instead of table definitions using *char(5)* as the type for columns containing zip codes, as in

```
CREATE TABLE t1 (... zip char(5))
```

the type ZIPCODE would be used:

```
CREATE TABLE t1 (... zip ZIPCODE)
```

Especially in large schemas, stronger typing always helps improve the semantics of the underlying data.

In ODBC we wanted to ensure that every user had the same ability to create tables, even if user-defined types were used. So in Microsoft SQL Server's case, the function *SQLGetTypeInfo* queries the server to return all of the types, including the user-defined types.

For applications that prompt the user through the table creation process, the availability of the user-defined types makes table creation much more functional than the availability only of base types. Microsoft Query is such an application. If a user-defined type called ZIPCODE were created in Microsoft SQL Server, Query would display the type in its dialog box for creating a table, as shown in Figure 6-9 on the following page.

Figure 6-9.
User-defined data types displayed in Microsoft Query.

Because each user-defined type is derived from a base type, it can always be mapped to one of the standard ODBC types.

I should mention one issue here, although it does not apply only to the Microsoft SQL Server ODBC driver. One of the unfortunate omissions in ODBC versions 1 and 2 was the ability to detect the "best fit" for an ODBC type that has multiple DBMS types mapped to it. For example, the ZIPCODE user-defined type would be returned from *SQLGetTypeInfo* with TYPE_NAME of ZIPCODE and a DATA_TYPE of SQL_CHAR. But the information for *char*, the general fixed-length character type on Microsoft SQL Server, also returns a DATA_TYPE of SQL_CHAR. If an application needs to convert a table from one data source to another, this presents a problem: how will it know which type to use when multiple types have been returned? A human could look at the types *char* and ZIPCODE and determine immediately which is more generic, but with a computer, considering all types from all data sources, it isn't always so simple.

Most applications resort to some heuristics, such as choosing the type name that most closely matches the ODBC type name (without the SQL_ prefix, of course). The ODBC type names are taken directly from the ANSI/ISO SQL standard; consequently, most DBMSs use these type names in their products.

In the example just mentioned, the first type to look for would be *char*, which happens to match the ODBC type SQL_CHAR. But when no match is found, most applications simply use the first data type returned from *SQLGetTypeInfo*. You'll see an example of how to do this kind of type matching in the Table Copy sample program in Part II.

In ODBC 2.10, a clarification was added to *SQLGetTypeInfo* so that ODBC 2.10 drivers must return the types in a certain order, beginning with the type most closely matching the ODBC type. This should eliminate most of the difficulty of determining which type to use.

6.9 Performance Tuning

The Microsoft SQL Server ODBC driver contains a few driver-specific options that can greatly enhance performance. Driver-specific options are supported by ODBC to allow applications to get maximum performance and functionality out of a driver and a DBMS. Of course, there is a tradeoff between using driver-specific options and having the application be interoperable. But the ability to fine tune performance is critical for applications that use ODBC for one particular backend or for writers of development tools who want to allow applications generated by the tool to be able to use all the capabilities of the backend.

The Microsoft SQL Server ODBC driver has two driver-specific options that enhance performance.

The first driver option that is useful for performance tuning is the ability to change the packet size. The packet size determines the number of bytes that are sent between the client and Microsoft SQL Server on a single read or write across the network. The default is 512 bytes. The driver and server will use as many 512-byte packets as necessary to complete a request. For example, a results set that is 600 bytes long (when represented in TDS format) will require two transmissions from the server to the client. If the packet size is increased with the SQL_PACKET_SIZE option in *SQLSetConnectOption*, larger results sets will produce fewer writes across the network. But keep in mind that the server sends only "full" packets to the client. For a complex query, it will take the server longer to fill a 2048-byte packet than a 512-byte packet; thus the initial response time for the first set of rows will be slower. However, if large amounts of data will be streamed to the client, larger packet sizes will improve performance. When the scrollable cursors in the Microsoft SQL Server 6 ODBC driver are used, setting the packet size to the size of the TDS representation for the rowset or slightly larger will also improve performance. That is, if each call to *SQLExtendedFetch* results in a rowset that fits in exactly one packet, there is no extra network interaction at all.

The second performance-related option is for prepared statements. By default, the Microsoft SQL Server ODBC driver generates a stored procedure when *SQLPrepare* is called. However, this is not always desirable if it is known that a statement will be executed only once or twice. Application development tools can use *SQLPrepare* unconditionally but allow the user of the tool to turn off the stored procedure generation for performance reasons when appropriate. The end user or system administrator can also set this option directly for a particular data source name from the ODBC Administrator Control Panel device. The Generate Stored Procedure For Prepared Statement checkbox in the ODBC Administrator dialog box controls stored procedure generation for prepared statements.

Regardless of the method used to set the option, when stored procedure generation is turned off, the SQL statement is sent directly to Microsoft SQL Server each time *SQLExecute* is called.

6.10 Summary

We've looked behind the scenes at Microsoft SQL Server's ODBC driver implementation. Overall, the main reason this driver performs well is that it is not a layer on top of DB-Library (the native Microsoft SQL Server API) but uses the same low-level network interface and data protocol as DB-Library. Client/server DBMSs can exploit this design to produce high-performance, full-featured ODBC drivers.

We've seen how the Microsoft SQL Server 4.2 ODBC driver uses the cursor library to provide scrollable, updatable, static cursors, and how the Microsoft SQL Server 6 ODBC driver improves on this functionality, providing the entire set of ODBC cursor types (static, keyset-driven, dynamic, mixed) by using the native cursor support in the server.

We've seen how the ODBC driver exposes the powerful Microsoft SQL Server features of user-defined data types and stored procedures in a way that allows their full functionality to be used without compromising interoperability.

Finally, we've seen how a driver makes use of advanced features in the server, such as scrollable cursors and stored procedures, while preserving the semantics of the ODBC API.

This concludes Part I of Inside ODBC. In Part I, I've tried to provide a good conceptual understanding of what ODBC is, including its architecture, some of its key features, and what its various components are and what they do. In Part II, we'll go beyond concepts and start doing some actual programming with ODBC.

PROGRAMMING WITH ODBC

In Part I we looked at the background and architecture of ODBC. Now it's time to roll up our sleeves and start coding! But before we begin, a brief explanation of my purposes is in order.

First, even though this part of the book is about programming with the ODBC API in Microsoft Windows, this book is not about programming for Windows. Many other reference materials are available for that purpose. The classic is Charles Petzold's *Programming Windows 3.1,* Third edition (Microsoft Press, 1992).

Second, because ODBC's focus is on database access, we're not going to spend much effort making pretty screens. That task is best left to application designers.

Third, because of the same reasons behind the first two points, for all of the examples in Chapter 7 I have tried to eliminate as much Windows-specific code as possible. In Chapter 8, we'll go through some very useful, complete sample programs that will demonstrate some of the major functional areas of ODBC and that include a slightly better user interface. For an ODBC example that has more user interface code, see the CRSRDEMO example included with the ODBC 2.0 SDK.

Finally, to reflect the different programming languages currently being used to develop ODBC applications, I have included samples written in C, C++, and Visual Basic, and I have provided an example of an OLE Automation server written in C and invoked by Visual Basic for Applications from Microsoft Excel.

CHAPTER SEVEN

Getting Started with ODBC Programming

This chapter presents some simple examples of ODBC programming. Before we actually start using ODBC function calls, however, I'd like to point out a few general principles about the ODBC API.

7.1 General ODBC Programming Principles

Here are a few pointers (no C pun intended) to keep in mind while you are working with ODBC.

7.1.1 ODBC's Use of Handles

Every ODBC function takes a 32-bit handle as its first argument. The handle provides a context for each function. From the application's point of view, the handle is an opaque value. It is sometimes referred to as a "magic cookie" because its contents are never read or modified by the application; they are just passed around. Windows programmers use handles all the time, so this shouldn't be a strange concept. In ODBC's case, the handle is actually a pointer to a structure in the ODBC Driver Manager.

A handle is used in three ways. First, it is used to return error information. Whenever an ODBC function returns an error code, the application must always, always call *SQLError* with the handle just passed to the function. The *SQLError* function uses the handle to retrieve all the errors.

A handle is also used to allow the Driver Manager to be polymorphic. That is, the Driver Manager uses a handle to determine which application called it and to which driver it should send the function call. The application can use a single piece of code to execute an SQL statement, but the handle's contents will dictate in which driver the function is actually executed.

The "every function takes a handle" design also allows handles to be used for multithreaded applications. When a handle is used, the application never has to protect against ambiguous concurrent executions because the handle always provides the appropriate context. By way of contrast, if you've used DB-Library on Windows NT in a multithreaded application, you're probably aware that the error and message handlers are global (in other words, they do not take any kind of context handle and are called by DB-Library for all errors on any connection by any thread) and that semaphores must be used to access error information.

There are three handles in ODBC: the environment handle, the connection handle, and the statement handle. As we saw in Chapter 5, they are hierarchical, as shown in Figure 7-1.

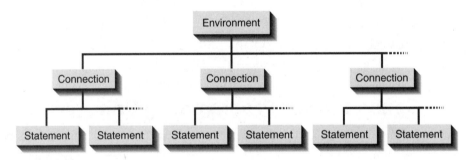

Figure 7-1.
ODBC handle hierarchy.

7.1.2 Length Arguments in ODBC Functions

Every variable-length character argument in ODBC has an associated length argument. More than one C programmer has questioned this design. Why not just use null-terminated strings? We didn't want to do that because from the beginning ODBC was designed to be used by many different programming languages, not just by C, and some languages do not have the ability to use variable-length strings unless the length is specified. COBOL is one such language, and, in fact, in the X/Open CLI you'll see both C and COBOL prototypes for each function. A second purpose for the length argument is to provide a place in which to hold NULL indicator values for data that flows to and from the data source. So any function that can send or receive a database value needs such a variable anyway.

7.1.3 Error Handling

Every ODBC function returns a value (the *return code*) that indicates the success or failure of the function call. The general idea behind ODBC's error handling design is to allow an application to use the return code value to determine the general outcome of the function. The application will then call the *SQLError* function to discover the details of an error only if the return code indicates that the function has failed or has produced some kind of warning. The design also assumes that a single function call in ODBC can produce multiple errors, so the *SQLError* function must be called repeatedly until it doesn't return any more error information.

The return codes in ODBC are defined in the following table:

ODBC Error Return Codes

#define Name	Actual Value	Meaning
SQL_INVALID_HANDLE	−2	An application programming error has occurred. Specifically, the environment, the connection, or the statement handle passed to the Driver Manager was invalid. For example, calling any ODBC function with a required handle that is null (0) will always generate this error.
SQL_ERROR	−1	The ODBC function failed. *SQLError* should be called to determine the reason. For example, *SQLExecDirect* will return SQL_ERROR when it is called with an SQL statement that contains a syntax error.
SQL_SUCCESS	0	The ODBC function succeeded. No further processing is needed; the program can continue.
SQL_SUCCESS_WITH_INFO	1	The ODBC function succeeded, but the driver or DBMS returned some kind of warning information that can be retrieved with *SQLError*. For example, a call to *SQLFetch* will return SQL_SUCCESS_WITH_INFO if a variable-length character column was truncated when retrieved.

(continued)

275

ODBC Error Return Codes *continued*

#define Name	Actual Value	Meaning
SQL_NO_DATA_FOUND	100	This return code is used when data is being fetched from the driver. It indicates that there is no more data to be retrieved. For example, a call to the *SQLFetch* function returns SQL_NO_DATA_FOUND when the cursor is positioned on the last row of a results set.
SQL_STILL_EXECUTING	2	This return code is used with asynchronous execution and indicates that the called function (for instance, *SQLExecDirect*) hasn't finished executing yet.
SQL_NEED_DATA	99	This return code is used when Blob data is being sent to the driver in chunks. It indicates that the driver is now ready for the application to supply the next chunk to the DBMS.

A common shortcut to detect the overall success or failure of a function is to combine SQL_SUCCESS and SQL_SUCCESS_WITH_INFO into a single macro, as in this line:

```
#define RC_SUCCESS(rc) (((rc)==SQL_SUCCESS)||((rc)==SQL_SUCCESS_WITH_INFO))
```

Then the code is a little easier to read. For example,

```
rc = SQLExecDirect(...)
if (rc == SQL_SUCCESS || rc == SQL_SUCCESS_WITH_INFO) {
/* success logic */

}
```

is a little more tedious than

```
rc = SQLExecDirect(...)
if (RC_SUCCESS(rc)) {
/* success logic */
}
```

You'll see some kind of macro combining these two return codes in nearly every ODBC program. The macro used in this book is a bit more efficient in terms of code size, but it isn't so obvious:

```
#define RC_SUCCESS(rc) (!((rc)>>1))
```

The proof of this macro's equivalence to the longer formulation shown previously is left as an exercise for the reader. (I've *always* wanted to say that!)

OK, that's enough preliminary information. Let's look at some code.

7.2　A "Hello World" Example in ODBC

If you are not familiar with C programming, this section heading probably doesn't make much sense. "Hello World" is a phrase used by C programmers as a generic name for the first program a programmer learns. As far as I can tell, "Hello World" originated with the original text on C programming, *The C Programming Language* (Brian W. Kernighan and Dennis M. Ritchie, Prentice Hall, 1978 and 1988).

Here's the original program:

```
main()
{
printf("Hello World\n");
}
```

This program does nothing more than display the words "Hello World" on the screen and then terminate.

Our first ODBC program displays two dialog boxes along the lines of the original "Hello World" program, as shown in Figure 7-2.

Figure 7-2.
The output of the ODBC Hello program.

Because ODBC is about databases, there will be more to our "Hello World" code than simply displaying that phrase on the screen—we've got to get some data from a database! We'll write a program called Hello that retrieves and displays all the lines of a text file (HELLO) using the Text file ODBC driver supplied on the CD included with this book.[1] For each line in HELLO we'll pop up a dialog box that displays the text from the file. The source code (HELLO.C) and the text file (HELLO) are in the ...\CHAPTERS\HELLO directory on the CD. The source code for the HELLO.C program is shown in Figure 7-3.

This isn't a "real" Windows-based program because it doesn't register a Windows class and doesn't create a window. But, as I said earlier, teaching programming for Windows is not the goal of this book; explaining ODBC programming is. Even with that in mind, this program leaves out a lot that you'll normally include in a serious application. For example, this program doesn't do any error checking. In Chapter 8 we'll use better software engineering techniques, but for now we'll just focus on the ODBC essentials.

First let's look at the include files. The WINDOWS.H file is obviously the master include file for Windows-based applications. The SQL.H and SQLEXT.H files define all the ODBC functions and a lot of useful #define constants for use in ODBC programs. You will use these files in every C program file that uses ODBC functions. Later, we'll combine these include files with some other include files to produce a precompiled header file that makes life simpler (and makes compiling faster).

The *WinMain* function is the entry point for a Windows-based program, just as *main* is the entry point for an MS-DOS–based program. We won't use any of the arguments (*hInstance* and so on) to *WinMain* in this program.

Next are the declarations for a return code variable (*rc*) and the three types of ODBC handles. SQL.H contains typedefs for the RETCODE, HENV, HDBC, and HSTMT types. Although we call these handles, they are actually 32-bit pointers. The last two declarations are for the variables that will hold the output data (*szData*) and the output length (*cbData*).

The first executable statement is a call to *SQLAllocEnv*, which allocates the environment handle:

```
SQLAllocEnv(&henv);
```

---

1. This driver is one of several included with this book. The entire set of drivers includes those for 16-bit and 32-bit versions of Microsoft Access 1.*x* and 2.0; Microsoft FoxPro 2.0, 2.5, and 2.6; dBASE III and IV; Paradox 3.*x* and 4.*x*; Microsoft Excel 3, 4, and 5; Text; and Microsoft SQL Server 4.2*x*. Also included are drivers for the 16-bit versions of Btrieve and Oracle 6 and 7. This entire set of drivers was released by Microsoft in December 1994 as the ODBC Driver Pack version 2.0.

```
/* "Hello World" program with an ODBC twist */
#include <windows.h>
#include <sql.h>
#include <sqlext.h>

#define MAX_DATA           100

int WINAPI WinMain (HANDLE hInstance, HANDLE hPrevInstance,
                    LPSTR lpszCmdLine, int nCmdShow)
{
RETCODE rc;              /* Return code for ODBC functions  */
HENV henv;              /* Environment handle              */
HDBC hdbc;              /* Connection handle               */
HSTMT hstmt;            /* Statement handle                */
char szData[MAX_DATA];  /* Variable to hold data retrieved */
SDWORD cbData;          /* Output length of data           */

SQLAllocEnv(&henv);
SQLAllocConnect(henv, &hdbc);
SQLConnect(hdbc, "hello", SQL_NTS, NULL, 0, NULL, 0);
SQLAllocStmt(hdbc, &hstmt);
SQLExecDirect(hstmt, "select * from hello", SQL_NTS);
for (rc = SQLFetch(hstmt); rc == SQL_SUCCESS;
     rc = SQLFetch(hstmt)) {
    SQLGetData(hstmt, 1, SQL_C_CHAR, szData, sizeof(szData),
               &cbData);
    MessageBox(NULL, szData, "ODBC", MB_OK);
    }
SQLFreeStmt(hstmt, SQL_DROP);
SQLDisconnect(hdbc);
SQLFreeConnect(hdbc);
SQLFreeEnv(henv);
return(TRUE);
}
```

Figure 7-3.
HELLO.C.

This ODBC function must be called before any other ODBC function in any application that uses ODBC. The environment handle is the global (parent) handle to which all other ODBC resources allocated for the application are attached. There is only one environment handle per application instance.

After the environment handle *henv* has been allocated we can use *SQLAllocConnect* to allocate a connection handle, associating this connection with the *henv* we just allocated, as shown in the code on the following page.

```
SQLAllocConnect(henv, &hdbc);
```

Now it is time to actually make the connection. "Connection" might seem like a misnomer in this context because we're simply going to retrieve data from a text file on the local hard disk, not "connect" to a server across the network. But remember, ODBC's primary design focus is on client/server DBMSs, hence this terminology is used for all data sources. For accessing desktop databases and flat files as in our example here, it helps if you visualize that we are connecting to the driver itself rather than to some other physical machine across the network.

In HELLO.C we're using the simplest of the three ODBC connection functions, *SQLConnect*:

```
SQLConnect(hdbc, "hello", SQL_NTS, NULL, 0, NULL, 0);
```

An enormous amount of activity is generated when this seemingly innocuous function call is executed. The arguments to *SQLConnect* indicate that we're using the connection handle we just allocated (the variable *hdbc*) and that we're going to connect to the data source named "hello." SQL_NTS indicates that the data source name is a null-terminated string, which is typical for C programs that pass strings. As I stated earlier, however, some programming languages do not use null-terminated strings, so the length value might be required. Here we could have specified the constant 5 or used the C runtime function *strlen*("hello"), but using SQL_NTS is a lot easier. The rest of the arguments are for the user ID and password (and associated lengths for those strings), which in this case are not relevant, so we can pass a NULL string and 0 length value for each. If the data source name we specified belonged to a DBMS that uses security, such as Microsoft SQL Server or Oracle, we would have had to supply these arguments.

How did I know to specify the data source name "hello"? What does that name mean, and how is it associated with the Text driver? Remember that a data source name in ODBC maps to a driver and to the data that the driver can access. In this case, if you ran the setup program provided with the CD for this book, it has automatically installed the Text driver and created a data source name, "hello," that references the Text driver. The setup program creates the "hello" data source name by calling the ODBC installer API, which adds a few lines to ODBC.INI[2] stating that "hello" uses the Text driver.

---

2. If you installed the *Inside ODBC* samples on Windows NT, HELLO uses the 32-bit Text driver, and the "hello" data source is stored in the registry instead of in ODBC.INI. Note that both 32-bit and 16-bit data sources are accessible from 16-bit applications, including the 16-bit ODBC Administrator. 32-bit applications (including the 32-bit ODBC Administrator) can access only 32-bit data sources.

In this example, when the Driver Manager receives the *SQLConnect* function from HELLO.EXE, it will look in the ODBC.INI file for an entry called "hello." This is what's in the ODBC.INI file for the "hello" data source:

```
[ODBC Data Sources]
hello=Microsoft Text Driver (*.txt; *.csv)
```

This specifies that the data source named "hello" uses the driver whose descriptive name is "Microsoft Text Driver (*.txt; *.csv)." The rest of the details for "hello" are given further down in the ODBC.INI file:

```
[hello]
Driver=C:\WINDOWS\SYSTEM\odbcjt16.dll
DefaultDir=.
DriverId=27
JetIniPath=odbcddp.ini
```

The information in these lines tells the Driver Manager the name of the actual driver DLL that must be loaded (ODBCJT16.DLL). The rest of the information is used only by the driver itself. Again, this was all created when the setup program on the CD called the necessary functions in the ODBC installer. (We'll talk more about the installer in section 7.3.) If you try to run this program without having the Text driver or a data source named "hello" installed, it won't do anything.

By the time the call to *SQLConnect* has returned, the Driver Manager has loaded the Text driver into memory,[3] called its *SQLConnect* entry point, and initialized itself with various parameters from various initialization files (such as ODBC.INI and ODBCDDP.INI). For the Text driver, a data source can be configured to use files either in a specific directory or in the current directory. We'll use the latter. Now we're ready to execute our one and only SQL statement for this program:

```
SQLExecDirect(hstmt, "select * from hello", SQL_NTS);
```

SQLExecDirect is the workhorse function in ODBC; it is what you use to send SQL strings to the driver. Depending on the type of driver, the SQL string is either sent across the network to the DBMS (as in a two-tier system) or executed directly within the driver (as in a one-tier system). The Text driver is, of course, a one-tier driver, so it executes the statement directly.

---

3. The Text driver, like all the desktop database drivers included on the CD, uses the Microsoft Jet engine, which has a fairly sophisticated SQL optimizer and many advanced capabilities. However, it is also quite large—all the required DLLs exceed 2 MB—so loading the driver is not, shall we say, instantaneous.

When the driver processes the *SQLExecDirect* call it must parse the SQL string and find the HELLO file it references. The HELLO file in our example will be treated like a table in a traditional DBMS. The driver must open the file and execute what the SQL string specifies. In this case, because there is no WHERE clause or any other complication, the driver simply needs to read all the columns and all the rows of the "table" HELLO.

Here are the contents of the HELLO file:

```
Hello World
Welcome to ODBC
```

Next we position to each row in the HELLO file using a loop containing the *SQLFetch* function, get the first column of data (the only column, in this case) using *SQLGetData*, and use the Windows *MessageBox* function to pop up a simple dialog box that displays the retrieved data:

```
for (rc = SQLFetch(hstmt); rc == SQL_SUCCESS; rc = SQLFetch(hstmt)) {
    SQLGetData(hstmt, 1, SQL_C_CHAR, szData, sizeof(szData), &cbData);
    MessageBox(NULL, szData, "ODBC", MB_OK);
    }
```

Because HELLO contains two lines (rows) of text, the *SQLFetch* loop will end after two iterations. If you add a few lines to the HELLO file, you can rerun the Hello program and see the new lines appear in addition to the original two.

SQLGetData is the simplest way to retrieve a column of data in ODBC. *SQLGetData* can be used only after *SQLFetch* has been called to position the cursor to a row. Then *SQLGetData* can retrieve the data in that row one column at a time. The column number is specified in the second argument. *SQLGetData* also allows data to be converted into the type desired by the application. The type SQL_C_CHAR is used here to indicate that the variable for output data, *szData*, is a character string and that that's the format in which we want the data. In this case no conversion actually happens, because the data is already in the form of a character string. However, this call to *SQLGetData* would have worked just as well if the data were a number or a date—the driver would have converted it to a character string. The fifth argument to *SQLGetData* specifies the length of the buffer that is supplied. In this case, I used the C *sizeof* operator on the *szData* buffer itself. The length is supplied so that the driver will not overwrite the end of a buffer—an error that almost always leads to a GP fault. Finally, the last argument (*cbData*, in this case) is the number of bytes actually written to the output data buffer. If the value retrieved in *szData* is NULL, the *cbData* variable contains a special value of SQL_NULL_DATA (−1) defined in SQL.H.

The code following the *SQLFetch* loop frees the various handles and the associated resources allocated by those handles.

```
SQLFreeStmt(hstmt, SQL_DROP);
SQLDisconnect(hdbc);
SQLFreeConnect(hdbc);
SQLFreeEnv(henv);
return(TRUE)
```

SQLFreeStmt, when used with the SQL_DROP option, frees the memory for the statement handle; *SQLDisconnect* terminates the connection with the driver; *SQLFreeConnect* frees the connection handle; and *SQLFreeEnv* frees the environment handle.

Hello is probably the simplest ODBC program you can write, but it isn't exactly the most useful program in the world. Using the Text driver to do SELECT * queries with no WHERE clause is just like opening the file, reading all the data, and then displaying the data, but it involves enormous overhead. In the next example we'll use the Text driver again, but this time we'll actually try something that does a better job of showing off the capabilities of SQL, and we'll see a few more ODBC features along the way.

7.3   ODBCFile: How to Perform Queries About Your File System

In this example we retrieve some data that is a little more relevant to you than the data in the HELLO example. First we generate a flat file that describes every file on your computer's hard disk. This gives us a more realistic text database to work with. Then we embellish the Hello program to create a program called ODBCFile that will tell you the name of the largest file that was created or modified between one and five days ago. This example shows you

- How to use the ODBC installer API function *SQLConfigDataSource* to dynamically create a new data source.

- How to use an SQL SELECT statement that includes an escape clause for an ODBC standard scalar function.

- How to use the ODBC functions *SQLNumResultCols, SQLDescribeCol,* and *SQLColAttributes* to obtain the number and descriptions of columns in the generated text file. The program doesn't really need this information, but I have included it to show why the SELECT statement does what it does.

Figure 7-4, starting on the following page, shows the source code for ODBCFile. (Note that again I have omitted the error handling code you'd normally include so that this example can focus on the ODBC issues.)

283

```
//  ODBCFile: ODBC program to generate and query a text file
#include "stdinc.h"
#include <odbcinst.h>
#include "common.h"
#include "progress.h"


#define MAX_DATA          300
#define MAX_COLNAME        50
#define MAX_ERROR_MSG     100


long GenFile(char *);
static char * szDIALOG_TITLE = "ODBCFile";
static char * szDSN = "odbcfile";


int WINAPI WinMain (HINSTANCE hInstance, HINSTANCE hPrevInstance,
                    LPSTR lpszCmdLine, int nCmdShow)
{
RETCODE rc;                     // Return code for ODBC functions
HENV    henv;                   // Environment handle
HDBC    hdbc;                   // Connection handle
HSTMT   hstmt;                  // Statement handle
char    szData[MAX_DATA];       // Variable to hold data retrieved
char *  pszData;                // Pointer to data retrieved
SDWORD  cbData;                 // Output length of data
char *  szSQL = "select * "
                    "from MyFiles "
                    "where f3 = "
                        "(select max(f3) "
                        "from MyFiles "
                        "where f4 between {fn now()} - 1 and "
                                "{fn now()} - 5)";
char * szDriverName = "Microsoft Text Driver (*.txt; *.csv)";
char * szAttributes =
    "DSN=odbcfile\0DefaultDir=\\\0DriverId=27\0";
SWORD   cCols;
SWORD   i;
char    szColName[MAX_COLNAME + 1];
char    szTypeName[MAX_COLNAME + 1];
SWORD   cbColName;
SWORD   fSQLType;
UDWORD  cbPrec;
SWORD   cbTypeName;
SWORD   cbScale;
SWORD   fNullable;
int     fOK;
long    nfiles;
```

Figure 7-4.
ODBCFILE.C.

Figure 7-4. *continued*

```
SQLAllocEnv(&henv);
SQLAllocConnect(henv, &hdbc);

    // Connect to the data source "odbcfile"; if not
    // successful, create it, generate text file, and reconnect

rc = SQLConnect(hdbc, szDSN, SQL_NTS, NULL, 0, NULL, 0);
if (rc != SQL_SUCCESS) {
    ShowProgress(NULL, hInstance, szDIALOG_TITLE);
    SetWorkingItem(
        "Generating text file with file names on hard disk");
    nfiles = GenFile("\\MyFiles");
    if (!nfiles) {
        MessageBox(NULL,
            "Cancelled!  Press OK to end ODBCFILE",
            szDIALOG_TITLE,
            MB_OK);
        goto abort;
        }
    wsprintf(szData, "File generated with %ld rows", nfiles);
    SetWorkingItem(szData);
    SetProgressText(
        "Creating data source 'odbcfile' and reconnecting");
    SQLConfigDataSource(NULL, ODBC_ADD_DSN, szDriverName,
        szAttributes);
    SQLConnect(hdbc, szDSN, SQL_NTS, 0, 0, 0, 0);
    StopProgress();
    }


fOK = MessageBox(NULL,
    "Ready to run query?", szDIALOG_TITLE, MB_YESNO);
if (fOK == IDNO)
    goto abort;

    // Allocate statement handle, execute query, and handle errors

SQLAllocStmt(hdbc, &hstmt);
ShowProgress(NULL, hInstance, szDIALOG_TITLE);
ShowCancel(FALSE);
vBusy();
SetWorkingItem("Executing Query...");
rc = SQLExecDirect(hstmt, szSQL, SQL_NTS);
vBusy();
if (rc != SQL_SUCCESS) {
    char    szSQLSTATE[6];
```

(continued)

285

Figure 7-4. *continued*

```
    SDWORD nErr;
    char   msg[MAX_ERROR_MSG + 1];
    SWORD  cbmsg;
    while(SQLError(0, 0, hstmt, szSQLSTATE, &nErr, msg,
                  sizeof(msg), &cbmsg) == SQL_SUCCESS) {
        wsprintf(szData,
            "Error!\nSQLSTATE = %s, Native err = %ld, msg = '%s'",
            szSQLSTATE, nErr, msg);
        MessageBox(NULL, szData, szDIALOG_TITLE, MB_OK);
        }
    }
else    {

        // Get and display metadata

    rc = SQLNumResultCols(hstmt, &cCols);
    szData[0] = '\0';
    for (i = 1; i <= cCols; i++) {
        rc = SQLDescribeCol(hstmt, i, szColName, MAX_COLNAME,
            &cbColName, &fSQLType, &cbPrec, &cbScale, &fNullable);
        rc = SQLColAttributes(hstmt, i, SQL_COLUMN_TYPE_NAME,
            szTypeName, sizeof(szTypeName), &cbTypeName, 0);
        wsprintf(szData + lstrlen(szData),
            "Column %d name = '%s'; type is %02d (%s); "
            "max length = %3ld\n",
            i, szColName, fSQLType, szTypeName, cbPrec);
        }
    MessageBox(NULL, szData, "ODBCFile: Columns in text file",
        MB_OK);

        // Get and display data

    for(rc = SQLFetch(hstmt); rc == SQL_SUCCESS;
        rc = SQLFetch(hstmt)) {
        szData[0] = '\0';
        pszData = szData;
        for(i = 1; i <= cCols; i++) {
            SQLGetData(hstmt, i, SQL_C_CHAR, pszData,
                MAX_DATA - (pszData - szData), &cbData);
            if (i < cCols) {
                pszData+=cbData;
                *pszData++ = '\t';
                }
            }
        MessageBox(NULL, szData, "ODBCFile:  Largest file "
            "modified between yesterday and 5 days ago", MB_OK);
```

Figure 7-4. *continued*

```
        SetWorkingItem("Fetching next row...");
        }
    }

    if (i)
        MessageBox(NULL,
            "All rows found, ODBCFILE is complete",
            szDIALOG_TITLE, MB_OK);
    else
        MessageBox(NULL,
            "No records found",
            szDIALOG_TITLE, MB_OK);

    // Clean up: drop and free all handles

SQLFreeStmt(hstmt, SQL_DROP);
abort:
SQLDisconnect(hdbc);
SQLFreeConnect(hdbc);
SQLFreeEnv(henv);
StopProgress();
return(TRUE);
}
```

The ODBCFile program starts off slightly differently than the Hello program. The #include directives for WINDOWS.H, ODBC.H, and ODBCEXT.H have been replaced by a single line:

```
#include "stdinc.h"
```

This is a precompiled header that includes all of the above include files plus a few more C runtime #includes. We'll be using STDINC.H throughout the rest of Part II.

The ODBCFile program allocates handles and connects the same way the Hello program did, but after the call to *SQLConnect* we'll check for an error. If we find one, we'll assume that it is because the data source name "odbcfile" isn't there. (It won't be there the first time you run the program.)

To generate the text file that will act as our database table for this program, we call the *GenFile* function. *GenFile* uses a utility library to generate a single row of data for each file on your hard disk. Each line will include the directory, the filename, the file size, and the date the file was created or last modified. For example, the line that describes WIN.COM (the program that launches Windows) on my computer looks like this:

```
\WINDOWS\,win.com,50904,1994-12-08 12:09
```

Depending on the size of your hard disk, the file generation process could take a minute or two. You'll see a dialog box that shows the progress of the file generation, and you can click the Cancel button to stop it at any time. The file it generates is called MYFILES in the root directory.

After MYFILES has been generated, we need to create the "odbcfile" data source. We use the ODBC installer function *SQLConfigDataSource* to create it. *SQLConfigDataSource* is the function that programmers use to specify a driver and its attributes from a program; end users can do the same thing using the ODBC Administrator from the Windows Control Panel. The variables *szDriverName* and *szAttributes* contain the driver description and those attributes with which I want to create the data source for the driver. Here are the variable declarations and the call to *SQLConfigDataSource*:

```
char * szDriverName = "Microsoft Text Driver (*.txt; *.csv)";
char * szAttributes = "DSN=odbcfile\0DefaultDir\\\0DriverId=27\0";
    ⋮
SQLConfigDataSource(hInstance, ODBC_ADD_DSN, szDriverName,
    szAttributes);
```

> **NOTE:** The *SQLConfigDataSource* function can also be used to modify or delete a DSN. To do this, specify the second argument as ODBC_CONFIG_DSN to modify or as ODBC_REMOVE_DSN to delete.

The driver is specified by its descriptive name as stored in ODBCINST.INI,[4] not by its actual DLL name. After *SQLConfigDataSource* is finished, a new entry will appear in ODBC.INI called "odbcfile." Now we will try to connect again using *SQLConnect*. This time the statement should succeed, since we just created the data source.

Now we are ready to use *SQLAllocStmt* to allocate the statement handle and to use *SQLExecDirect* to run the query contained in the variable *szSQL*. Just what does this complicated query do? Here is the SQL text, reformatted a bit for readability:

```
select *
from MyFiles
where f3 = (
    select max(f3)
    from MyFiles
    where f4 between {fn now()} - 1 and {fn now()} - 5
    )
```

---

4. The ODBCINST.INI file is used to store information about the installed drivers. The ODBC.INI file is used to associate drivers with a data source name.

The first and second lines tell the DBMS to select all the columns from the MYFILES file. The WHERE clause that starts on the third line says that we're interested only in the row in which the f3 column (the file size) is the largest for all the rows in which the f4 column (the date and time of the latest write to the file) is between one and five days ago. Or, to put that all more succinctly: we are asking the DBMS to find the largest file that has been written to between one and five days ago.

Note the use of the curly braces, { }, in this query. The curly braces are the delimiters for the ODBC *escape clause,* which is used when the driver needs to translate something from a standard syntax to a driver-specific or DBMS-specific syntax. We discussed the various kinds of escape clauses in Chapter 5 (section 5.8.2.3). The expression *{fn now( )}* shows the use of the ODBC escape clause for the ODBC scalar function called *now.* The letters *fn* tell the driver that the next item is one of the ODBC scalar functions. As you might guess, the *now* scalar function returns the current date and time.

I used the ODBC escape clause instead of the native syntax of the Text driver for the *now* scalar function because this way, if I ever want this application to be able to use another DBMS, I won't have to rewrite that portion of the query (assuming that the ODBC driver for the other DBMS supports the ODBC *now* function, of course).

When the query is finished[5] (which could take awhile, depending on the size of MYFILES), we check the return code *rc* for success or failure. If it fails (which it shouldn't, unless the driver is not installed or the *GenFile* function has failed), we call the *SQLError* function to get the standard error code (SQLSTATE), the native error number, and the message text. In general, most ODBC programs call *SQLError* after any ODBC function returns an error. The call to *SQLError* is placed in a *while* loop because it is possible that multiple errors can be returned from a driver. We discussed the error handling capabilities of *SQLError* in Chapter 4 (section 4.2.3.5).

If the query has succeeded, we use *SQLNumResultCols* to place the number of columns in the result into the variable *cCols. SQLNumResultCols* is used whenever the number of columns in a results set is unknown. Although I didn't need to use it here, it is a good idea to use *SQLNumResultCols* with SELECT * queries because the definition of the table might change.

---

5. Unfortunately, even if you'd like to stop the query you cannot. This is because the Text driver does not support asynchronous processing, so you have no choice but to wait.

Once we know the number of columns, we use that information to loop through each column, retrieving the descriptive information about each column with the function *SQLDescribeCol*. All such descriptive information about returned data is called *metadata*. As with *SQLNumResultCols*, *SQLDescribeCol* isn't needed here; I am calling this function only to show the data types in the generated text file. Usually when you hard-code a query so that it expects certain column names and types in a table, as we are doing in ODBCFILE.C, you wouldn't need to call *SQLDescribeCol*—you would already know the description of the data in the query. But for this example it is valuable to see the data type information so that you can better understand the query we are executing. The call to *SQLDescribeCol* looks like this in ODBCFILE.C:

```
SQLDescribeCol(hstmt, i, szColName, MAX_COLNAME, &cbColName, &fSQLType,
&cbPrec, &cbScale, &fNullable);
```

SQLDescribeCol returns the most commonly used metadata in a single function call. This includes the column's name (*szColName*); its ODBC data type (*fSQLType*); the defined length of the column (*cbPrec*); its scale (for DECIMAL, NUMERIC, and TIMESTAMP types), which is the number of digits to the right of the decimal point (*cbScale*); and a flag that states whether the column can contain null values (*fNullable*). The data type information returned in *fSQLType* is a number that corresponds to the type numbers defined in ODBC. (The ODBC types and their meanings were described in section 5.6 of Chapter 5.) Drivers are required to map data types into the types defined by ODBC so that applications will know what C data type to use for the output variable passed to *SQLGetData*.

The information returned by *SQLDescribeCol* might not contain all the metadata you want. For the ODBCFile example I also want to show the native data type names for the columns in the text file, but this information isn't included in the metadata returned by *SQLDescribeCol*. The more general metadata function is *SQLColAttributes*. *SQLColAttributes* takes an input parameter that describes the kind of metadata you want, and then it returns the metadata. The nice thing about *SQLColAttributes* is that it is very general; not only is there a long list of metadata elements to choose from, but driver writers can also expose additional elements specific to the driver and data source. Of course, once you use a driver-specific element you've lost the ability to be interoperable with other drivers, but if you followed the discussion in section 5.7 of Chapter 5, you'll remember that one of the fundamental design goals of ODBC was to allow application writers—not the ODBC API—to make the decision about the level of interoperability. Here is the call to *SQLColAttributes* in ODBCFILE.C:

```
SQLColAttributes(hstmt, i, SQL_COLUMN_TYPE_NAME, szTypeName,
sizeof(szTypeName), &cbTypeName, 0);
```

For the given column number (*i*) we specify the *fDesc* argument to be SQL_COLUMN_TYPE_NAME, and the driver returns the type name in the variable *szTypeName*. In this example I concatenate all the metadata information for *SQLDescribeCol* and *SQLColAttributes* into one long string that is displayed after the loop.

After the metadata is displayed, the *SQLFetch* loop is used to position to each row. For every row, the inner loop calls *SQLGetData* to retrieve each column, just as we did in the Hello program. As with the metadata, I concatenate all the information for each row and display it with a call to *MessageBox*.

Finally, once the results of the query have been displayed, the usual cleanup procedure is performed: each handle is freed and the connection is dropped.

When you run the ODBCFile program for the first time, you'll see a dialog box stating that the text file and data source need to be generated. After the generation has been done, as long as you keep the "odbcfile" data source around, you won't have to regenerate the MYFILES file or the data source for another five days. (If the file is not regenerated after five days, the query will not return any rows.) Subsequent executions of the program will immediately connect and go on to the next step, which is the dialog box that announces that the program is ready to execute the query. When the query is completed, the metadata is displayed, followed by the data returned by the query. The data includes the directory name, the filename, the file's size, and its write date. You might see the dialog box more than once if you happen to have more than one file of exactly the same size that happens to be the largest. You might not see anything at all if no files on your disk have been modified between one and five days ago. To regenerate the text file, delete the "odbcfile" data source using the ODBC Administrator and run the ODBCFile program again.

I hope that this example demonstrates adequately that you can do powerful things with SQL and a simple Text driver. Although I wouldn't recommend building a real database application using the Text driver, it can be extremely useful for importing and exporting data to different database formats. However, performance will never be very good with this driver because it has no indexes.

Obviously, using the power of SQL with the file system would make the most sense if the driver talked directly to the file system. Could such a driver be written? Of course! But to my knowledge no one has ever written such a driver, although I was tempted to do so for this book. We're not quite done with the file system yet, however.

The next example demonstrates the dramatic performance gains that can be achieved when you use a driver that supports indexes, and, of course, it demonstrates more elements of the ODBC API.

7.4 ODBCAcc: More Fun with Your File System

In this example we continue to embellish the ODBCFile program. This example uses two different drivers—one that uses indexes (the Microsoft Access driver) and one that does not (the Text driver)—to show their effects on performance. Several new techniques are introduced:

- How to use the installer API to create a Microsoft Access database

- How to use multiple connection and statement handles

- How to bind columns and parameters with *SQLBindCol* and *SQLBindParameter*

- How to use *SQLPrepare* and *SQLExecute*

- How to use *SQLTransact*

The ODBCAcc program builds on the ODBCFile program by copying all the rows in the text file that was generated by ODBCFile to a Microsoft Access database. Then it runs two queries on both the Text driver and the Microsoft Access driver. The execution time is measured and displayed for each query on each driver.

Figure 7-5 shows the source code for ODBCACC.C.

```
#include "stdinc.h"
#include <odbcinst.h>
#include "stdio.h"
#include "time.h"
#include "common.h"
#include "progress.h"


#define MAX_DATA          300
#define MAX_COLNAME        50
static void RunQuery(HDBC, char * pszSQL, char * pszTitle);
static void fCopyText(HDBC hdbc, HDBC hdbc2);

int WINAPI WinMain (HINSTANCE hInstance, HINSTANCE hPrevInstance,
                    LPSTR lpszCmdLine, int nCmdShow)
{
```

Figure 7-5.
ODBCACC.C.

Figure 7-5. *continued*

```
HENV    henv;             // Environment handle
HDBC    hdbc;             // Connection handle
HDBC    hdbc2;            // Connection handle
char    szSQL1[] =
    "select * "
    "from MyFiles "
    "where f3 = ( "
        "select max(f3) "
        "from MyFiles "
        "where f4 "
        "between {fn now()} - 1 and {fn now()} - 5 "
        ")";
char    szSQL2[] =
    "select * "
    "from MyFiles "
    "where f2 in  ( "
        "select f2 "
        "from MyFiles "
        "where f3 > 350000 "
        "group by f2 "
        "having(count(*) > 1) "
        ") "
    "order by f2";
char    szDriverName[] = "Microsoft Access Driver (*.mdb)";
char    szAttributes[] = "DSN=odbcacc\0DefaultDir=\\\0"
                        "DriverId=25\0DBQ=odbcacc.mdb\0";
char    szAttributesCreateMDB[] =
                        "CREATE_DB=\\odbcacc.mdb General\0";
int     fOK;

ShowProgress(NULL, hInstance, "ODBCACC");
ShowCancel(FALSE);

    // Create Microsoft Access database file ODBCACC.MDB
SQLConfigDataSource(NULL, ODBC_ADD_DSN, szDriverName,
    szAttributesCreateMDB);

    // Add data source "odbcacc" for the new database
SetWorkingItem("Creating Access database ODBCACC.MDB...");
SQLConfigDataSource(NULL, ODBC_ADD_DSN, szDriverName,
    szAttributes);

    // Allocate handles and connect to Text and MS Access drivers
SQLAllocEnv(&henv);
```

(continued)

Figure 7-5. *continued*

```
SQLAllocConnect(henv, &hdbc);
SetWorkingItem("Connecting to data sources odbcfile and odbcacc");
SQLConnect(hdbc, "odbcfile", SQL_NTS, NULL, 0, NULL, 0);
SQLAllocConnect(henv, &hdbc2);
SQLConnect(hdbc2, "odbcacc", SQL_NTS, NULL, 0, NULL, 0);

fOK = MessageBox(0, "Create and copy text to "
    "Microsoft Access table?", "ODBCAcc", MB_YESNO);
if (fOK == IDYES)
    // Populate Microsoft Access table from text file
    fCopyText(hdbc, hdbc2);

fOK = MessageBox(0, "Run queries?", "ODBCAcc", MB_YESNO);
if (fOK == IDYES) {
    // Run both queries against both drivers
    RunQuery(hdbc, szSQL1, "Text Driver - "
        "Largest file changed in the last 5 days");
    RunQuery(hdbc2, szSQL1, "Microsoft Access Driver - "
        "Largest file changed in the last 5 days");
    RunQuery(hdbc, szSQL2, "Text Driver - "
        "Duplicate files larger than 350 KB");
    RunQuery(hdbc2, szSQL2, "Microsoft Access Driver - "
        "Duplicate files larger than 350 KB");
    }

  // Disconnect and free connection handles
SQLDisconnect(hdbc);
SQLDisconnect(hdbc2);
SQLFreeConnect(hdbc);
SQLFreeConnect(hdbc2);
SQLFreeEnv(henv);
StopProgress();
return(TRUE);
}
//////////////////////////////////////////////////////////////////
// RunQuery - Executes input SQL string
//
// Returns:  Nothing
//////////////////////////////////////////////////////////////////

void RunQuery(
    HDBC hdbc,        // Connection handle
    char * pszSQL,    // SQL string to execute (without table name)
    char * pszTitle   // Dialog box title
  )
{
```

Figure 7-5. *continued*

```
HSTMT      hstmt;
DWORD      t1;
DWORD      t2;
RETCODE    rc;         // Return code for ODBC functions
char       szData[MAX_DATA];
char *     pszData;
SWORD      cCols;
SWORD      i;
char       szColName[MAX_COLNAME + 1];
char       szTypeName[MAX_COLNAME + 1];
SWORD      cbColName;
SWORD      fSQLType;
UDWORD     cbPrec;
SWORD      cbTypeName;
SWORD      cbScale;
SWORD      fNullable;
SDWORD     cbData;

SQLAllocStmt(hdbc, &hstmt);
MessageBox(NULL, "Ready to run query?", pszTitle, MB_OK);
SetWorkingItem("Executing query...");
SetProgressText(pszTitle);
vBusy();
t1 = GetTickCount();
rc = SQLExecDirect(hstmt, pszSQL, SQL_NTS);
t2 = GetTickCount();
SetWorkingItem("Complete");
SetProgressText("");
vBusy();

wsprintf(szData, "Execution time = %ld:%ld seconds",
    (long) (t2 - t1) / 1000L,
    (long) (t2 - t1) % 1000L
    );
MessageBox(0, szData, pszTitle, MB_OK);
if (rc != SQL_SUCCESS) {
    char szSQLSTATE[6];
    long nErr;
    char msg[100];
    short cbmsg;
    while(SQLError(0, 0, hstmt, szSQLSTATE, &nErr, msg, 100,
        &cbmsg) == SQL_SUCCESS) {
        wsprintf(szData, "Error! sqlstate = %s, native err = "
            "%ld, msg = '%s'", szSQLSTATE, nErr, msg);
        MessageBox(NULL, szData, "ODBCAcc", MB_OK);
        }
    }
```

(continued)

Figure 7-5. *continued*

```
    else    {
        SQLNumResultCols(hstmt, &cCols);
        szData[0] = '\0';
        for (i = 1; i <= cCols; i++) {
            SQLDescribeCol(hstmt, i, szColName, MAX_COLNAME,
                &cbColName, &fSQLType, &cbPrec, &cbScale,
                &fNullable);
            SQLColAttributes(hstmt, i, SQL_COLUMN_TYPE_NAME,
                szTypeName, sizeof(szTypeName), &cbTypeName,
                0);
            wsprintf(szData + lstrlen(szData),
                "Column %d name = '%s'; type is %02d (%s); "
                "max length = %3ld\n",
                i, szColName, fSQLType, szTypeName, cbPrec);
            }
            MessageBox(NULL, szData,
                "ODBCAcc: Column descriptions", MB_OK);
        }
    for(rc = SQLFetch(hstmt); rc == SQL_SUCCESS;
        rc = SQLFetch(hstmt)) {
        szData[0] = '\0';
        pszData = szData;
        for(i = 1; i <= cCols; i++)  {
            SQLGetData(hstmt, i, SQL_C_CHAR, pszData,
                MAX_DATA - (pszData - szData), &cbData);
            if (i < cCols)  {
                pszData += cbData;
                *pszData++ = '\t';
                }
            }
        MessageBox(NULL, szData, pszTitle, MB_OK);
        }
    SQLFreeStmt(hstmt, SQL_DROP);
}

//////////////////////////////////////////////////////////////////
// fCopyText - Imports table from Text driver to Microsoft
//             Access database using INSERT statements and
//             SQLPrepare/SQLExecute
//
// Returns:  Nothing
//////////////////////////////////////////////////////////////////

void fCopyText(HDBC hdbc, HDBC hdbc2)
{
```

Figure 7-5. *continued*

```
HSTMT              hstmt;
HSTMT              hstmt2;
char               szData[MAX_DATA];
SDWORD             cbData1;
SDWORD             cbData2;
SDWORD             cbData3;
SDWORD             cbData4;
char               f1[MAX_DATA + 1];
char               f2[MAX_DATA + 1];
SDWORD             lf3;
TIMESTAMP_STRUCT tsf4;
DWORD              t1;
DWORD              t2;
DWORD              rowcount;
RETCODE            rc;          // Return code for ODBC functions

SQLAllocStmt(hdbc, &hstmt);
SQLAllocStmt(hdbc2, &hstmt2);

SetWorkingItem("Creating Access table 'MyFiles'");
SQLExecDirect(hstmt2, "drop table MyFiles", SQL_NTS);

SQLExecDirect(hstmt2, "create table MyFiles ("
    "f1 text(255), "
    "f2 text(15), "
    "f3 long, "
    "f4 datetime)",
    SQL_NTS);

SQLBindCol(hstmt, 1, SQL_C_CHAR, f1, MAX_DATA, &cbData1);
SQLBindCol(hstmt, 2, SQL_C_CHAR, f2, MAX_DATA, &cbData2);
SQLBindCol(hstmt, 3, SQL_C_LONG, &lf3, sizeof(lf3), &cbData3);
SQLBindCol(hstmt, 4, SQL_C_TIMESTAMP, &tsf4, sizeof(tsf4),
    &cbData4);

SQLBindParameter(hstmt2, 1, SQL_PARAM_INPUT, SQL_C_CHAR,
    SQL_CHAR, 15, 0, f1, sizeof(f1), &cbData1);
SQLBindParameter(hstmt2, 2, SQL_PARAM_INPUT, SQL_C_CHAR,
    SQL_CHAR, 255, 0, f2, sizeof(f2), &cbData2);
SQLBindParameter(hstmt2, 3, SQL_PARAM_INPUT, SQL_C_LONG,
    SQL_INTEGER, 0, 0, &lf3, sizeof(lf3),&cbData3);
SQLBindParameter(hstmt2, 4, SQL_PARAM_INPUT, SQL_C_TIMESTAMP,
    SQL_TIMESTAMP, 0, 0, &tsf4, 0, &cbData4);

SQLSetConnectOption(hdbc2, SQL_AUTOCOMMIT, SQL_AUTOCOMMIT_OFF);
```

(continued)

297

Figure 7-5. *continued*

```
    SQLPrepare(hstmt2,
        "insert into MyFiles(f1, f2, f3, f4) values (?, ?, ?, ?)",
        SQL_NTS);
    rc = SQLExecDirect(hstmt, "select * from MyFiles", SQL_NTS);
    t1 = GetTickCount();

    SetWorkingItem("Copying records from text file to Access");
    ShowCancel(TRUE);
    for(rowcount = 0, rc = SQLFetch(hstmt); rc == SQL_SUCCESS;
        rc = SQLFetch(hstmt)) {
        SQLExecute(hstmt2);
        rowcount++;
        if (rowcount % 10 == 0 ) {
            wsprintf(szData, "%ld records copied", rowcount);
            SetProgressText(szData);
            if (fCancel())
                break;
        }
    }

    SetProgressText("");
    SQLTransact(SQL_NULL_HENV, hdbc2, SQL_COMMIT);
    t2 = GetTickCount();
    wsprintf(szData, "Copy completed "
        "in %ld:%ld seconds; %ld records/sec",
        (long) (t2 - t1) / 1000L,
        (long) (t2 - t1) % 1000L,
        (long) (t2 - t1 >= 1000L) ?
            (rowcount / ((t2 - t1) / 1000L)) : rowcount
        );
    SetWorkingItem(szData);
    SQLFreeStmt(hstmt, SQL_DROP);
    ShowCancel(FALSE);
    SQLExecDirect(hstmt2,
        "create index f2idx on MyFiles(f2)", SQL_NTS);
    SQLExecDirect(hstmt2,
        "create index f3idx on MyFiles(f3)", SQL_NTS);
    SQLExecDirect(hstmt2,
        "create index f4idx on MyFiles(f4)", SQL_NTS);
    SQLTransact(SQL_NULL_HENV, hdbc2, SQL_COMMIT);
    SQLFreeStmt(hstmt2, SQL_DROP);
    SQLSetConnectOption(hdbc2, SQL_AUTOCOMMIT, SQL_AUTOCOMMIT_ON);
}
```

7.4.1 Creating a Microsoft Access Database

The first thing this program does is create a Microsoft Access database using the *SQLConfigDataSource* function with some driver-specific keywords. In this case, the attribute string specifies that a Microsoft Access database called ODBCACC should be created in the root directory. The code is shown here:

```
char    szDriverName[] = "Microsoft Access Driver (*.mdb)";
⋮
char    szAttributesCreateMDB[] =
                    "CREATE_DB=\\odbcacc.mdb General\0";
⋮
SQLConfigDataSource(hInstance, ODBC_ADD_DSN, szDriverName,
    szAttributesCreateMDB);
```

After the database file has been created, the environment handle and two connection handles are allocated. The calls to *SQLConnect* then make the connection to the Text driver using the DSN "odbcfile" and to the Microsoft Access driver using the newly created DSN "odbcacc."

Next the user must choose whether to import the text data to the Microsoft Access database. The import must be done at least once so that the queries that follow can be run. The import is handled by the *fCopyText* function, which we'll discuss shortly.

The user must then choose whether to run the queries. If the user chooses the Yes button, four calls to the *RunQuery* function are made to run the queries. Following the four calls, the program does the usual cleanup.

7.4.2 Copying Data into the Database

The *fCopyText* function shows one common technique for inserting data into a table.[6] First, statement handles are allocated and the table MyFiles is dropped (if it exists) and created using calls to *SQLExecDirect*, as shown here:

```
SQLExecDirect(hstmt2, "drop table MyFiles", SQL_NTS);

SQLExecDirect(hstmt2, "create table MyFiles ("
    "f1 text(255), "
    "f2 text(15), "
    "f3 long, "
    "f4 datetime)",
    SQL_NTS);
```

If the table MyFiles doesn't exist, the first call to *SQLExecDirect* will return an error. We will ignore the error because we want to create a new table anyway.

---

6. In the next example in this series, we look at a less obvious technique that provides much better performance for some desktop database drivers that support the ODBC Level 2 function *SQLSetPos*.

Next we use *SQLBindCol* to bind all the columns we'll be retrieving from the text file. The first *SQLBindCol* statement is shown here:

```
SQLBindCol(hstmt, 1, SQL_C_CHAR, f1, MAX_DATA, &cbData1);
```

SQLBindCol looks very similar to the *SQLGetData* function we used in the previous example, and in fact the two accomplish the same result. The main difference is that when *SQLBindCol* is used it is typically called outside the fetch loop and the data is not returned immediately (as it is with *SQLGetData*) but is returned later. Like *SQLGetData*, *SQLBindCol* relies on calls to *SQLFetch* or *SQLExtendedFetch* to position the cursor to the next row in the results set. When *SQLBindCol* is used, the specified variable is automatically filled with the data from the results set—no other function needs to be called. The driver stores the address of the variable supplied for each bound column and places the data there each time a row is fetched. As with *SQLGetData*, conversions can be specified in the arguments to *SQLBindCol*. In this example, the four calls bind the variables *f1*, *f2*, *lf3*, and *tsf4* to columns f1, f2, f3, and f4. Note that the type of each variable must correspond to the *fCType* argument to *SQLBindCol*. In this case, the variables consist of two character strings, one long integer, and one timestamp. Every time *SQLFetch* is called, the four variables will receive the values of the next row in the results set; the function converts the values to the appropriate representation specified by the C type. For the character data, nothing needs to be done. For the long integer and timestamp columns, the text representation of the data stored in the text file will be converted to the type specified by the SQL_C type. The remaining calls to *SQLBindCol* are shown here:

```
SQLBindCol(hstmt, 2, SQL_C_CHAR, f2, MAX_DATA, &cbData2);
SQLBindCol(hstmt, 3, SQL_C_LONG, &lf3, sizeof(lf3), &cbData3);
SQLBindCol(hstmt, 4, SQL_C_TIMESTAMP, &tsf4, sizeof(tsf4),
    &cbData4);
```

Following the *SQLBindCol* calls are four calls to *SQLBindParameter*, the first of which is shown here:

```
SQLBindParameter(hstmt2, 1, SQL_PARAM_INPUT, SQL_C_CHAR,
    SQL_CHAR, 15, 0, f1, sizeof(f1), &cbData1);
```

SQLBindParameter is to SQL parameters what *SQLBindCol* is to columns in a results set. In this case, we are binding to the same variables used to retrieve the data. This is perfect; we won't have to do any copying in our program at all, and neither will the drivers. Once the data is retrieved from the Text driver, the Microsoft Access driver will be able to use it because the driver knows the addresses of the variables specified in *SQLBindCol*.

The next line specifies that our copy will be subject to transaction control:

```
SQLSetConnectOption(hdbc2, SQL_AUTOCOMMIT, SQL_AUTOCOMMIT_OFF);
```

By default, ODBC applications run in *autocommit mode,* which means that every executable statement is considered to be an atomic action. Because we want to specify that multiple statements should be considered to be one atomic unit of work for the Microsoft Access driver, we must turn off autocommit by using *SQLSetConnectOption,* as shown above.

Now it is time to retrieve the data from the text file and insert it into the Microsoft Access database. First the INSERT statement is prepared using the *SQLPrepare* function call:

```
SQLPrepare(hstmt2,
    "insert into MyFiles(f1, f2, f3, f4) values (?, ?, ?, ?)",
    SQL_NTS);
```

> **NOTE:** *SQLPrepare* should be used only when the SQL statement will be executed several times. If it will be executed only once or twice, *SQLExecDirect* is a better choice.

The INSERT statement is then parsed and optimized by the Microsoft Access driver; each parameter represents the corresponding variable specified in *SQLBindParameter.*

Next the query to get all the rows from the text file MYFILES is executed:

```
SQLExecDirect(hstmt, "select * from MyFiles", SQL_NTS);
```

Finally, we use *SQLFetch* to retrieve every row from the text file, and for each row we use *SQLExecute* to execute the INSERT statement previously prepared:

```
for(rowcount = 0, rc = SQLFetch(hstmt); rc == SQL_SUCCESS;
    rc = SQLFetch(hstmt)) {
    SQLExecute(hstmt2);
    rowcount++;
    ⋮
```

As each call to *SQLFetch* is made, the bound variables *f1, f2, lf3,* and *tsf4* get the values from the current row of the text file, and the call to *SQLExecute* causes the Microsoft Access driver to take the values in those variables and insert them into the MyFiles table.

After the fetch loop is finished, we commit the transaction using the *SQLTransact* function:

```
SQLTransact(SQL_NULL_HENV, hdbc2, SQL_COMMIT);
```

The rest of the function displays the execution time, creates the indexes on the Microsoft Access table, and cleans up the statement handles.

7.4.3 Executing Queries Against the Text Driver and the Microsoft Access Driver

The *RunQuery* function uses the same technique that was used in ODBCFile to execute statements and retrieve data. The calls from *WinMain* pass a connection handle for either the Text driver or the Microsoft Access driver, the SQL string to be executed (including placeholders for the table name), and a title for the dialog box that will be used to display the results:

```
RunQuery(hdbc, szSQL1, "Text Driver - "
    "Largest file changed in the last 5 days");
RunQuery(hdbc2, szSQL1, "Microsoft Access Driver - "
    "Largest file changed in the last 5 days");
RunQuery(hdbc, szSQL2, "Text Driver - "
    "Duplicate files larger than 350 KB");
RunQuery(hdbc2, szSQL2, "Microsoft Access Driver - "
    "Duplicate files larger than 350 KB");
```

You should see a fairly dramatic difference between the performance of the two drivers. Remember that we created indexes on the table using the Microsoft Access driver, whereas the Text driver has no ability to create or use indexes. The first query is the same one we used in ODBCFile: show the largest file that was modified between one and five days ago. In my tests, the Microsoft Access driver always ran the query at least 10 times faster than the Text driver.

The second query is more difficult to execute. It finds all the files on your hard disk that have the same name and are larger than 350 KB. Let's look at the SQL code in more detail:

```
select *
from MyFiles
where f2 in (
    select f2
    from MyFiles
    where f3 > 350000
    group by f2
    having (count(*) > 1)
    )
order by f2
```

This query uses a subquery on the f2 column to return all the filenames for which the file size is greater than 350 KB and that appear more than once (in other words, those files that have the same filename but that are in different directories on your hard disk). Finally, it sorts the results by filename.

Again the Microsoft Access driver outperforms the Text driver by a wide margin. (By the way, if you find identical files in this list—those files whose date, time, and file size are the same—you might be able to delete some of them and save some disk space.)

The final example in this chapter presents an alternative version of the *fCopyText* function that demonstrates more features of the ODBC API.

7.5 ODBCAcc2: Fast Inserts for Level 2 Desktop Drivers

In this example we look at one last twist on the ODBCFile program to show a high-performance alternative to the INSERT statement shown in the previous example. This technique works only for drivers that support the ODBC Level 2 functions *SQLExtendedFetch* and *SQLSetPos*. It will probably not affect the performance of client/server data sources, but for desktop database drivers it can provide a dramatic performance improvement.

The only difference between this example and ODBCAcc is the action of *fCopyText*. Instead of using an INSERT statement in SQL, we'll use a special feature of *SQLSetPos*: the ADD operation.

Figure 7-6 shows the new *fCopyText* function.

```
#define ROWSET  1
void fCopyText(HDBC hdbc, HDBC hdbc2)
{
    HSTMT            hstmt;
    HSTMT            hstmt2;
    char             szData[MAX_DATA];
    SDWORD           cbData1;
    SDWORD           cbData2;
    SDWORD           cbData3;
    SDWORD           cbData4;
    char             f1[MAX_DATA + 1];
    char             f2[MAX_DATA + 1];
    SDWORD           lf3;
    TIMESTAMP_STRUCT tsf4;
    DWORD            t1;
    DWORD            t2;
    DWORD            rowcount;
    UDWORD           r;
    UWORD            rgfRowStat[ROWSET];
    RETCODE          rc;          // Return code for ODBC functions

    SQLAllocStmt(hdbc, &hstmt);
    SQLAllocStmt(hdbc2, &hstmt2);
```

Figure 7-6. *(continued)*

The fCopyText *function in ODBCACC2.C.*

303

Figure 7-6. *continued*

```
    SetWorkingItem("Creating Access table 'MyFiles'");

    SQLExecDirect(hstmt2, "drop table MyFiles" , SQL_NTS);

    SQLExecDirect(hstmt2, "create table MyFiles ("
        "f1 text(255), "
        "f2 text(15), "
        "f3 long, "
        "f4 datetime)",
        SQL_NTS);
SQLFreeStmt(hstmt2,SQL_CLOSE);

    // Set statement options for the cursor that will be used
    // to insert rows
    SQLSetStmtOption(hstmt2, SQL_CONCURRENCY, SQL_CONCUR_VALUES);
    SQLSetStmtOption(hstmt2, SQL_CURSOR_TYPE,
        SQL_CURSOR_KEYSET_DRIVEN);
    SQLSetStmtOption(hstmt2, SQL_ROWSET_SIZE, ROWSET);

    // Bind columns of output cursor
    SQLBindCol(hstmt2, 1, SQL_C_CHAR, f1, MAX_DATA, &cbData1);
    SQLBindCol(hstmt2, 2, SQL_C_CHAR, f2, MAX_DATA, &cbData2);
    SQLBindCol(hstmt2, 3, SQL_C_LONG, &lf3, sizeof(lf3), &cbData3);
    SQLBindCol(hstmt2, 4, SQL_C_TIMESTAMP, &tsf4, sizeof(tsf4),
        &cbData4);

    // Tell Microsoft Access driver to use transactions
    SQLSetConnectOption(hdbc2, SQL_AUTOCOMMIT, SQL_AUTOCOMMIT_OFF);

    // Bind columns from Text driver
    SQLBindCol(hstmt, 1, SQL_C_CHAR, f1, MAX_DATA, &cbData1);
    SQLBindCol(hstmt, 2, SQL_C_CHAR, f2, MAX_DATA, &cbData2);
    SQLBindCol(hstmt, 3, SQL_C_LONG, &lf3, sizeof(lf3), &cbData3);
    SQLBindCol(hstmt, 4, SQL_C_TIMESTAMP, &tsf4, sizeof(tsf4),
        &cbData4);

    // Select all data from Text driver
    SQLExecDirect(hstmt, "select * from MyFiles", SQL_NTS);

    // Open the cursor that will be used to add new rows
    // for Microsoft Access driver
    SQLExecDirect(hstmt2, "select * from MyFiles", SQL_NTS);

    // Position the cursor so SetPos can be used
    SQLExtendedFetch(hstmt2, SQL_FETCH_FIRST, 1, &r, rgfRowStat);
    t1 = GetTickCount();

    SetWorkingItem("Copying records from text file to Access");
    ShowCancel(TRUE);
```

Figure 7-6. *continued*

```
    // Fetch all rows using Text driver
    for(rowcount = 0, rc = SQLFetch(hstmt); rc == SQL_SUCCESS;
        rc = SQLFetch(hstmt)) {

        // For each row in Text driver, use SetPos to add the row
        // to Microsoft Access table
        rc = SQLSetPos(hstmt2, 0, SQL_ADD, SQL_LOCK_NO_CHANGE);
        if (rc != SQL_SUCCESS)
            break;
        rowcount++;
        if (rowcount % 10 == 0 ) {
            wsprintf(szData, "%ld records copied", rowcount);
            SetProgressText(szData);
            if (fCancel())
                break;
        }
    }

    SetProgressText("");
    SQLTransact(SQL_NULL_HENV, hdbc2, SQL_COMMIT);
    t2 = GetTickCount();
    wsprintf(szData, "Copy completed "
        "in %ld:%ld seconds; %ld records/sec",
        (long) (t2 - t1) / 1000L,
        (long) (t2 - t1) % 1000L,
        (long) (t2 - t1 >= 1000L) ?
            (rowcount / ((t2 - t1) / 1000L)) : rowcount
        );
    SetWorkingItem(szData);
    SQLFreeStmt(hstmt, SQL_DROP);
    SQLFreeStmt(hstmt2, SQL_CLOSE);
    ShowCancel(FALSE);

    // Add indexes to Microsoft Access table
    SQLExecDirect(hstmt2,
        "create index f2idx on MyFiles(f2)", SQL_NTS);
    SQLExecDirect(hstmt2,
        "create index f3idx on MyFiles(f3)", SQL_NTS);
    SQLExecDirect(hstmt2,
        "create index f4idx on MyFiles(f4)", SQL_NTS);
    SQLTransact(SQL_NULL_HENV, hdbc2, SQL_COMMIT);
    SQLFreeStmt(hstmt2, SQL_DROP);

    // Turn off transactions for remainder of program
    SQLSetConnectOption(hdbc2, SQL_AUTOCOMMIT, SQL_AUTOCOMMIT_ON);
}
```

Instead of using parameters and *SQLBindParameter*, in this example we bind the columns for input and output and then do a SELECT on the Microsoft Access table into which we are going to insert the data. Now this seems strange at first; why do a SELECT on an empty table? But remember from the discussion of the file orientation of desktop databases in Chapter 2 (section 2.2) that the SELECT statement is acting just like the traditional File Open operation. The call to *SQLSetPos* then acts like the file I/O function that writes to the file. These actions are shown in the following code:

```
// Open the cursor that will be used to add new rows
// for Microsoft Access driver
SQLExecDirect(hstmt2, "select * from MyFiles", SQL_NTS);

// Position the cursor so SetPos can be used
SQLExtendedFetch(hstmt2, SQL_FETCH_FIRST, 1, &r, rgfRowStat);
t1 = GetTickCount();
⋮
// Fetch all rows using Text driver
for(rowcount = 0, rc = SQLFetch(hstmt); rc == SQL_SUCCESS;
    rc = SQLFetch(hstmt)) {

    // For each row in Text driver, use SetPos to add the row
    // to Microsoft Access table
    rc = SQLSetPos(hstmt2, 0, SQL_ADD, SQL_LOCK_NO_CHANGE);
    if (rc != SQL_SUCCESS)
        break;
    rowcount++;
⋮
```

If you use the drivers supplied on the sample CD, you should find that copying the data from the Text driver to the Microsoft Access driver is five or six times faster than using the INSERT technique in ODBCAcc. This is mostly due to the fact that Jet, the underlying SQL engine for the Microsoft Access driver, opens and closes the Microsoft Access MDB file every time an SQL INSERT statement is executed but leaves it open for the cursor method that uses *SQLSetPos*.

This ends our brief tour of ODBC programming. You have now seen the basic programming techniques used in ODBC programs. But we have not yet done anything with client/server DBMSs or used many of the interoperability features. Stay tuned, because in the next chapter we're going to look at some much more sophisticated ODBC programs that will do just that.

C H A P T E R   E I G H T

ODBC at Work

In this chapter we look at 11 complete programs that show a variety of ways to use ODBC. Many of these programs are useful utilities in their own right, quite apart from their usefulness as teaching tools. However, the main value of these samples is in their source code, which shows you how to program in ODBC. Five of the programs are written in C, two in C++, and four in Visual Basic. One of the C++ programs is an OLE Automation server that includes an application written in Visual Basic for Applications (VBA) that is invoked from Microsoft Excel 5.

All the programs are included on the sample CD that comes with this book. If you run the setup program from the CD, icons will appear in Program Manager or on the Start menu for each executable program[1] to make each easy to run. If you are running Windows NT, you'll get both 16-bit and 32-bit versions of each C and C++ sample. If you are running Windows 3.x or Windows 95, you'll get only the 16-bit samples. All the source code and other files necessary to build each sample are included. The complete source code for each sample is contained in its own subdirectory within the SAMPLES directory. To install the samples, run SETUP.EXE from the root directory on the CD.

Following is a brief description of each program.

The Benchmark Sample (BENCH)   The ODBC benchmark sample is a C program that is loosely based on the TPC-B benchmark, a widely used benchmark for testing OLTP performance in client/server DBMSs. The benchmark consists of four tables that track bank transactions, including tables for branches, tellers, and accounts. A fourth table, history, keeps an audit log of all changes made. Each transaction contains three updates, one single-row select, and one insert. As an option, BENCH allows the user to do a 100-row query with each

---

1. Except for the REGISTER program, which has no user interface.

transaction to simulate a more interactive application. BENCH also includes an integrated loader that populates the tables with data for the benchmark.

The goals for BENCH are twofold:

1. BENCH can be used to measure the effect on performance of three different execution paradigms: building SQL strings dynamically and executing them with *SQLExecDirect*, using *SQLPrepare* and *SQLExecute* with bound parameters using *SQLBindParameter*, and using a stored procedure with bound parameters (if supported by the DBMS).

2. BENCH can be used as a comparison tool to judge the performance of ODBC drivers for OLTP application use. The most meaningful comparisons will be between drivers for the same DBMS. For example, using BENCH to compare two drivers for Oracle 7 will be more meaningful than using it to compare an Oracle driver to a Sybase driver unless all the software (except the ODBC driver and the DBMS) and hardware are identical for the two tests.

In addition to its use as a utility, BENCH demonstrates some advanced ODBC programming techniques, including:

- How to use *SQLDriverConnect* to connect to a data source

- How to call stored procedures from ODBC

- How to execute SQL statements in asynchronous mode

- How to use *SQLGetInfo* to determine various characteristics of the data source, such as support for stored procedures and asynchronous processing

The Table Copy Sample (TBLCPY)　The ODBC table copy sample is a C program that is used to move schema and data between data sources.

TBLCPY allows the user to copy schema information (tables and indexes) from one data source to another. It uses a Wizard format to guide the user through the operation, prompting the user for information in several steps to perform the overall copy. The user can customize many of the options, including the objects to be created, the amount of data to be copied, and whether to show the SQL statements generated during the process.

TBLCPY demonstrates the following advanced ODBC programming techniques:

■ How to use three of the ODBC catalog functions—*SQLTables*, *SQLColumns*, and *SQLStatistics*—to retrieve the list of tables, columns, and indexes for a data source

■ How to use *SQLGetTypeInfo* to map data types from one data source to another

■ How to retrieve and insert long data values using *SQLGetData* and *SQLPutData*

■ How to use *SQLGetInfo* to handle tricky SQL syntax problems related to delimited identifiers, qualifiers, and long data values

The Type Declaration Generator Sample (TYPEGEN) TYPEGEN is a C program that generates source code for C and Visual Basic. It is useful for creating ODBC programs that use multirow cursors with row-wise binding. Given an input SQL query, it generates a C structure or a Visual Basic user-defined type declaration and generates calls to *SQLBindCol* that match the columns of the query. TYPEGEN also generates a C test function that can be pasted into the main program to test the ODBC bindings with calls to *SQLExtendedFetch*.

The code generated by TYPEGEN demonstrates the following ODBC programming techniques:

■ How to use *SQLSetStmtOption* and *SQLBindCol* to do row-wise binding for multirow cursors

■ How to generate the correct user-defined type definitions in Visual Basic to use multirow binding in ODBC

■ How to call *SQLExtendedFetch* to scroll a multirow cursor

The SQL Executer Sample (EXECUTER) The ODBC SQL Executer sample is a C program that executes SQL statements under various ODBC settings. Most of the performance-related features demonstrated with EXECUTER are also in BENCH (such as the use of *SQLExecDirect* vs. *SQLPrepare* and *SQLExecute*, and the use of asynchronous execution), but a few features are shown only in the EXECUTER program, including:

■ The use of the Query timeout in *SQLSetStmtOption*.

■ The use of *SQLMoreResults*, which is the function ODBC uses to support the return of data from batched SQL statements, stored procedures that return multiple results sets, and any other features of a

DBMS that return multiple results sets with execution of a single statement. (The use of the COMPUTE BY clause in Microsoft SQL Server is an example of the latter.)

Because most of the code shows concepts similar to those demonstrated in BENCH, this chapter doesn't discuss EXECUTER beyond this brief description. But remember, the source code is located on the CD for you to study and use.

The DSN Registration Sample (REGISTER)   In the samples directory of the CD you'll find a directory called REGISTER. The REGISTER directory contains an ODBC utility called REGISTER that creates, removes, and modifies DSNs using the ODBC installer API functions *SQLConfigDataSource* and *SQLGetInstalledDrivers*. REGISTER is a C program used by the Inside ODBC setup program to generate the HELLO DSN used by the HELLO example in Chapter 7 and some sample DSNs that can be used for the benchmark sample.

No icon is generated for REGISTER during setup because there is no need to run the program once setup has been run. (Running the program unchanged simply duplicates a portion of the setup process.) However, the source code for REGISTER is included on the CD because it is a handy piece of code to have around if you are building an ODBC application and want to create one or more DSNs when your application is installed. REGISTER hard-codes a DSN list in a structure, so to add other DSNs to an application you must change the list to reflect the driver and DSN attributes you want and rebuild the application. Because the use of *SQLConfigDataSource* is covered in Chapter 7, the source code for the REGISTER sample is not discussed further in this chapter.

The Simple C++ Class Library for ODBC Sample (CPPSMPL)   The CPPSMPL sample is a C++ program that provides a drastically simplified programming interface to ODBC. It exposes only the ability to make a connection, execute SQL statements, and retrieve all the results from SELECT statements into a column object. Two classes, *ODBCExecute* and *ODBCColumn*, encapsulate the necessary ODBC functions to provide this simple data access abstraction.

CPPSMPL shows how the ODBC API can easily be wrapped by a simple C++ class library. Although it is possible to write an application using only this simple class library, it is more likely that you'll use CPPSMPL as the basis to write your own C++ class library tailored to your specific application.

The OLE Automation Server Sample (ODBCAUTO)   The OLE Automation server sample follows the same theme as CPPSMPL but adds the ability to invoke the simple programming interface as an inproc OLE Automation server. This sample is written in C++ but also uses code generated by the Microsoft Visual C++ Foundation Classes for the OLE "plumbing" required to create an OLE Automation server. Included in this sample is a Microsoft Excel spreadsheet with a small Visual Basic for Applications (VBA) program to invoke the server. You can enter an SQL statement on the spreadsheet, execute it with a button that invokes the VBA code, and see the results returned to the spreadsheet.

Similar to CPPSMPL, ODBCAUTO provides the foundation for you to build a more comprehensive OLE Automation server for data access using ODBC.

The Simple ODBC for Visual Basic Sample (VBODBC)   The VBODBC sample is a Visual Basic 3.0 program that provides a simple programing model for ODBC. The VBODBC programming model is a bit more powerful than the models provided by CPPSMPL and ODBCAUTO; it supports a fetch model and the ability the use some of the scrollable cursor capabilities of ODBC in addition to the option to fetch all the results at execution time. VBODBC also shows you how to use the grid control supplied with Visual Basic to display re-sults from a query.

VBODBC demonstrates:

- ▓ How to write a Visual Basic application using the high-level API provided in VBODBC.

- ▓ How to use a variety of cursor models in ODBC with *SQLFetch* and *SQLExtendedFetch*.

- ▓ How to use *SQLSetPos* and *SQLGetData* instead of binding to support multirow cursors with *SQLExtendedFetch*.

- ▓ How to use *SQLSetStmtOption* and *SQLGetInfo* to set ODBC cursor options.

The Visual Basic ODBC Binding and Multirow Cursors Sample (VBFETCH)
The VBFETCH sample demonstrates how to do row-wise binding of multirow cursors (also known as *fat cursors*) in Visual Basic. Because row-wise binding is useful primarily for results sets whose structures are known when the application is written, two fixed results sets are used instead of an arbitrary query. In addition to demonstrating how to do binding, VBFETCH shows how to use the status array returned from *SQLExtendedFetch* to determine the status of each row in the rowset. Finally, VBFETCH shows the correct way to declare Visual Basic variables so that ODBC binding can be used.

The Visual Basic Stored Procedures Sample (VBSPROCS)
The Visual Basic stored procedures sample demonstrates the creation and execution of various stored procedures. The sample demonstrates the principles that allow communication between stored procedures and an application using the ODBC {call...} syntax and *SQLBindParameter*.

The stored procedures sample demonstrates the following ODBC techniques:

- Creating and executing stored procedures with
  - No parameters
  - Input parameters
  - Output parameters
  - Input and output parameters
  - Return values
  - Combinations of the above
- Binding parameters for input, output, and return values
- Binding and retrieving results from a stored procedure

Stored procedures can be generated in VBSPROCS for Microsoft SQL Server or Oracle 7.

The Hotel Reservation Sample (VBENTRY)
The hotel reservation sample is a crude hotel reservation system that demonstrates how to use the ODBC API directly for a specific application.

The hotel reservation sample demonstrates the following ODBC techniques:

- How to use *SQLExtendedFetch* to scroll through results, using *SQLSetPos* to perform updates and deletes

- How a keyset-driven cursor reflects updates and deletes made to a results set

- How to send and retrieve data types in their native format to and from Visual Basic variables

- How to use a variety of native Visual Basic controls with the ODBC API

Now let's look at the samples in more detail.

8.1 The Benchmark Sample (BENCH)

This section takes a look at the BENCH sample. First it discusses the overall purpose of the standard TPC-B benchmark (on which BENCH is based) and how it relates to the BENCH sample. Then the discussion moves to the various elements of BENCH's user interface and concludes with a look at how various portions of the benchmark are implemented with ODBC.

8.1.1 Background of the TPC-B Benchmark

The BENCH sample is loosely based on the TPC-B benchmark defined by the Transaction Processing Performance Council, a nonprofit organization that was founded to define transaction processing and database benchmarks. The council includes representatives from nearly every major hardware and software vendor that provides online transaction processing. The TPC-B is a database stress test that simulates hundreds or thousands of transactions in batch mode and models activities such as a rollup of daily sales orders as conducted by a central MIS department. According to the TPC-B Specification, Clause 1.1.1:

> This benchmark is stated in terms of a hypothetical bank. The bank has one or more branches. Each branch has multiple tellers. The bank has many customers, each with an account. The database represents the cash position of each entity (branch, teller, and account) and a history of recent transactions run by the bank. The transaction represents the work done when a customer makes a deposit or a withdrawal against a host account. The transaction is performed by a teller at some branch.

The table definitions are very simple, as shown on the following page.

The Account Table

Column	Data Type
account	INTEGER
branch	INTEGER
balance	FLOAT
filler	CHAR(84)

The Teller Table

Column	Data Type
teller	INTEGER
branch	INTEGER
balance	FLOAT
filler	CHAR(84)

The Branch Table

Column	Data Type
branch	INTEGER
fillerint	INTEGER
balance	FLOAT
filler	CHAR(84)

The History Table

Column	Data Type
histid	INTEGER
account	INTEGER
teller	INTEGER
branch	INTEGER
amount	FLOAT
timeoftxn	TIMESTAMP
filler	CHAR(22)

Each transaction involves five operations: three updates, one select, and one insert. The operations begin with a deposit or a withdrawal from an account, as shown here:

```
UPDATE    account
    SET   balance = balance + ?
    WHERE account = ?
```

The first question mark is a placeholder for the amount of the deposit (if the value is a positive number) or the withdrawal (if the value is a negative number), and the second question mark is a placeholder for the account number.

Next the new balance is selected from the account that was just updated:

```
SELECT    balance
    FROM  account
    WHERE account = ?
```

The question mark is a placeholder for the account number that was used in the first update.

Then a particular teller's balance is updated with the deposit or withdrawal amount:

```
UPDATE    teller
    SET   balance = balance + ?
    WHERE teller  = ?
```

As in the update for the account table, the first question mark is a placeholder for the amount of the deposit or the withdrawal. The second question mark is a placeholder for the teller number. Performing this update simulates the change of the balance in a particular teller's cash drawer.

Next the balance of the branch is updated with the deposit or withdrawal amount:

```
UPDATE    branch
    SET   balance = balance + ?
    WHERE branch  = ?
```

Again, the first question mark is a placeholder for the amount of the deposit or the withdrawal. The second question mark is a placeholder for the branch number. Performing this update simulates the change of the total deposits held by a particular branch.

Finally, a record is written to the history table to record the account, teller, branch, amount, and time of the transaction:

```
INSERT history1
    (histid, account, teller, branch, amount, timeoftxn, filler)
VALUES
    (?, ?, ?, ?, ?, ?, ?)
```

315

In the standard benchmark, all these operations must occur within a single transaction. The number of transactions that are run in a given period of time provides the comparison metric of transactions per second (TPS). The higher the TPS, the better the performance. When the benchmark is run, various statistics are captured, including the TPS, the total number of transactions, and the number of transactions that finish in less than 1 second.

8.1.2 Differences Between the Standard TPC-B Benchmark and the ODBC Sample (BENCH)

Compared to TPC-B, BENCH omits a lot of the complexities regarding multiple-client synchronization and scalability. BENCH also has an option that adds a query that returns 100 rows to simulate mixed query and update usage. Variations in code for binding, fetching, and converting data in the driver can have an impact on performance. The 100-row fetch will expose driver inefficiencies in this area.

Each DBMS vendor typically writes code for the TPC-B benchmark that works only with its own DBMS and is hard-coded to use specific performance features of the DBMS. The BENCH ODBC benchmark is written to be used with a number of different data sources, and it allows developers to select high-performance features by checking various *SQLGetInfo* options.

Finally, whereas typical benchmarks use two separate programs—one to load the data and one to execute the benchmark—BENCH has an integrated loader program that makes it easier to create the tables that are used in the benchmark and the data necessary to populate those tables.

The number of rows in each table and some indexing options can be changed through the user interface to BENCH so that the impact on performance of different-size tables can be easily measured. For public disclosure purposes, the standard TPC-B benchmark requires a minimum number of rows: 100,000 account rows, 10 teller rows, and 1 branch row. The BENCH defaults use 1000 accounts, 100 tellers, and 10 branches so that loading the tables will not take so long.

8.1.3 The BENCH User Interface

BENCH performs four major functional tasks: connecting to the data source, loading the benchmark tables, running the benchmark, and cleaning up. The loader creates and populates the tables used in the benchmark (branches, tellers, accounts, and the history table). To run the benchmark you enter the number of runs, the amount of time to allot to each run, and which execution options you want. The cleanup portion drops the tables and indexes created by the loader.

8.1.3.1 Connecting to the Data Source

BENCH uses the simplest form of *SQLDriverConnect* to establish the connection to the desired data source. To connect, you select Connect from the File menu, as shown in Figure 8-1.

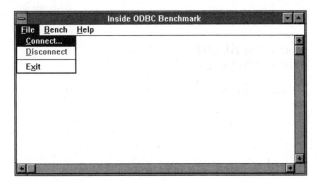

Figure 8-1.
Using the BENCH program to connect to the data source.

Because no DSN is specified in the arguments to *SQLDriverConnect*, the ODBC Driver Manager displays the Data Sources dialog box, as shown in Figure 8-2.

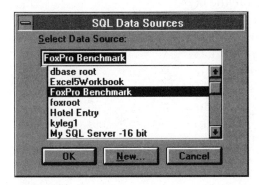

Figure 8-2.
Selecting the data source from the Driver Manager's Data Sources dialog box.

For your convenience, if you elect to install the Microsoft Access or FoxPro driver included on the CD, the Inside ODBC setup program will create a data source for the driver. The data sources are called Access Benchmark and

FoxPro Benchmark, respectively.[2] Each can be used with the BENCH program and with the data source's respective driver. Of course, other drivers can be used; these were provided so that you would have something to use without having to configure a data source yourself.

Once the connection to the desired data source has been made, the loader, the benchmark, and the cleanup operations can be performed from the Bench menu.

8.1.3.2 Loading the Benchmark Tables

The loader is invoked from the Bench menu, as shown in Figure 8-3.

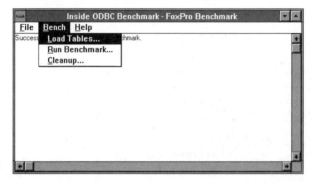

Figure 8-3.
Invoking the loader.

The loader has several options. The dialog box that contains these options is shown in Figure 8-4.

As you can see in Figure 8-4, you can create and load each table that is used in the benchmark as well as create indexes. The number of records to load in each table can also be specified. The settings are saved in standard Windows INI format in a file called BENCH.INI.

The Schema From DBMS combo box requires a bit of explanation. You might recall from the discussion of data types in Chapter 5 (section 5.6) that ODBC exposes the native data types of DBMSs to applications rather than defining a set of standard types and requiring drivers to parse and convert CREATE TABLE statements. The BENCH program contains templates for the native data types for all the drivers included on the CD, plus several templates for popular DBMSs and one template called ANSI that uses data type names taken from the SQL-92 standard.

---

2. If you ran the Inside ODBC setup program on Windows NT, the data sources will be generated for the 32-bit versions of the drivers. For Windows 95 and Windows 3.*x*, the 16-bit versions are used.

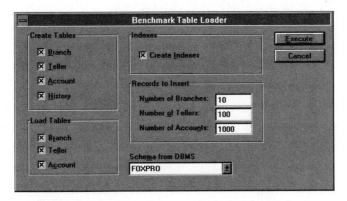

Figure 8-4.
The Benchmark Table Loader option dialog box.

8.1.3.3 Running the Benchmark

When you select Run Benchmark from the Bench menu, the Execute Benchmark dialog box is displayed, as shown in Figure 8-5.

The benchmark will be run as many times as specified and for the number of minutes specified. By default, the benchmark is run once for 5 minutes. There are three options for executing the SQL statements, one of which (Use Stored Procedures) is disabled or enabled depending upon calls made to *SQLGetInfo* at connect time.

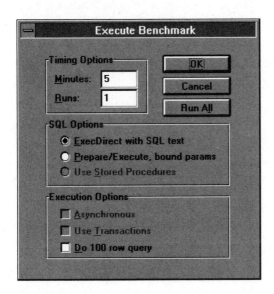

Figure 8-5.
The Execute Benchmark dialog box.

319

The first SQL option, ExecDirect With SQL Text, dynamically constructs the SQL statements for the transaction every time. The C function *sprintf* is used to provide the current values of the account number, teller number, branch number, and so on for every SQL statement. For example, the update of the account table uses the following code fragment:

```
static const char gszUPD_ACCOUNTS[] =
    "UPDATE account SET balance = balance + (%f) WHERE account = %ld";
    ⋮
sprintf(szStmt, gszUPD_ACCOUNTS, dDelta, nAcctNum);
fRtn = fExecuteSql(lpBench, szStmt);
```

At execution time, an actual update statement might look like this:

```
UPDATE account SET balance = balance + (-15.0000) WHERE account = 145
```

In this model, the *application* converts everything to text before executing it.

The second SQL option in Figure 8-5, Prepare/Execute, Bound Params, does not convert the values for each statement to text but instead uses *SQLBindParameter* outside the main loop to bind the variables that hold the account number, balance, and so on to parameters used in each SQL statement. For example, the code to bind the parameters for the update account statement looks like this:

```
SQLAllocStmt(lpBench->hdbc, &hstmtUpdAcct);
fSuccess &= fSQLBindParameter(hwnd, hstmtUpdAcct, 1, SQL_PARAM_INPUT,
                SQL_C_DOUBLE, SQL_DOUBLE, sizeof(double), 0,
                &dDelta, sizeof(dDelta), NULL);
fSuccess &= fSQLBindParameter(hwnd, hstmtUpdAcct, 2, SQL_PARAM_INPUT,
                SQL_C_LONG, SQL_INTEGER, sizeof(SDWORD), 0,
                &nAcctNum, sizeof(nAcctNum), NULL);
if(fSuccess) {
    do {
        rc = SQLPrepare(hstmtUpdAcct,
            "update account set balance = balance + ? where account = ?",
            SQL_NTS);
        } while(SQL_STILL_EXECUTING == rc);
```

With the Prepare/Execute option, in contrast to the ExecDirect With SQL Text option, the application does not convert the values to text using *sprintf*. Instead, the contents of each variable are used by the driver directly because the address of each variable is passed to the driver in the call to *SQLBindParameter*. Ideally, neither the driver nor the DBMS will have to convert these values at all but will be able to store or search for them in their native form. If the driver and data source are optimized to support parameters in this way, this option will show a significant performance improvement over the first option.

Each SQL statement uses its own statement handle. In the main loop that runs the transaction, each statement is executed with a call to the *SQLExecute* function. The code that updates the account table is:

```
do {
    rc = SQLExecute(hstmtUpdAcct);
    } while(SQL_STILL_EXECUTING == rc);
```

The calls to *SQLExecute* and *SQLPrepare* are in a loop that will continue to execute as long as the return code is SQL_STILL_EXECUTING. This is an example of how to use ODBC's asynchronous execution mode. If these statements were time consuming, it would be wise to call the Windows *Yield* function in Windows 3.1–based programs or to create a separate thread for the code that executes the benchmark (the *fRunTrans* function in EXECUTE.C) in Windows 95 and Windows NT.

The third and last option in the SQL Options group is the Use Stored Procedures option. If the driver and data source are capable of supporting stored procedures, the Use Stored Procedures checkbox will be enabled. Selecting it will generally produce the best benchmark results. As in the Prepare/Execute option, bound parameters are used to send all the input and output arguments to the data source. The key difference between this model and the Prepare/Execute model is that in this model all the SQL statements are contained within the stored procedure, which should provide even better performance. The entire transaction (three updates, one select, and one insert) is executed by invoking the stored procedure with ODBC's standard stored procedure syntax:

```
{CALL ODBC_BENCHMARK(?,?,?,?,?,?,?)}
```

Of course, the DBMS must have such a stored procedure defined for it. Examples for Microsoft SQL Server and Oracle 7 are provided on the CD and are discussed in section 8.1.4.3.

Figure 8-5 also shows three execution options. If the driver reports that it can support asynchronous execution, the Asynchronous checkbox will be enabled and you can test the effect of asynchronous execution on performance.

The Use Transactions checkbox is enabled if the driver reports that it supports transactions. If it does support transactions, selecting the checkbox wraps all the SQL commands in a transaction (which is the assumed mode of operation in the standard TPC-B benchmark). However, if you clear the checkbox you can test the effect of ODBC's autocommit mode, in which every statement is committed individually. This option has no effect when stored procedures are used.

If the Do 100 Row Query checkbox is selected, in addition to the usual TPC-B statements a query is executed to select and fetch 100 rows from the accounts table using *SQLExecDirect*. The row data is retrieved and converted into character strings using *SQLBindCol* and *SQLFetch*.

To try all the options automatically, click the Run All button. Every valid option for the current driver will be run, which is the easiest way to see the effects of the various options on performance.

Alternatively, after all the options have been set, manually click the OK button to start the benchmark for a single run. For each run, the statistics are displayed on the screen. Figure 8-6 shows a sample of the statistics that are displayed.

```
Starting benchmark run number: 1
Max branch = 10, Max teller = 100, Max account = 1000
Benchmark finished.
Calculating statistics:
    SQL options used:           Params
    Transaction time:           61.000000
    Environmental overhead:     -1.000000
    Total transactions:         158
    Transactions per second:    2.590164
    % less than 1 second:       100.000000
    % 1 < n < 2 seconds:        0.000000
    Average processing time:    0.386076
```

Figure 8-6.
Statistics displayed by BENCH.

The statistics are also written to a text file called ODBCBNCH.CSV and can be input into a spreadsheet program such as Microsoft Excel to plot the results of several runs. The file contains the date and time of the run, the data source name, the options selected, and all the statistics shown in Figure 8-6. For example, to use Microsoft Excel to chart the results, you can open ODBCBNCH.CSV and select the first four columns, as shown in Figure 8-7. Then press the F11 key, and voilà, you have a nice chart of the average TPS of each data source, as shown in Figure 8-8.

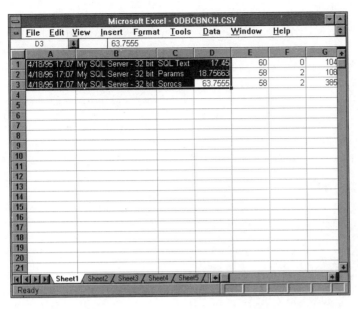

Figure 8-7.
Selecting data to chart from ODBCBNCH.CSV in Microsoft Excel.

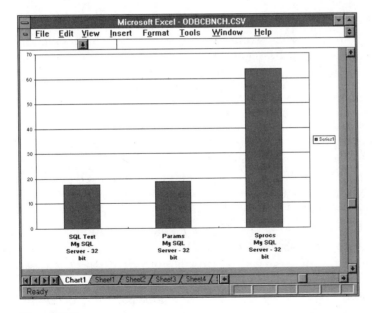

Figure 8-8.
Chart of transactions per second from BENCH.

The chart in Figure 8-8 shows the effect of using the three different SQL options for the Microsoft SQL Server driver. The performance improvement attained by using Prepare/Execute and parameters vs. *SQLExecDirect* and SQL text is only marginal; but, as expected, there is a huge gain when the stored procedures method is used.

8.1.3.4 Cleaning Up

After a benchmark run, you can drop some or all of the tables and indexes from the data source by selecting Cleanup from the Bench menu. The resulting dialog box is shown in Figure 8-9.

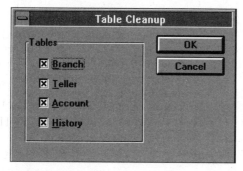

Figure 8-9.
The Table Cleanup dialog box.

Using Cleanup is not required if you want to run the benchmark again, however, because the history table is cleared automatically on each run, and reloading the three data tables each time is unnecessary.

8.1.4 Inside BENCH

The overall structure of BENCH is quite simple. The initialization and Windows housekeeping code is in BENCH.C. The *WndProc* function handles the usual window management events (create, size, and destroy) and the commands menu. ODBC connections are managed in the *OnConnect* function in BENCH.C and in COMMON.C (which contains a set of useful ODBC helper functions). The *vDisplayLoad* function is the top-level routine for the loader, and *ExecuteBench* manages the benchmark execution code. Cleanup is handled in—you guessed it—CLEANUP.C.

Much of the necessary state information for BENCH is passed via a structure of type BENCHINFO. One global instance of the structure called *gBenchInfo* is declared in BENCH.C. The loader code in LOADER.C uses a separate structure called *RunCfg*, which contains a pointer to *gBenchInfo*. The execution code in EXECUTE.C uses a pointer to *gBenchInfo* called *lpBench*. The Windows handle and the ODBC environment, connection, and main statement handles used throughout BENCH reside in *BenchInfo*.

8.1.4.1 Connecting to the Data Source

Choosing Connect from the File menu calls the *OnConnect* function in BENCH.C. The *fDoConnect* helper function is used to make the connection. *fDoConnect* calls the ODBC function *SQLDriverConnect* with a null data source name. The rest of the connection process is handled by the Driver Manager and the driver. If the connection is successful, a statement handle is allocated and returned by *fDoConnect*.

After the connection is made, five calls are made to *SQLGetInfo* to get the data source name, to get the name of the DBMS, to test whether stored procedures are supported by the DBMS, to test whether transactions are supported, and to test for the appropriate scalar function to use to generate the current time and date. The flag for stored procedures will be used to enable or disable the Use Stored Procedures checkbox when the benchmark run is configured. Finally, a call to *SQLSetConnectOption* determines whether asynchronous execution is supported. Flags are set so that the corresponding checkboxes in the Execute Benchmark dialog box can be enabled or disabled appropriately.

Figure 8-10 shows the code for the *OnConnect* function in BENCH.C.

```
//////////////////////////////////////////////////////////////////////
// OnConnect - Do a connection
//
// Returns:  Nothing
//////////////////////////////////////////////////////////////////////
void OnConnect(
    HWND hwnd,                          // Parent window
    lpBENCHINFO lpBench                 // Application info
    )
{
    char      szBuff[256];
    SWORD     sTxnCapable;
    long      ulDTFunc;
    RETCODE   rc;

    if(fDoConnect(hwnd, lpBench->henv, lpBench->hdbc,
        &lpBench->hdbc, NULL, &lpBench->hstmt)) {
        // Gather connection information for later use
        //
        SQLGetInfo(lpBench->hdbc,
                    SQL_DATA_SOURCE_NAME,
                    lpBench->szDSN,
                    sizeof(lpBench->szDSN),
                    NULL);
```

Figure 8-10.   *(continued)*

The OnConnect *function in BENCH.C.*

Figure 8-10. *continued*

```
SQLGetInfo(lpBench->hdbc,
               SQL_DBMS_NAME,
               lpBench->szDBMS,
               sizeof(lpBench->szDBMS),
               NULL);
SQLGetInfo(lpBench->hdbc,
               SQL_PROCEDURES,
               szBuff,
               sizeof(szBuff),
               NULL);

if ('Y' == *szBuff ) {
    rc=SQLProcedures(lpBench->hstmt, NULL, 0, NULL, 0,
        "ODBC_BENCHMARK", SQL_NTS);
    if ( SQL_SUCCESS != rc
        || SQL_SUCCESS != SQLFetch(lpBench->hstmt) )
        *szBuff = 'N';
    SQLFreeStmt(lpBench->hstmt, SQL_CLOSE);
    }
lpBench->fProcsSupported = (*szBuff == 'Y');

SQLGetInfo(lpBench->hdbc,
               SQL_TXN_CAPABLE,
               &sTxnCapable,
               sizeof(sTxnCapable),
               NULL);
lpBench->fCommitSupported = sTxnCapable > 0;

SQLGetInfo(lpBench->hdbc,
               SQL_TIMEDATE_FUNCTIONS,
               &ulDTFunc,
               sizeof(ulDTFunc),
               NULL);
if (ulDTFunc & SQL_FN_TD_NOW)
    lpBench->pszDateTimeSQLFunc = "now";
else if (ulDTFunc & SQL_FN_TD_CURDATE)
    lpBench->pszDateTimeSQLFunc = "curdate";
else
    lpBench->pszDateTimeSQLFunc = NULL;

// Set title of application with DSN for user
//
wsprintf(szBuff, "%s - %s", (LPCSTR)gsz_WIN_TITLE,
    (LPCSTR)lpBench->szDSN);
SetWindowText(hwnd, szBuff);

// Determine whether asynchronous processing is supported
// by setting the value to its default, which has no
// effect other than to tell us whether it is supported
//
```

Figure 8-10. *continued*

```
        rc = SQLSetStmtOption(lpBench->hstmt, SQL_ASYNC_ENABLE,
            SQL_ASYNC_ENABLE_OFF);
        lpBench->fAsyncSupported = RC_SUCCESSFUL(rc);

        // Set defaults for execution--use all features
        // supported
        lpBench->fExecAsync = lpBench->fAsyncSupported;
        lpBench->fUseCommit = lpBench->fCommitSupported;
        lpBench->fSQLOption =
            lpBench->fProcsSupported ? IDX_SPROCS : IDX_PLAINSQL;
        lpBench->fDoQuery = FALSE;
        lpBench->fClearHistory = FALSE;

        // Give user some feedback
        //
        Printf(lpBench, "Successfully connected to %s.\r\n",
            (LPCSTR)lpBench->szDSN);
        }
    }
```

The function *fDoConnect* in COMMON.C allocates the connection handle and calls *SQLDriverConnect* with a NULL input connection string:

```
if(SQL_SUCCESS != SQLAllocConnect(henv, &hdbcNew))
    return FALSE;
rc = SQLDriverConnect(hdbcNew, hDlg,
                NULL, 0,  // Input connect string is NULL
                szConnOut, sizeof(szConnOut), NULL,
                SQL_DRIVER_COMPLETE);
```

The Driver Manager and the driver take care of the rest of the connection.

8.1.4.2 Using the Loader to Insert Data

The function *vDisplayLoad* in LOADER.C displays the option dialog box that was shown in Figure 8-4. Then it calls the *fBuildBench* function, which is also in LOADER.C. Depending upon the options the user selects in the dialog box, *fBuildBench* will call functions to create tables (using *vCreateTables*), to create indexes (using *vCreateIndices*), or to load each table with data (using *vLoadBranch*, *vLoadTeller*, or *vLoadAccount*).

The SQL statement CREATE TABLE is used to create each table. Each SQL string is stored in a global variable (*szCreateBranch*, *szCreateTeller*, or *szCreateAccount*) and is executed with *SQLExecDirect*. However, because the tables can be created on any of several DBMSs, the data type names are not provided in the global strings.

The data types to be used in the CREATE TABLE statement for each table are derived from the template specific to the DBMS that you select in the loader dialog box, as discussed in section 8.1.3.2. It would be possible to use *SQLGetTypeInfo* to query the data source and then map the types according to what the data source supported, but there is another sample that does that (TBLCPY). Although the method here is not as comprehensive as the *SQLGetTypeInfo* approach, the templates will handle a number of different data sources. If you use a driver that isn't supported directly, it's fairly easy to add another template: near the beginning of LOADER.C are several tables with data type names. Add the new type names and the template at the end of each table and recompile, and you should be off and running.

The loading of the data into each table is handled via bound parameters and the prepare-and-execute method. For example, the code that loads the data for the teller table in the *vLoadTeller* function first binds one parameter for each column, again using data types derived from the DBMS template that was selected in the loader dialog box. The code in *vLoadTeller* prepares the INSERT statement, binds the parameters for each column in the teller table, and calls *SQLExecute* in a loop, as shown in Figure 8-11. The code for loading data into the branch and account tables is similar.

```
const char szInsertTeller[]  =
    "insert into %s (teller, branch, balance, filler) "
    "values (?, ?, ?, ?)";
⋮
// Prepare the insert statement
wsprintf(szSQLBuffer, szInsertTeller, szTeller);
rc = SQLPrepare(lpRunCfg->lpBenchInfo->hstmt, szSQLBuffer,
    SQL_NTS);

// Bind each variable to its parameter marker
// Teller ID
rc = fSQLBindParameter(lpRunCfg->lpBenchInfo->hwndMain,
    lpRunCfg->lpBenchInfo->hstmt, 1, SQL_PARAM_INPUT,
    SQL_C_LONG, BindTypeMap[uwBindIdx].swInt,
    BindTypeMap[uwBindIdx].uwInt, 0, (PTR)&udwTeller, 0, 0);

// Branch ID
rc = fSQLBindParameter(lpRunCfg->lpBenchInfo->hwndMain,
    lpRunCfg->lpBenchInfo->hstmt, 2, SQL_PARAM_INPUT,
    SQL_C_LONG, BindTypeMap[uwBindIdx].swInt,
    BindTypeMap[uwBindIdx].uwInt, 0, (PTR)&udwBranch, 0, 0);
```

Figure 8-11.
Loading data with the vLoadTeller *function.*

Figure 8-11. *continued*

```
// Balance
rc = fSQLBindParameter(lpRunCfg->lpBenchInfo->hwndMain,
    lpRunCfg->lpBenchInfo->hstmt, 3, SQL_PARAM_INPUT,
    SQL_C_DOUBLE, BindTypeMap[uwBindIdx].swFloat,
    BindTypeMap[uwBindIdx].uwFloat, 0, (PTR) &dBalance, 0, 0);

// Filler char
rc = fSQLBindParameter(lpRunCfg->lpBenchInfo->hwndMain,
    lpRunCfg->lpBenchInfo->hstmt, 4, SQL_PARAM_INPUT,
    SQL_C_CHAR, BindTypeMap[uwBindIdx].swChar,
    sizeof(lpRunCfg->szTemp) - 1, 0, lpRunCfg->szTemp,
    sizeof(lpRunCfg->szTemp) - 1, &cbFiller);
⋮
// Insert records
for(udwTeller=1; udwTeller <= lpRunCfg->udwMaxTeller;
    udwTeller++) {
    udwBranch = (UDWORD)((rand() % lpRunCfg->udwMaxBranch) + 1);
    rc = SQLExecute(lpRunCfg->lpBenchInfo->hstmt);
    if (RC_NOTSUCCESSFUL(rc)) {
        Printf(lpRunCfg->lpBenchInfo, (LPSTR)szInsertFailure,
            udwTeller);
        break;
        }
```

8.1.4.3 Executing the Benchmark

The code that executes the benchmark is located in EXECUTE.C. The main function, *ExecuteBench*, displays an option dialog box and then executes the benchmark according to the options that are set. The *fRunTrans* function in EXECUTE.C handles the chores for running the benchmark in one of three ways:

- Using standard SQL UPDATE, SELECT, and INSERT statements with *SQLExecDirect*. In this case the values to be inserted and updated are put into a string (using *sprintf*), which in turn is used as an argument to *SQLExecDirect*.

- Using *SQLBindParameter* and the *SQLPrepare* and *SQLExecute* method for execution.

- Using a stored procedure, which must be created separately according to the syntax supported by the DBMS. The stored procedure must be called ODBC_BENCHMARK, and it must take seven parameters. For example, the code on the next page shows the stored procedure used for Microsoft SQL Server version 4.21.

```
CREATE PROCEDURE ODBC_BENCHMARK
    @histid   int;
    @acct     int,
    @teller   int,
    @branch   int,
    @delta    float,
    @balance  float output,
    @filler   char(22)
AS
BEGIN TRANSACTION
UPDATE    account
    SET   balance = balance + @delta
    WHERE account = @acct
SELECT    @balance = balance
    FROM  account
    WHERE account = @acct
UPDATE    teller
    SET   balance = balance + @delta
    WHERE teller  = @teller
UPDATE    branch
    SET   balance = balance + @delta
    WHERE branch  = @branch
INSERT history
    (histid, account, teller, branch, amount, timeoftxn, filler)
VALUES
    (@histid, @acct, @teller, @branch, @delta, getdate(), @filler)
COMMIT TRANSACTION
```

The stored procedure used for Oracle looks like this:

```
create procedure ODBC_BENCHMARK(
    vhistid IN  number,
    acct    IN  number,
    vteller IN  number,
    vbranch IN  number,
    delta   IN  float,
    balance OUT float,
    vfiller IN  char)
is
BEGIN
update account set balance = balance + delta where account = acct;
update teller set balance = balance + delta where teller = vteller;
update branch set balance = balance + delta where branch = vbranch;
insert INTO history
    (histid, account, teller, branch, amount, timeoftxn, filler)
values
    (vhistid, acct, vteller, vbranch, delta, SYSDATE, vfiller);
COMMIT WORK;
END  ODBC_BENCHMARK;
```

For the stored procedure method, *SQLBindParameter* is called for every parameter, as in the code shown for the loader. At execution time, the entire transaction is executed by the standard ODBC stored procedure syntax:

```
{CALL ODBC_BENCHMARK(?,?,?,?,?,?,?)}
```

Each parameter is passed in its native format. The output parameter for the new balance in the account is retrieved in the sixth parameter. Notice that the declaration for this parameter declares a parameter type of SQL_PARAM_INPUT_OUTPUT:

```
fSQLBindParameter(hwnd, lpBench->hstmt, 6, SQL_PARAM_INPUT_OUTPUT,
    SQL_C_DOUBLE, SQL_DOUBLE, sizeof(double), 0,
    &dBalance, sizeof(dBalance), NULL);
```

Each time the stored procedure finishes, the new value of the balance column will be available in the variable *dBalance*.

The main loop of the benchmark is in *fRunTrans* in EXECUTE.C. The loop is controlled by the time that is entered in the Execute Benchmark dialog box and by any error that occurs. First, within the loop, the values for the account number, teller number, branch number, and the amount of the transaction are randomly generated, as shown in Figure 8-12.

```
while((dDiff <= dTimeToRun) && !fDone) {
    // Generate random data for each field and amount
    //
    nAcctNum = ((rand() * rand()) % lpBench->udwMaxAccount) + 1;
    assert(nAcctNum > -1);

    nBranchNum = (rand() % lpBench->udwMaxBranch) + 1;
    assert(nBranchNum > -1);

    nTellerNum = (rand() % lpBench->udwMaxTeller) + 1;
    assert(nTellerNum > -1);

    // Arbitrarily set bank transaction to a random amount
    // no greater than the number of tellers. The type of
    // transaction (deposit or withdrawal) is determined
    // by the C runtime function 'time' being even or odd.
    dDelta = ((rand() % lpBench->udwMaxTeller) + 1) *
        (double)(((long)time(NULL) % 2) ? 1 : -1);

    // Add 1 to transaction counter
    ++lpBench->nTrnCnt;

    // Obtain the start time for this transaction
    time(&tTransStartTime);
```

Figure 8-12.
Generating the values in EXECUTE.C.

Next the options selected for execution are checked, and the appropriate execution model is used, as shown in Figure 8-13.

```
// Stored procedure method
if(IDX_SPROCS == lpBench->fSQLOption) {
    SetWorkingItem(
        "Executing stored procedure with parameters");
    fRtn = fExecuteSprocCall(lpBench);
    if(!fRtn)
        fDone = TRUE;
}

// Prepare/Execute with parameters
else if (IDX_PARAMS == lpBench->fSQLOption) {
    SetWorkingItem(
        "Executing prepared statement with parameters");

    // Update account
    do {
        rc = SQLExecute(hstmtUpdAcct);
        } while(SQL_STILL_EXECUTING == rc);
    if(SQL_SUCCESS != rc)
        vShowErrors(lpBench->hwndMain, NULL, NULL,
            hstmtUpdAcct);

    // Select new balance for the account just updated
    if (RC_SUCCESSFUL(rc)) {
        do {
            rc = SQLExecute(hstmtSelBal);
            } while(SQL_STILL_EXECUTING == rc);
        if(SQL_SUCCESS != rc)
            vShowErrors(lpBench->hwndMain, NULL, NULL,
                hstmtSelBal);
        else {
            SDWORD cbBal;
            SQLFetch(hstmtSelBal);
            SQLGetData(hstmtSelBal, 1, SQL_C_DOUBLE,
                &dBalance, 0, &cbBal);
            SQLFreeStmt(hstmtSelBal, SQL_CLOSE);
            }
        }

    // Update teller
    if (RC_SUCCESSFUL(rc)) {
```

Figure 8-13.

Selecting the execution options and executing in EXECUTE.C.

Figure 8-13. *continued*

```
            do {
                rc = SQLExecute(hstmtUpdTeller);
                } while(SQL_STILL_EXECUTING == rc);
            if(SQL_SUCCESS != rc)
                vShowErrors(lpBench->hwndMain, NULL, NULL,
                    hstmtUpdTeller);
            }

        // Update branch
        if (RC_SUCCESSFUL(rc)) {
            do {
                rc = SQLExecute(hstmtUpdBranch);
                } while(SQL_STILL_EXECUTING == rc);
            if(SQL_SUCCESS != rc)
                vShowErrors(lpBench->hwndMain, NULL, NULL,
                    hstmtUpdBranch);
            }

        // Insert into history table
        if (RC_SUCCESSFUL(rc)) {
            do {
                rc = SQLExecute(hstmtInsHist);
                } while(SQL_STILL_EXECUTING == rc);
            if(SQL_SUCCESS != rc)
                vShowErrors(lpBench->hwndMain, NULL, NULL,
                    hstmtInsHist);
            }
        if (SQL_SUCCESS != rc)
            fDone = TRUE;
        else
            fDone = !fExecuteQuery(lpBench, TRUE);
        }   // Prepare/Execute w/params

// For SQLExecDirect with SQL text method,
// build SQL string with all values
//
else {
    SetWorkingItem(
        "Executing SQL text with no parameters");

    if(!(fRtn = fExecuteTrans(lpBench, lpBench->nTrnCnt,
        nAcctNum, nTellerNum,
        nBranchNum, &dBalance, dDelta)))
        fDone = TRUE;
}
```

The stored procedure method calls the *fExecuteSprocCall* function, which calls *SQLExecute* on the main hstmt, which contains the call to the stored procedure.

The Prepare/Execute with parameters method is handled inline. Notice that each SQL statement has its own hstmt. This is necessary because the bound parameters are different for each statement. In each case, the statement is executed by simply calling *SQLExecute.*

The *SQLExecDirect* with SQL text method calls the *fExecuteTrans* function, which calls *sprintf* with the input values for each statement and executes each statement with *SQLExecDirect.*

After execution, the transaction is ended using *SQLTransact.* If an error occurred, the transaction is rolled back; otherwise it is committed. The *fUseCommit* flag is checked and *SQLTransact* is executed only if the user selected the option specifying that transactions should be used:

```
// Commit the transaction based on success
// Note: For stored procedure method this has no effect;
// the commit happens in the sproc
if(lpBench->fUseCommit) {
    rc = SQLTransact(NULL, lpBench->hdbc,
        (UWORD)((fRtn) ? SQL_COMMIT : SQL_ROLLBACK));
    fRtn &= RC_SUCCESSFUL(rc);
    }
```

That's the end of the transaction, so the only thing left to do is to determine the time it took, compute some running statistics, and update the display, as shown in Figure 8-14.

```
// Get the end time and the elapsed time
//
time(&tTransEndTime);
dTransDiff = difftime(tTransEndTime, tTransStartTime);
lpBench->dDiffSum += dTransDiff;

// Track 1-second and 2-second transactions
//
if(dTransDiff <= 1)
    ++lpBench->nTrnCnt1Sec;
if(dTransDiff > 1 && dTransDiff <= 2)
    ++lpBench->nTrnCnt2Sec;
```

Figure 8-14.
The endgame of the fRunTrans *function.*

Figure 8-14. *continued*

```
// Get elapsed time now to see whether we should quit
//
time(&tCurTime);
dDiff = difftime(tCurTime, tStartTime);
// Every five transactions, see whether we need to cancel
//
if(0 == (lpBench->nTrnCnt % 5)) {
    char    szBuff[50];
    wsprintf(szBuff, "%ld transactions processed",
        lpBench->nTrnCnt);
    SetProgressText(szBuff);
    if(fCancel()) {
        fDone = TRUE;
        fRtn = TRUE;
        Printf(lpBench, "*** Cancelled ***\r\n");
    }
}
} // end main loop
```

When the loop terminates, the statistics are summarized, displayed, and written to the ODBCBNCH.CSV file.

Overall, the benchmark demonstrates how to use ODBC to do parameter and column binding, how to execute stored procedures, and how to work with asynchronous execution. BENCH can also be used to compare ODBC drivers in a very fair way.

8.2 The Table Copy Sample (TBLCPY)

In this example we tackle one of the more vexing problems that developers encounter when writing an interoperable database application with ODBC: copying the table definition and the data for a table from one data source to another while trying to match as closely as possible the semantics of the data types in the original table. This includes the way in which each data source handles Blobs, user-defined types, and other special data types such as currency types and auto-increment columns. It is not an easy problem to solve; TBLCPY comprises more than 5000 lines of C code!

Like BENCH, TBLCPY is a very useful utility in its own right, regardless of whether you ever look at or modify the source code. You can use TBLCPY as a general-purpose import/export utility between two data sources. If you find that you frequently use TBLCPY for one particular combination of data sources, you can build a separate version of TBLCPY that is tuned to get the best performance from each data source using specific SQL extensions or programming techniques. For instance, the example at the end of Chapter 7 demonstrated that using cursors and *SQLSetPos* is much faster than using *SQLPrepare* and *SQLExecute* with INSERT statements when copying data into tables using the desktop database drivers for applications such as Microsoft Access and FoxPro. As another example of performance-tuning for a specific data source, you could build a Microsoft SQL Server–specific version of TBLCPY that uses the Level 2 *SQLParamOptions* function available in the Microsoft SQL Server 6 driver to increase the speed of inserts into Microsoft SQL Server 6.

TBLCPY is written more in the style of the Chapter 7 examples than in the style of BENCH. That is, it doesn't register a window class and create a main window but instead uses a series of dialog boxes similar to the Wizards found in many Microsoft applications. Each dialog box prompts the user through one step of the table copying process, allowing the user to backtrack to a previous step at any time.

Let's first take a high-level programming overview of this utility. It uses the ODBC functions *SQLTables* and *SQLColumns* to enumerate the tables and columns for a data source. Once a table has been selected, TBLCPY uses the *SQLStatistics* function to enumerate the indexes that can be copied. Then *SQLGetTypeInfo* is used to determine the best fit between the data type information of the source table and that of the destination table. Finally the destination table and indexes are created, and the data is copied from the source to the destination using *SQLBindCol* to bind the columns of the source table and *SQLBindParameter* to bind parameters for the INSERT statement on the destination table. If large text or binary columns are involved, the Blob handling functions *SQLGetData* and *SQLPutData* are used to read and write the data in pieces.

8.2.1 Initialization and General Control Flow

TBLCPY has four major steps, each with an associated dialog box. The four steps are as follows:

1. Connect to the data source from which data will be copied, and select the table to copy.

2. Display and select the indexes to copy.

3. Connect to the data source to which data will be copied, and specify the table name.

4. Create the destination table and copy the data. This step actually includes several components, including a few more dialog boxes that show the actual type mapping used and, if you want, the SQL statements generated.

The control flow between each step of the Wizard is handled in the TBLCPY.C code. The necessary windows initialization code, including the *WinMain* entry point, is also handled in TBLCPY.C. An array of function pointers is used to store the entry points for each step of the Wizard. The declaration of the function pointer array and the code for *WinMain* is shown in Figure 8-15.

```
// Track functions used for steps in the Wizard
//
STEPPROC procs[] = {
    fDoStep1,
    fDoStep2,
    fDoStep3,
    fDoStep4
    };
    ⋮
int WINAPI WinMain (HINSTANCE hInstance,
                    HINSTANCE hPrevInstance,
                    LPSTR     lpszCmdLine,
                    int       nCmdShow)
{
int nReturn;
    if (Init(hInstance, hPrevInstance, lpszCmdLine, nCmdShow)) {
        nReturn = DoMain(hInstance);
        Cleanup();
        }
    return nReturn;
}
```

Figure 8-15.
The function pointer array declaration and WinMain *code for TBLCPY.*

The *Init* function (not shown) allocates the environment handle with *SQLAllocEnv* and assigns the resulting *henv* to a global structure, *gcpInfo*. The *gcpInfo* structure is used to pass around the ODBC handles and several other settings throughout the program. Following the call to *Init*, the *DoMain* function is called. *DoMain* manages the flow of control between each dialog box. The *DoMain* function is shown in Figure 8-16 on the following page.

```
int  DoMain(HANDLE hInstance)
{
    int         iDlg;
    HWND        hwnd = NULL;

    Ctl3dRegister(hInstance);
    Ctl3dAutoSubclass(hInstance);

    // Call each step. The return value will be either the next
    // step to run or END_WIZARD when we are all done.
    //
    iDlg = DO_STEP1;
    while(END_WIZARD != iDlg)
        iDlg = (*procs[iDlg])(hwnd, hInst, &gcpInfo);

    Ctl3dUnregister(hInstance);

    return TRUE;
}
```

Figure 8-16.
The DoMain *function of TBLCPY.*

The calls to *Ctl3dRegister* and *Ctl3dAutoSubclass* give the dialog boxes three-dimensional visual effects. The *while* loop that controls the Wizard uses an indirect function call for each element in the *proc* array. The *proc* array elements contain the function pointers to *fDoStep1, fDoStep2, fDoStep3,* and *fDoStep4.* These functions always return the step of the Wizard to execute next (either the next step or the previous step). If the user cancels or finishes, the function returns the value END_WIZARD, which terminates the loop. The *Ctl3dUnregister* function performs the necessary cleanup for the 3-D visual controls, and that ends the program.

Let's look at the ODBC features used in each step of TBLCPY.

8.2.2 Step 1: Connect and Display the Table List

In step 1 we call *SQLDriverConnect* to connect to the desired data source. Then we use the *SQLTables* function to obtain the list of tables from which we can copy.

The code for step 1 of TBLCPY is in STEP1.C and begins with the *fDoStep1* function, which simply launches the dialog box for step 1. The real work happens in the window procedure (*Step1WndProc*) used by the dialog box. All the steps are structured in this way. Figure 8-17 shows the code for *fDoStep1.* The dialog box for step 1 is shown in Figure 8-18.

```
int fDoStep1(
    HWND hwnd,                  // Parent window handle
    HINSTANCE hInst,            // Instance handle that owns dialog box
    lpCOPYINFO pCopyInfo        // Copy information
    )
{
    DLGPROC dlgproc;
    int         nRtn=END_WIZARD;

    dlgproc = MakeProcInstance((FARPROC)Step1WndProc, hInst);
    switch(DialogBoxParam(hInst, MAKEINTRESOURCE(IDD_FROM_INFO),
                hwnd, dlgproc, (LPARAM)pCopyInfo)) {
        case IDOK:
            nRtn = DO_STEP2;
            break;

        case IDCANCEL:
            break;

        default:
            assert(0);
            break;
    }

    FreeProcInstance((FARPROC) dlgproc);

    return nRtn;
}
```

Figure 8-17.
The fDoStep1 *code in STEP1.C.*

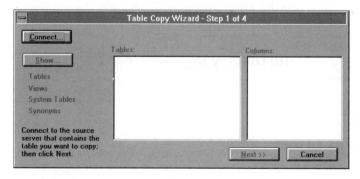

Figure 8-18.
*The dialog box used for connecting to the input data source in step 1
of TBLCPY.*

When the Connect button is clicked, the function *fDoFromConnect* is called in the WM_COMMAND case of the main message switch statement in *Step1WndProc*. The *fDoFromConnect* function handles the connection process for the data source from which we'll be copying the table. The connection process includes actually making the connection and making a number of calls to *SQLGetInfo* to get information that we'll need later. Figure 8-19 shows the code for *fDoFromConnect*.

```
BOOL fDoFromConnect(
    HWND hDlg,                              // Parent window handle
    lpCOPYINFO pCopyInfo                    // Copy struct information
    )
{
    assert(NULL!=pCopyInfo && NULL!=hDlg);

    if(fDoConnect(hDlg, pCopyInfo->henv,
                    pCopyInfo->hFromConn, &pCopyInfo->hFromConn,
                    pCopyInfo->szFromConn,
                    &pCopyInfo->hFromStmt)) {
        // Do some cleanup
        //
        vMaskKeyword(pCopyInfo->szFromConn, "PWD", '*');
        SQLGetInfo(pCopyInfo->hFromConn,
                    SQL_DATA_SOURCE_NAME,
                    pCopyInfo->szFromDsn,
                    sizeof(pCopyInfo->szFromDsn),
                    NULL);
        SQLGetInfo(pCopyInfo->hFromConn,
                    SQL_IDENTIFIER_QUOTE_CHAR,
                    pCopyInfo->szFromIDQuote,
                    sizeof(pCopyInfo->szFromIDQuote),
                    NULL);
        *pCopyInfo->szFromDBMS = '\0';
        SQLGetInfo(pCopyInfo->hFromConn,
                    SQL_DBMS_NAME,
                    pCopyInfo->szFromDBMS,
                    sizeof(pCopyInfo->szFromDBMS),
                    NULL);
```

Figure 8-19.
The fDoFromConnect *code in step 1.C.*

Figure 8-19. *continued*

```
        pCopyInfo->ulGetDataExt = 0L;
        SQLGetInfo(pCopyInfo->hFromConn,
                    SQL_GETDATA_EXTENSIONS,
                    &pCopyInfo->ulGetDataExt,
                    sizeof(pCopyInfo->ulGetDataExt),
                    NULL);

        // Reset all strings that will affect processing of this
        // dialog box. This doesn't mean every member for step 1.
        //
        *pCopyInfo->szFromTable = '\0';
        *pCopyInfo->szColList = '\0';

        vResetIndexInfo(pCopyInfo);

        return TRUE;
        }

    return FALSE;
    }
```

The *fDoConnect* function in COMMON.C takes care of the actual connection. Yes, this is the same *fDoConnect* function we used in BENCH. As demonstrated previously, *fDoConnect* uses the ODBC function *SQLDriverConnect* to manage the user interface for the connection and also allocates a statement handle, which it returns in the last argument (which in this case would be *pCopyInfo->hFromStmt*).

The output connection string from *SQLDriverConnect* is returned in *pCopyInfo->szFromConn*. Because we are going to display the string on the screen, we need to ensure that the password is not displayed if we connect to a data source that has a security system. The call to *vMaskKeyword* (also located in COMMON.C) will replace each character of any password entered with an asterisk (*). You might wonder why the driver returns the password in the connection string at all. With a completed connection string, if we need to make a second connection to the same data source or merely want to retry a connection after a network failure, we can do so "under the covers" without having to bother the user to enter the information again. The second connection attempt would be made by calling *SQLDriverConnect* again, but this time the connection string would be supplied on input as the *szConnStrIn* argument. If the *fDriverComplete* argument in the *SQLDriverConnect* function is set to SQL_DRIVER_COMPLETE, the connection would happen as before, but without user intervention. We don't have an auto-reconnect feature in TBLCPY, but I thought it was worth explaining why passwords are returned.

Following the call to *vMaskKeyword*, several calls are made to *SQLGetInfo*. SQL_DATA_SOURCE_NAME and SQL_DBMS_NAME are used only for display purposes, but it would be useful to take some time to discuss SQL_IDENTIFIER_QUOTE_CHAR and SQL_GETDATA_EXTENSIONS.

SQL_IDENTIFIER_QUOTE_CHAR is obtained from the driver so that we can use *delimited identifiers*. Delimited identifiers are used by the SQL-92 standard (and by ODBC) to allow SQL identifiers (for example, table names, column names, and index names) to contain characters that are not otherwise legal as part of an identifier. For example, no DBMS allows blanks to be embedded in a nondelimited column name, so you could never create a table in SQL with the following syntax:

```
CREATE TABLE THIS_WILL_NOT_WORK (First Name VARCHAR(25))
```

However, if you use a delimited identifier, the column name First Name is not a problem:

```
CREATE TABLE THIS_WILL_WORK ("First Name" VARCHAR(25))
```

The double quotation mark is used to delimit the identifier First Name. But, as you might guess, not all DBMSs use the *same* character to delimit their identifiers! Although SQL-92 specifies that the double quotation mark is the delimiter, some products use that character for other purposes and so return another character for the identifier delimiter. A popular delimiter character is the grave accent, also known as the back quote (`). The call to *SQLGetInfo*, shown here, returns the character we'll use to enclose all identifiers in our SQL statements so that tables and columns containing special characters such as blanks will still work.

```
SQLGetInfo(pCopyInfo->hFromConn,
           SQL_IDENTIFIER_QUOTE_CHAR,
           pCopyInfo->szFromIDQuote,
           sizeof(pCopyInfo->szFromIDQuote),
           NULL);
```

The second interesting call to *SQLGetInfo* is the one that retrieves SQL_GETDATA_EXTENSIONS, which returns information about the ways that *SQLGetData* can be used to provide more functionality than is required by the ODBC specification, such as the order in which *SQLGetData* can access column information in a results set. For example, some drivers support calling *SQLGetData* for any column in any order, whereas others support retrieving columns only in ascending order. This is because some drivers buffer an entire row and keep it until the next row is fetched, while others do no buffering in the driver at all, so after the data has been received from the DBMS and placed into the application's buffers, the driver has no way to return it again if the application were to ask for it. The latter functionality is the only required behavior for *SQLGetData*, but because several drivers and applications support extensions, this *SQLGetInfo* option comes in handy. Other *SQLGetData* extensions specify the operations that can be done when binding with *SQLBindCol* is used with *SQLGetData*.

In our case, we'll be checking for the SQL_GD_ANY_ORDER extension to determine the most efficient and functional way to handle the transfer of Blob data from one data source to another. If *SQLGetData* can be called only in ascending column order, the SELECT list will have to be rearranged to put all the Blob columns at the end so that the *SQLGetData/SQLPutData* loop can be called in the proper sequence.

After we have connected and have retrieved the *SQLGetInfo* settings just described, control returns to *Step1WndProc*, and, if the connection was successful, the function *vResetTableList* is called. In *vResetTableList* the ODBC function *SQLTables* is used to retrieve the list of tables from the data source. *SQLTables* can return not only base tables but also views, system tables, and synonyms. The table types to return are specified in the *szTableType* argument to *SQLTables*. In our case, the user can select the desired table types by clicking the Show button in the step 1 dialog box. The default is to retrieve only base tables and views.

SQLTables typically launches a query against the system catalog of the DBMS. The results are processed like any query, so after the call to *SQLTables*, the typical processing loop for a cursor is used. The result columns from *SQLTables* are shown and explained in the table on the following page.

Column Name	Data Type	Comments
TABLE_QUALIFIER	VARCHAR(128)	Table qualifier identifier. This value is NULL if table qualifiers are not applicable to the data source. If a driver supports qualifiers for some tables but not for others, as could be the case when the driver retrieves data from different DBMSs, it returns an empty string ("") for those tables that do not have qualifiers.
TABLE_OWNER	VARCHAR(128)	Table owner identifier. This value is NULL if table owners are not applicable to the data source. If a driver supports owners for some tables but not for others, as could be the case when the driver retrieves data from different DBMSs, it returns an empty string ("") for those tables that do not have owners.
TABLE_NAME	VARCHAR(128)	Table identifier.
TABLE_TYPE	VARCHAR(128)	Table type identifier. This value is one of the following: TABLE, VIEW, SYSTEM TABLE, ALIAS, GLOBAL TEMPORARY, LOCAL TEMPORARY, SYNONYM, or a data source–specific type identifier.
REMARKS	VARCHAR(254)	A description of the table.

In our example we use *SQLBindCol* to get only the table owner name and the table name. Figure 8-20 shows the relevant code from *vResetTableList*.

```
    vGetTypes(szTypes, pCopyInfo);
    rc = SQLTables(pCopyInfo->hFromStmt,
                NULL, 0,
                NULL, 0,
                NULL, 0,
                (UCHAR FAR *)szTypes, SQL_NTS);
    if(RC_SUCCESSFUL(rc)) {
        if(SQL_SUCCESS_WITH_INFO == rc)
            vShowErrors(hwndTblList, NULL, NULL,
                pCopyInfo->hFromStmt);

        // Bind the user and table name for the list
        //
        fRtn = fSQLBindCol(hwndTblList, pCopyInfo->hFromStmt,
                        2, SQL_C_CHAR,
                        szUser, sizeof(szUser), &cbUser);
        fRtn &= fSQLBindCol(hwndTblList, pCopyInfo->hFromStmt,
                        3, SQL_C_CHAR,
                        szTable, sizeof(szTable), &cbTbl);
        if(!fRtn)
            goto clean_up;

        // Fetch all tables
        //
        rc = SQLFetch(pCopyInfo->hFromStmt);
        while(RC_SUCCESSFUL(rc)) {
            // Show users any info messages received
            //
            if(SQL_SUCCESS_WITH_INFO == rc)
                vShowErrors(hwndTblList, NULL, NULL,
                    pCopyInfo->hFromStmt);
        // If there is a user, format buffer in a familiar way
        //
        if((SQL_NULL_DATA != cbUser) && (*szUser)) {
            wsprintf(szFmtBuff, "%s.%s",
                (LPCSTR)szUser,
                (LPCSTR)szTable);
            nRow = (WPARAM)SendMessage(hwndTblList, LB_ADDSTRING,
                        0, (LPARAM)szFmtBuff);
            dwTableLoc = lstrlen(szUser) + 1;
            }
```

Figure 8-20. *(continued)*

The vResetTableList *code in step 1.C.*

Figure 8-20. *continued*

```
    else {
        nRow = (WPARAM)SendMessage(hwndTblList, LB_ADDSTRING,
                            0, (LPARAM)szTable);
        dwTableLoc = 0;
        }
    ⋮

    // Fetch next table
    //
    rc = SQLFetch(pCopyInfo->hFromStmt);
    }
}
```

Once the table names are displayed, the user can choose the Show button to specify the table types he or she wants. When a table name is selected from the list box, the column names for that table are retrieved. The step 1 dialog box, as it appears after the table name has been selected, is shown in Figure 8-21. Here we use *SQLColumns* much like we did *SQLTables*. The *SQLColumns* function is called from the *vResetColInfo* function that is invoked when the user selects a table name from the list box. Figure 8-22 shows the relevant code in *vResetColInfo*.

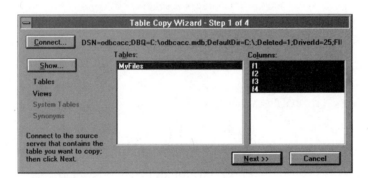

Figure 8-21.
The step 1 dialog box as it appears after table selection.

The results set from *SQLColumns* contains a lot of information about a column, including its data type, length, nullability, and so forth. Here we are interested only in the fourth column in the results set, the column name, so that is the only column specified in *SQLBindCol*.

```
       rc = SQLColumns(pCopyInfo->hFromStmt,
               NULL, 0,
               NULL, 0,
               (UCHAR FAR *)pCopyInfo->szFromTable, SQL_NTS,
               NULL, 0);
   if(RC_SUCCESSFUL(rc)) {
       if(SQL_SUCCESS_WITH_INFO == rc)
           vShowErrors(hwndColList, NULL, NULL,
               pCopyInfo->hFromStmt);

       // Bind the table name for the list
       //
       rc = SQLBindCol(pCopyInfo->hFromStmt, 4, SQL_C_CHAR,
                       szColumn, sizeof(szColumn), NULL);
       if(RC_NOTSUCCESSFUL(rc)) {
           vShowErrors(hwndColList, NULL, NULL,
               pCopyInfo->hFromStmt);
           goto clean_up;
           }

       // Fetch all the columns
       //
       rc = SQLFetch(pCopyInfo->hFromStmt);
       while(RC_SUCCESSFUL(rc)) {
           if(SQL_SUCCESS_WITH_INFO == rc)
               vShowErrors(hwndColList, NULL, NULL,
                   pCopyInfo->hFromStmt);
           SendMessage(hwndColList, LB_ADDSTRING,
                       0, (LPARAM)szColumn);
           rc = SQLFetch(pCopyInfo->hFromStmt);
           }
       }
```

Figure 8-22.
The vResetColInfo *code.*

When all the column names have been retrieved and displayed in the
list box, every column in the list box is selected by default so that all columns
in the table will be copied. However, the user can choose to copy only a few
columns by clicking on only those columns of interest. A fair amount of code
in STEP1.C allows the user to see the effects of selecting a different table type
with the Show button (which requires a new call to *SQLTables* to display the
correct table list) and selecting a different table in the Tables list box (which

requires a new call to *SQLColumns* to display the correct columns in the Columns list box). I've found that the step 1 dialog box is a handy tool for viewing the tables in a particular data source and the columns in each table. You simply click the table name to see the column names.

That's it for step 1. We've made the connection to the data source from which we'll copy the table, selected the table to copy, and selected the columns to copy within the table. Now it's time for step 2.

8.2.3 Step 2: Retrieve and Display Indexes

In step 2 we retrieve and display all indexes that are defined on the table that was selected in step 1. The dialog box displayed in step 2 is shown in Figure 8-23.

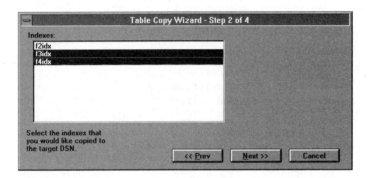

Figure 8-23.
The dialog box for selecting indexes to copy in step 2 of TBLCPY.

All the code for step 2 is contained in—you guessed it—STEP2.C. Just as *fDoStep1* did for step 1, the *fDoStep2* function creates the step 2 dialog box, and the real action takes place in *Step2WinProc*. The ODBC function used to obtain index information is another catalog function that operates like *SQLTables* and *SQLColumns*: *SQLStatistics*. The *SQLStatistics* function is called from *vResetIndexList* in STEP2.C. Figure 8-24 shows the relevant code from *vResetIndexList*.

```
rc = SQLStatistics(pCopyInfo->hFromStmt,
        NULL, 0,
        NULL, 0,
        (UCHAR FAR *)pCopyInfo->szFromTable, SQL_NTS,
        SQL_INDEX_ALL, SQL_ENSURE);
```

Figure 8-24.
The vResetIndexList *code from STEP2.C.*

Figure 8-24. *continued*

```
if(RC_SUCCESSFUL(rc)) {
    if(SQL_SUCCESS_WITH_INFO == rc)
        vShowErrors(hwndDexList, NULL, NULL,
            pCopyInfo->hFromStmt);

    // Bind the index information
    //
    fRtn = fSQLBindCol(hwndDexList, pCopyInfo->hFromStmt, 3,
        SQL_C_CHAR, szTable, sizeof(szTable), &cbWhoCares);
    fRtn &= fSQLBindCol(hwndDexList, pCopyInfo->hFromStmt, 4,
        SQL_C_SHORT, &fNonUnique, sizeof(fNonUnique), &cbUnique);
    fRtn &= fSQLBindCol(hwndDexList, pCopyInfo->hFromStmt, 6,
        SQL_C_CHAR, szIndex, sizeof(szIndex), &cbIndex);
    fRtn &= fSQLBindCol(hwndDexList, pCopyInfo->hFromStmt, 7,
        SQL_C_SHORT, &iType, sizeof(iType), &cbWhoCares);
    fRtn &= fSQLBindCol(hwndDexList, pCopyInfo->hFromStmt, 8,
        SQL_C_SHORT, &iColDex, sizeof(iColDex), &cbWhoCares);
    fRtn &= fSQLBindCol(hwndDexList, pCopyInfo->hFromStmt, 9,
        SQL_C_CHAR, szCol, sizeof(szCol), &cbWhoCares);
    fRtn &= fSQLBindCol(hwndDexList, pCopyInfo->hFromStmt, 10,
        SQL_C_CHAR, szCollation, sizeof(szCollation),
        &cbCollation);

    if(fRtn) {
        // Fetch all the index information
        //
        rc = SQLFetch(pCopyInfo->hFromStmt);
        while(RC_SUCCESSFUL(rc)) {
            if(SQL_SUCCESS_WITH_INFO == rc)
                vShowErrors(hwndDexList, NULL, NULL,
                    pCopyInfo->hFromStmt);

            // We care only about indexes, so
            // ignore table statistics
            //
            if(SQL_TABLE_STAT != iType) {
                if(SQL_NULL_DATA == cbIndex)
                    *szIndex = '\0';

                // Add this column information to the list
                //
                if(1 == iColDex)
                    ++iDex;
                fAscending = (SQL_NULL_DATA == cbCollation) ||
                            ('A' == *szCollation);
```

(continued)

Figure 8-24. *continued*

```
            if(!fAddIndexInfo(hwndDexList,
                        iDex, &pCopyInfo->pIndexInfo,
                        (FALSE==fNonUnique &&
                            SQL_NULL_DATA!=cbUnique),
                        szIndex,
                        szTable,
                        iColDex, szCol,
                        fAscending))
            goto clean_up;

        // New indexes are added to the list box
        //
        if(1 == iColDex) {
            SendMessage(hwndDexList, LB_ADDSTRING,
                        0, (LPARAM)szIndex);
            ++pCopyInfo->iIndexes;
            }
        }

        rc = SQLFetch(pCopyInfo->hFromStmt);
        }
    }
}
```

A lot of information is returned from *SQLStatistics* (13 columns in all), and we're going to use about half of it (7 columns). Here is the description of each column returned from *SQLStatistics*, as given in the *Microsoft ODBC 2.0 Programmer's Reference*:

Column Name	Data Type	Comments
TABLE_QUALIFIER	VARCHAR(128)	Table qualifier identifier of the table to which the statistic or index applies. This value is NULL if table qualifiers are not applicable to the data source. If a driver supports qualifiers for some tables but not for others, as could be the case when the driver retrieves data from different DBMSs, it returns an empty string ("") for those tables that do not have qualifiers.

(continued)

continued

Column Name	Data Type	Comments
TABLE_OWNER	VARCHAR(128)	Table owner identifier of the table to which the statistic or index applies. This value is NULL if table owners are not applicable to the data source. If a driver supports owners for some tables but not for others, as could be the case when the driver retrieves data from different DBMSs, it returns an empty string ("") for those tables that do not have owners.
TABLE_NAME	VARCHAR(128) not NULL	Table identifier of the table to which the statistic or index applies.
NON_UNIQUE	SMALLINT	Value that indicates whether the index prohibits duplicate values. This value is TRUE if the index values can be nonunique and FALSE if the index values must be unique. NULL is returned if TYPE is SQL_TABLE_STAT.
INDEX_QUALIFIER	VARCHAR(128)	Identifier used to qualify the index name in a DROP INDEX statement. NULL is returned if an index qualifier is not supported by the data source or if TYPE is SQL_TABLE_STAT. If a non-NULL value is returned in this column, that value must be used to qualify the index name in a DROP INDEX statement; if NULL is returned, the TABLE_OWNER name should be used to qualify the index name in the statement.
INDEX_NAME	VARCHAR(128)	Index identifier. If TYPE is SQL_TABLE_STAT, NULL is returned.

(continued)

continued

Column Name	Data Type	Comments
TYPE	SMALLINT not NULL	Type of information being returned. SQL_TABLE_STAT indicates a statistic for the table. SQL_INDEX_CLUSTERED indicates a clustered index. SQL_INDEX_HASHED indicates a hashed index. SQL_INDEX_OTHER indicates another, data source–specific, type of index.
SEQ_IN_INDEX	SMALLINT	Column sequence number in index (starting with 1). If TYPE is SQL_TABLE_STAT, NULL is returned.
COLUMN_NAME	VARCHAR(128)	Column identifier. If the column is based on an expression, such as SALARY + BENEFITS, the expression is returned; if the expression cannot be determined, an empty string is returned. If the index is a filtered index, each column in the filter condition is returned; this may require more than one row. NULL is returned if TYPE is SQL_TABLE_STAT.
COLLATION	CHAR(1)	Sort sequence for the column. *A* specifies ascending; *D* specifies descending; NULL is returned if column sort sequence is not supported by the data source or if TYPE is SQL_TABLE_STAT.
CARDINALITY	INTEGER	Cardinality of the table or index. This value is the number of rows in the table if TYPE is SQL_TABLE_STAT; it is the number of unique values in the index if TYPE is not SQL_TABLE_STAT; NULL is returned if the value is not available from the data source.

(continued)

continued

Column Name	Data Type	Comments
PAGES	INTEGER	Number of pages used to store the index or table. This value is the number of pages for the table if TYPE is SQL_TABLE_STAT, and it is the number of pages for the index if TYPE is not SQL_TABLE_STAT. NULL is returned if the value is not available from the data source or if the number of pages is not applicable to the data source.
FILTER_CONDITION	VARCHAR(128)	If the index is a filtered index, this is the filter condition, such as SALARY > 30000. If the filter condition cannot be determined, this is an empty string. This value is NULL if the index is not a filtered index, if it cannot be determined whether the index is a filtered index, or if TYPE is SQL_TABLE_STAT.

The information we retrieve in the columns of the results set from *SQLStatistics* will be used to try to create indexes on the table to which we're copying that have the same characteristics as the original indexes. The most important characteristics are whether the index enforces unique values (as indicated in the NON_UNIQUE column), the type of index (clustered or hashed, as indicated in the TYPE column), and whether the index is collated in ascending or descending order (as indicated in the COLLATION column).

As with *SQLTables* and *SQLColumns*, first we call the function and then we bind the columns and use *SQLFetch* to retrieve the results. *SQLStatistics* returns information about both base tables and indexes. We're interested only in information about indexes, so in the fetch loop you'll see the check that excludes table information by checking the *iType* bound column from the results set:

```
if(SQL_TABLE_STAT != iType) {
```

We'll call *fAddIndexInfo* to add each index to the global data structure, and then we'll add only the index names to the list box in step 2. The user can choose to create any set of indexes (or none at all) on the table that will be created in the output data source.

8.2.4 Step 3: Connect and Specify Copy Options

In step 3 (STEP3.C) we go through another connection sequence to select the output data source. Figure 8-25 shows the step 3 dialog box.

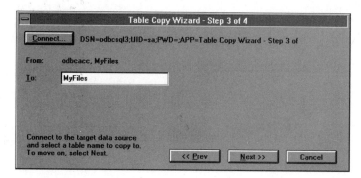

Figure 8-25.
The appearance of the step 3 dialog box after connecting to the output data source.

This sequence is very similar to what happened in step 1: click the Connect button, select the desired destination data source, and click OK. In the code, we check a few more *SQLGetInfo* items. The items that are checked are listed here:

- **SQL_DATA_SOURCE_READ_ONLY**   If the driver reports that the data source is read-only, we will not be able to create the table. A message box is displayed that prompts the user to select a different data source if this occurs.

- **SQL_SPECIAL_CHARACTERS**   If the data source allows non-alphanumeric characters in identifiers, we'll need to translate any characters that are not legal in the input table, column, and index names when creating the new objects in the output data source. The SQL_SPECIAL_CHARACTERS option returns a string of the nonalphanumeric characters that are valid to use in identifiers.

- **SQL_NEED_LONG_DATA_LEN** Some data sources require that the length of Blob column data be sent prior to the actual data. If this is the case, we'll need to handle that during the copy process. The SQL_NEED_LONG_DATA_LEN option returns *Y* (yes) if the length is needed and *N* (no) if the data can be streamed to the data source without specifying the length up front.

- **SQL_MAX_COLUMN_NAME_LEN** We will need to be sure that the column names from the input table don't exceed the maximum length that is allowed in the output table. The option SQL_MAX_COLUMN_NAME_LEN returns an integer that indicates the maximum number of characters allowed for a column in the output data source.

That's it for step 3. At this point we have established connections to the input and output data sources; we have retrieved the table, column, and index information from the input table; and we have retrieved all the *SQLGetInfo* data we need for the final step.

8.2.5 Step 4: Create the Table and Copy the Data

Step 4 presents one more dialog box that prompts the user to set the final output options before the copy process is actually begun. The copy process itself comprises many smaller steps. Figure 8-26 shows the step 4 dialog box.

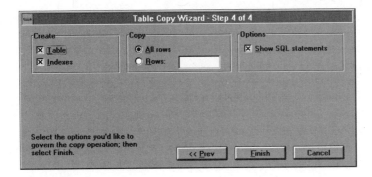

Figure 8-26.
The dialog box for selecting output options in step 4 of TBLCPY.

In this dialog box the user can specify whether indexes should be created, whether the number of rows copied should be limited, and whether the SQL statements should be displayed as they are generated.

When the Finish button is clicked in the dialog box, the options are copied into the *pCopyInfo* data structure. Now we get to the real heart of TBLCPY, beginning with the *nCopyTable* function, located in COPY.C.

The *nCopyTable* function is a three-step, high-level control routine and is itself in Wizard format. The Wizard guides you through:

1. Performing the SELECT on the input table and obtaining all the necessary metadata on each column

2. Determining from the input table and column information the mapping to the output table and column information, and executing the CREATE TABLE and CREATE INDEX statements

3. Copying the data, including special handling of Blob data

Figure 8-27 presents the code for *nCopyTable* that shows the overall flow of control.

```
int nCopyTable(
    lpCOPYINFO pCopyInfo,           // Copy information
    UDWORD * pnRecords              // Copied records
    )
{
    HWND      hwnd=NULL;            // We don't really have one
    int       nRtn=END_WIZARD;     // Assume success
    assert(pCopyInfo);

    // Get descriptions of each column
    //
    if(END_WIZARD == (nRtn = nDescInfo(hwnd, pCopyInfo))) {
        // Create the table and indexes if required
        //
        if(END_WIZARD == (nRtn = nCreateSchema(hwnd, pCopyInfo))) {
            // Finally, copy all the data
            //
            nRtn = nCopyData(hwnd, pCopyInfo, pnRecords);
            }
        }

    return nRtn;
}
```

Figure 8-27.
The flow of control in nCopyTable.

8.2.5.1 Getting the Metadata from the Input Table

The *nDescInfo* function (located in TYPEMAP.C) builds a SELECT statement using the selected columns from the input table, displays the statement to the user if the user chose that option in the step 4 dialog box, executes the statement with *SQLExecDirect*, and retrieves the metadata using a combination of *SQLDescribeCol* and *SQLColAttributes*. Figure 8-28 shows the code for *nDescInfo*.

```
int nDescInfo(
    HWND hwnd,                      // Window handle for errors
    lpCOPYINFO pCopyInfo            // Copy information
    )
{
    int         nRtn=1;             // Assume we'll fail; allow reselect
    RETCODE     rc;                 // Return code from ODBC functions
    lpCOLDESC   pColInfo;           // Data type output for each column
    int         idex;              // Index for columns
    LPCSTR      pszCol;             // Pointer for column list
    LPSTR       pszSqlStmt;         // Base address from SELECT statement
    LPSTR       pszStr;             // Moving pointer for efficiency

    assert(pCopyInfo);

    // Format a SELECT statement by listing all columns
    // the user chose to copy
    //
    pszSqlStmt = (LPSTR)malloc(MAX_STMT);
    if(!pszSqlStmt) {
        vOutOfMemory(hwnd);
        goto clean_up;
        }

    // Create the column list first in standard order
    //
    lstrcpy(pszSqlStmt, "SELECT ");
    pszStr = pszSqlStmt + lstrlen(pszSqlStmt);
    pszCol = pCopyInfo->szColList;
    while(*pszCol) {
        GetQuotedID(pszStr,
            pCopyInfo->szFromIDQuote, (LPSTR)pszCol);
        pszCol += lstrlen(pszCol) + 1;
        if(*pszCol != '\0')
            lstrcat(pszStr, ", ");
        pszStr += lstrlen(pszStr);
        }
```

Figure 8-28. *(continued)*
The nDescInfo *code.*

357

Figure 8-28. *continued*

```
// Add the table name with correct quoting
//
lstrcat(pszStr, " FROM ");
pszStr += lstrlen(pszStr);
GetQuotedID(pszStr, pCopyInfo->szFromIDQuote,
    pCopyInfo->szFromTable);

// Finally, add a bogus WHERE clause. Because we want this
// statement to get only metadata, we'll try to tell the
// server not to actually get rows.
//
lstrcat(pszStr, " WHERE 0 = 1");

// If user wants to see the statement, show it
//
if(pCopyInfo->fDisplaySql)
    iClipMessageBox(hwnd, MB_OK | MB_ICONINFORMATION,
            sz_SHOW_SQL, pszSqlStmt);

// Execute the query and retrieve the results
//
rc = SQLExecDirect(pCopyInfo->hFromStmt, pszSqlStmt, SQL_NTS);
if(RC_SUCCESSFUL(rc)) {
    rc = SQLNumResultCols(
        pCopyInfo->hFromStmt, &pCopyInfo->iCols);
    if(RC_SUCCESSFUL(rc)) {
        // Allocate memory for the descriptions of each column
        //
        pCopyInfo->pColumns =
            (lpCOLDESC)GlobalAllocPtr(GHND,
            pCopyInfo->iCols * sizeof(COLDESC));
        if(!pCopyInfo->pColumns) {
            vOutOfMemory(hwnd);
            return nRtn;
            }
        memset(pCopyInfo->pColumns, 0,
            (pCopyInfo->iCols * sizeof(COLDESC)));

        // For each column, get the metadata and store it
        //
        for(idex = 0 ;  idex < pCopyInfo->iCols;  idex++) {
            pColInfo = &pCopyInfo->pColumns[idex];
            rc = SQLDescribeCol(pCopyInfo->hFromStmt,
                        (UWORD)(idex + 1),
                        NULL, 0, NULL,
                        &pColInfo->fSqlType,
```

Figure 8-28. *continued*

```
                                &pColInfo->cbPrecision,
                                &pColInfo->ibScale,
                                &pColInfo->fNullable);
            if(RC_NOTSUCCESSFUL(rc))
                goto clean_up;

            // Get the type of the column for mapping
            //
            rc = SQLColAttributes(pCopyInfo->hFromStmt,
                        (UWORD)(idex + 1),
                        SQL_COLUMN_TYPE_NAME,
                        &pColInfo->szFromType,
                        sizeof(pColInfo->szFromType),
                        NULL,
                        NULL);
            if(RC_NOTSUCCESSFUL(rc))
                goto clean_up;

            // Get the display size in case this column gets
            // converted to char
            //
            rc = SQLColAttributes(pCopyInfo->hFromStmt,
                        (UWORD)(idex + 1),
                        SQL_COLUMN_DISPLAY_SIZE,
                        NULL,
                        sizeof(pColInfo->cbDspSize),
                        NULL,
                        &pColInfo->cbDspSize);
            if(RC_NOTSUCCESSFUL(rc))
                goto clean_up;

            // If this is a money column, we'll try to find a
            // money column
            //
            rc = SQLColAttributes(pCopyInfo->hFromStmt,
                        (UWORD)(idex + 1),
                        SQL_COLUMN_MONEY,
                        NULL,
                        sizeof(pColInfo->fIsMoney),
                        NULL,
                        &pColInfo->fIsMoney);
            if(RC_NOTSUCCESSFUL(rc))
                goto clean_up;
        }
    nRtn = END_WIZARD;
    }
}
```

(continued)

Figure 8-28. *continued*

```
    // Clean up the statement handle
    //
clean_up:
    if(pszSqlStmt)
        free(pszSqlStmt);
    if(RC_NOTSUCCESSFUL(rc))
        vShowErrors(hwnd, NULL, NULL, pCopyInfo->hFromStmt);
    SQLFreeStmt(pCopyInfo->hFromStmt, SQL_CLOSE);
    SQLFreeStmt(pCopyInfo->hFromStmt, SQL_UNBIND);

    return nRtn;
}
```

The column list that was generated in step 1 for the input table is stored in *pColInfo->szColList*. The list uses null character delimiters to separate the column names, and an extra null byte is placed at the end. This setup allow us to step through the list with a pointer that is incremented by the string length of the current column name, as is done in the loop that builds the SELECT list. Here's the code that builds the SELECT list:

```
pszCol = pCopyInfo->szColList;
while(*pszCol) {
    GetQuotedID(pszStr, pCopyInfo->szFromIDQuote, (LPSTR)pszCol);
    pszCol += lstrlen(pszCol) + 1;
    if(*pszCol != '\0')
        lstrcat(pszStr, ", ");
    pszStr += lstrlen(pszStr);
    }
```

Note the call to the *GetQuotedID* function for the column and table names in the SELECT statement. This function uses the information we obtained about delimited identifiers, described in step 1, to determine the correct character to use to delimit each column name. The call to *GetQuotedID* is made again for the table name.

After the SQL string has been constructed using delimited identifiers, it is executed with *SQLExecDirect.* The standard metadata (column name, type, and length) is obtained with *SQLDescribeCol*, but we also need to know the type name, the display length, and whether any columns have a money or currency attribute to do the best fit possible when we map the actual data types to the output data source. For the latter metadata, we use *SQLColAttributes.*

You might be wondering why we didn't obtain all this information by calling *SQLColumns* instead of executing a SELECT statement with a bogus WHERE clause and processing the metadata. There are two reasons. First of all, the *SQLColumns* function does not return as much information. For example, *SQLColumns* does not return the display size of a column, which is available with *SQLColAttributes*. It should, but it doesn't. The second reason for not using *SQLColumns* is that the user might have selected only a few columns to copy, and *SQLColumns* only allows you to get either one column or all columns of a table. We need to keep track of which data type belongs in which column, so it is a lot easier to do the SELECT on just the columns we need rather than trying to shuffle the results from *SQLColumns* into the appropriate place in the *pCopyInfo->pColumns* array.

At this point we return to the high-level routine *nCopyTable*. Now we have most of the information we need to do the most gnarly part of TBLCPY: the data type mapping.

8.2.5.2 Mapping the Types and Creating the Output Table and Indexes

The next function called in *nCopyTable* is *nCreateSchema*, which controls the steps for mapping the types, creating the output table, and creating the output indexes, if any. The code for *nCreateSchema* is shown in Figure 8-29.

```
int nCreateSchema(
    HWND hwnd,                          // Window handle for errors
    lpCOPYINFO pCopyInfo                // Copy information
    )
{
    int         nRtn=END_WIZARD;        // Assume success
    assert(pCopyInfo);

    // First, map all the data types
    //
    if(END_WIZARD == (nRtn = nMapType(hwnd, pCopyInfo))) {
        // Show user the mapped data types
        //
        DspDataTypes(hwnd, hInst, pCopyInfo);

        // If all types are mapped correctly, create the table
        //
        if(pCopyInfo->fCopySchema)
            nRtn = nCreateTable(hwnd, pCopyInfo);

        // Finally, create the indexes (if desired)
        //
        if(END_WIZARD == nRtn && pCopyInfo->fCopyIndexes)
            nRtn = nCreateIndexes(hwnd, pCopyInfo);
    }

    return nRtn;
}
```

Figure 8-29.
The nCreateSchema *code.*

361

The data type mapping process consists of three functions, which are contained in the *nMapType* function in TYPEMAP.C. In *nMapType*, the columns for the eventual call to *SQLGetTypeInfo* are bound. Each input column is then passed to *fFindTypeMatch* in a loop. The loop is shown in Figure 8-30.

```
// Loop through each column and find a mapping data type
//
for(idex = 0; idex < pCopyInfo->iCols; idex++) {
    pColInfo = &pCopyInfo->pColumns[idex];
    if(!fFindTypeMatch(hwnd,
        pCopyInfo->hToStmt, pColInfo, &sInfo))
        goto clean_up;

    // Finish init based on mapped type
    //
    pColInfo->fCType =
        GetCTypeFromSqlType(pColInfo->fSqlType);
    SetMappedInfo(pColInfo, &sInfo);
    pCopyInfo->fConvertNulls |= pColInfo->fConvertNulls;

    // Determine whether this column will need to handle long
    // data. This is the case only when the target needs to
    // know the precision of a data column before the data is
    // given to it and when a column has a long data type.
    //
    if((SQL_LONGVARCHAR == pColInfo->fToSqlType ||
        SQL_LONGVARBINARY == pColInfo->fToSqlType) &&
        pCopyInfo->fNeedLongDataLen) {
        // Store the index of the column in the array of
        // columns requiring this support
        //
        pCopyInfo->rgnColNLD[pCopyInfo->nHandleNLD] = idex;
        ++pCopyInfo->nHandleNLD;
        }
    }
```

Figure 8-30.
Passing columns to fFindTypeMatch *in a loop.*

In *fFindTypeMatch*, the loop will examine every possible type that might be a fit for the type of the source column. If all else fails, the function will make the output type a character string. A lot of heuristics are applied to this process, but, generally speaking, the algorithm for finding a type match for an input column in *fFindTypeMatch* is as follows:

1. If the source column's ODBC type number (SQL_INTEGER or SQL_CHAR, for instance) and type name (such as INTEGER or CHAR) match those of a possible type, map the source column to that type above all others. This will take care of one of the more difficult problems related to user-defined types (UDTs) mentioned in Chapter 6, section 6.8, in which a data source with UDTs might have several types that match the ODBC type. For example, the ZIPCODE type we saw in section 6.8 would be returned from *SQLGetTypeInfo* along with the CHAR data type. But if the input type name was "CHAR", the match on the type name would choose "CHAR" over "ZIPCODE" for the output type name, even though both types are the ODBC type SQL_CHAR.

2. Find a type in the same type *family,* of which there are six:

   Integers (TINYINT, SMALLINT, INTEGER, and BIGINT)

   Fixed-point exact numeric types (DECIMAL and NUMERIC)

   Approximate numeric types (REAL, FLOAT, and DOUBLE)

   Characters (CHAR, VARCHAR, and LONG_VARCHAR)

   Binary types (BINARY, VARBINARY, and LONG_VARBINARY)

   Date/time types (DATE, TIME, and TIMESTAMP)

3. "Promote" the type to one in a more general type family. For example, an integer can always be represented by a fixed-point exact numeric type or by an approximate numeric type if an integer type is not available in the output data source.

4. Use a character type. You might lose the semantics of the data type, but the data itself will be preserved. For example, converting a floating-point value to a character string loses the semantics of the original type (preventing you from performing arithmetic operations on the character string) but preserves all the data.

The loop uses flags during the matching process to keep track of the best match that has been found so far for the source data type. The MATCH_FULL flag indicates that a suitable match has been found and the process is done, MATCH_NAME indicates that a type name match has been found, MATCH_PREC indicates that the precision or length in the output data source is long enough to handle the input column, and MATCH_DFT indicates that it was necessary to default to a character or binary data type.

Several special cases are checked. For instance, the use of data types that have the AUTO_INCREMENT attribute is checked and avoided because typically these types cannot accept inserts. Columns that have the MONEY attribute should be used in cases for which both the input and the output data source support them (assuming that the output precision and scale are sufficient to handle the input type). Finally, in all cases the column definition length must be checked for variable-length data to ensure that no truncation will occur.

All the information about the output data type to be used is obtained by calling *SQLGetTypeInfo* with the input argument for the ODBC type of the input column. Recall that *SQLGetTypeInfo* returns all the data types in the DBMS for a given ODBC type. We looked at *SQLGetTypeInfo* in detail in Chapter 5. After the call to *SQLGetTypeInfo*, we call *SQLFetch* to get the first type in the output data source that matches the ODBC type that is compatible with the input column.

Figure 8-31 shows the code for *fFindTypeMatch*, which is found in TYPEMAP.C.

```
BOOL fFindTypeMatch(
    HWND hwnd,                  // Window for errors
    HSTMT hstmt,                // Statement handle to find results on
    lpCOLDESC pColInfo,         // Column we're trying to match up
    lpGETTYPEINFO psInfo        // Type info to return if successful
    )
{
    RETCODE     rc;             // Return code for status
    UWORD       uTypesUsed;     // Flag to avoid promotion recursion
    SWORD       fSrcType;       // Original type we wanted to match
    UWORD       uMatch;         // Match mask
    GETTYPEINFO sMatch;         // Potential matches
    GETTYPEINFO sDftType;       // Default type if no match found

    // Set all values to defaults
    //
    uTypesUsed = 0;
    fSrcType = pColInfo->fSqlType;
    uMatch = 0;
    memset(&sMatch, 0, sizeof(GETTYPEINFO));
    memset(&sDftType, 0, sizeof(GETTYPEINFO));
    psInfo->fSqlType = pColInfo->fSqlType;

    while(!(uMatch & MATCH_FULL)) {
```

Figure 8-31.
The fFindTypeMatch *code in TYPEMAP.C.*

Figure 8-31. *continued*

```
// Get type info for the given SQL type
//
rc = SQLGetTypeInfo(hstmt, psInfo->fSqlType);
if(RC_NOTSUCCESSFUL(rc)) {
    vShowErrors(hwnd, NULL, NULL, hstmt);
    return FALSE;
    }

rc = SQLFetch(hstmt);
while(RC_SUCCESSFUL(rc) && !(uMatch & MATCH_FULL)) {
    // Disallow auto-increment fields (see note in header)
    //
    if((SQL_NULL_DATA != psInfo->cbAutoInc) &&
        (TRUE == psInfo->fAutoInc))
        ;

    // Try to map currency types to other currency types
    //
        // Source type is money
    else if(pColInfo->fIsMoney &&
        // But target is not
        !psInfo->fMoney &&
        // And we have a potential match
        (uMatch & (MATCH_PREC | MATCH_NAME)))
        ;
    else {
        // Exact name type matches take precedence
        //
        if(fExactNameMatch(psInfo->fSqlType,
            psInfo->szTypeName) &&
            (pColInfo->cbPrecision <=
            (UDWORD)psInfo->cbMaxPrec)) {
            if(!pColInfo->fIsMoney)
                uMatch |= MATCH_FULL;
            else {
                uMatch |= MATCH_NAME;
                uMatch &= ~MATCH_PREC;
                }
            memcpy(&sMatch, psInfo, sizeof(GETTYPEINFO));
            }
        // No name match. If this type handles our
        // precision, it might work.
        //
        else if(!(uMatch & MATCH_NAME) &&
            (pColInfo->cbPrecision <=
            (UDWORD)psInfo->cbMaxPrec)) {
```

(continued)

Figure 8-31. *continued*

```
                        uMatch |= MATCH_PREC;
                        memcpy(&sMatch, psInfo, sizeof(GETTYPEINFO));
                        }

                // If we have a potential match stored, and if
                // there is a money match, use it regardless
                //
                if(uMatch && pColInfo->fIsMoney && psInfo->fMoney)
                    uMatch |= MATCH_FULL;
                }

            // If there is no match, see if this is a large
            // binary or character type. We'll save this as
            // the last possible match.
            //
            if(!(uMatch & MATCH_FULL)) {
                if(fIsCharType(psInfo->fSqlType) ||
                    fIsBinType(psInfo->fSqlType)) {
                    // We have a char or binary type, which is
                    // good for defaults. Now be sure we take
                    // only the largest one.
                    //
                    if((UDWORD)sDftType.cbMaxPrec <
                        pColInfo->cbPrecision &&
                        psInfo->cbMaxPrec > sDftType.cbMaxPrec) {
                        memcpy(&sDftType, psInfo,
                            sizeof(GETTYPEINFO));
                        uMatch |= MATCH_DFT;
                        }
                    }
                }

            // Get next row if we're not done
            //
            if(!(uMatch & MATCH_FULL))
                rc = SQLFetch(hstmt);
            } // End loop through this type

    // Remove any pending results or states
    //
    SQLFreeStmt(hstmt, SQL_CLOSE);

    // If there is no exact name match, check for a precision
    // match
    //
    if(!pColInfo->fIsMoney &&
        !(uMatch & MATCH_FULL) && (uMatch & MATCH_PREC))
        uMatch |= MATCH_FULL;
```

Figure 8-31. *continued*

```
            // If there is still no match, promote the data type
            // and try again
            //
            if(!(uMatch & MATCH_FULL))
                if(!fGetPromotedType(&psInfo->fSqlType, &uTypesUsed))
                    {
                    // If there is any sort of match besides default,
                    // use it
                    //
                    if(uMatch & (~MATCH_DFT))
                        uMatch |= MATCH_FULL;
                    // Else if we have a default match, it's not
                    // ideal, but we'll try it
                    //
                    else if(uMatch & MATCH_DFT) {
                        memcpy(&sMatch, &sDftType,
                            sizeof(GETTYPEINFO));
                        uMatch |= MATCH_FULL;
                        }
                    // Else we are out of luck
                    //
                    else {
                        iMessageBox(hwnd, MB_ICONEXCLAMATION | MB_OK,
                                sz_ERROR, sz_NO_TYPES_CORRESPOND,
                                GetSqlTypeName(fSrcType));
                        return FALSE;
                        }
                    }

        } // End while no match

    // If we found a match, return it to caller
    //
    if(uMatch & MATCH_FULL) {
        memcpy(psInfo, &sMatch, sizeof(GETTYPEINFO));

        // Check whether the source allows NULLs and our target
        // does not. This might require NULL fixups at copy data
        // time.
        //
        pColInfo->fConvertNulls =
            (SQL_NO_NULLS == psInfo->fNullable &&
             SQL_NO_NULLS != pColInfo->fNullable);
        }

    return (uMatch & MATCH_FULL);
}
```

The type escalation is handled in *fGetPromotedType*, which is simply a large switch statement that encodes the rules for promoting a type to the next compatible type if an exact match is not found. Figure 8-32 shows the code for *fGetPromotedType*.

```
BOOL fGetPromotedType(
    SWORD * pfSqlType,                    // The input type
    UWORD * puType                        // Bitmask for types used
    )
{
    switch(*pfSqlType) {
        // Character family. Track usage since other families
        // will recurse back to SQL_CHAR.
        //
        case SQL_CHAR:
            if(*puType & CHR_VARCHAR_CHECKED)
                return FALSE;
            *pfSqlType = SQL_VARCHAR;
            break;

        case SQL_VARCHAR:
            // Promote VARCHAR to CHAR first and then
            // to LONGVARCHAR
            //
            if(*puType & CHR_LONGVARCHAR_CHECKED)
                return FALSE;
            else if(*puType & CHR_CHAR_CHECKED)
                *pfSqlType = SQL_LONGVARCHAR;
            else
                *pfSqlType = SQL_CHAR;
            break;

        case SQL_LONGVARCHAR:
            if(*puType & CHR_CHAR_CHECKED)
                return FALSE;
            *pfSqlType = SQL_CHAR;
            break;


        // Integer family
        //
        case SQL_BIT:
            *pfSqlType = SQL_TINYINT;
            break;
```

Figure 8-32.
The fGetPromotedType *code.*

Figure 8-32. *continued*

```
case SQL_TINYINT:
    *pfSqlType = SQL_SMALLINT;
    break;

case SQL_SMALLINT:
    *pfSqlType = SQL_INTEGER;
    break;

case SQL_INTEGER:
    *pfSqlType = SQL_BIGINT;
    break;

case SQL_BIGINT:
    *pfSqlType = SQL_NUMERIC;
    break;


// Floating-point type family. FLOAT and DOUBLE actually
// have the same precision, so do a mutual promotion (that
// is, allow FLOAT to become DOUBLE and DOUBLE to become
// FLOAT) before going to CHAR.
//
case SQL_REAL:
    *pfSqlType = SQL_FLOAT;
    break;

case SQL_FLOAT:
    if(*puType & FLT_DOUBLE_CHECKED)
        *pfSqlType = SQL_CHAR;
    else
        *pfSqlType = SQL_DOUBLE;
    break;

case SQL_DOUBLE:
    if(*puType & FLT_FLOAT_CHECKED)
        *pfSqlType = SQL_CHAR;
    else
        *pfSqlType = SQL_FLOAT;
    break;

// Fixed-point exact numerics. Ordering of the two types
// is unimportant--for our purposes they have exactly the
// same semantics.
//
case SQL_NUMERIC:
    *pfSqlType = SQL_DECIMAL;
    break;
```

(continued)

Figure 8-32. *continued*

```
        case SQL_DECIMAL:
            *pfSqlType = SQL_REAL;
            break;


        // Binary types
        //
        case SQL_BINARY:
            *pfSqlType = SQL_VARBINARY;
            break;

        case SQL_VARBINARY:
            *pfSqlType = SQL_LONGVARBINARY;
            break;

        case SQL_LONGVARBINARY:
            *pfSqlType = SQL_CHAR;
            break;


        // Date/Time family
        //
        case SQL_DATE:
            *pfSqlType = SQL_TIMESTAMP;
            break;

        case SQL_TIME:
            *pfSqlType = SQL_TIMESTAMP;
            break;

        case SQL_TIMESTAMP:
            *pfSqlType = SQL_CHAR;
            break;

        // We're in trouble if we arrive here
        //
        default:
            assert(0);
            return SQL_CHAR;
        }

    // Set checking flags to avoid rechecks
    //
    switch(*pfSqlType) {
        case SQL_CHAR:
            *puType |= CHR_CHAR_CHECKED;
            break;
```

Figure 8-32. *continued*

```
        case SQL_VARCHAR:
            *puType |= CHR_VARCHAR_CHECKED;
            break;

        case SQL_LONGVARCHAR:
            *puType |= CHR_LONGVARCHAR_CHECKED;
            break;

        case SQL_FLOAT:
            *puType |= FLT_FLOAT_CHECKED;
            break;

        case SQL_DOUBLE:
            *puType |= FLT_DOUBLE_CHECKED;
            break;
        }

    return TRUE;
}
```

Once the types have all been mapped and the lengths of the output column definitions calculated, a dialog box is displayed that shows the results of the type mapping. The column definitions for the input and the output tables are shown side by side so you can see how well they map. Figure 8-33 shows the data type comparison dialog box as it appears when the table from the Chapter 7 examples is being copied to Microsoft SQL Server.

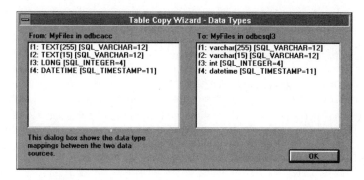

Figure 8-33.
Example data type matching dialog box.

When the user clicks OK in the dialog box, the actual CREATE TABLE statement is generated in the *nCreateTable* function in COPY.C. (Index creation is less complicated because there are fewer choices. You can find the

371

code that creates the CREATE INDEX statements in the *nCreateIndexes* function in COPY.C.)

Subsequent dialog boxes display the SQL statements generated. Finally, the status dialog box showing the records being copied is displayed. The status dialog box is shown in Figure 8-34.

Figure 8-34.
The status dialog box.

8.2.5.3 Copying the Data: Focus on Copying Blob Data

The data is copied using the standard *SQLPrepare* and *SQLExecute* method with parameters bound using *SQLBindParameter*. We've seen this technique in previous examples, but TBLCPY handles one operation that the others do not: working with Blob data. ODBC supports the ability to retrieve and send data in pieces for columns that map to the ODBC SQL_LONGVARCHAR and SQL_LONGVARBINARY types. The *SQLGetData* and *SQLPutData* functions are used for this purpose.

The function *nCopyData* in COPY.C handles the process of reading the data from the input data source and copying it to the output source. When the INSERT statement is prepared, a separate variable is used to specify the length of the long data parameter, as shown in this code fragment from the *nPrepareInsert* function in COPY.C:

```
static SDWORD gcbDataAtExec=SQL_DATA_AT_EXEC;
    ⋮
rc = SQLBindParameter(pCopyInfo->hToStmt,
    (UWORD)(nCol + 1 ),       // Parameter number
    SQL_PARAM_INPUT,          // Input value for insert
    pColInfo->fCType,         // Source data type
    pColInfo->fToSqlType,     // Target data type
    pColInfo->cbToPrecision,  // Precision of column (not data)
    pColInfo->ibScale,        // Scale of column
    (PTR)nCol,                // Store index
    0,                        // Not applicable for data-at-exec
    &gcbDataAtExec);          // Indicates we'll supply values at
                              //   runtime
```

The value of the *gcbDataAtExec* variable must be the #define value SQL_DATA_AT_EXEC. For ODBC 2.0 drivers and applications, the macro SQL_LEN_DATA_AT_EXEC(*length*) can be used because it allows drivers that need to know the total length of the long data column up front to specify it here. The description of *SQLBindParameter* in the *Microsoft ODBC 2.0 Programmer's Reference* describes in more detail how the macro is used. TBLCPY uses this macro when it is rebinding columns to handle data sources that need to know the total length before they can send any data.

Parameters whose values are not specified until execution time are known as *data-at-execution* parameters. Note that for the address of the data (the *rgbValue* argument of *SQLBindParameter*) we are actually passing the parameter number in the variable *nCol* (which also corresponds to the column number from which we are going to read). We'll be able to retrieve this value at execution time and use it to identify the parameter for which we need to supply the value.

With data-at-execution parameters, the application cannot simply change the value of the variable that is bound to a parameter and have the driver automatically get the new value when *SQLExecute* is called. It's a bit more complicated than that.

When *SQLExecute* is called and there are data-at-execution parameters (as in the preceding code fragment), the driver returns from *SQLExecute* with a special return code: SQL_NEED_DATA. Then the application can get the value from the *rgbValue* argument that is specified to *SQLBindParameter* by calling *SQLParamData*. In our case, the value is the parameter number for which we need to supply data. We use that information to call *SQLGetData* for the column data and then call *SQLPutData* to send the value to the driver iteratively. Figure 8-35 shows the code that handles data-at-execution parameters.

```
RETCODE HandleNeedData(
    HWND hwnd,                      // Window for errors
    lpCOPYINFO pCopyInfo,           // Copy information
    PTR pDataAtExec                 // Data pointer for transfer
    )
{
    RETCODE     rc;                 // Status
    int         nIndex;             // Index of the parameter
    lpCOLDESC   pColInfo;           // Column info
    SDWORD      cbVal;              // Bytes in progress
```

Figure 8-35.

(continued)

The code that handles data-at-execution parameters.

373

Figure 8-35. *continued*

```
// Use SQLParamData to retrieve the index of the column
// for which we need data. This was specified during
// SQLBindParameter.
//
rc = SQLParamData(pCopyInfo->hToStmt, (PTR)&nIndex);
while(SQL_NEED_DATA == rc) {
    assert(nIndex < pCopyInfo->iCols);
    pColInfo = &pCopyInfo->pColumns[nIndex];

    // Get the first chunk of data if we haven't already
    // done so
    //
    if(!pCopyInfo->fTruncNLD)
        rc = SQLGetData(pCopyInfo->hFromStmt,
                        pColInfo->nColInRslt,
                        pColInfo->fCType,
                        pDataAtExec,
                        MAX_INLINE_BUFF,
                        &cbVal);
    else {
        // Otherwise, get the length by decoding the macro
        //
        cbVal = -pColInfo->cbFetched +
            SQL_LEN_DATA_AT_EXEC_OFFSET;
        rc = SQL_SUCCESS;
        }

    while(RC_SUCCESSFUL(rc)) {
        // Adjust the retrieved bytes for the null terminator
        // if truncation occurred. The null is not included
        // with the put.
        //
        cbVal = min(cbVal, MAX_INLINE_BUFF);
        if((cbVal >= MAX_INLINE_BUFF) &&
                (SQL_C_CHAR == pColInfo->fCType))
            cbVal -= 1;

        // Continue to put chunks until none are left
        //
        rc = SQLPutData(pCopyInfo->hToStmt,
                        pDataAtExec,
                        cbVal);
        if(RC_NOTSUCCESSFUL(rc))
            goto clean_up;
```

Figure 8-35. *continued*

```
                // If we are truncating long data columns, move on
                //
                if(pCopyInfo->fTruncNLD)
                    rc = SQL_NO_DATA_FOUND;
                // Get the next chunk
                //
                else
                    rc = SQLGetData(pCopyInfo->hFromStmt,
                                pColInfo->nColInRslt,
                                pColInfo->fCType,
                                pDataAtExec,
                                MAX_INLINE_BUFF,
                                &cbVal);
            }

            // Determine whether any other columns need data
            //
            if(SQL_NO_DATA_FOUND == rc || RC_SUCCESSFUL(rc))
                rc = SQLParamData(pCopyInfo->hToStmt, (PTR)&nIndex);
            }

clean_up:
    if(RC_NOTSUCCESSFUL(rc)) {
        vShowErrors(hwnd, NULL, NULL, pCopyInfo->hFromStmt);
        vShowErrors(hwnd, NULL, NULL, pCopyInfo->hToStmt);
        }
    return rc;
}
```

Handling long data is one of the most complex parts of ODBC; I hope that the TBLCPY example has made it a bit clearer.

Overall, the copy process fetches from the input data source and calls *SQLExecute* on the output data source, handling long data as necessary.

That's all for TBLCPY. In the next example, we look at a useful code generator for developers who want to use ODBC cursors with row-wise binding.

8.3 The Type Declaration Generator Sample (TYPEGEN)

In this example we look at a utility that generates C and Visual Basic 3.0 type declarations suitable for building programs that use ODBC's scrollable cursors. Specifically, TYPEGEN generates a structure (which Visual Basic calls a *user-defined type*) that matches the columns in any given query so that row-wise binding can be used, and it also generates the calls to *SQLBindCol* that use elements in the data structure. For testing purposes, TYPEGEN also generates a C function that calls *SQLExtendedFetch* and dumps the results of several fetch types (FIRST, NEXT, PRIOR, RELATIVE, and ABSOLUTE). The test function can be appended to TYPEGEN's main program (MAIN.C) and invoked from the menu.

TYPEGEN is useful for vertical applications or for any application in which the queries are known at the time the application is constructed. The code generated by TYPEGEN can be copied into the actual application code. Because TYPEGEN doesn't teach any new ODBC programming concepts, I focus on how it can be used as a tool, rather than looking at the TYPEGEN source code.

You should recall from Chapter 5 (section 5.4.2.2) that row-wise binding is most useful when the results set of a query is known in advance and when you want to make a data structure in your program match the results from the query. In TYPEGEN, the structure is generated from the query you enter.

Let's go through an example. Figure 8-36 shows the TYPEGEN application window with the Connect menu item selected from the File menu. Selecting Connect ultimately calls *SQLDriverConnect* to make the connection. Once the connection is made, the Execute item from the Map menu can be selected. Execute displays the Map Data Types dialog box, as shown in Figure 8-37.

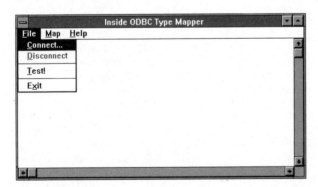

Figure 8-36.
TYPEGEN connecting to the data source.

You can enter any SQL SELECT statement in the edit control. In Figure 8-37 I've typed a very simple query. You can choose to generate either a C typedef or a Visual Basic 3.0 Type definition. The test program is generated only when you choose C output, so this discussion focuses on C type generation. We discuss row-wise binding in Visual Basic in the VBFETCH example in section 8.7, so you'll have to wait until then to learn more about Visual Basic.

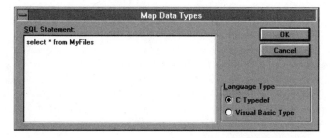

Figure 8-37.
The Map Data Types dialog box in TYPEGEN.

When the OK button is chosen, the statement is executed. If there were no errors, you'll see some C (or Visual Basic) code spewing out onto the screen. Figure 8-38 shows the code that is generated when the query in Figure 8-37 is run against the MyFiles table in the odbcfile data source from Chapter 7.

```
// TypeGen automated code generated: Tue Oct 18 01:12:45 1995
// From data source: odbcfile
// SQL statement: select * from MyFiles

typedef struct _DATAMAP {
    char                F1[254+1]; // Column: 'F1', precision: 255
    SDWORD              cbF1;      //    Length/null indicator for 'F1'
    char                F2[254+1]; // Column: 'F2', precision: 255
    SDWORD              cbF2;      //    Length/null indicator for 'F2'
    long                F3;        // Column: 'F3', precision: 10
    SDWORD              cbF3;      //    Length/null indicator for 'F3'
    TIMESTAMP_STRUCT F4;           // Column: 'F4', precision: 16
    SDWORD              cbF4;      //    Length/null indicator for 'F4'
    } DATAMAP, FAR * lpDATAMAP;

// TO DO: Set the size of your rowset
#undef ROWSET_SIZE
#define ROWSET_SIZE 10
static DATAMAP rgData[ROWSET_SIZE];


static BOOL SetRowsetOptions(HWND hwnd, HSTMT hstmt)
{
    RETCODE    rc;
```

Figure 8-38.
Code generated by TYPEGEN.

(continued)

377

Figure 8-38. *continued*

```
   // TO DO: Add other desired statement options here
   //    (such as SQL_CONCURRENCY)
   SQLSetStmtOption(hstmt,SQL_KEYSET_SIZE, ROWSET_SIZE);
   rc = SQLSetStmtOption(hstmt, SQL_CURSOR_TYPE,
      SQL_CURSOR_KEYSET_DRIVEN);
   if (RC_SUCCESSFUL(rc))  {
      rc = SQLSetStmtOption(hstmt, SQL_ROWSET_SIZE,
         ROWSET_SIZE);
      if (RC_SUCCESSFUL(rc))
         rc = SQLSetStmtOption(hstmt, SQL_BIND_TYPE,
            sizeof(DATAMAP));
      }
   if (RC_NOTSUCCESSFUL(rc))
      vShowErrors(hwnd, NULL, NULL, hstmt);
   return RC_SUCCESSFUL(rc);
}


static BOOL BindDataCols(HWND hwnd, HSTMT hstmt)
{
   BOOL            fRtn=TRUE;
   fRtn &= fSQLBindCol(hwnd, hstmt, 1, SQL_C_CHAR,
      &rgData[0].F1, sizeof(rgData[0].F1), &rgData[0].cbF1);
   fRtn &= fSQLBindCol(hwnd, hstmt, 2, SQL_C_CHAR,
      &rgData[0].F2, sizeof(rgData[0].F2), &rgData[0].cbF2);
   fRtn &= fSQLBindCol(hwnd, hstmt, 3, SQL_C_LONG,
      &rgData[0].F3, sizeof(rgData[0].F3), &rgData[0].cbF3);
   fRtn &= fSQLBindCol(hwnd, hstmt, 4, SQL_C_TIMESTAMP,
      &rgData[0].F4, sizeof(rgData[0].F4), &rgData[0].cbF4);
   return fRtn;
}



/////////////////////////////////////////////////////////////////
// OnCTest - Generated code to test binding and SQLExtendedFetch
//
// Returns:  Nothing
/////////////////////////////////////////////////////////////////

struct {
   UWORD   fFetchType;
   char *  pszFetchType;
   SDWORD  nFetchRows;
} rgTest[] ={
SQL_FETCH_FIRST,    "SQL_FETCH_FIRST", 0,
SQL_FETCH_NEXT,     "SQL_FETCH_NEXT", 0,
```

Figure 8-38. *continued*

```
SQL_FETCH_PRIOR,    "SQL_FETCH_PRIOR", 0,
SQL_FETCH_RELATIVE, "SQL_FETCH_RELATIVE", 1,
SQL_FETCH_RELATIVE, "SQL_FETCH_RELATIVE", -1,
SQL_FETCH_ABSOLUTE, "SQL_FETCH_ABSOLUTE", 5,
0,                  0,                   0
};

void OnCTest(
    HWND hwnd,                          // Parent window
    lpMAPINFO lpMap                     // Application info
    )
{

HDBC    hdbc;
HSTMT   hstmt;
RETCODE rc;
UWORD   rgfStatus[ROWSET_SIZE];
UDWORD  nrows;
int     cTest, cRow;


SQLAllocConnect(lpMap->henv, &hdbc);
SQLSetConnectOption(hdbc,SQL_ODBC_CURSORS, SQL_CUR_USE_IF_NEEDED);
Printf(lpMap, "Connecting to 'odbcfile'\r\n");
SQLDriverConnect(hdbc, hwnd, "DSN=odbcfile", SQL_NTS, NULL, 0,
    NULL, SQL_DRIVER_COMPLETE);
SQLAllocStmt(hdbc, &hstmt);
if (!SetRowsetOptions(hwnd, hstmt))
    return;
if (!BindDataCols(hwnd, hstmt))
    return;

Printf(lpMap, "Executing 'select * from MyFiles'\r\n");
if(!fSQLExecDirect(hwnd, hstmt, "select * from MyFiles"))
    return;

for(cTest = 0; rgTest[cTest].fFetchType; cTest++) {
    Printf(lpMap, "\r\n****** Fetch %s %d ******\r\n\r\n",
        rgTest[cTest].pszFetchType, rgTest[cTest].nFetchRows);
    rc = SQLExtendedFetch(hstmt, rgTest[cTest].fFetchType,
        rgTest[cTest].nFetchRows, &nrows, rgfStatus);
    if (rc != SQL_SUCCESS) {
        vShowErrors(hwnd, NULL, NULL, hstmt);
        if (rc != SQL_SUCCESS_WITH_INFO)
            goto cleanup;
    }
```

(continued)

Figure 8-38. *continued*

```
    for (cRow = 0; cRow < nrows; cRow++)
        Printf(lpMap,
            "%.80s\t%.80s\t%10ld\t%04d-%02d-%02d "
                "%02d:%02d:%02d.%ld\r\n",
            rgData[cRow].F1,
            rgData[cRow].F2,
            rgData[cRow].F3,
            rgData[cRow].F4.year,rgData[cRow].F4.month,
            rgData[cRow].F4.day,rgData[cRow].F4.hour,
            rgData[cRow].F4.minute,rgData[cRow].F4.second,
            rgData[cRow].F4.fraction
            );
    }

cleanup:
SQLFreeStmt(hstmt, SQL_DROP);
SQLDisconnect(hdbc);
SQLFreeConnect(hdbc);
}
```

Keep in mind as we go through this example that the code shown in Figure 8-38 is not the code *in* TYPEGEN but the code *generated by* TYPEGEN.

The first thing you'll see in the generated output is the structure definition. There are two structure elements for each column in the results set: one for the column data and one for the output length (indicator) variable. The data type of each structure element is generated according to the ODBC data type returned from the query; the element name itself is given the column name from the query. In this example there are four columns, corresponding to the columns f1, f2, f3, and f4 in the table MyFiles. There are two character strings (the ODBC type SQL_CHAR), one long integer (SQL_INTEGER), and one timestamp (SQL_TIMESTAMP). The type is then given the name *DATAMAP*.

Next is a #define for the rowset size and a declaration of *rgData*, which is the array of structures. The *rgData* array is the data structure that will act as the virtual window over the results set. The size of the rowset generated is 10 rows by default, but you can change it to whatever you want.

The *SetRowsetOptions* function that follows sets up a statement handle to contain the desired cursor options that are set with *SQLSetStmtOption*. TYPEGEN uses *SQLGetInfo* to check the cursor options supported by the driver and generates the statement option for a dynamic, keyset-driven, or static cursor (in that order) depending on what is supported by the driver.

The default for CONCURRENCY (ready-only) is assumed, but you can always add another call to *SQLSetStmtOption* in the generated code to set it. The last call to *SQLSetStmtOption* sets the binding style to row-wise binding:

```
rc = SQLSetStmtOption(hstmt, SQL_BIND_TYPE, sizeof(DATAMAP));
```

Instead of passing an option value, as is typical with *SQLSetStmtOption*, in this case we must pass a positive integer that specifies the length of one "row" of the structure. The driver will use this to compute the offsets to each column in every row.

Next is the code for *BindDataCols*. This function calls *SQLBindCol* for each column that is generated by the query. The code in TYPEGEN, CMAP.C (VBMAP.C for Visual Basic), uses information obtained by *SQLDescribeCol* and *SQLColAttributes* to get all the type information about each column. Both the data item and the output length item of the first structure element are passed as arguments to *SQLBindCol*, as shown in this call for the third column:

```
fRtn &= fSQLBindCol(hwnd, hstmt, 3, SQL_C_LONG,
    &rgData[0].F3, sizeof(rgData[0].F3), &rgData[0].cbF3);
```

Although it is possible to bind the columns in an order that is different from that of the structure definition, the ODBC cursor library and probably some drivers make use of a nice optimization if the memory for the bound columns is contiguous. With this optimization the cursor library can do a single memory move call from its local cache into the array of structures. If the memory is not contiguous, each column has to be copied separately.

Following *BindDataCols* is the generated test function, *OnCTest*. (Remember that you won't see this test function if you choose Visual Basic instead of C.) *OnCTest* uses the generated code to perform scrolling operations with *SQLExtendedFetch*. *OnCTest* does the following:

- It connects to the same data source that was used for the query.

- It uses the generated functions *SetRowsetOptions* and *BindDataCols* to initialize the cursor options and bind the columns.

- It executes the same query that we used originally, but *OnCTest* actually retrieves the data into the array of structures (*rgData*) with *SQLExtendedFetch*.

- It makes a few arbitrary calls to *SQLExtendedFetch* with a variety of fetch types, as specified in the *rgType* array.

- It displays the data in a crude fashion in the main window of TYPEGEN.

Here is the call to *SQLExtendedFetch*:

```
rc = SQLExtendedFetch(hstmt, rgTest[cTest].fFetchType,
    rgTest[cTest].nFetchRows, &nrows, rgfStatus);
```

You'll notice that the *rgData* array does not appear in the arguments—the *SQLExtendedFetch* function knows where to put the data because of the earlier calls to *SQLBindCol* on the same *hstmt*. After a single call to *SQLExtendedFetch*, the *rgData* array contains the specified number of rows (in this case, 10). Then a *for* loop is used to display every column in every row in the array. The format for the data is always

```
rgData[row_number].column_name
```

When the data type is itself represented as a structure, the type's structure members must be used, as shown in this example for the f4 column with the TIMESTAMP_STRUCT:

```
rgData[cRow].F4.year,rgData[cRow].F4.month,rgData[cRow].F4.day,
    rgData[cRow].F4.hour,rgData[cRow].F4.minute,rgData[cRow].F4.second,
    rgData[cRow].F4.fraction
```

So how do you get all this to actually run? Fortunately, a few hooks are built into TYPEGEN itself so that you don't have to write a separate program to try it out. Here are the steps you need to follow:

1. Select all the generated code, starting with the comment

   ```
   // TypeGen automated code generated: ...
   ```

   and copy it to the Clipboard. (Pressing Ctrl-C works just fine.)

2. Exit the TYPEGEN program.

3. Using Windows Notepad or your favorite editor, open MAIN.C in the source directory for TYPEGEN. (This will probably be C:\INODBC\SAMPLES\TYPEGEN, unless you chose a different install directory.)

4. Move to the end of the MAIN.C file.

5. Paste the code from the Clipboard.

6. Find the call to *OnCTest*, which is located in the *WndProc* procedure. You'll see a comment about removing the comment on the call to *OnCTest*:

```
case IDM_TEST:
     // Uncomment OnCTest() when the generated code
     // has been appended to this file
     ⋮
//        OnCTest(hwnd, &gMapInfo);
     return FALSE;
```

Remove the comment.

7. Exit to the MS-DOS or Windows NT command line. Go to the ...\SAMPLES\TYPEGEN directory and enter

   ```
   build
   ```

   or, if you are running Windows NT and want to build the 32-bit version, enter

   ```
   build drop32
   ```

8. If the build is successful, you can rerun TYPEGEN. This time, instead of choosing Connect from the File menu, choose Test.

The code you pasted into MAIN.C will be executed. Figure 8-39 shows the output from the ODBCFile example.

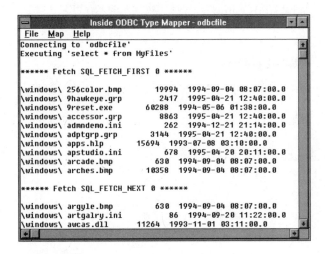

Figure 8-39.
Output from OnCTest-*generated code.*

I hope that this example has given you a useful tool for understanding and using row-wise binding and scrollable cursors in ODBC. This is the last sample written in C. Next we're going to turn our attention to another programming language, C++.

8.4 The Simple C++ Class Library for ODBC Sample (CPPSMPL)

In this example we look at a set of simple C++ classes that encapsulate the bare essentials of ODBC functionality. You could write an extremely simple application using only these classes, but it's more likely that you would want to use these as a starting point to write your own classes. Alternatively, you could use the simple classes supplied with the ODBC SDK or one of the more powerful C++ class libraries currently on the market. A brief list of these appears at the end of this section.

The functionality in CPPSMPL is limited to making a connection, executing an SQL statement and retrieving the entire results set into an array of column objects, and accessing that array with member functions. There is no fetch model, no update capability, and no use of any advanced ODBC features. Obviously, this approach is practical only for very simple applications that retrieve small amounts of data.

8.4.1 The CPPSMPL User Interface

The user interface for CPPSMPL is about as simple as an ODBC application can be. Figure 8-40 shows the main window for CPPSMPL with the File menu displayed.

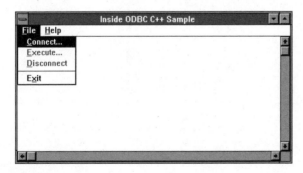

Figure 8-40.
The File menu for CPPSMPL.

Once you are connected, you can execute any SQL statement by choosing Execute from the File menu, which displays a simple dialog box, as shown in Figure 8-41.

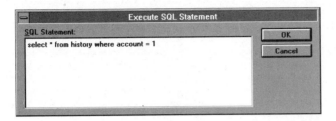

Figure 8-41.
The Execute dialog box in CPPSMPL.

When you choose OK, the SQL statement is executed and the results are displayed in the main window, as shown in Figure 8-42. To disconnect from the data source, select the Disconnect item from the File menu.

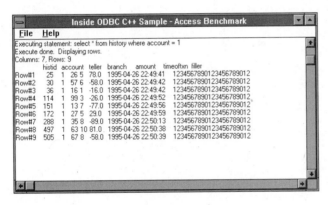

Figure 8-42.
Output of an SQL statement in CPPSMPL.

That's the whole user interface! The C++ code that underlies the Connect and Execute menu items is much more interesting.

8.4.2 Inside CPPSMPL: The Application Programming Model

In this section we see what the simple class library defined in CPPSMPL provides for the application programmer. Using the classes appears quite a bit different from using straight ODBC calls. For one thing, you won't see any

ODBC handles in the application code. You won't see explicit column binding either. All you'll see are the high-level calls to connect, execute, and disconnect and the access functions to retrieve data. Data is retrieved much as though the entire results set were an array of structures, but in an object-oriented fashion. Let's look at the details.

The CPPSMPL sample includes only two high-level classes: *CODBCExec* and *CODBCColumn*. The *CODBCExec* class connects to the data source, executes SQL statements, and disconnects. The *CODBCColumn* class handles binding and data retrieval.

When the Connect item from the File menu is selected, the *OnConnect* function in CPPSMPL.CPP is called. Here is the code for *OnConnect*:

```
void OnConnect(
    HWND hwnd,                          // Parent window
    lpCPPSMPL lpInfo                    // Application info
    )
{
    char        szBuff[256];

    lpInfo->odbc.SetParentWindow(hwnd);
    if(lpInfo->odbc.fConnect("")) {
        // Set title of application with DSN for user
        //
        wsprintf(szBuff, "%s - %s", (LPCSTR)gsz_WIN_TITLE,
            (LPCSTR)lpInfo->odbc.GetDSNName());
        SetWindowText(hwnd, szBuff);

        // Give user some feedback
        //
        Printf(lpInfo, "Successfully connected to %s.\r\n",
            (LPCSTR)lpInfo->odbc.GetDSNName());
        }
}
```

All the action happens in the line of code that calls the *fConnect* method of the instance variable *odbc*:

```
    if(lpInfo->odbc.fConnect("")) {
```

The *lpInfo* variable is a pointer to a structure that is similar to the informational structures we've seen in earlier examples (such as *lpBench* in BENCH, *lpCopyInfo* in TBLCPY, and *lpMap* in TYPEGEN). The variable *odbc* is part of that structure and is declared as an instance of the *CODBCExec* class:

```
typedef struct _CPPSMPL {
    // Global info
    //
    HWND        hwndMain;       // Main window handle
    HWND        hwndOut;        // Output window for logging info
    HFONT       hFont;          // Font for output window
    HGLOBAL     hEditMem;       // Memory handle to increase output window
    HINSTANCE   hInst;          // Instance handle of this application
    int         nHelpCnt;       // Load count on help file

    // ODBC handles
    //
    CODBCExec   odbc;           // Our class instance
} CPPSMPL, FAR * lpCPPSMPL;
```

The *CODBCExec::fConnect* function takes a connection string as an input argument and handles all the chores of making the connection. We'll see how it works in section 8.4.3.

When the Execute item from the File menu is selected, the function *OnExecute* in CPPSMPL.CPP is called. Figure 8-43 shows the code for the *OnExecute* function.

```
void OnExecute(
    HWND hwnd,                          // Parent window
    lpCPPSMPL lpInfo                    // Application info
    )
{
    char        szSql[DFT_SQL_STMT + 1];
    CODBCExec * podbc;

    if(IDOK == GetSqlText(hwnd, lpInfo->hInst, szSql)) {
        Printf(lpInfo, "Executing statement: %s\r\n",
            (LPCSTR)szSql);

        podbc = &lpInfo->odbc;
        if(podbc->fExecSql(szSql)) {
            Printf(lpInfo, "Execute done. Displaying rows.\r\n");
            Printf(lpInfo, "Columns: %d, Rows: %ld\r\n",
                podbc->GetColumnCnt(), podbc->GetRowCnt());
```

Figure 8-43. *(continued)*

The code for OnExecute.

Figure 8-43. *continued*

```
            // Disable redraw of window until results are shown.
            // The edit control is actually very pokey, and it
            // gives the impression that the query is slow when
            // it is not.
            //
            ShowWindow(lpInfo->hwndOut, SW_HIDE);
            HCURSOR hOld = SetCursor(LoadCursor(NULL,
                MAKEINTRESOURCE(IDC_WAIT)));

            if(podbc->HasResultsSet()) {
                CODBCColumn *    prgColInfo;
                CODBCColumn *    pColInfo;
                UDWORD           nRows = podbc->GetRowCnt();
                UWORD            nCols = podbc->GetColumnCnt();
                LPCSTR           pszData;
                SDWORD           cbVal;

                // Get the column descriptors for fetching data
                //
                prgColInfo = podbc->GetColDesc();

                // Display column heads
                for(UWORD col = 0;  col < nCols;  col++) {
                    pColInfo = &prgColInfo[col];
                    Printf(lpInfo, "\t%s", pColInfo->GetColName());
                    }
                Printf(lpInfo, "\r\n");

                // Loop through each row and display its data
                //
                for(UDWORD row = 0;  row < nRows;  row++) {
                    Printf(lpInfo, "Row#%lu", row + 1);

                    // For this row, display each column value
                    //
                    for(UWORD col = 0;  col < nCols;  col++) {
                        pColInfo = &prgColInfo[col];
                        pColInfo->GetRowData(row + 1,
                            (PTR *)&pszData, &cbVal);

                        Printf(lpInfo, "\t%s",
                            (SQL_NULL_DATA == cbVal) ?
                            (LPCSTR)"<null>" : (LPCSTR)pszData);
                        }  // column loop
                    (Printf(lpInfo, "\r\n");
                    }  // row loop
                }  // has results
```

Figure 8-43. *continued*

```
                // Show the results
                //
                SetCursor(hOld);
                ShowWindow(lpInfo->hwndOut, SW_SHOW);
                } // successful execute
        }
    }
```

In *OnExecute* a pointer (*podbc*) to the *CODBCExec* class is declared so that we can use it as a shorthand notation for referencing the instance variable *odbc* in the *lpInfo* structure:

```
podbc = &lpInfo->odbc;
```

The call to *GetSqlText* displays the dialog box that prompts for the SQL statement, and it returns the SQL string in the variable *szSql*.

The SQL statement is executed by calling the *fExecSql* method of the *CODBCExec* class:

```
if(podbc->fExecSql(szSql)) {
```

After execution all the data from the SQL statement will have been retrieved, and a *CODBCColumn* object will have been created for each column in the results set (if the statement was a SELECT statement). Now we can use the member functions to access the data.

If rows have been returned, we can get the number of rows and the number of columns with the *CODBCExec::GetRowCnt* and *CODBCExec::GetColumnCnt* member functions. We can get a pointer to the array of *CODBCColumn* objects by using the *GetColDesc* member function:

```
prgColInfo = podbc->GetColDesc();
```

Then we can do a nested loop to print out all the data. In the innermost loop, we get the *CODBCColumn* object for the current column with

```
pColInfo = &prgColInfo[col];
```

Then we use the member function *GetRowData* to get the data for the desired row into the variable *pszData*. The output length and null indicator are returned in *cbVal*.

```
pColInfo->GetRowData(row + 1, (PTR *)&pszData, &cbVal);
```

That's the gist of the application programming model as it is used in CPPSMPL. Now let's look at how it's implemented in the class library.

8.4.3 Inside CPPSMPL: The Class Code

As you might guess from its description in the *CODBCExec* class, the *fConnect* member function is simply a thin wrapper around *SQLDriverConnect*. It also allocates all the ODBC handles and stores them in private member variables. Figure 8-44 shows the code for *CODBCExec::fConnect* from CPPODBC.CPP.

```
BOOL CODBCExec::fConnect(
    LPCSTR pszConnStr          // Input connection string; see the
                               // SQLDriverConnect function
    )
{
    RETCODE         rc;

    assert(NULL == m_hdbc);          // Don't call if connected

    // Allocate the environment handle for this application
    //
    rc = SQLAllocEnv(&m_henv);
    if(RC_SUCCESSFUL(rc)) {
        // Allocate a connection handle
        //
        rc = SQLAllocConnect(m_henv, &m_hdbc);
        if(RC_SUCCESSFUL(rc)) {
            // Connect to the data source of choice
            //
            rc = SQLDriverConnect(m_hdbc, m_hwnd,
                    (UCHAR FAR *)pszConnStr, SQL_NTS,
                    NULL, 0, NULL,
                    SQL_DRIVER_COMPLETE);
            if(RC_SUCCESSFUL(rc)) {
                // Allocate a statement handle
                //
                rc = SQLAllocStmt(m_hdbc, &m_hstmt);
                if(RC_SUCCESSFUL(rc)) {
                    GatherConnectInfo();
                    return TRUE;
                    } // alloc stmt
                } // connect

        } // alloc hdbc
```

Figure 8-44.
The code for CODBCExec::fConnect.

Figure 8-44. *continued*

```
        } // alloc henv

    // An error occurred. Show the messages to the user and
    // free up any handles that were allocated.
    //
    ShowAllErrors();
    vDisconnect();

    return FALSE;
}
```

Execution of the SQL statement is handled with *SQLExecDirect* inside *CODBCExec::fExecSql*, as shown in Figure 8-45.

```
BOOL CODBCExec::fExecSql(
    LPCSTR pszSqlStr                        // SQL string to execute
    )
{
    RETCODE       rc;
    BOOL          fRtn = TRUE;
    int           iRtn = TRUE;
    CODBCColumn   *pColInfo;

    assert(pszSqlStr);

    // Execute the statement directly
    //
    rc = SQLExecDirect(m_hstmt, (UCHAR FAR *)pszSqlStr, SQL_NTS);
    if(RC_SUCCESSFUL(rc)) {
        // Destroy the old column info; then gather the new info
        //
        vDestroyColumns();
        if(fGetResultsCols()) {
            ⋮
```

Figure 8-45.
The code for CODBCExec::fExecSql.

The rest of *fExecSql* sets up the column binding, allocates the array of *CODBCColumn* objects, and retrieves all the data into the array. The binding is accomplished via the *fGetResultsCols* function, as shown in Figure 8-46 on the following page.

```
BOOL CODBCExec::fGetResultsCols(void)
{
    RETCODE      rc;
    BOOL         fRtn = FALSE;    // Assume failure
    CODBCColumn * pColInfo;       // Working pointer for each column

    rc = SQLNumResultCols(m_hstmt, &m_nCols);
    if(RC_SUCCESSFUL(rc)) {
        fRtn = TRUE;
        if(m_nCols > 0) {
            // The executed statement produced a results set
            //
            assert(NULL == m_rgColumns);
            if(NULL != (m_rgColumns = new CODBCColumn[m_nCols])) {
                // Loop through each column and gather metadata
                //
                for(SWORD col = 0;  col < m_nCols;  col++) {
                    pColInfo = &m_rgColumns[col];
                    if(!pColInfo->InitToColumn(col + 1, m_hstmt,
                                      GetGrowRate(),
                                      GetMaxBinding(), m_hwnd)) {
                        fRtn = FALSE;
                        break;
                        }
                    } // for
                } // allocate column array
            } // results set present
        }
}
```

Figure 8-46.
The fGetResultsCols *function.*

The number of columns is retrieved by *SQLNumResultCols* into *m_nCols*, which is used to allocate the correct number of *CODBCColumn* objects:

```
if(NULL != (m_rgColumns = new CODBCColumn[m_nCols])) {
```

Then, for each *CODBCColumn* object, the function *InitToColumn* is called. This function ultimately allocates some memory, stores the metadata using *SQLDescribeCol* and *SQLColAttributes*, and calls *SQLBindCol* to do the actual binding of the row data.

Back in *fExecSql*, we now fetch all the rows (up to the maximum number of rows, which was set in the variable *m_ulMaxRows*) and call *SetDataRow* to copy each bound value to its correct row position:

```
    ⋮
m_ulRtndRows = 0;
rc = SQL_SUCCESS;
while(RC_SUCCESSFUL(rc) && (m_ulRtndRows < m_ulMaxRows) &&
                      fRtn && (TRUE == iRtn)) {
    // Fetch each row, keeping count
    //
    rc = SQLFetch(m_hstmt);
    if(RC_SUCCESSFUL(rc)) {
        ++m_ulRtndRows;

        // For each column, transfer the bound data to the
        // correct row number
        //
        for(SWORD col = 0;  col < m_nCols;  col++) {
            pColInfo = &m_rgColumns[col];
            if((iRtn = pColInfo->SetDataRow(m_hstmt, m_ulRtndRows,
                             m_hwnd)) < 0) {
        ⋮
```

That's the heart of the class library implementation. Many other helpful member functions that we didn't cover here are contained in both the *CODBCExec* and the *CODBCColumn* classes. You can see these classes in the CPPODBC.H file. The implementations are in CPPODBC.CPP.

In the next example we use this same simple class library to help us write an OLE Automation server for ODBC.

REFERENCES

For further information about C++ class libraries for ODBC, refer to the following products:

Microsoft Visual C++ Development System and Tools, version 2.0, Microsoft Corporation, 1995.

Microsoft Open Database Connectivity Software Development Kit, version 2.10, Microsoft Corporation. Available on Microsoft Developer Network (MSDN) Development Platform; released quarterly.

winPAK, version1.0, Faison Computing, Inc., Irvine, CA. Call 1-800-500-6535 for more information.

odbc/ClassLib, version 2.0, South Wind Design, Inc., Ann Arbor, MI. Call 1-800-89-S-WIND for more information.

WinClient, WinClient Technologies, Inc., Seattle, WA. Call 1-800-959-8515 for more information.

8.5 The OLE Automation Server Sample (ODBCAUTO)

The ODBCAUTO sample is an OLE Automation server for ODBC that supports the functionality of the simple classes that are described in CPPSMPL. The sample was built using the Visual C++ Microsoft Foundation Classes (MFC) and, obviously, makes use of many concepts from OLE 2. To run the example you must also have Visual Basic for Applications (VBA) supplied in Microsoft Excel version 5. This book, however, does not attempt to explain MFC, OLE, VBA, or Microsoft Excel; several references that will give you more information about those topics are listed at the end of this section.

The main purposes of this sample are to show how a simple set of wrapper functions for ODBC can be invoked as an inproc OLE Automation server and to provide you with the source code so that you can embellish the interface yourself.

8.5.1 The User Interface for ODBCAUTO in Microsoft Excel 5

The user interface for this sample is provided by Microsoft Excel. When you start the OLE Automation server sample from the icon in the Inside ODBC program group, the Microsoft Excel spreadsheet file USEAUTO.XLS is opened. The screen shown in Figure 8-47 appears.

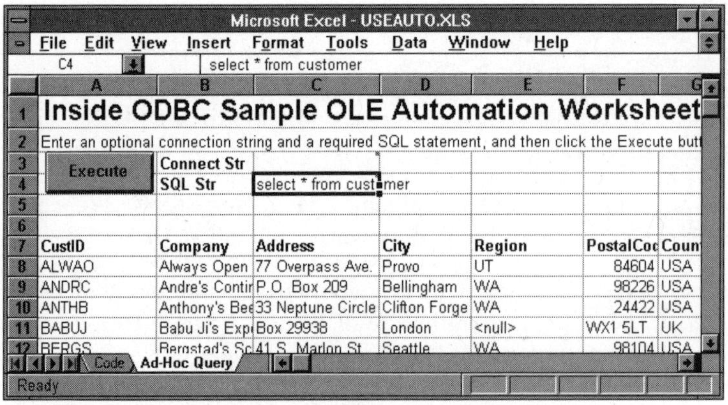

Figure 8-47.
The USEAUTO.XLS OLE Automation sample.

You can fill in a connection string in cell C3, or you can ignore this cell and leave the connection user interface to *SQLDriverConnect*, as we did in previous examples. The SQL string in cell C4 must be valid for the data source you choose. When you click the Execute button, you will be prompted for any necessary information to complete the connection, and then the SQL string will be executed and the results (if any) will be displayed in the spreadsheet, starting in row 7.

That's it for the user interface. Let's see what's going on under the covers.

8.5.2 The Visual Basic for Applications Programming Model

When the Execute button is clicked, a VBA function named *AdHocQuery* is invoked. You can see the code by clicking on the Code tab near the bottom of the Microsoft Excel window. The *AdHocQuery* function is shown in Figure 8-48.

```
' Takes the given SQL string and executes
' it after connecting to a data source
Function AdHocQuery()
    Dim nColCnt As Integer
    Dim nColNum As Integer
    Dim nRowCnt As Long
    Dim nRowNum As Long
    Dim szColName As String
    Dim szColData As String
    Dim szSql As String
    Dim szConnectStr As String
    Dim nBaseRow As Integer

    nBaseRow = 7

    ' Create an object with our given prog-id
    '
    Set MyQuery = CreateObject("inodbc.ExecSql")

    szConnectStr = ActiveSheet.Cells(3, 3).Value
    If (MyQuery.Connect(szConnectStr) = True) Then
        ' Execute the SQL statement we are given
        '
        szSql = ActiveSheet.Cells(4, 3).Value
        If (MyQuery.ExecSql(szSql) = True) Then
            ' Get the count of columns in the result; then
            ' populate the spreadsheet with the results
            nColCnt = MyQuery.ColumnCount
            nRowCnt = MyQuery.RowCount
            Call ClearOldResults(nBaseRow)
```

Figure 8-48.   *(continued)*
The AdHocQuery *function.*

Figure 8-48. *continued*

```
            For nColNum = 1 To nColCnt
                ' Set the current column number and display
                ' the title
                '
                MyQuery.SetCurCol (nColNum)
                szColName = MyQuery.GetColName
                ActiveSheet.Cells(nBaseRow, nColNum).Font.Bold =
                    True
                ActiveSheet.Cells(nBaseRow, nColNum).Value =
                    szColName

                ' Show every row for this column. The auto object
                ' is optimized for contiguous access, so this is
                ' faster than going one row at a time for each
                ' column. Note that the data has already been
                ' retrieved from the driver; we are populating
                ' only the spreadsheet now.
                '
                For nRowNum = 1 To nRowCnt
                    szColData = MyQuery.GetRowData(nRowNum)
                    ActiveSheet.Cells(nBaseRow + nRowNum,
                    nColNum).Value = szColData
                Next nRowNum
            Next nColNum
        End If

        ' Disconnect
        '
        MyQuery.Disconnect
    End If

End Function

' Removes the contents of an old query
Sub ClearOldResults(nBaseRow As Integer)
    Dim anchor_cell
    ActiveSheet.Cells(nBaseRow, 1).Select
    anchor_cell = ActiveCell.Address
    ActiveCell.End(xlDown).Select
    ActiveCell.End(xlToRight).Select
    Range(anchor_cell, ActiveCell).Select
    Selection.Clear
    ActiveSheet.Cells(nBaseRow, 1).Select
End Sub
```

After some declarations and an assignment statement, you see the statement

```
Set MyQuery = CreateObject("inodbc.ExecSql")
```

The *CreateObject* function is built into VBA. It creates an OLE Automation object when supplied with a prog-id (the string "inodbc.ExecSql" in this case). The string must be in the form

```
application.object_type
```

In our example the application name is *inodbc* and the object type is *ExecSql*. What actually happens here is that after a lot of OLE 2 "plumbing," a DLL (ODBCAUTO.DLL for 32-bit Excel or ODBCAU16.DLL for 16-bit Excel) containing the ODBC classes that were discussed in CPPSMPL is loaded, and a reference to the OLE Automation object is stored in the VBA variable *MyQuery*. We'll go into a bit more detail in section 8.5.3 about how some of the plumbing works, but for now it is enough to know that *MyQuery* can be used just like an instance of the *CODBCExec* class in CPPSMPL.

Next the connection string is retrieved from the worksheet and the *Connect* method is called:

```
szConnectStr = ActiveSheet.Cells(3, 3).Value
If (MyQuery.Connect(szConnectStr) = True) Then
    ⋮
```

As you might guess, this ultimately calls *SQLDriverConnect* with the input connection string to connect to the data source.

If the connection is successful, the program gets the SQL statement from the worksheet and executes it:

```
szSql = ActiveSheet.Cells(4, 3).Value
If (MyQuery.ExecSql(szSql) = True) Then
    ⋮
```

If you're thinking that this will ultimately call *CODBCExec::fExecSql*, you're right!

Finally, we do a results processing loop that is similar to the one we did for CPPSMPL. We start by getting the number of columns and rows that were returned with *MyQuery.ColumnCount* and *MyQuery.RowCount*:

```
nColCnt = MyQuery.ColumnCount
nRowCnt = MyQuery.RowCount
```

Then, for each column, we set the column number:

```
MyQuery.SetCurCol (nColNum)
```

After getting and displaying the column name, we get all the rows for the column with

```
szColData = MyQuery.GetRowData(nRowNum)
```

and display them in the spreadsheet.

That's the application programming model in a nutshell. The similarities to CPPSMPL should be clear. Now let's look at what's going on to make it all work together.

8.5.3 Inside ODBCAUTO.DLL and How We Get There from Visual Basic for Applications

The code that actually makes ODBC calls is located in ODBCAUTO.DLL (or ODBCAU16.DLL, for 16-bit Excel). How does the call to *CreateObject*, which is made in the VBA code, relate to ODBCAUTO.DLL? Here is the code that calls *CreateObject*:

```
Set MyQuery = CreateObject("inodbc.ExecSql")
```

First VBA uses the argument to *CreateObject* (known as the *program id* or simply *prog-id*) to look for an entry in the registry by that name. Using the *regedt32* program in Windows NT, we find the registry entry for inodbc.ExecSql in HKEY_CLASSES_ROOT. Within the registry entry is the CLSID, as shown in Figure 8-49.

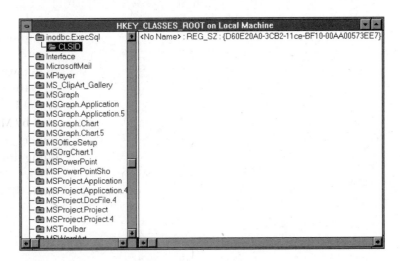

Figure 8-49.
The registry editor showing the entry for inodbc.ExecSql and the CLSID.

The inodbc.ExecSql registry entry was created by the Inside ODBC set-up program. The file containing the entries that the setup creates is located with the sample code for ODBCAUTO in ODBCAUTO.REG.

VBA then uses the CLSID from inodbc.ExecSql to find yet another entry in the registry, as shown in Figure 8-50.

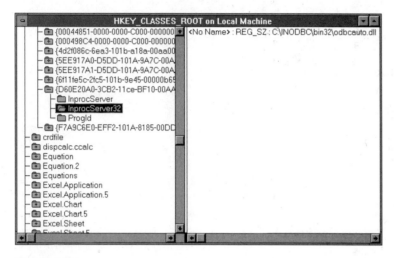

Figure 8-50.
The CLSID registry entry for inodbc.ExecSql, showing the reference to ODBCAUTO.DLL.

Here, at last, we see the reference to ODBCAUTO.DLL under the InprocServer32 entry for the CLSID. The call to the *CreateObject* function ultimately causes the ODBCAUTO.DLL to be loaded, and through the wonders of OLE and MFC, the necessary interfaces are initialized to access the methods of the *CODBCExec* and *ODBCColumn* objects in ODBCAUTO.DLL.

When a method such as *Connect* is invoked, code generated by MFC is used to map the string passed from VBA (which would be "Connect" in this case) to the OLE Automation library and then to the corresponding function address in ODBCAUTO.DLL. The generated code from MFC that does the mapping for all the methods is located in AUTOEXEC.CPP and is shown in Figure 8-51 on the following page.

```
BEGIN_DISPATCH_MAP(CAutoExec, CCmdTarget)
    //{{AFX_DISPATCH_MAP(CAutoExec)
    DISP_PROPERTY_EX(CAutoExec, "ColumnCount", GetColumnCount,
        SetNotSupported, VT_I2)
    DISP_FUNCTION(CAutoExec, "Connect", Connect, VT_BOOL,
        VTS_BSTR)
    DISP_FUNCTION(CAutoExec, "ExecSql", ExecSql, VT_BOOL,
        VTS_BSTR)
    DISP_FUNCTION(CAutoExec, "Disconnect", Disconnect, VT_EMPTY,
        VTS_NONE)
    DISP_FUNCTION(CAutoExec, "SetCurCol", SetCurCol, VT_EMPTY,
        VTS_I2)
    DISP_FUNCTION(CAutoExec, "GetColName", GetColName, VT_BSTR,
        VTS_NONE)
    DISP_FUNCTION(CAutoExec, "GetRowData", GetRowData, VT_BSTR,
        VTS_I4)
    DISP_FUNCTION(CAutoExec, "RowCount", RowCount, VT_I4,
        VTS_NONE)
    //}}AFX_DISPATCH_MAP
END_DISPATCH_MAP()
```

Figure 8-51.
The MFC code for mapping methods, from AUTOEXEC.CPP.

When the VBA call

```
MyQuery.Connect(szConnectStr)
```

is made, the string "Connect" is mapped to the actual function *Connect*, for which a stub was generated by MFC. Code was added to the stub to call the function that actually does the work, which in this case is the *fConnect* method:

```
BOOL CAutoExec::Connect(LPCTSTR pszConnStr)
{
    return m_ODBCExec.fConnect(pszConnStr);
}
```

The *m_ODBCExec* variable is an instance of the class *CODBCExec*, and the implementation for *fConnect* is located in CPPODBC.CPP, just as it was in CPPSMPL. All the other functions are handled in exactly the same way.

Although we didn't touch on any of the details of OLE Automation, the example should give you enough of a start to allow you to add your own embellishments for ODBC.

For the final set of examples, we turn our attention to Visual Basic version 3 and look at several ways ODBC can be used in the Visual Basic environment.

REFERENCES

For further information about OLE, MFC, and Microsoft Excel, consult the following references:

Kraig Brockschmidt, *Inside OLE 2*, Microsoft Press, 1994.

OLE 2 Programmer's Reference, Microsoft Corporation, 1993.

Microsoft Visual C++ Development System and Tools, version 2.0, Microsoft, 1995.

Microsoft Excel 5 documentation, Microsoft Corporation, 1993.

The Visual Basic Samples

The final four samples are written in Visual Basic. If you have Visual Basic installed on your machine and intend to look at the source code for these samples, you should know a few things about how each sample is organized.

First, in each sample you'll see four modules in the project. The modules are called ODBCOR_G.BI, ODBCOR_M.BI, ODBEXT_G.BI, and ODBEXT_M.BI. These modules include all the ODBC #defines and ODBC function prototypes from the ODBC C header files SQL.H and SQLEXT.H, respectively.

Second, most of the code that calls ODBC directly is in a BAS module; the code that is contained in the Visual Basic forms uses a higher level interface that simplifies some of the details and the C orientation of the ODBC API.

Finally, if you decide to use these modules as the basis for your own applications, pay close attention to how variables are declared and passed to ODBC functions. The correct use of ByVal and user-defined types is imperative, but it isn't always obvious when to use what. Trust me; it took a lot of e-mail to the Visual Basic developers to figure out how to do some things!

With these comments in mind, let's delve in the world of ODBC and Visual Basic....

8.6   The Simple ODBC for Visual Basic Sample (VBODBC)

VBODBC embellishes the high-level, connect-and-execute type of interface that we used in CPPSMPL and ODBCAUTO by adding a fetch model that uses ODBC scrollable cursors. VBODBC is not intended to teach you how to program in Visual Basic but is intended to provide specific information about how to interface Visual Basic and ODBC. In addition, VBODBC provides a simple query tool and a nicer output model for cursors than we have seen in any of the C or C++ examples.

Unlike the previous examples, VBODBC supports scrollable cursors with *SQLExtendedFetch* and shows the use of two of the catalog functions, *SQLTables* and *SQLColumns*.

This discussion follows the format that was used in the previous examples. First the user interface is described; then the application programming model that uses the simple interface to ODBC is discussed; and finally the implementation of the simple interface is described, showing how it calls ODBC directly.

8.6.1   The VBODBC User Interface

The user interface for VBODBC provides the usual simple connection functionality, the ability to execute SQL statements, and the ability to scroll around the results set using a variety of options. Figure 8-52 shows the main Visual Basic form for VBODBC.

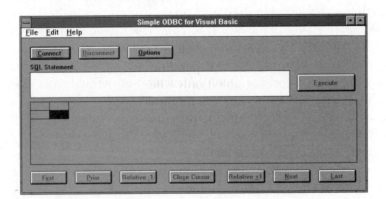

Figure 8-52.
The main form for VBODBC.

The Connect and Disconnect buttons duplicate the functionality found in the File menu that was shown in the previous examples. (The File menu items are included here too, but the buttons are easier to use.) Once you are connected to the data source, you can enter any SQL statement in the edit control and click the Execute button (or choose Execute from the File menu). As a convenience, you can also enter the word *tables* to call *SQLTables*, which will show you a list of the tables that you can access, as shown in Figure 8-53. You can also enter the word *columns* to call *SQLColumns*, which will show you a list of all columns for all tables.

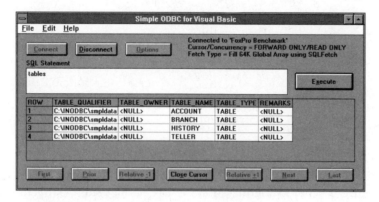

Figure 8-53.
The result of calling SQLTables *in VBODBC.*

The Options button can be used to set the various cursor options. By default, VBODBC operates like CPPSMPL: it executes the SQL statements and fetches all the results into memory (into the grid control, in this case). The Options button enables you to use a true fetch model to get the data and allows you to set many of the cursor capabilities available in ODBC.

The Options button is enabled only when there is no open cursor, so you might need to click the Close Cursor button at the bottom of the window before you can set options for the ODBC cursor types and for how the data will be fetched.

The ODBC Cursor Options dialog box can be displayed either before or after you have connected to a data source. If you use the dialog box before connection, all cursor options for multirow cursors can be set, even if the driver for the data source cannot support some of the options. If you use the options dialog box after connecting, however, the code uses *SQLGetInfo* to enable only the options supported by the driver. The ODBC Cursor Options dialog box is shown in Figure 8-54 on the following page.

403

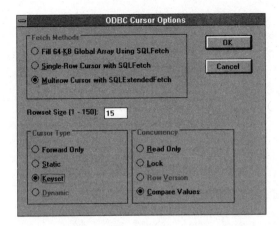

Figure 8-54.
The ODBC Cursor Options dialog box in VBODBC.

In the Fetch Methods area of the dialog box, you can choose from the following options:

■ **Fill 64-KB Global Array Using *SQLFetch*** This option fetches all the data after Execute is clicked in the main window and stores it (up to 64 KB) in memory as we did in the CPPSMPL example. In this case the scroll buttons at the bottom of the main window will be disabled, and the grid control can be manipulated directly because it already contains all the data.

■ **Single-Row Cursor With *SQLFetch*** This option uses a single-row cursor with *SQLFetch* and *SQLGetData*. In this case you will see only one row at a time in the output grid, and only the Next button in the main window will be enabled.

■ **Multirow Cursor With *SQLExtendedFetch*** This option uses a multi-row cursor with *SQLExtendedFetch*, using *SQLSetPos* to position the cursor within the rowset and *SQLGetData* to fill the rowset. All the scroll buttons at the bottom of the main window will be enabled when this option is selected. You don't have to use *SQLBindCol* with *SQLExtendedFetch*; the *SQLSetPos* and *SQLGetData* technique used in VBODBC accomplishes the same multirow fetch model, although a bit more coding is involved. We'll see exactly how this is done in section 8.6.3. (An example dedicated to using *SQLBindCol* with *SQLExtendedFetch*, VBFETCH, will demonstrate some of the challenges presented by Visual Basic's memory model when binding in ODBC is used.)

The lower half of the options dialog box contains the three standard control options for cursors: the rowset size, the cursor type, and the concurrency control setting. We discussed these options in Chapter 5 (section 5.5). The grid control on the main window will be filled with the number of rows specified in the rowset. Scrolling operations apply to the entire rowset.

That concludes our quick tour through the user interface of VBODBC. Next let's look at the programming model that underlies the main features of this application.

8.6.2 Inside VBODBC: The Application Programming Model

The simple ODBC application programming model for VBODBC consists of six functions:

■ **ODBC_Connect(***hwnd, DSN, UserId, Password***)** This function connects to the data source. The application can supply the input data source name (DSN), user ID, and password. However, empty strings can also be supplied for *DSN, UserId*, and *Password*, in which case the Driver Manager and the driver will prompt the user for the information. Here is the code that is executed when the Connect button is clicked:

```
If (True = ODBC_Connect((frmMain.hWnd), "", "", "")) Then
    Call SetControlStatus(gConnect.fConnected)
End if
```

■ **ODBC_Execute(***SQL***)** This function executes the input SQL string. When the Execute button is clicked, the following code is executed:

```
If (ODBC_Execute((txtSQL.Text))) Then
⋮
```

txtSQL.Text is the contents of the edit control that contains the SQL statement.

■ **ODBC_ExtFetch(***FetchDir, Rownum***)** This function fetches a set of rows in the direction specified by *FetchDir*. This direction can be SQL_FETCH_NEXT, SQL_FETCH_RELATIVE, SQL_FETCH_PRIOR, and so forth. If *FetchDir* is either SQL_FETCH_RELATIVE or SQL_FETCH_ABSOLUTE, the *Rownum* argument indicates the relative or absolute row number to fetch. The scroll buttons at the bottom of the window use *ODBC_ExtFetch*. For example, here is the code that is executed when the Next button is clicked:

```
If (ODBC_ExtFetch(SQL_FETCH_NEXT, 0)) Then
⋮
```

Here is the code that is executed when the Relative −1 button is clicked:

```
If (ODBC_ExtFetch(SQL_FETCH_RELATIVE, -1)) Then
    ⋮
```

- ■ **ODBC_Fetch**   This function fetches the next row and is used only for single-row, forward-only cursors.
- ■ **ODBC_Close**   This function closes the cursor that is currently open.
- ■ **ODBC_Disconnect**   This function disconnects from the data source.

To control the cursor options and to get information about results sets, the application uses the variable *gExecute*, which is declared as a user-defined type called TypeExecute. Figure 8-55 shows the definition of TypeExecute and *gExecute* in VBODBC.BAS.

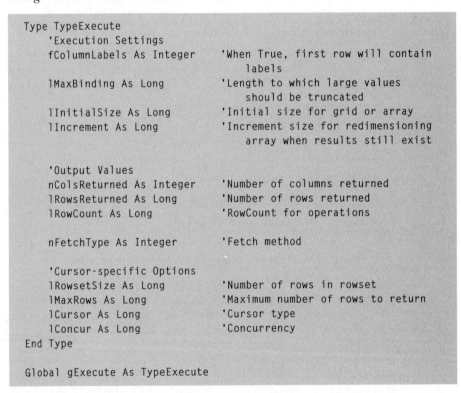

```
Type TypeExecute
    'Execution Settings
    fColumnLabels As Integer       'When True, first row will contain
                                       labels
    lMaxBinding As Long            'Length to which large values
                                       should be truncated
    lInitialSize As Long           'Initial size for grid or array
    lIncrement As Long             'Increment size for redimensioning
                                       array when results still exist


    'Output Values
    nColsReturned As Integer       'Number of columns returned
    lRowsReturned As Long          'Number of rows returned
    lRowCount As Long              'RowCount for operations


    nFetchType As Integer          'Fetch method


    'Cursor-specific Options
    lRowsetSize As Long            'Number of rows in rowset
    lMaxRows As Long               'Maximum number of rows to return
    lCursor As Long                'Cursor type
    lConcur As Long                'Concurrency
End Type

Global gExecute As TypeExecute
```

Figure 8-55.
The definition of TypeExecute and gExecute *in VBODBC.BAS.*

The *gExecute* variable is used by the VBODBC application to set the various fetch options and cursor options from the Options menu when the OK button is pressed, as shown in the following code:

```
'Store option values
If gExecute.nFetchType < 2 Then
    gExecute.lRowsetSize = 1
    gExecute.lCursor = SQL_CURSOR_FORWARD_ONLY
    gExecute.lConcur = SQL_CONCUR_READ_ONLY
Else
    'Check to see whether we have a valid rowset size range
    If (Val(txtRowset.Text) < 1 Or Val(txtRowset.Text) > 150) Then
        MsgBox "Invalid Rowset Size", MB_OK + MB_ICONSTOP
        txtRowset.SetFocus
        Exit Sub
    End If

    gExecute.lRowsetSize = Val(txtRowset.Text)

    'Set global cursor type and concurrency based on
    'values set in control arrays. This code relies on the
    'fact that the cursor types in ODBC are numbered zero
    'through three and concurrency types one through four.
    For i = 0 To 3
        If CursorType(i) = True Then
            gExecute.lCursor = i
        End If
        If Concurrency(i + 1) = True Then
            gExecute.lConcur = i + 1
        End If
    Next i
End If
```

Two other procedures are very valuable if you use VBODBC to build your own application. The first is *FillResultsArray*, which takes as an input argument the number of rows to retrieve into memory; the second is *FillGridFromArray*, which takes as input arguments the name of a grid control and the number of rows to display in the grid. For example, when the Next button is clicked, the following logic is used to retrieve the next rowset of data and fill the grid control for both multirow and single-row fetch options:

```
If (gExecute.nFetchType = MULTIROW_FETCH) Then
    If (ODBC_ExtFetch(SQL_FETCH_NEXT, 0)) Then
        fOK = FillResultsArray(gExecute.lRowsetSize)
        Call FillGridFromArray(grdResults, gExecute.lRowsetSize)
    End If
Else
    If ODBC_Fetch() Then
        fOK = FillResultsArray(1)
        Call FillGridFromArray(grdResults, 1)
    End If
End If
```

This is a lot easier than using *printf* format specifiers, as we did in CPPSMPL, and it looks better too!

To conclude our discussion of this example, let's see what's behind this easy-to-use, six-function application layer.

8.6.3 Inside VBODBC: How the Application Layer Is Implemented

As you might guess, of the six functions *ODBC_Connect* is the easiest to implement. Aside from building up a connection string with the input arguments, all *ODBC_Connect* does is allocate the environment handle and a connection handle, call *SQLDriverConnect*, and allocate a statement handle.

ODBC_Execute is a bit more involved because the statement options have to be set using *SQLSetStmtOption* and the checks for the special keywords *tables* and *columns* have to be made. Other than that, it is just a straight call to *SQLExecDirect*. Figure 8-56 shows the code for *ODBC_Execute* in VBODBC.BAS.

```
Function ODBC_Execute (szSQLString As String) As Integer
Dim rc As Integer
Dim fOK As Integer

    'Initialize return value
    ODBC_Execute = False

    'Clean up statement handle
    fOK = ODBC_Close()

    'Set cursor options for ExtendedFetch
    If gExecute.nFetchType = MULTIROW_FETCH Then
        'Set the rowset size
        rc = SQLSetStmtOption(ByVal gConnect.pHstmt,
            SQL_ROWSET_SIZE, gExecute.lRowsetSize)
        If (False = CheckSuccess(HNDL_HSTMT, gConnect.pHstmt, rc))
            Then
            MsgBox "Prior message meant the rowset size of " &
                gExecute.lRowsetSize &
                " could not be set; prior value will be used.",
                MB_OK + MB_ICONINFORMATION
        End If

        'Set the cursor type
        rc = SQLSetStmtOption(ByVal gConnect.pHstmt,
            SQL_CURSOR_TYPE, gExecute.lCursor)
        If (False = CheckSuccess(HNDL_HSTMT, gConnect.pHstmt, rc))
            Then
            MsgBox "Prior message meant the cursor type
                was not valid; prior value will be used.",
```

Figure 8-56.
The code for ODBC_Execute.

Figure 8-56. *continued*

```
            MB_OK + MB_ICONINFORMATION
    End If


    'Set the concurrency
    rc = SQLSetStmtOption(ByVal gConnect.pHstmt,
        SQL_CONCURRENCY, gExecute.1Concur)
    If (False = CheckSuccess(HNDL_HSTMT, gConnect.pHstmt, rc))
        Then
        MsgBox "Prior message meant the concurrency type
            was not valid; prior value will be used.",
            MB_OK + MB_ICONINFORMATION
    End If


    'Set the maximum number of rows to retrieve from the DBMS
    rc = SQLSetStmtOption(ByVal gConnect.pHstmt, SQL_MAX_ROWS,
        gExecute.1MaxRows)
    If (False = CheckSuccess(HNDL_HSTMT, gConnect.pHstmt, rc))
        Then
        MsgBox "Prior message meant the maximum number of rows
            could not be set; prior value will be used.",
            MB_OK + MB_ICONINFORMATION
    End If

End If


If (0 = StrComp(szSQLString, "tables", 1)) Then
    rc = SQLTables(ByVal gConnect.pHstmt, ByVal 0&, SQL_NTS,
        ByVal 0&, SQL_NTS, ByVal 0&, SQL_NTS,
        ByVal 0&, SQL_NTS)
    If (True = CheckSuccess(HNDL_HSTMT, gConnect.pHstmt, rc))
        Then
        ODBC_Execute = True
        Exit Function
    End If
    GoTo cleanup
End If


If (0 = StrComp(szSQLString, "columns", 1)) Then
    rc = SQLColumns(ByVal gConnect.pHstmt, ByVal 0&, SQL_NTS,
        ByVal 0&, SQL_NTS, ByVal 0&, SQL_NTS,
        ByVal 0&, SQL_NTS)
    If (True = CheckSuccess(HNDL_HSTMT, gConnect.pHstmt, rc))
        Then
        ODBC_Execute = True
        Exit Function
    End If
    GoTo cleanup
End If
```

(continued)

Figure 8-56. *continued*

```
    'Execute DML and DDL operations
    rc = SQLExecDirect(ByVal gConnect.pHstmt, ByVal szSQLString,
        SQL_NTS)
    If (True = CheckSuccess(HNDL_HSTMT, gConnect.pHstmt, rc)) Then
        ODBC_Execute = True
        Exit Function
    End If

cleanup:
    fOK = ODBC_Close()

End Function
```

The *ODBC_ExtFetch* function is a very straightforward mapping to the *SQLExtendedFetch* function:

```
Function ODBC_ExtFetch (lFetchDir As Long, iRow As Long) As Long
Dim lRows As Long

    ODBC_ExtFetch = 0
    ReDim gnRowStatus(gExecute.lRowsetSize)

    rc = SQLExtendedFetch(ByVal gConnect.pHstmt, lFetchDir, iRow, lRows,
        gnRowStatus(0))

    If (SQL_NO_DATA_FOUND = rc) Then
        MsgBox "No more records exist in the direction you are
            fetching", MB_OK + MB_ICONINFORMATION
        Exit Function
    End If

    If (CheckSuccess(HNDL_HSTMT, gConnect.pHstmt, rc)) Then
        ODBC_ExtFetch = lRows
    End If
End Function
```

Note the use of a very nice Visual Basic feature: the dynamic resizing of arrays. The status array for *SQLExtendedFetch*, *gnRowStatus*, can be redimensioned to match the rowset size very easily.

ODBC_Fetch is nearly identical to *ODBC_ExtFetch*, so I won't bother to show the code. It simply uses a call to *SQLFetch* instead of to *SQLExtendedFetch* and doesn't have to bother with the status array.

ODBC_Close and *ODBC_Disconnect* are thin wrappers for *SQLFreeStmt* and *SQLDisconnect*.

Finally, the code for *FillResultsArray* merits some discussion. Recall that there are three ways to retrieve data: get it all up front (up to 64 KB of memory), get a single row, or get multiple rows per fetch using the rowset size specified in the ODBC Cursor Options dialog box. If we want to retrieve the entire result, we simply call *SQLFetch* and *SQLGetData* for every row and column, dynamically increasing the array size by 10 rows as needed. Figure 8-57 shows the first portion of *FillResultsArray*, which includes the code for the first option.

```
Function FillResultsArray (lCursorSize As Long) As Integer
Dim i As Integer
Dim j As Integer
Dim pHstmt As Long

    pHstmt = gConnect.pHstmt
    'Initialize return value
    FillResultsArray = True

    On Error GoTo ErrHandler

    'Resize the arrays to hold the data
    ReDim gszResults(gExecute.nColsReturned, lCursorSize)
    ReDim gcbResults(gExecute.nColsReturned, lCursorSize)

    'Determine the routine to call to retrieve the data
    Select Case gExecute.nFetchType
        Case FETCH_64K
            'Retrieve all the data available or up to the
            'amount that will fit in a 64-KB block using
            'SQLFetch and SQLGetData
            gExecute.lRowsReturned = 0

            While (rc <> SQL_NO_DATA_FOUND)
                i = gExecute.lRowsReturned
                For j = 0 To (gExecute.nColsReturned - 1)
                    'Initialize the string buffer
                    gszResults(j, i) =
                        String(glDisplaySize(j) + 1, 0)
                    rc = SQLGetData(ByVal pHstmt, j + 1,
                        SQL_C_CHAR, ByVal gszResults(j, i),
                        glDisplaySize(j), gcbResults(j, i))

                    'If an error occurred on SQLGetData
                    If (rc = SQL_ERROR) Then
                        gszResults(j, i) = "<ERROR>"
                    End If
```

Figure 8-57. *(continued)*

The first portion of FillResultsArray *showing the code that retrieves all data up front.*

Figure 8-57. *continued*

```
                        'If SQL_NULL_DATA was returned
                        If (gcbResults(j, i) = SQL_NULL_DATA) Then
                            gszResults(j, i) = "<NULL>"
                        End If
                    Next j

                    'Increment the count of rows and get the next row
                    gExecute.lRowsReturned =
                        gExecute.lRowsReturned + 1
                    rc = SQLFetch(ByVal pHstmt)

                    If (lCursorSize <= (gExecute.lRowsReturned + 1))
                        Then
                        lCursorSize = lCursorSize + 10
                        ReDim Preserve
                            gszResults(gExecute.nColsReturned,
                            lCursorSize)
                        ReDim Preserve
                            gcbResults(gExecute.nColsReturned,
                            lCursorSize)
                    End If

                    'If an error occurs or no data is found, return
                    If (rc <> SQL_NO_DATA_FOUND) Then
                        If (CheckSuccess(HNDL_HSTMT,
                            gConnect.pHstmt, rc) = False) Then
                            rc = SQL_NO_DATA_FOUND
                        End If
                    End If
                Wend
            ⋮
```

For the single-row fetch case, the code is quite simple: the application just calls *SQLGetData* on each column for the next row and then returns.

```
Case SINGLE_FETCH
    'Retrieve a single row of data using SQLGetData
    'and SQLFetch
    i = 0
    For j = 0 To (gExecute.nColsReturned - 1)
        'Initialize the string buffer
        gszResults(j, i) = String(glDisplaySize(j) + 1, 0)
        rc = SQLGetData(ByVal pHstmt, j + 1, SQL_C_CHAR,
            ByVal gszResults(j, i), glDisplaySize(j), gcbResults(j, i))
```

continued

```
        'If an error occurred on SQLGetData
        If (rc = SQL_ERROR) Then
            gszResults(j, i) = "<ERROR>"
        End If

        'If SQL_NULL_DATA was returned
        If (gcbResults(j, i) = SQL_NULL_DATA) Then
            gszResults(j, i) = "<NULL>"
        End If
    Next j
```

The multirow fetch case is a bit tricky because we are not using binding to automatically get multiple rows with a single call to *SQLExtendedFetch*. (You'll see why in the next example.) So we must explicitly position to each row in the multirow cursor with *SQLSetPos*, and then we can use the *SQLGetData* function as usual. Figure 8-58 shows the portion of *FillResultsArray* that handles multirow fetch.

```
Case MULTIROW_FETCH
    'Retrieve a rowset cursor's worth of data using SQLGetData
    'and SQLExtendedFetch
    For i = 0 To (lCursorSize - 1)
        If (gnRowStatus(i) = SQL_ROW_SUCCESS) Then
            'Position to the correct row to call SQLGetData on
            rc = SQLSetPos(ByVal pHstmt, i + 1, SQL_POSITION,
                SQL_LOCK_NO_CHANGE)

            For j = 0 To (gExecute.nColsReturned - 1)
                'Initialize the string buffer
                gszResults(j, i) = String(glDisplaySize(j) + 1, 0)
                rc = SQLGetData(ByVal pHstmt, j + 1, SQL_C_CHAR,
                    ByVal gszResults(j, i), glDisplaySize(j),
                    gcbResults(j, i))

                'If an error occurred on SQLGetData
                If (rc = SQL_ERROR) Then
                    gszResults(j, i) = "<ERROR>"
                End If

                'If SQL_NULL_DATA was returned
                If (gcbResults(j, i) = SQL_NULL_DATA) Then
                    gszResults(j, i) = "<NULL>"
                End If
            Next j
        End If
    Next i
```

Figure 8-58.
The portion of FillResultsArray *that handles multirow fetch.*

I think you'll find VBODBC a useful starting point from which you can build your own Visual Basic applications that use ODBC directly but that hide most of the C flavor of ODBC.

In the next example, we delve a little deeper into the issues of using ODBC binding with Visual Basic.

8.7 The Visual Basic ODBC Binding and Multirow Cursors Sample (VBFETCH)

This example demonstrates how to do row-wise binding in Visual Basic. The most natural data structure for row-wise binding—an array of structures—has some definite idiosyncrasies in Visual Basic that need to be handled carefully to ensure that the memory is laid out correctly.

As you might recall from Chapter 5 (section 5.4.2.2), row-wise binding is useful when the structure of the results set is known in advance. In the VBFETCH example we use the output from two catalog functions, *SQLTables* and *SQLColumns*, for the row-wise binding output.

8.7.1 The VBFETCH User Interface

The user interface for VBFETCH is very similar to the interface for VBODBC except that instead of an edit control in which you can enter an arbitrary SQL string, VBFETCH has only the two buttons labeled SQLTables and SQLColumns. Figure 8-59 shows the main window for VBFETCH after the connection has been made and the SQLTables button has been clicked.

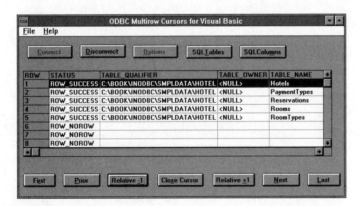

Figure 8-59.
The main form for VBFETCH.

The Connect and Disconnect buttons handle the connection and disconnection operations by calling *SQLDriverConnect* and *SQLDisconnect.* The File menu contains Connect and Disconnect items that call the same code. Clicking the Options button displays the dialog box, shown in Figure 8-60, in which the cursor type and concurrency control options can be set. The options dialog box also includes a check box that allows you to load the cursor library.

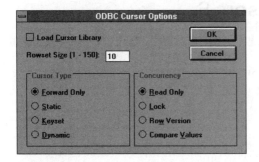

Figure 8-60.
The options dialog box in VBFETCH.

Once the desired options have been set, you can click the SQLTables button on the main window to call the *SQLTables* function (which lists the available tables), or click the SQLColumns button to call *SQLColumns* (which lists all the columns of one or more tables). The results are displayed in the grid control, and the scrolling operations are controlled with the buttons along the bottom of the form. When the table list is displayed, you can select a table name and then click SQLColumns to see the columns for only that table. Otherwise, clicking the SQLColumns button shows all the columns for all the tables in the list.

One more ODBC feature is used in the user interface of VBFETCH. This is one that we didn't explore in VBODBC: the use of the *status array* in *SQLExtendedFetch.* In the VBFETCH grid control, you'll see one more column to the right of the row number. This column contains the value that is in the status array for each row in the rowset. ODBC defines several possible values for the status array:

- **SQL_ROW_SUCCESS** This value indicates that the row was fetched successfully.

- **SQL_ROW_DELETED** This value indicates that the row was deleted (for dynamic and keyset-driven cursors only).

415

■ **SQL_ROW_ERROR**   This value indicates that the row could not be retrieved.

■ **SQL_ROW_ADDED**   This value indicates that the row is a new row that was added by your application.

■ **SQL_ROW_NOROW**   This value indicates that the end of the results set was reached and that the row of the rowset does not contain any data.

In VBFETCH, you'll probably see only the SQL_ROW_SUCCESS and SQL_ROW_NOROW values because it is unlikely that other users will make any changes to the system tables that would be reflected in *SQLTables* or *SQLColumns*.

8.7.2   How to Perform Row-Wise Binding in Visual Basic

Before we look at the code for VBFETCH, let's go through a simple example to explain the concepts behind row-wise binding in Visual Basic.

Because Visual Basic has extensive string management capabilities, it is not always clear how Visual Basic allocates memory for its string variables. This is of no consequence when you are staying within the Visual Basic environment, but when you are calling into C DLLs such as ODBC, it matters a lot. Internally, Visual Basic uses either fixed-length strings or variable-length strings. Only fixed-length strings can be used for ODBC row-wise binding. Variable-length strings actually have a length prefixed to the string data, and they are subject to being moved to a different location in memory when Visual Basic's memory manager needs to compact space. For these two reasons, trying to use variable-length Visual Basic strings for binding with *SQLBindCol* in ODBC would be a disaster; ODBC doesn't use length-prefixed strings, and it requires the data to remain in a fixed location as long as the string data is bound.

To declare a fixed-length string in Visual Basic, simply specify the length in the declaration, as in:

```
Dim str1 As String * 25
```

For row-wise binding, memory for all returned columns must be allocated in one contiguous chunk so that one row of data follows another. Thus, the best data structure to use for row-wise binding is an array of structures, known in Visual Basic terminology as an *array of user-defined types*. Further complications arise when you use Visual Basic strings within user-defined types, but fortunately there is a way to make everything work.

To allocate a user-defined type in Visual Basic so that it can be used with ODBC row-wise binding, each string variable must be declared as a separate type with the appropriate length. For example, the following can be used in Visual Basic to declare a string variable of length 25:

```
Type TypeFixedStr25
    strData As String * 25
End Type
```

Then the fixed-string type can be used in another type definition for row-wise binding, such as

```
Type TypeCustomer
    Name As TypeFixedStr25
    lName As Long
    InterestRate As Double
    lInterestRate As Long
End Type
```

For ODBC row-wise binding, each data element in the user-defined type (for example, *Name* and *InterestRate* in the TypeCustomer example just shown) must have a corresponding length or indicator variable (which would be *lName* and *lInterestRate* in TypeCustomer) for reporting output lengths and whether the data was NULL.

Next, because Visual Basic doesn't have the equivalent of the C *sizeof* operator, the total size of the user-defined type must be explicitly defined so that the size can be passed to *SQLSetStmtOption* when we specify the bind type. One way to do this is to declare a global constant and place it in the code immediately after the definition of the user-defined type, as shown in this example:

```
Global Const SizeofTypeCustomer = 41
```

Alternatively, you could use the *Len* function to compute the length at runtime, but you must be sure to redimension the array first and use one element of the array as the argument to *Len*, as in *Len(Customer(0))*. In VBFETCH, the array is dimensioned after the call to *SQLSetStmtOption* sets the bind type to row-wise binding, so the length constant is used.

To declare the array of the user-defined type, you can either hard-code the number of rows, as in

```
Global Customer(15) As TypeCustomer
```

or you can omit the number of rows and fill it in later, as in

```
Global Customer() As TypeCustomer
```

The latter case has the advantage of allowing you to dimension the array to the rowset size, which might vary, depending on the application. For example, if the application allows the user to set the rowset size (as VBFETCH does) or dynamically sets the rowset size based on the number of rows that can be displayed at one time, it is better not to hard-code the dimension of the array in the declaration. If you do, you can't use *ReDim* in the code to change its size.

Now let's look at how the ODBC function calls work. To specify row-wise binding, *SQLSetStmtOption* is used with the SQL_BIND_TYPE option and the length of the user-defined type. Here is an example for the *Customer* variable shown above:

```
SQLSetStmtOption(hstmt, SQL_BIND_TYPE, SizeofTypeCustomer)
```

The rowset size, cursor type, and concurrency option are also set with *SQLSetStmtOption*. For example, the rowset size is set to 15 with the code:

```
RowSetSize = 15
SQLSetStmtOption(hstmt, SQL_ROWSET_SIZE, RowSetSize)
```

Next the TypeCustomer array and the status array are dimensioned according to the number of rows in the rowset, and each data element of *Customer* is bound with *SQLBindCol*:

```
ReDim Customer(RowSetSize)
ReDim RowStatus(RowSetSize)

rc = SQLBindCol(ByVal hstmt, 1, SQL_C_CHAR, Customer(0).Name,
    Len(Customer(0).Name), Customer(0).lName)
rc = SQLBindCol(ByVal hstmt, 2, SQL_C_DOUBLE, Customer(0).InterestRate,
    8, Customer(0).lInterestRate)
```

Note that the data element and the output length for a single results column are both specified in one call to *SQLBindCol*.

The SQL SELECT statement can be executed with *SQLExecDirect*:

```
SQLExecDirect (hstmt,
    "select name, rate from customer where city = 'Boston'", SQL_NTS);
```

The data can be retrieved with *SQLExtendedFetch*:

```
SQLExtendedFetch(ByVal hstmt, lFetchDir, 1, lRows, RowStatus(0))
```

When the call to *SQLExtendedFetch* returns, the elements in the *Customer* array will have been set and can be accessed using the form

```
Customer(row_number).element_name.string_type_name
```

for strings and the form

```
Customer(row_number).element_name
```

for nonstrings. For example, to display the fifth customer name and the corresponding interest rate, the syntax is

```
MsgBox "Customer name = " & Customer(4).Name.strData &
    ";  Interest rate = " & Customer(4).InterestRate
```

Note in particular the reference to the customer name. To access string data, you *do not* simply use the form given to *SQLBindCol*; you must also tack on the type name of the string. In other words, for the *Customer* user-defined type, it is not correct to use:

```
MsgBox "Customer name = " & Customer(4).Name          ' not valid!
```

But it is correct to specify:

```
MsgBox "Customer name = " & Customer(4).Name.strData    ' valid
```

Also note that arrays in Visual Basic are zero-based (although this can be overridden with the *Option Base* statement), so the fifth element is actually *Customer(4)*.

8.7.3 Inside VBFETCH

Let's see how the VBFETCH example implements row-wise binding for the two queries it handles: *SQLTables* and *SQLColumns*. The types are declared in the file VBFETCH.BAS, as shown in Figure 8-61.

```
' Stub Type to force contiguous memory when embedded in another
' structure
'
Type TypeFixedStr128
    strData As String * 128
End Type


'
' SQLTables Constants and Field Definitions
'
Global Const SizeofTypeTables = 660
Type TypeTables
    szQualifier As TypeFixedStr128
    lQualifier As Long
    szOwner As TypeFixedStr128
```

Figure 8-61.   *(continued)*
Type declarations in VBFETCH.BAS.

Figure 8-61. *continued*

```
        lOwner As Long
        szTableName As TypeFixedStr128
        lTableName As Long
        szTableType As TypeFixedStr128
        lTableType As Long
        szRemarks As TypeFixedStr128
        lRemarks As Long
End Type
Global gTables() As TypeTables


'
' SQLColumns Field Definitions
'
Global Const SizeofTypeColumns = 832
Type TypeColumns
        szQualifier As TypeFixedStr128
        lQualifier As Long
        szOwner As TypeFixedStr128
        lOwner As Long
        szTableName As TypeFixedStr128
        lTableName As Long
        szColumnName As TypeFixedStr128
        lColumnName As Long
        nDataType As Integer
        lDataType As Long
        szTypeName As TypeFixedStr128
        lTypeName As Long
        nPrecision As Long
        lPrecision As Long
        nLength As Long
        lLength As Long
        nScale As Integer
        lScale As Long
        nRadix As Integer
        lRadix As Long
        nNullable As Integer
        lNullable As Long
        szRemarks As TypeFixedStr128
        lRemarks As Long
End Type
Global gColumns() As TypeColumns
```

When the SQLTables button is clicked in the main window, the Visual Basic *cmdTables_Click* function is called. This function sets the size of the type in a global information structure called *gOptions.lRowBindSize* using the constant *SizeofTypeTables*. Then *cmdTables_Click* calls *ODBC_Execute* with the query to be executed. This is the same *ODBC_Execute* we used in VBODBC. Here is the relevant code fragment from *cmdTables_Click*:

```
gOptions.1RowBindSize = SizeofTypeTables
If (ODBC_Execute("tables")) Then
    ⋮
    Call cmdNext_Click
    ⋮
End If
```

In *ODBC_Execute*, the statement options for the rowset size, the cursor type, and the concurrency are set with *SQLSetStmtOption*. The *ODBC_Execute* code checks for the string "tables" and, if it finds it, executes *ODBC_Tables*. The *ODBC_Tables* function binds the columns with *SQLBindCol* and calls *SQLTables*, as shown in Figure 8-62. Note the use of *ReDim* to dimension the *gTables* array and the *gnRowStatus* status array to the rowset size. Each call to *SQLBindCol* takes the data and output length element of the *gTables* array.

```
Function ODBC_Tables (pHstmt As Long) As Integer
Dim rc As Integer

    rc = SQLTables(ByVal pHstmt, ByVal 0&, SQL_NTS,
        ByVal 0&, SQL_NTS, ByVal 0&, SQL_NTS, ByVal 0&, SQL_NTS)

    If (SQL_SUCCESS_WITH_INFO = rc) Then
        MsgBox "SQLTables returned SQL_SUCCESS_WITH_INFO; most
            likely the options chosen are not valid for this
            results set type. The actual error message follows.",
            MB_ICONINFORMATION
        Call PostError(HNDL_HSTMT, pHstmt)
    End If

    If (True = CheckSuccess(HNDL_HSTMT, gConnect.pHstmt, rc)) Then
        On Error GoTo ErrTables

        'Reset arrays to rowset size
        ReDim gTables(gOptions.1RowsetSize)
        ReDim gnRowStatus(gOptions.1RowsetSize)

        ' Bind the columns to a memory address
        rc = SQLBindCol(ByVal pHstmt, 1, SQL_C_CHAR,
            gTables(0).szQualifier, MAX_QUALIFIER,
            gTables(0).1Qualifier)
```

Figure 8-62.   *(continued)*
The ODBC_Tables *function.*

421

Figure 8-62. *continued*

```
        rc = SQLBindCol(ByVal pHstmt, 2, SQL_C_CHAR,
            gTables(0).szOwner, MAX_OWNER,
            gTables(0).lOwner)
        rc = SQLBindCol(ByVal pHstmt, 3, SQL_C_CHAR,
            gTables(0).szTableName, MAX_TABLENAME,
            gTables(0).lTableName)
        rc = SQLBindCol(ByVal pHstmt, 4, SQL_C_CHAR,
            gTables(0).szTableType, MAX_TABLETYPE,
            gTables(0).lTableType)
        rc = SQLBindCol(ByVal pHstmt, 5, SQL_C_CHAR,
            gTables(0).szRemarks, MAX_REMARKS,
            gTables(0).lRemarks)


        ODBC_Tables = True
    End If
    Exit Function

ErrTables:
    If (Err = 14) Then        'Out of string space
        fOK = MsgBox("Out of string space; rowset size too large",
            MB_ICONSTOP)
        ODBC_Tables = False
        Exit Function
    Else
        Resume Next
    End If

End Function
```

After the call to *ODBC_Tables* finishes, *ODBC_Execute* returns and the *cmdNext_Click* function is called:

```
Sub cmdNext_Click ()
    frmMain.MousePointer = HOUR_GLASS
    If (ODBC_ExtFetch(SQL_FETCH_NEXT, 0)) Then
        If (RSLT_TABLES = gOptions.nResultType) Then
            Call FillGridFromTablesArray(grdResults)
        Else
            Call FillGridFromColumnsArray(grdResults)
        End If
    End If
    frmMain.MousePointer = ARROW
End Sub
```

In *cmdNext_Click*, the function *ODBC_ExtFetch* is called, followed by a call to either the *FillGridFromTablesArray* function or the *FillGridFromColumnsArray* function, depending on which button was clicked. You might recall from the VBODBC example that *ODBC_ExtFetch* is just a wrapper for *SQLExtendedFetch*.

In *FillGridFromTablesArray*, each bound column is copied to the grid control for display. Here is a fragment from *FillGridFromColumnsArray* that demonstrates how strings are handled differently from other data types:

```
Select Case y
    ⋮
    Case 5
    strTemp = gColumns(x).szColumnName.strData
    cbValue = gColumns(x).lColumnName

    Case 6
    strTemp = Str(gColumns(x).nDataType)
    cbValue = gColumns(x).lDataType

    Case 7
    strTemp = gColumns(x).szTypeName.strData
    cbValue = gColumns(x).lTypeName

    Case 8
    strTemp = Str(gColumns(x).nPrecision)
    cbValue = gColumns(x).lPrecision
    ⋮
End Select

If (SQL_NULL_DATA = cbValue) Then
    grdResult.Text = "<NULL>"
Else
    grdResult.Text = Left(strTemp, cbValue)
End If
```

Note that for the string data in *Case 5* and *Case 7* the string type name (*strData*) is used in addition to the type member names (*szColumnName* and *szTypeName*), whereas for the numeric types (*lDataType* and *lPrecision*) only the member names are used.

I hope that this example clarifies how to use row-wise binding within Visual Basic. If you really want to build an application that uses row-wise binding, you should make use of the TYPEGEN sample to generate the Visual Basic type definitions and the calls to *SQLBindCol*.

In the next example, we look at another advanced feature of ODBC: invoking stored procedures from Visual Basic.

8.8 The Visual Basic Stored Procedures Sample (VBSPROCS)

In this example we look at how to invoke stored procedures from Visual Basic using ODBC's standard stored procedure syntax. The sample creates and executes some example stored procedures for Microsoft SQL Server (which will also work on Sybase SQL Server) and Oracle 7.

Stored procedures are extremely important to client/server DBMS performance. Often, whether an application runs well or runs poorly is determined by where the different parts of the application are executed: on the client or on the server. The server portion of the application often relies on stored procedures to do the job.

If your client programming environment is Visual Basic and if stored procedures are used to manipulate the data in the DBMS, you will find the VBSPROCS example useful because it shows you how to use ODBC to execute stored procedures, including how to handle input and output parameters, return values, and results sets.

8.8.1 The VBSPROCS User Interface

The user interface for VBSPROCS is quite simple: the user connects to a data source, chooses the target DBMS (Microsoft SQL Server or Oracle), chooses the type of parameters to use in the stored procedure, and sees the results on the screen. Figure 8-63 shows the main window for VBSPROCS.

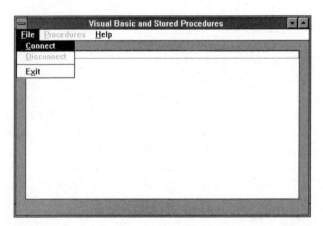

Figure 8-63.
The main window for VBSPROCS.

After a successful connection has been accomplished with the function *SQLDriverConnect*, another dialog box is displayed to retrieve the name of the DBMS product to be used, as shown in Figure 8-64.

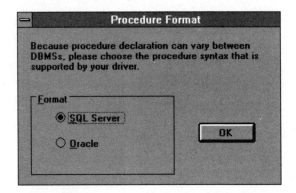

Figure 8-64.
The Procedure Format dialog box.

Now, it may seem a bit strange to be prompting for information specific to a DBMS. After all, isn't ODBC all about interoperability? Unfortunately, the only thing that is even remotely similar between DBMSs with regard to stored procedures is the method used to invoke them; the syntax for *creating* the stored procedures is very different. Because we wanted to have the VBSPROCS example work "out of the box" for both Microsoft SQL Server and Oracle, the syntax for creating the stored procedures is embedded in the Visual Basic source code. However, we'll also see that the syntax for invoking the stored procedures from Visual Basic is exactly the same for Microsoft SQL Server as it is for Oracle: both use ODBC's *call* escape sequence.

In the user interface for VBSPROCS, the Procedures menu contains options that allow you to designate the type of stored procedure you want to create and execute. Figure 8-65 on the following page shows the items on the Procedures menu.

As you can see, the options allow you to create and execute stored procedures with no parameters, with input parameters only, with output parameters only, with a return value, or in a mixed form with two input parameters, one output parameter, and a return value.

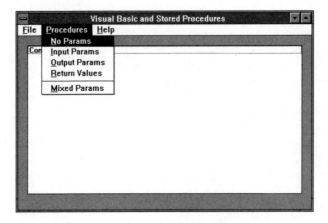

Figure 8-65.
Procedures menu items.

When you select an item, the code creates one or more example stored procedures and executes them, displaying the statements used to create each stored procedure, the standard ODBC syntax used to invoke the procedure, and any output values that are returned. Figure 8-66 shows the results of selecting the Mixed Params item from the Procedures menu for Microsoft SQL Server.

Figure 8-66.
The results of selecting the Mixed Params item from the Procedures menu.

Selecting the other items on the Procedures menu generates similar output. Next we look at the Visual Basic code that creates and executes the stored procedures.

8.8.2 Inside VBSPROCS

We've already looked at enough code that shows how *SQLDriverConnect* makes the connection, so we'll skip over the whole connection process here except to say that you can assume that a valid connection exists and that a statement handle has been allocated.

We will look at the code only for the Mixed Params item on the Procedures menu. The code for the other items is similar.

When the Mixed Params item is selected from the Procedures menu, the procedure *MNU_SPROCS_MIXEDPARAMS_Click* is called. This procedure clears the output window, displays a status message, and calls *ExecMixedParams* with the previously allocated statement handle:

```
Sub MNU_SPROCS_MIXEDPARAMS_Click ()

    frmMain.MousePointer = HOUR_GLASS

    out = ""
    Call DisplayMsg("Example of using stored procedure with INPUT/OUTPUT
        parameters and return values", 0)
    fOK = ExecMixedParams(gHandles.pHstmt)

    frmMain.MousePointer = ARROW

End Sub
```

In *ExecMixedParams* we check for the type of DBMS and call the appropriate function:

```
Function ExecMixedParams (pHstmt As Long) As Integer

    If (gHandles.nProcType = PROC_SQLSERVER) Then
        fOK = SQLMixedParams(pHstmt)
    Else
        fOK = OraMixedParams(pHstmt)
    End If

End Function
```

Let's look at the Oracle version in *OraMixedParams*. The *OraMixedParams* function performs five major steps:

1. It creates the stored procedure *vbMixed1*, which has two input parameters, one output parameter, and a return value. All parameters and the return value are floating-point numbers.

2. It binds the return value and parameters with *SQLBindParameter* to Visual Basic variables of type DOUBLE.

3. It sets the values of the input parameters and executes the stored procedure *vbMixed1* with *SQLExecDirect*.

4. It displays the output parameter and return value.

5. It drops the stored procedure.

Figure 8-67 shows the code for *OraMixedParams*.

```
Function OraMixedParams (pHstmt As Long) As Integer
Const SP_Divide = "vbMixed1"
Const SP_DivideExecute = "{?=Call vbMixed1 (?, ?, ?)}"
Dim rc As Integer
Dim fOK As Integer
Dim dReturn As Double
Dim dDividend As Double
Dim dDivisor As Double
Dim dQuotient As Double
Dim cbValue As Long
Dim i as Integer
Dim szProc As String
Dim crlf As String

    crlf = Chr(13) + Chr(10)

    szProc = "create function vbMixed1 " + crlf
    szProc = szProc + "  (PDividend IN number, " + crlf
    szProc = szProc + "   PDivisor  IN number, " + crlf
    szProc = szProc + "   PQuotient IN OUT number) " + crlf
    szProc = szProc + "RETURN number " + crlf
    szProc = szProc + "as " + crlf
    szProc = szProc + "begin " + crlf
    szProc = szProc + "  PQuotient := PDividend / PDivisor; " +
        crlf
```

Figure 8-67.
The code for OraMixedParams.

Figure 8-67. *continued*

```
szProc = szProc + "   IF PQuotient > 100 THEN " + crlf
szProc = szProc + "      return 1; " + crlf
szProc = szProc + "   ELSE " + crlf
szProc = szProc + "      return 0; " + crlf
szProc = szProc + "   END IF; " + crlf
szProc = szProc + "end;" + crlf


If (False = CreateProc(pHstmt, SP_Divide, szProc)) Then
    OraMixedParams = False
    GoTo OraMixedCleanup
End If


'Bind the buffers and values for the parameters
'of the stored procedure
rc = SQLBindParameter(ByVal pHstmt, 1, SQL_PARAM_OUTPUT,
    SQL_C_DOUBLE, SQL_NUMERIC, 8, 0, dReturn, 8, cbValue)
rc = SQLBindParameter(ByVal pHstmt, 2, SQL_PARAM_INPUT,
    SQL_C_DOUBLE, SQL_NUMERIC, 8, 0, dDividend, 8, cbValue)
rc = SQLBindParameter(ByVal pHstmt, 3, SQL_PARAM_INPUT,
    SQL_C_DOUBLE, SQL_NUMERIC, 8, 0, dDivisor, 8, cbValue)
rc = SQLBindParameter(ByVal pHstmt, 4, SQL_PARAM_INPUT_OUTPUT,
    SQL_C_DOUBLE, SQL_NUMERIC, 8, 0, dQuotient, 8, cbValue)


Call DisplayMsg("Executing: SQLExecDirect(hstmt, '" +
    SP_DivideExecute + "', " + "SQL_NTS)", 0)
Randomize


'Execute the stored procedure several times with different
'parameter values
For i = 1 To 15
    dDividend = Int(1000 * Rnd)
    dDivisor = Int(10 * Rnd + 1)


    rc =
        SQLExecDirect(ByVal pHstmt, SP_DivideExecute, SQL_NTS)
    If (True = CheckSuccess(HNDL_HSTMT, pHstmt, rc)) Then
        'Display the return value and parameters
        Call DisplayMsg(Str(dDividend) + " DIV " +
            Str(dDivisor) + " = " + Str(dQuotient) +
            ";  Return value = " + Str(nReturn), 4)
    End If
Next i
Call DisplayMsg("", 0)
```

(continued)

Figure 8-67. *continued*

```
    'Remove the procedure just created
OraMixedCleanup:
    rc = SQLExecDirect(ByVal pHstmt, (DropFuncMsg + SP_Divide),
        SQL_NTS)


    'Clean up handles
    '---------------------------------------------------
    rc = SQLFreeStmt(ByVal pHstmt, SQL_CLOSE)
    fOK = CheckSuccess(HNDL_HSTMT, pHstmt, rc)
    rc = SQLFreeStmt(ByVal pHstmt, SQL_RESET_PARAMS)
    fOK = CheckSuccess(HNDL_HSTMT, pHstmt, rc)
End Function
```

The Oracle stored procedure *vbMixed1* simply divides the first parameter by the second, puts the quotient in the third (the output parameter), and sets the return value to 1 or 0 depending on whether the quotient was greater than 100. The following code shows the text of the stored procedure formatted for better readability. (The procedure is actually called a *function* in Oracle because a value is returned.)

```
create function vbMixed1 (
    PDividend IN number,
    PDivisor  IN number,
    PQuotient IN OUT number)
RETURN number
as
BEGIN
    PQuotient := PDividend / PDivisor;
    IF PQuotient > 100 THEN
        return 1;
    ELSE
        return 0;
    END IF;
END;
```

In the Visual Basic code, the function *CreateProc* is called to send the text of the procedure to Oracle. *CreateProc* first drops the procedure if one already exists by that name and then uses *SQLExecDirect* to send the text.

Next the Visual Basic variables are bound to the return value and Oracle function parameters with *SQLBindParameter*. Note that the third argument to *SQLBindParameter* is the parameter type (input, input/ouput, or output). For the return value the type is SQL_PARAM_OUTPUT; for the input params the type is SQL_PARAM_INPUT; and for the final parameter the type is

SQL_PARAM_INPUT_OUTPUT, even though the input value is not used in the Oracle function:

```
rc = SQLBindParameter(ByVal pHstmt, 1, SQL_PARAM_OUTPUT,
    SQL_C_DOUBLE, SQL_NUMERIC, 8, 0, dReturn, 8, cbValue)
rc = SQLBindParameter(ByVal pHstmt, 2, SQL_PARAM_INPUT,
    SQL_C_DOUBLE, SQL_NUMERIC, 8, 0, dDividend, 8, cbValue)
rc = SQLBindParameter(ByVal pHstmt, 3, SQL_PARAM_INPUT,
    SQL_C_DOUBLE, SQL_NUMERIC, 8, 0, dDivisor, 8, cbValue)
rc = SQLBindParameter(ByVal pHstmt, 4, SQL_PARAM_INPUT_OUTPUT,
    SQL_C_DOUBLE, SQL_NUMERIC, 8, 0, dQuotient, 8, cbValue)
```

Also note that the input data type is SQL_C_DOUBLE, corresponding to the Visual Basic variables of type DOUBLE, but the data type of the parameter is type SQL_NUMERIC. This shows that *SQLBindParameter*, like *SQLGetData* and *SQLBindCol*, supports the ability to convert data types by simply specifying the desired types in the argument list.

After the parameters are bound, we enter a loop in which the Oracle function is executed 15 times with *SQLExecDirect* and the results are displayed. The string used in *SQLExecDirect* uses the ODBC standard syntax for stored procedures:

```
Const SP_DivideExecute = "{?=Call vbMixed1 (?, ?, ?)}"
    ⋮
rc = SQLExecDirect(ByVal pHstmt, SP_DivideExecute, SQL_NTS)
```

The curly braces indicate to the driver that an ODBC escape clause is being used, and the keyword *Call* means that the escape clause is a stored procedure invocation (rather than a scalar function or a date/time literal). In the Oracle driver example, the escape clause gets translated by the driver to

```
EXECUTE vbMixed1 (parameter_list)
```

Finally, we delete the Oracle function from the Oracle DBMS and clean up the statement handle:

```
rc = SQLExecDirect(ByVal pHstmt, (DropFuncMsg + SP_Divide),
    SQL_NTS)

    'Clean up handles
    '-----------------------------------------
    rc = SQLFreeStmt(ByVal pHstmt, SQL_CLOSE)
    fOK = CheckSuccess(HNDL_HSTMT, pHstmt, rc)
    rc = SQLFreeStmt(ByVal pHstmt, SQL_RESET_PARAMS)
    fOK = CheckSuccess(HNDL_HSTMT, pHstmt, rc)
End Function
```

That's it for this example. All the other items on the Procedures menu are handled similarly.

In the next example, we look at a complete Visual Basic application for a simple hotel registration system that is written directly to the ODBC API.

8.9   The Hotel Reservation Sample (VBENTRY)

VBENTRY is a crude hotel reservation system that demonstrates how to write Visual Basic applications that use ODBC directly. The hypothetical user of this application is a hotel reservation agent who books and checks the status of reservations at one of four hotels. However, keep in mind that the main purpose of this application is to show you how to use the ODBC API from Visual Basic, so a lot of what would normally be included in a real hotel system is missing. For example, there is little enforcement of the "business rules" that would normally make up a part of any production software application. You would normally expect a hotel reservation program to ensure that the same room wasn't booked by two different parties at the same time. Although VBENTRY does some limited checking for this situation and others like it, you should not consider this sample to be the basis for a real hotel reservation system; VBENTRY's true value is as a demonstration tool that shows you how the ODBC function calls are used.

VBENTRY was written to work with the Microsoft Access driver. The Microsoft Access database that describes the hotels and the rooms is called HOTEL.MDB and is located in the SMPLDATA directory. If you installed the samples on the companion CD, you will see a data source name, Hotel Entry, that refers to HOTEL.MDB. Although the Microsoft Access driver is the target, VBENTRY is reasonably portable, as long as the target driver is capable of supporting keyset-driven cursors and performing updates and deletes via *SQLSetPos.* I was able to use the TBLCPY sample to copy the tables from the Hotel Entry data source to a Microsoft SQL Server 6 database, change the Hotel Entry data source to refer to the Microsoft SQL Server driver, and run VBENTRY against Microsoft SQL Server with no code changes whatsoever.

8.9.1   The VBENTRY Database Schema

There are five tables in the VBENTRY database schema. Their relationships are shown in Figure 8-68.

The PaymentTypes, Hotels, and RoomTypes tables are all lookup tables. The heart of the system is the Reservations table, which contains one row for every reservation made, and the Rooms table, which contains the set of valid room numbers and other information for each hotel.

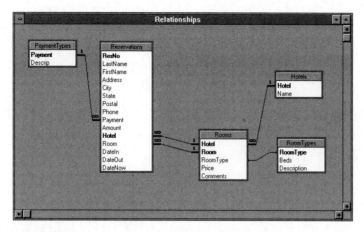

Figure 8-68.
The database schema for VBENTRY.

8.9.2 The VBENTRY User Interface

The user interface for VBENTRY consists of a main MDI form from which you can display either or both of the forms that do the real work: the reservation form and the confirmation form. The main form in VBENTRY is shown in Figure 8-69.

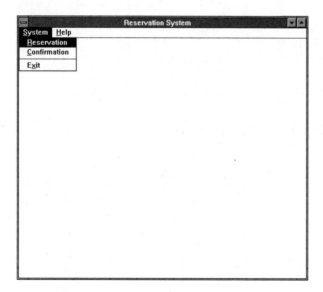

Figure 8-69.
The main MDI form of VBENTRY.

The reservation form allows the agent to enter new reservation information, including the guest information (name, address, and so forth), the room number, the dates of the stay, and the payment type. The confirmation form allows the agent to review reservations and query the database for all or some of the reservations made at a particular hotel.

8.9.2.1 The Reservation Form

The reservation form is displayed by choosing Reservation from the System menu. The form is shown in Figure 8-70.

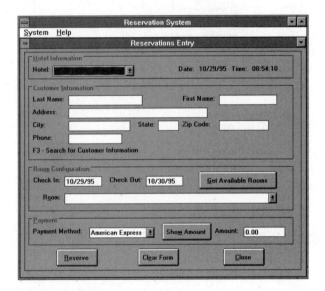

Figure 8-70.
The reservation form in VBENTRY.

The first thing the reservation agent would do is select the hotel. To display the list of hotel names, the agent clicks the combo box labeled Hotel. Then the desired hotel can be selected from the list.

Next the reservation agent would typically get the information about the guest and enter it into the controls in the Customer Information section of the form. Pressing the F3 key while the reservation form is displayed allows the agent to search for a particular guest's name in the database and retrieve all the pertinent information about the person. (The reservation agent can then ask, "Have you stayed with us before, Mr. X?" and, if so, can retrieve the previous address information and verify it verbally with the prospective guest rather than rekeying it.) The customer search dialog box is shown in Figure 8-71.

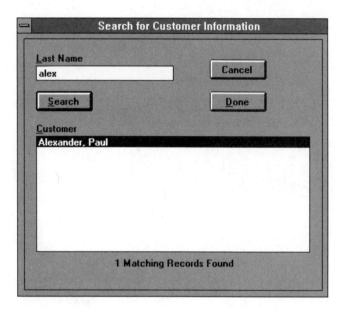

Figure 8-71.
The customer search dialog box.

The agent can type in the first few letters of the customer's last name and click the Search button to find the name. If more than three letters are typed, the search will be started automatically. When a name is selected and the agent clicks the Done button, the guest information is displayed in the reservation form.

After the guest information has been entered or selected, the check-in and check-out dates can be entered (with the default being one night starting on today's date) and the Get Available Rooms button can be clicked to assign the first available room. The reservation agent can then select an alternative room from the Room combo box if necessary. Once the check-in and check-out dates have been entered and the room number has been assigned, the Show Amount button can be used to compute the cost for the stay. (This equals the number of nights times the cost of the room per night.) Finally, the payment type can be selected from the Payment Method combo box. Figure 8-72 on the following page shows a completed reservation form.

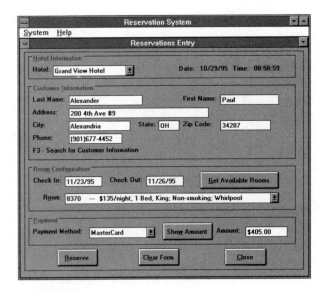

Figure 8-72.

A completed reservation form.

After all the information is entered, the reservation is completed when the agent clicks the Reserve button. An information dialog box that gives a confirmation number for the reservation is displayed.

8.9.2.2 The Confirmation Form

The confirmation form is displayed by choosing Confirmation from the System menu. The form is shown in Figure 8-73.

First a hotel must be selected from the Hotel combo box. Then the agent can enter all or part of a last name into the Last Name edit control, if desired. Clicking the Query button shows all the reservations that match the specified last name for the selected hotel. The buttons at the bottom of the form can be used to scroll through the reservations.

The information can be updated by changing the data in the controls and clicking the Update button. The word *UPDATED* will appear in red letters on the form, as shown in Figure 8-74. (*UPDATED* will also appear if someone else updated a reservation after the agent ran the query.) The reservation can be deleted by clicking the Delete button. As the agent scrolls, the "hole" left by the deletion in the results set will appear, because VBENTRY uses a keyset-driven cursor. If the agent reruns the query, the deleted record will not appear.

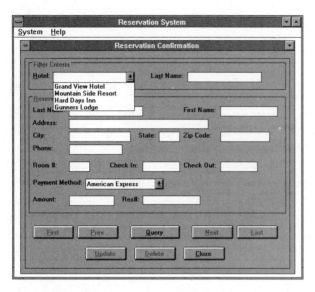

Figure 8-73.
The confirmation form with the hotel list displayed.

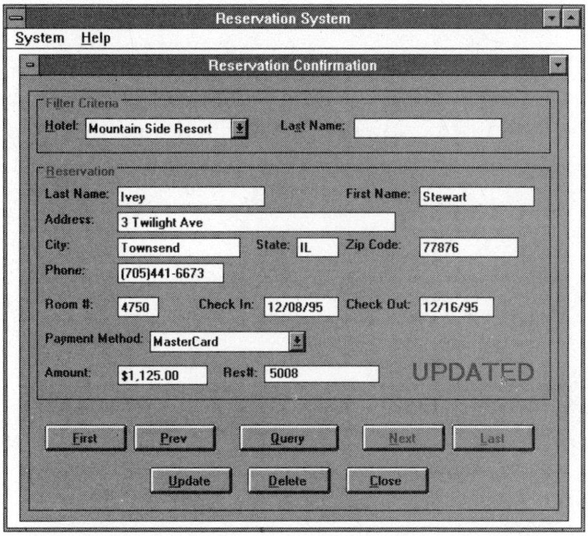

Figure 8-74.
The confirmation form as it appears after a reservation has been updated.

That's what the VBENTRY sample does. Let's see some of the code that makes it happen.

8.9.3 Inside VBENTRY

VBENTRY contains a lot of code, but I'll cover only some of the major points here.

8.9.3.1 Connecting to the Hotel Entry Data Source

Unlike the other samples we've seen in this chapter, VBENTRY doesn't use a completely generic connection model that allows the user to select any data source. It still uses *SQLDriverConnect*, but it does so with a hard-coded connection string of "DSN=Hotel Entry", which skips the Driver Manager dialog box that prompts for the data source name. You might have noticed that there is no menu or button to initiate a connection. That is because the connection happens when the application starts up. If the data source doesn't require any further information to make the connection, as is the case with the Microsoft Access driver, there is no need for further interaction with the user. But if the Hotel Entry data source referred to Microsoft SQL Server, the dialog box that prompts for the user name and password would be displayed by the driver. Here is the code that makes the connection from CONNECT.BAS:

```
rc = SQLDriverConnect(ByVal Handles.pHdbc, MDIMain.hWnd,
    "DSN=Hotel Entry", SQL_NTS, "", 0, 0, SQL_DRIVER_COMPLETE)
```

8.9.3.2 Filling Combo Boxes

Many of the combo boxes in this example use hard-coded SQL SELECT statements to retrieve the information needed to fill them. The Hotel combo box is no exception: it is filled with the contents of the Hotels table. Figure 8-75 shows the code to fill the Hotel combo box. This code is located in CURSOR.BAS.

```
Function PopulateHotels (nControl As Control) As Integer
Const HOTELS_SQL1 =
    "select Hotel, Name from Hotels order by Hotel"
Dim fHotels As Integer
Dim fOK As Integer
Dim szName As TYPESTR_51
Dim lHotel As Long
Dim cbHotel As Long
Dim cbName As Long

    'Initialize return value
    PopulateHotels = False
```

Figure 8-75.
The code to fill the Hotel combo box.

Figure 8-75. *continued*

```
'Execute the SELECT statement
rc = SQLExecDirect(Handles.pMiscHstmt, HOTELS_SQL1, SQL_NTS)
If (CheckSuccess(HNDL_HSTMT, Handles.pMiscHstmt, rc) = True)
    Then

    'Bind buffers for hotel information
    rc = SQLBindCol(Handles.pMiscHstmt, 1, SQL_C_ULONG,
        lHotel, 4, cbHotel)
    rc = SQLBindCol(Handles.pMiscHstmt, 2, SQL_C_CHAR,
        szName, MAX_HOTELNAME, cbName)

    'Fetch the data from the results set
    rc = SQLFetch(Handles.pMiscHstmt)
    While ((rc = SQL_SUCCESS) Or (rc = SQL_SUCCESS_WITH_INFO))
        'Skip SQL_NULL_DATA cases
        If ((cbName <> SQL_NULL_DATA)
            And (cbHotel <> SQL_NULL_DATA)) Then
            nControl.AddItem szName.strData
            nControl.ItemData(nControl.NewIndex) = lHotel
            fHotels = True
        End If
        rc = SQLFetch(Handles.pMiscHstmt)
    Wend

    If (fHotels = True) Then
        PopulateHotels = True
    End If
End If

'Close statement handle and unbind
rc = SQLFreeStmt(Handles.pMiscHstmt, SQL_CLOSE)
fOK = CheckSuccess(HNDL_STMT, Handles.pMiscHstmt, rc)
rc = SQLFreeStmt(Handles.pMiscHstmt, SQL_UNBIND)
fOK = CheckSuccess(HNDL_STMT, Handles.pMiscHstmt, rc)

End Function
```

The *PopulateHotels* function uses *SQLExecDirect*, *SQLBindCol*, and *SQLFetch* to execute the SELECT statement and retrieve the hotel information. For each row, the hotel name is added to the combo box with the *AddItem* method, and the matching *ItemData* array element is set to the hotel number:

```
nControl.AddItem szName.strData
nControl.ItemData(nControl.NewIndex) = lHotel
```

Note that we are employing the same technique here that we used in VBFETCH to ensure that fixed-length string variables will be used by Visual Basic. The variable is declared with a user-defined type, as is done for the *szName* variable here:

```
Type TYPESTR_51
    strData As String * 51
End Type

Dim szName As TYPESTR_51
```

Then it is bound using the variable name:

```
rc = SQLBindCol(Handles.pMiscHstmt, 2, SQL_C_CHAR,
    szName, MAX_HOTELNAME, cbName)
```

But to reference the actual data, the underlying type name (the *strData* type, in this case) is used:

```
nControl.AddItem szName.strData
```

8.9.3.3 Filling the Room Combo Box

One of the tricky parts of VBENTRY is ensuring that no two reservations at a single hotel claim the same room for any overlapping set of dates. Fortunately, the SQL query itself takes care of the most difficult part. Although most of the VBENTRY code that takes data from the screen and constructs a query uses *SQLBindParameter*, the code to construct the query to get the valid set of room numbers uses a lot of string concatenation. Figure 8-76 shows the code to get the rooms.

```
Function PopulateRooms (pHstmt As Long, nControl As Control)
    As Integer
Dim fRooms As Integer
Dim fOK As Integer
Dim nRoom As Integer
Dim cbRoom As Long
Dim cbHotelNo As Long
Dim szDateIn As String
Dim szDateOut As String
Dim szSQL As String
Dim nBeds As Integer
Dim szDesc As TYPESTR_51
Dim dPrice As Double
Dim cbIgnore As Long
```

Figure 8-76.
The code to get the rooms.

Figure 8-76. *continued*

```
'Initialize return value
PopulateRooms = False

'Execute the SELECT statement
szDateIn = "{ts '19" & Mid$(Reserve.txtDateIn, 7, 2) & "-"
    & Mid$(Reserve.txtDateIn, 1, 2) & "-"
    & Mid$(Reserve.txtDateIn, 4, 2) & " 00:00:00.000'}"
szDateOut = "{ts '19" & Mid$(Reserve.txtDateOut, 7, 2) & "-"
    & Mid$(Reserve.txtDateOut, 1, 2) & "-"
    & Mid$(Reserve.txtDateOut, 4, 2) & " 00:00:00.000'}"

szSQL =
    "select Room, Beds, Description from Rooms, RoomTypes "
szSQL = szSQL
    & "where Hotel = " & DSNStruct.lHotelNo & " and "
szSQL = szSQL
    & "RoomTypes.RoomType = Rooms.RoomType and Room not in ( "
szSQL = szSQL & "select Room from Reservations "
szSQL = szSQL
    & "where Hotel = " & DSNStruct.lHotelNo & " and "
szSQL = szSQL & szDateIn & " between DateIn and DateOut and "
szSQL = szSQL & szDateOut & " between DateIn and DateOut"
szSQL = szSQL & ") "
szSQL = szSQL & "order by Room"

rc = SQLExecDirect(ByVal pHstmt, szSQL, SQL_NTS)

If (CheckSuccess(HNDL_HSTMT, pHstmt, rc) = True) Then

    'Bind buffers for room information
    rc = SQLBindCol(ByVal pHstmt, 1, SQL_C_USHORT, nRoom,
        2, cbRoom)
    rc = SQLBindCol(ByVal pHstmt, 2, SQL_C_USHORT, nBeds,
        2, cbIgnore)
    rc = SQLBindCol(ByVal pHstmt, 3, SQL_C_CHAR, szDesc,
        Len(szDesc), cbIgnore)
    rc = SQLBindCol(ByVal pHstmt, 4, SQL_C_DOUBLE, dPrice,
        0, cbIgnore)

    'Fetch data from results set
    rc = SQLFetch(ByVal pHstmt)
    nControl.Clear
    While ((rc = SQL_SUCCESS) Or (rc = SQL_SUCCESS_WITH_INFO))
```

(continued)

Figure 8-76. *continued*

```
            'Skip SQL_NULL_DATA cases
            If (cbRoom <> SQL_NULL_DATA) Then
                nControl.AddItem Trim$(Str$(nRoom) & "    --- $"
                    & dPrice & "/night, " & nBeds & " Bed"
                    & IIf(nBeds > 1, "s", "") & ", "
                    & szDesc.strData & ")")
                fRooms = True
            End If
            rc = SQLFetch(ByVal pHstmt)
        Wend

        If (fRooms = True) Then
            PopulateRooms = True
            nControl.ListIndex = 0
        End If
    End If

    'Close statement handle and unbind
    rc = SQLFreeStmt(ByVal pHstmt, SQL_CLOSE)
    fOK = CheckSuccess(HNDL_STMT, pHstmt, rc)
    rc = SQLFreeStmt(ByVal pHstmt, SQL_UNBIND)
    fOK = CheckSuccess(HNDL_STMT, pHstmt, rc)
    rc = SQLFreeStmt(ByVal pHstmt, SQL_RESET_PARAMS)
    fOK = CheckSuccess(HNDL_STMT, pHstmt, rc)

End Function
```

The query uses a subselect on the Reservations table to exclude any rooms that are already assigned to reservations that begin or end on a date that overlaps the dates on the current reservation form.

The *PopulateRooms* function is called when the Get Available Rooms button is clicked.

8.9.3.4 Using Scrollable Cursors in the Confirmation Form

The confirmation form uses the scrolling capabilities of the driver to display all the reservation information for a hotel. It uses a one-row rowset, so the complexity of managing arrays in Visual Basic won't be an issue here as it was in VBFETCH. A global variable, *HotelData,* is used to bind all the columns that are displayed on the screen. (*HotelData* is declared using the user-defined type TypeHotelStruct.) Then the *SQLExtendedFetch* function is called for each button used to scroll the data. The code to execute the query is contained in *RetrieveHotelData* in CURSOR.BAS, as shown in Figure 8-77.

```
Function RetrieveHotelData (pHstmt As Long, lHotel As Long,
    szLastName As String) As Integer
Const HOTEL_DATA_SQL1 = "select LastName, FirstName, Address,
    City, State, Postal, Phone, Payment, Amount, Hotel, Room,
    DateIn, "
Const HOTEL_DATA_SQL2 = "DateOut, ResNo from reservations
    where (Hotel = "
Const HOTEL_DATA_SQL3 = " and LastName like '"
Const HOTEL_DATA_SQL4 = "%') order by LastName"
Dim rc As Integer
Dim fOK As Integer
Dim wRowStatus As Integer
Dim dwCrow As Long
Dim SQL As String

    'Initialize return value
    RetrieveHotelData = False

    'Clear statement handle
    rc = SQLFreeStmt(pHstmt, SQL_CLOSE)

    'Build SQL statement
    SQL = HOTEL_DATA_SQL1 + HOTEL_DATA_SQL2
    SQL = SQL + Str(lHotel) + HOTEL_DATA_SQL3 + szLastName
    SQL = SQL + HOTEL_DATA_SQL4

    'Execute the SELECT statement
    rc = SQLExecDirect(pHstmt, SQL, SQL_NTS)
    If (CheckSuccess(HNDL_HSTMT, pHstmt, rc) = True) Then
        'Bind data buffers
        If (BindHotelStruct(pHstmt, HotelData, 0) = True) Then
            'Get first record or, if none, a new entry form
            If (MoveRecord(pHstmt, MOVE_FIRST) = True) Then
                RetrieveHotelData = True
            End If
        End If
    End If

End Function
```

Figure 8-77.
The code to execute the query.

443

BindHotelStruct calls *SQLBindCol* for each column in the results set. The *MoveRecord* function calls *SQLExtendedFetch* with the appropriate fetch direction. Some of the code from *MoveRecord* is shown in Figure 8-78.

```
    ⋮
Select Case nMoveType
    Case MOVE_NEXT
        rc = SQLExtendedFetch(ByVal pHstmt, SQL_FETCH_NEXT, 1,
            cRow, HotelData.rgfRowStatus)

        'Off the end of the results set
        If (rc = SQL_NO_DATA_FOUND) Then
            'If this routine was called and HotelStatus.rc
            'is set to SQL_NO_DATA_FOUND, no records are
            'in the results set
            If (HotelStatus.rc = SQL_NO_DATA_FOUND) Then
                HotelStatus.fFirstRecord = True
                HotelStatus.fLastRecord = True
                Exit Function
            End If

            'If we have indicated that we are on the first
            'record, we have no need to try to move backward
            'because it will always fail
            ' If (HotelStatus.fFirstRecord = False) Then
                HotelStatus.rc = rc
                If (False = MoveRecord(pHstmt, MOVE_PREV)) Then
                    HotelStatus.fNoRecords = True
                    HotelStatus.rc = SQL_SUCCESS
                    MoveRecord = True
                    Exit Function
                End If
            ' End If
            MsgBox "At last record", MB_OK + MB_ICONINFORMATION
            HotelStatus.rc = SQL_SUCCESS
            HotelStatus.fLastRecord = True
        Else
            HotelStatus.fFirstRecord = False
            GoTo MoveRecordSuccess
        End If
    ⋮
```

Figure 8-78.
Some code from MoveRecord.

8.9.3.5 Using *SQLSetPos* to Update and Delete

When the cursor is positioned on a row, clicking the Update or the Delete button will perform the corresponding operation on the current row using *SQLSetPos*. Here is the code that is called when the Update button is clicked:

```
Function UpdtRecord () As Integer
Dim rc As Integer
Dim fBool As Integer

    'Initialize return value
    UpdtRecord = True
    Call TransferToBuffers(HotelData)

    'Update reservation
    rc = SQLSetPos(ByVal Handles.pConfirmHstmt, 1, SQL_UPDATE,
        SQL_LOCK_NO_CHANGE)
    If (CheckSuccess(HNDL_HSTMT, Handles.pConfirmHstmt, rc) = False)
        Then
        UpdtRecord = False
    End If

End Function
```

The *TransferToBuffers* function ensures that the current data on the form is reflected in the current bound buffers in the global variable *HotelData*. Then the call to *SQLSetPos* with the SQL_UPDATE flag stores the values in the current bound buffers in the database. The deletion process is similar, except that no call to *TransferToBuffers* is needed.

The row status array is used with *SQLExtendedFetch* to detect the presence of an updated or a deleted record in the results set. The row status array, *rgfRowStatus*, is stored in the global variable *HotelData*. The *SetButtonStatus* function is used to display the value in the status array after every call to *SQLExtendedFetch*. Here is the relevant code from *SetButtonStatus*:

```
If (HotelData.rgfRowStatus = SQL_ROW_DELETED) Then
    lblRecStatus.Visible = True
    lblRecStatus.Caption = "DELETED"
Else
    If (HotelData.rgfRowStatus = SQL_ROW_UPDATED) Then
        lblRecStatus.Visible = True
        lblRecStatus.Caption = "UPDATED"
    Else
        lblRecStatus.Visible = False
    End If
End If
```

That covers the highlights of VBENTRY. I hope you'll find the code useful for developing your own applications that use ODBC directly.

This concludes Chapter 8 and thus our discussion of all of the sample code on the companion CD. In the last chapter of the book, Chapter 9, we'll take a brief look at what's ahead for ODBC.

REFERENCES

For further information on programming with ODBC, consult the following references:

Tom Johnston, *ODBC Developers Guide,* Howard W. Sams & Company, 1994.

Ken North, *Windows Multi-DBMS Programming: Using C++, Visual Basic, ODBC, OLE 2 and Tools for DBMS Projects,* John Wiley & Sons, Inc., 1995.

Michael Stegman, Robert Signore, and John Creamer, *The ODBC Solution: Open Database Connectivity in Distributed Environments,* McGraw-Hill, 1994.

Robert Gryphon et al., *Using ODBC 2, Special Edition,* Que Corporation, 1995.

Bill Whiting, *Teach Yourself ODBC in Twenty-One Days,* Howard W. Sams & Company, 1994.

CHAPTER NINE

What's Ahead for ODBC

In this final chapter we look briefly at the next versions of ODBC, versions 2.5 and 3.0, which at the time of this writing are still in the design and prototype stage.

9.1 ODBC 2.5

ODBC 2.5 will add the necessary features to ODBC to support Microsoft Windows 95, as well as a few other enhancements. ODBC 2.5 will be a 32-bit–only release and will include the following major features:

- A new uninstall API that allows removal of ODBC components from the Windows NT and Windows 95 registries.

- Use of Windows 95's native 3-D controls. This makes it unnecessary to supply CTL3D32.DLL for Windows 95. (However, Windows NT will still use CTL3D32.DLL.)

- Cleaner architecture for localization. All the code that would need to be localized for all the core components will be centralized in one DLL. The material that will be moved from existing DLLs to a common DLL in ODBC 2.5 includes all error-message strings and all dialog boxes.

- Support for systemwide DSNs. Currently, all data sources on Windows NT and Windows 95 are registered as "user" information. Therefore, they cannot be shared or used by all users of a particular machine, nor can they be used by system services, which have no user associated with them at all. ODBC 2.5 will provide the ability to create a system data source name (system DSN). A system DSN can be accessed by all users of a machine and by system services. The data source names currently created by default will be called user data source names (user DSNs). ODBC 2.5 will continue to provide the same functionality for user DSNs that was provided with previous versions of the ODBC installer.

■ Modification of the standard and extended header files SQL.H and SQLEXT.H to align them with changes in the X/Open CLI specification. The SQL.H file was designed to contain the definitions from the X/Open specification, and the SQLEXT.H file was designed to contain all the Microsoft extensions. Because the X/Open specification has now incorporated many ODBC Level 1 and Level 2 extensions, these header files are out of alignment. ODBC 2.5 will align these header files to the new standard.

ODBC 2.5 will probably be on the market by the time you read this.

9.2   ODBC 3.0

ODBC 3.0 will be a major functional release. Keep in mind that what I describe here can (and most likely will) change before ODBC 3.0 is released sometime in 1996.

Three major categories of enhancements are planned for ODBC 3.0:

■ Alignment with the ISO CLI standard

■ Support for OLE data access

■ New or improved functionality as requested by developers

Let's look at each of these individually.

9.2.1   Alignment with the ISO CLI Standard

The X/Open CLI specification was finalized in April 1995, and ANSI and ISO finalization is expected by mid-1995. All but one of the enhancements to the ISO CLI are simply variants of existing ODBC functions. In these cases, ODBC 3.0 will map most of the new ISO functions on top of existing ODBC functions with simple macros and implement the rest with the addition of a small amount of code in the Driver Manager. The other enhancement, the addition of *descriptors,* is a significant enhancement to the extensibility of ODBC that will, among other things, make dealing with metadata more consistent than it is with the current collection of ODBC metadata functions (*SQLDescribeCol* and *SQLColAttributes* for result columns, and *SQLBindParameter* for parameters).

Note that it will be the goal of the ODBC 3.0 Driver Manager to support existing applications on top of new ISO CLI-compliant drivers. It will not be a goal of ODBC 3.0 to support ISO-compliant applications on top of existing drivers. The ODBC 3.0 Driver Manager will support ODBC 3.0–compliant applications that use ODBC 2.x–compliant drivers by mapping the ODBC 3.0 functions to the equivalent ODBC 2.x functions whenever possible. Obviously, ODBC 3.0–compliant applications will not be able to use new ODBC 3.0 functionality with an ODBC 2.x driver. The ODBC 3.0 Driver Manager will also support ODBC 2.x applications that use ODBC 3.0 drivers by doing "reverse" mapping of ODBC 2.x functions to their equivalents in ODBC 3.0.

Let's look a bit more closely at how ODBC 3.0 will be enhanced to support the ISO CLI standard.

9.2.1.1 Variants to Existing ODBC Functions

Following are some examples of the ISO CLI functions that are variants of existing ODBC functions. The list is not comprehensive, but it will give you a good overview of this category of changes for ODBC 3.0.

A Generic Handle Allocation Function   ODBC 2.x has a different function to allocate and free each kind of handle (environment, connection, and statement). In ODBC 3.0, an additional function, *SQLAllocHandle*, will allocate any of the existing handles plus one new kind of handle for descriptors. As you might guess, *SQLAllocHandle* looks just like *SQLAllocConnect* and *SQLAllocStmt* except that *SQLAllocHandle* has an additional argument to specify the handle type (environment, connection, statement, or descriptor). Here is the function prototype for *SQLAllocHandle*:

```
RETCODE SQLAllocHandle(INTEGER HandleType, HANDLE InputHandle,
                       HANDLE * OutputHandle)
```

Applications using ODBC 3.0 will be able to use *SQLAllocHandle* instead of the individual allocation functions, and if an ODBC 2.x driver is used, the Driver Manager will map *SQLAllocHandle* to the appropriate handle function in the driver.

New and Renamed Option Functions   ODBC 2.x has functions to set and get options on connection handles and statement handles. In ODBC 3.0 there will also be a function to set and get environment options. All the functions have been extended and renamed to support variable-length arguments better than ODBC 2.x does. The new functions are *SQLGetEnvAttr*, *SQLGetConnectAttr*, *SQLGetStmtAttr*, *SQLSetEnvAttr*, *SQLSetConnectAttr*, and *SQLSetStmtAttr*. Each *Get* function has two new arguments in addition to those for the equivalent

ODBC 2.*x* options. The new arguments describe the input and output length of string attributes. Each *Set* function has one additional argument, the input length. Here is the definition of one of the new functions, *SQLGetConnectAttr*:

```
SQLGetConnectAttr(
    HDBC hDBC,
    UWORD fAttribute,
    PTR rgbValue,
    SWORD cbValueMax,
    SWORD * pcbValue
    )
```

Calling *SQLGetConnectAttr* is equivalent to calling *SQLGetConnectOption*. The *SQLGetConnectAttr* call includes buffer length (*cbValueMax*) and output data length (*pcbValue*) arguments, which can be NULL if the length is defined by the attribute (as is the case with the ODBC 2.*x* defined options). The Driver Manager will map calls to *SQLGetConnectOption* from ODBC 1.0 and ODBC 2.*x* applications to *SQLGetConnectAttr* in an ODBC 3.0 driver, as shown here:

```
#define SQLGetConnectOption(hDBC,fOption,vParam) \
        SQLGetConnectAttr(hDBC,fAttribute,vParam,NULL,NULL)
```

New and Extensible Error Handling   In ODBC 2.*x*, if an application wants to retrieve the error information that is returned when an ODBC function returns SQL_ERROR or SQL_SUCCESS_WITH_INFO, it calls *SQLError*. ODBC 3.0 will introduce the concept of a *diagnostics data structure* and two new functions—*SQLGetDiagRec* and *SQLGetDiagField*—that access the fields of this data structure. *SQLError* will be mapped on top of these two functions. The advantage of this method is that the diagnostics data structure is extensible, so other types of error information can be added. The *SQLError* function can return only the types of error information specified in the arguments, which is not extensible. For example, in ODBC 3.0 you will be able to obtain the data source name that returned the error by requesting the SERVER_NAME attribute in *SQLGetDiagField*. A second advantage is that reading data from the descriptor area is nondestructive; that is, you can read the same diagnostic record more than once. This is useful if several components need to read the same diagnostic information or if truncation of the error message occurs. In the latter case the error message can be read again with a larger buffer to avoid the truncation.

Many other similar changes in ODBC 3.0 are related to conformance with the ISO CLI standard. To get a more comprehensive look at the new standard, refer to a copy of the X/Open CLI CAE (Common Applications Environment) specification, which is available from X/Open.

9.2.1.2 Descriptors

A *descriptor* is a data structure that holds information about either columns in a results set or parameters in an SQL statement. Descriptors are accessed via *descriptor handles,* which are allocated with the ODBC 3.0 function *SQLAllocHandle* using SQL_HANDLE_DESC as the HandleType argument and a connection handle as the InputHandle argument. A descriptor is used to describe one of the following:

- A set of zero or more parameters. There are two types of parameter descriptors:

  - ❑ The *application parameter descriptor,* which holds information about variables that are used to specify information about a parameter that is set by the application

  - ❑ The *driver parameter descriptor,* which holds information about the same parameter after any data conversion that the application might specify has occurred

  An application will have to operate on the application parameter descriptor to set its fields before it can execute any SQL statement that contains parameters, such as

  ```
  SELECT name, amtdue FROM customer WHERE city = ? and amtdue > ?
  ```

  Applications will be able to specify different data types in the driver parameter descriptor to achieve data conversion for arguments.

- A single row or multiple rows of result data. There are two types of row descriptors:

  - ❑ The *driver row descriptor,* which holds the description of a row from the database

  - ❑ The *application row descriptor,* which holds the description of the same row after any data conversion that the application might specify has occurred

  The application will operate on the application row descriptor whenever column data from the database must appear in application variables.

Descriptor Fields Each descriptor contains a single copy of the *descriptor header,* described below, and zero or more *descriptor records,* described in the list following the descriptor header list. The data type of each field is specified with a new ODBC 3.0 function, *SetDescField.* For an application parameter descriptor or a driver parameter descriptor, each record describes one parameter. For an application row descriptor or a driver row descriptor, each record describes one column of data.

Descriptor Header Fields Each descriptor has two header fields:

- **COUNT** This field specifies the number of records that contain data. In general, the component that sets the data structure (the application or the driver) must also set the COUNT field to show how many records exist. An application does not have to specify the number of records to reserve room for when it allocates an instance of this data structure. As the application specifies the contents of the records, the driver will take any required action to ensure that the descriptor handle refers to a data structure of adequate size.

- **ALLOC_TYPE** This field specifies whether the descriptor was allocated automatically by the driver or explicitly by the application. The application can obtain but not modify this field.

Descriptor Record Fields Each descriptor record has the following fields:

- **TYPE** A numeric value that specifies the SQL data type.

- **LENGTH** A numeric value that specifies the defined length of a character column. The value is expressed as the number of characters in the column. For example, with multibyte character sets such as UNICODE and shift JIS the LENGTH field will be less than the OCTET_LENGTH field, which is the number of bytes. (See the description of OCTET_LENGTH below.)

- **PRECISION** A numeric value. This denotes the applicable precision for a numeric data type.

- **SCALE** A numeric value. This denotes the applicable scale for a numeric data type. For DECIMAL and NUMERIC data types, this is the defined scale. It is undefined for all other data types.

- **NULLABLE** A numeric value. For row descriptors, this is set to SQL_NULLABLE if the column accepts NULL values, to SQL_NO_NULLS if the column does not accept NULL values, or to SQL_NULLABLE_UNKNOWN if it is not known whether the column accepts NULL values. For driver parameter descriptors, this is always set to SQL_NULLABLE because dynamic parameters are always NULLABLE. The application cannot modify the value of this field for driver parameter descriptors.

- **NAME** A character string field. For row descriptors, this contains the column alias, if it applies. If the column alias does not apply, the column name is returned. In either case, UNNAMED is set to SQL_NAMED. If there is no column name or column alias, an empty string is returned and UNNAMED is set to SQL_UNNAMED. For driver parameter descriptors, this is always set to SQL_UNNAMED because dynamic parameters do not have names. The application cannot set the value of this field for driver parameter descriptors.

- **UNNAMED** See the description for NAME. The application cannot set the value of this field for driver parameter descriptors.

- **DATETIME_INTERVAL_CODE** An integer date/time subcode whose value distinguishes the types DATE, TIME, and TIMESTAMP. Its value can be SQL_CODE_DATE, SQL_CODE_TIME, or SQL_CODE_TIMESTAMP.

- **OCTET_LENGTH** The length, in bytes, of a character string data type. This value always excludes the NULL terminator for driver row descriptors and always includes it for application row descriptors. Parameter descriptors use this field only for output or input-output parameters.

- **INDICATOR_PTR** A pointer to the indicator variable. For application row descriptors, this contains SQL_NULL_DATA if the column value is NULL. Otherwise, it is 0. For application parameter descriptors, this field is set to SQL_NULL_DATA to specify a NULL parameter value.

- **DATA_PTR** The pointer to a variable that contains the parameter value (for parameter descriptors) or the column value (for row descriptors).

■ **OCTET_LENGTH_PTR**   The pointer to a variable that contains the total length, in bytes, of a parameter (for parameter descriptors) or of a bound column value (for row descriptors). For application parameter descriptors, this value is ignored for all argument types except character string and binary.

An application accesses these fields by calling *SQLGetDescField* and *SQLSetDescField* with the appropriate descriptor handle. These two functions and the associated fields in the descriptor provide the same functionality that is supported by several of the ODBC 2.*x* data retrieval and metadata functions: *SQLBindParameter, SQLNumResultCols, SQLNumParams, SQLDescribeCol, SQLBindCol, SQLGetData,* and *SQLColAttributes.*

Descriptors will also support something currently not possible in ODBC 2.*x*: the sharing of metadata across statement handles. In ODBC 2.*x*, if you have two statement handles, each containing an SQL statement that uses identical parameters, you must call *SQLBindParameter* for all parameters on both handles. With descriptors, you specify the information once, and then you can associate the same descriptor with multiple statement handles on the same connection. You can even share descriptors across connection handles by using the new ODBC 3.0 function *SQLCopyDesc* to create a descriptor with the same information.

9.2.2 Support for OLE Data Access

A set of OLE interfaces for manipulating tabular data is currently under development at Microsoft. These interfaces define a common mechanism for OLE applications within a Component Object Model (COM) environment so that the applications can read, share, and interact with all types of data.

To make sure that these interfaces work well with ODBC data, Microsoft will provide a component similar to the Driver Manager that exposes the OLE objects and that interfaces directly on top of ODBC drivers. This component will work with any 32-bit ODBC 2.*x* or later driver. Of course, many of the features being added to ODBC in the 3.0 version provide richer and more efficient functionality for the type of data management provided by these OLE interfaces. An ODBC 3.0 driver that supports these extensions will provide better performance and richer functionality in the OLE environment. However, these features are generally useful in any case. Some of the features are described below. They fall into two broad categories: binding enhancements and positioning enhancements.

■ **Binding enhancements**

❑ **Multiple bindings per column**   ODBC 3.0 will support the ability to bind the same column to multiple memory locations, possibly with different conversions, in a single fetch.

❑ **Options for binding long data**   In ODBC 2.*x*, long variable-length data is always bound to a fixed-size location. When fetching multiple long variable-length values in a single fetch, from multiple columns and even from multiple rows, the application must allocate a fixed amount of space for each value. This is true even if some of the columns contain only a small amount of actual data, because the application doesn't know which columns contain a small amount of data and which contain more data. ODBC 3.0 will introduce a new binding style that allows the application to specify a single buffer into which all such variable-length data can be copied. The data in this buffer is compacted; rather than preserving a fixed maximum size for each element, the driver lays out the data end to end and uses a bound pointer to indicate the position in the variable-length buffer at which each column's data is stored. This allows for a more efficient use of the data buffer.

❑ **Quick rebinding**   In many cases, an application has a buffer area that is capable of containing many rows. A call to *SQLFetch* or *SQLExtendedFetch* might fill in only some of those rows in the buffer. Wouldn't it be nice if the application could now make use of the remaining space in the buffer area for the next set of rows? In other words, it would be nice to have a way to say: "My current bind area starts at location *x*. I now want to move my bindings to an offset from location *x*." This operation essentially consists of modifying each binding by a specified offset. The only way to do this in ODBC 2.*x* is to rebind each column, which is a lot of work. In ODBC 3.0, a new descriptor header field called BIND_OFFSET is added to support quick rebinding.

■ **Positioning enhancements**

❑ **FETCH Find**   The ability to position to a record within an already open cursor will be added. This is discussed in section 9.2.3.3.

❑ **Enhanced bookmark support**   Support for variable-length bookmarks will be added.

9.2.3 New or Improved Functionality as Requested by Developers

A number of new enhancements in ODBC 3.0 have been requested by developers who use ODBC to build applications or drivers. In some cases, features from the work in progress in the standards groups are being incorporated into ODBC 3.0. Following is a brief overview of some of the new features planned for ODBC 3.0.

9.2.3.1 Better Support for Large Objects

In ODBC 2.x, when an application creates a results set that happens to have long data in one or more of its columns, all the data for that large object flows down from the server when the application fetches a row. Consider the following scenario: A user is looking through a table called Pictures that contains the names of people and their pictures, the latter of which are in a long varbinary column. The application has executed the statement SELECT * FROM PICTURES. Ideally, what the application could now do is display the peoples' names and let the user choose a name for which to display the picture. In ODBC 2.x, the application would either get all the pictures and cache them or it would get only the names and issue another SELECT statement to get the picture values.

It would be helpful if the application could get the name and get a pointer or a handle to the picture column. Then, when the user requests to view the picture, the application can use the handle to ask the server to flow the picture data down to it. As it happens, the next ISO SQL standard, code-named *SQL-3*, will have a concept that comes close to doing this very thing: the concept of *locators*.

There are two different locator types whose use is based on the data type:

- **Binary large object locator type**   This is defined by the type SQL_C_BINARY_LOCATOR. This type of locator is used to identify binary values.

- **Character large object locator type**   This is defined by the type SQL_C_CHAR_LOCATOR. This type of locator is used to identify character values.

A new function is introduced in the ODBC API to operate on locators:

```
SQLLocator(hstmt, fOperation, hLocator, fCType,
          rgbValue, cbValueMax, pcbValue)
```

The *SQLLocator* function performs the operation indicated by *fOperation* on the locator specified in *hLocator.* The value of *fCType* is either SQL_C_CHAR or SQL_C_BINARY. The use of *rgbValue, cbValueMax,* and *pcbValue* depends on the value of *fOperation,* which can be one of the following:

- **SQL_LOCATOR_GET_DATA** *SQLLocator* gets the data into the buffer pointed to by *rgbValue. cbValueMax* is the maximum length of the *rgbValue* buffer. If *fCType* is SQL_C_CHAR, this must also include space for the null termination byte. The semantics and usage of *pcbValue* are similar to those of this argument in *SQLBindCol* in *SQLGetData.*

- **SQL_LOCATOR_HOLD** If the driver supports holdable locators (locators that persist across transaction boundaries), the *SQLLocator* function holds the locator that is specified in *hLocator. fCType* is either SQL_C_CHAR_LOCATOR or SQL_C_BINARY_LOCATOR. *rgbValue, cbValueMax,* and *pcbValue* are not used.

- **SQL_LOCATOR_FREE** *SQLLocator* frees the locator specified in *hLocator.* Again, *rgbValue, cbValueMax,* and *pcbValue* are not used.

Locators will also support random access within long data columns.

9.2.3.2 Support for Arrays of Parameters with Row-Wise Binding

In ODBC 2.*x* it is not possible to perform the equivalent of row-wise binding for parameter values. That is, you cannot take an array of structures filled with data values and hand it to ODBC to send to the DBMS. In ODBC 3.0, arrays of parameters with row-wise binding will be supported.

9.2.3.3 Support for FETCH Find

Programmers have made various requests to enhance the ODBC cursor model to include the ability to find a row in the results set based on a predicate. Consider, for example, an application that implements a list box that lists names; with a typical FETCH find facility the user presses the F key and the application scrolls down to all the first names that begin with the letter *F.* This would amount to fetching the rowset whose first row satisfies the predicate *WHERE name LIKE 'F%'.* ODBC 3.0 will support the ability to define a limited set of predicates that can be used to position to a row in a results set through the use of new *fFetchType* options on *SQLExtendedFetch.*

9.2.3.4 Cross-Platform Portability Enhancements

At several locations in the ODBC API, pointers to long and short integers are passed. On SPARCs and many other processor chips, these pointers must be properly aligned or a "Bus Error" core dump will result. To help solve this problem, ODBC 3.0 will add a new connection attribute that checks for pointer alignment.

9.2.3.5 Clarification of Column Label, Column Alias, and So Forth

In ODBC 2.*x*, it isn't clear whether the column name that is returned by *SQLDescribeCol* and *SQLColAttributes* is the column name, the column alias, or the column label; nor is it clear what drivers should return in different situations. In order to end this confusion, ODBC 3.0 will add two new fields to a descriptor record:

- **COLUMN_LABEL**   Returns the heading/label if the underlying data source supports it; returns an empty string if not.

- **BASE_COLUMN_NAME**   Returns the base column name for this results set column. If there isn't one (as in the case of columns that are expressions), an empty string is returned.

Note also that the NAME field of the descriptor record returns the column alias, if it applies. If it does not apply, it returns the column name.

9.2.3.6 Clarification of the Updatability of a Column

In ODBC 2.*x*, the *SQLColAttributes* function returns an attribute called SQL_COLUMN_UPDATABLE, which indicates whether the column in the results set is updatable. However, in many cases, a results set column might not be updatable even though the base column is updatable. For example, in results sets based on a one-to-many join, the column from the "many" table is not updatable.

Furthermore, the updatability of a column in a results set is a different piece of information than the updatability of the underlying column in the table. The latter piece of information belongs to the results set of *SQLColumns*. Accordingly, ODBC 3.0 will add the following column to the end of the results set of *SQLColumns*:

- **UPDATABLE**   A smallint, not NULL. The column is described by the values for the defined constants:

      SQL_ATTR_READONLY
      SQL_ATTR_WRITE
      SQL_ATTR_READWRITE_UNKNOWN

This describes the updatability of the column in the results set. If it is unclear whether or not the column is updatable, SQL_ATTR_READWRITE_UNKNOWN must be returned.

9.2.3.7 Specification of the Number of Concurrent Asynchronous Statements

Consider a driver or a DBMS that has multiple active statements and that allows you to have multiple statement streams at any time, but that allows only one statement at a time to be asynchronously executed. If *hstmt1* is in the SQL_STILL_EXECUTING state, *hstmt2* cannot be executed until *hstmt1* finishes execution (in other words, until *hstmt1* returns SQL_SUCCESS). In ODBC 2.*x*, there is no way for an application to know this type of information. To solve this, ODBC 3.0 will add a new information option to *SQLGetInfo*, as described here:

- **SQL_ASYNC_CONCURRENT_STATEMENTS** Returns a 16-bit integer value specifying the maximum number of active concurrent statements that the driver can support on a given *hdbc*. If there is no specified limit or if the limit is unknown, this value is 0.

9.2.3.8 Definition of a Structure to Store Numeric and Decimal Data

ODBC 3.0 defines a structure for the storage of SQL_DECIMAL and SQL_NUMERIC numbers just like those for SQL_C_TIME, SQL_C_DATE, SQL_C_TIMESTAMP, and so forth. When an application fetches SQL_TIME, SQL_DATE, or SQL_TIMESTAMP data, it can elect to get that data formatted into a known ODBC format, such as SQL_C_TIME, SQL_C_DATE, or SQL_C_TIMESTAMP. It can also provide data in those formats when binding parameters.

In ODBC 2.*x*, numeric and decimal types of data can be stored only as SQL_C_CHAR data on the client, which requires data conversion even when copying data from one data source that supports NUMERIC or DECIMAL to another that also supports NUMERIC or DECIMAL. ODBC 3.0 will provide a C structure to store decimal and numeric data, making such facilities available to these data types as well:

```
#define MAXNUMERICLEN 16
typedef struct dbnumeric
{    // Internal representation of NUMERIC data type
    BYTE    precision; // Precision
    BYTE    scale;      // Scale
    BYTE    sign;       // Sign (1 if positive, 0 if negative)
    BYTE    val[MAXNUMERICLEN];    // Value
} SQL_C_NUMERIC;
```

9.2.3.9 A Better Installer API

The current installer API is very weak with regard to error handling. For example, in ODBC 2.*x* the *SQLConfigDataSource* function returns FALSE if an error occurs, but that's all you find out. You are unable to get further error information from a function like *SQLError*. In ODBC 3.0 a new set of installer functions and a new installer error function, *SQLInstallError*, will handle error information in a more comprehensive way.

Full support for uninstall of all ODBC components will also be included in ODBC 3.0.

9.3 Summary

This chapter has given you a taste of what's in store for upcoming releases of ODBC. As long as DBMS vendors and standards bodies continue to innovate, ODBC will ensure that applications can use all those innovations in an interoperable way.

ODBC and Standards Groups

This appendix provides a brief tour of the various industry consortia and standards bodies that have influenced ODBC's development.

The SQL Access Group

The SQL Access Group was formed in 1989. Its mission was to accelerate the acceptance of formal standards to increase *portability* (to allow a program to run on various hardware platforms with a minimum of reprogramming) and *interoperability* (to allow a program to access diverse data sources across a network) for database applications.

To fulfill this mission, the group initially targeted two technologies: embedded SQL for portability and RDA (remote data access) as a standard data protocol for interoperability. Early on, some members felt that the group also needed to champion the cause of a CLI in addition to embedded SQL. Eventually (in 1991) work was started on the CLI. (See the sidebars in Part I for the inside story about this issue.)

Every major DBMS vendor, with the notable exception of IBM, participated in the SQL Access Group in its first few years. Over time, the working relationship between X/Open and the SQL Access Group became closer, however, and IBM became a welcome addition to the technical meetings under the auspices of X/Open.

The group met every four to six weeks. There were three subgroups within the SQL Access Group: the management committee, which provided overall guidance and administrative support; the API/CLI technical committee, which worked on the embedded SQL and CLI specifications; and the FAP (formats and protocols) committee, which worked on the RDA specification. The companies that actively participated in the process sent representatives to the subgroup meetings, although not every company sent representatives to the meetings of all three subgroups.

The CLI technical committee worked with a *base document* that represented the current state of the specification. Members brought change proposals to every meeting to modify the specification in some way. The change proposals were debated and voted on by the committee members. Proposals that were accepted were given to the editor of the base document, and the proposed changes were merged into the base document to create the next version. The base document was modified in this way until the committee believed it had accomplished the intended goal. The document was then handed over to X/Open for publication. The document was also submitted to the ANSI and ISO SQL committees for consideration as a new binding style for SQL (in addition to embedded SQL and module language).

The SQL Access Group formally merged with X/Open in late 1994 and continues to pursue its objective as a technical working group within X/Open.

ODBC and the SQL Access Group

The base document for the SQL Access Group's CLI specification was a subset of an early version of ODBC (which we at Microsoft were then calling SQL Connectivity). After the subset was accepted by the SQL Access Group as the base document, a technical committee was formed in September 1991 to do further work on it. After nearly a year of meetings, the first version, called the Snapshot, was published by X/Open.

In March 1992, Microsoft produced the first beta of ODBC and hosted a developer's conference. In September of that year, Microsoft released version 1.0 of ODBC. A subset of ODBC was based on the SQL Access Group's CLI specification as it existed in the spring of 1992. However, the SQL Access Group's technical committee continued to embellish the CLI specification, causing increasing divergence between the CLI and ODBC. In early 1994, the SQL Access Group decided to align the CLI to work as much as possible with ODBC's Level 1 conformance while still keeping the numerous improvements the committee had made to the specification.

In turn, Microsoft's current plan is to take the new features added by the CLI committee and include those in ODBC version 3.0.

X/Open

X/Open worked closely with the SQL Access Group to assimilate the group's specifications into X/Open's extensive set of documentation known as the X/Open Portability Guide (XPG). X/Open acted as the publishing arm of the SQL Access Group.

X/Open has a slightly different role than formal standards groups in that X/Open helps developers with portability concerns. X/Open will even define additions to a standard specification to help developers achieve portability when the standards bodies do not. For example, the SQL standard does not offer any syntax to support the creation and deletion of indexes, yet these are crucial to every commercial DBMS. Rather than being silent on this issue, X/Open defines a simple syntax for basic indexing functionality and leaves it to the DBMS vendors to add extended features if such features are needed or desired.

However, X/Open is committed to following ISO standards when they exist. X/Open will make extensions or modifications only when some technical area isn't defined or must be further defined in order to facilitate portability.

X/Open did not have any direct involvement with ODBC. Its only connection to ODBC is through its work with the SQL Access Group.

ANSI

As mentioned in Chapter 1, ANSI is a U.S. government agency that sets standards in many areas of commerce and industry. ANSI standards exist in many areas of computer technology, including programming languages and database languages such as SQL. The ANSI committee that works with database languages is called X3H2. The committee typically meets five or six times each year. The X3H2 committee defined the first SQL standard in 1986, and the most recent standard was completed in 1992.

The ANSI committee does not work in isolation from other countries, however. At the international standards level, ANSI is just one member (with one vote). Delegates from the ANSI committee are selected to represent the U.S. position at ISO meetings, which occur twice each year.

In October 1992, the working draft of the SQL Access Group CLI specification was submitted to the ANSI SQL committee. That document was approved as a new base document and was eventually added as another binding style in addition to embedded SQL and module language in the SQL-92 standard.

The ANSI committee has been working cooperatively with the SQL Access Group and X/Open to enhance the CLI specification. Most of the technical matters are dealt with by the SQL Access Group and X/Open, with ANSI acting primarily as a conduit to the larger standards body, ISO.

ISO

ISO is a worldwide federation of national standards bodies. ANSI is one such national body that participates at the international level. Other actively involved standards bodies include those of the United Kingdom, Canada, Japan, Germany, and France.

In November 1992, the CLI specification that was submitted to ANSI by the SQL Access Group the previous month was submitted to the ISO DBL (database language) committee in Canberra, Australia. This document was accepted as the ISO CLI base document.

In August 1994, ISO approved a series of changes that brings the ISO version of the CLI very close to ODBC Level 1 conformance. As I stated earlier, Microsoft intends to make the necessary changes to ODBC in version 3.0 to comply with the ISO standard CLI so that a subset of ODBC will conform to the ISO standard CLI.

As of this writing, there is a possibility that the ISO CLI will be approved as a formal international standard as early as the ISO DBL editing meeting in Ottawa, Ontario, in mid-1995. If all the editing changes are accepted, the CLI would become an addendum to the current SQL-92 standard.

REFERENCE

Jim Melton and Alan R. Simon. *Understanding the New SQL: A Complete Guide.* Morgan Kaufman Publishers, 1993. Appendix F has an excellent description of national and international standards organizations.

INDEX

Italic page-number references indicate figures, listings, and tables.

Special Characters

4GLs (fourth-generation languages), 54–55

A

Access. *See* Microsoft Access
access plan, 33
active (connected) state, 146
adaptive programming, 216–17
AdHocQuery function, *395–96*
ad hoc query tools, 9
aggregates, scrolling, 192–93
ALLOCATE cursor statement, 47–48
allocated state, 146
American National Standards Institute. *See* ANSI
ANSI (American National Standards Institute), 4, 463
API conformance
  Core, 219
  introduced, 218
  Level 1, 219–20
  Level 2, 220–21
APIs (application programming interfaces)
  defined, 3, 4
  "Microsoft Scrollable Cursor API" paper, 166
  ODBC (*see* ODBC)
application developer's database connectivity perspective, 11–14, *12*
application parameter descriptors, 451
application programming interfaces. *See* APIs
application row descriptors, 451
applications
  distributed, 13
  DLL use, 129–30
  introduced, 101, 102, *102*
  ODBC design and, 18–19
  walkthrough of a simple request
    connection function called, 131, *132*

applications, walkthrough of a simple request,
  continued
    connection handle allocated, 130, *131*
    DLL use, 129–30
    driver handle allocation functions called by Driver Manager, 134, *134*
    driver loaded by Driver Manager, 132, *133*
    environment handle allocated, 130, *131*
    results data, 139, *140*
    server connected, 134–35, *136*
    SQL statement executed, 137–39, *138, 139*
approximate numeric (floating-point) data types, 198, 201, *201*
arrays
  of parameters, 457
  of structures, 162–64, *163*
asynchronous execution, 156–57
asynchronous statements, concurrent, 459
AUTO_COMMIT mode, 264
autocommit mode, 301
auto-increment data type, 202, 211
auto mode installation, 232
/AUTO switch, 232

B

badminton cursor model, 252–53, *253*
base document, 462
BCP (bulk copy), 238
BENCHINFO structure, 324
BENCH sample program (benchmark testing)
  background of the TPC-B benchmark, 313–16, *314*
  chart of transactions per second, *323*
  differences between the TPC-B benchmark and the sample program, 316
  endgame of the *fRunTrans* function, *334–35*
  generating the values in EXECUTE.C, *331*

Kyle Geiger

Kyle Geiger is the architect of Microsoft's Open Database Connectivity (ODBC). He has had 14 years of experience in the computer industry and has been working on database connectivity issues since he joined Microsoft in 1988. Kyle has had several roles in the ODBC group, including development manager and general manager. He has been a featured speaker at many database trade shows and events. Kyle also served as the first chairman of the SQL Access Group's API/CLI Technical Committee. Prior to joining Microsoft, Kyle was a software engineer at Wang Laboratories, where he worked on numerous desktop database products. He holds a masters degree in software engineering from the Wang Institute of Graduate Studies and a bachelor of science degree in computer science from the University of Washington. Kyle can be reached on the Internet at *kyleg@microsoft.com*.

Brian Tschumper

Brian Tschumper is currently an ODBC software design engineer in the developer division of Microsoft. When he joined Microsoft in 1993, Brian worked on the ODBC Test team writing test code and internal tools for the ODBC Software Development Kit 2.0. Prior to joining Microsoft, Brian designed and implemented several custom software systems on the IBM AS/400. He graduated from Mankato State University in 1993 with a bachelor of science degree in computer science. Brian can be reached on the Internet at *briants@microsoft.com*.

Jason Zander

Jason Zander is currently a software design engineer in the developer division of Microsoft. Since joining Microsoft in 1992, he has worked on the ODBC Test team writing test code, samples, and test tools, including the ODBC Test Tool for the Software Development Kit 2.0. As an intern at IBM, he worked on the implementation of DRDA for the IBM AS/400. Jason graduated from Mankato State University in 1992 with a bachelor of science degree in computer science. Jason can be reached on the Internet at *jasonz@microsoft.com*.

The manuscript for this book was prepared and submitted to Microsoft Press in electronic form. Text files were prepared using Microsoft Word 6.0 for Windows. Pages were composed by Microsoft Press using Aldus PageMaker 5.0 for Windows, with text in New Baskerville and display type in Helvetica Bold. Composed pages were delivered to the printer as electronic prepress files.

Cover Graphic Designer
Rebecca Geisler

Interior Graphic Designer
Kim Eggleston

Interior Graphic Artist
Michael Victor

Principal Compositor
Barbara Remmele

Principal Proofreader/Copy Editor
Lisa Theobald

Indexer
Foxon-Maddocks Associates

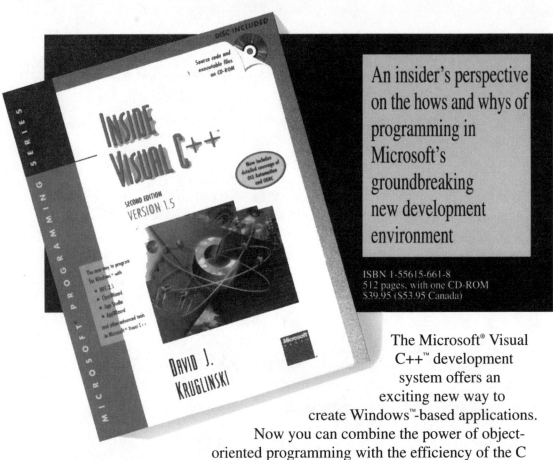

WELCOME TO THE WORLD OF WINDOWS® 95

The MICROSOFT® WINDOWS® 95 RESOURCE KIT provides you with all of the information necessary to plan for and implement Windows 95 in your organization.

ISBN 1-55615-863-7
1376 pages, $49.95 (67.95 Canada)
Three - 3.5" disks

Details on how to install, configure, and support Windows 95 will save you hours of time and help ensure you get the most from your computing investment. This exclusive Microsoft publication, written in cooperation with the Windows 95 development team, is the perfect technical companion for network administrators, support professionals, systems integrators, and computer professionals.

The MICROSOFT WINDOWS 95 RESOURCE KIT contains important information that will help you get the most out of Windows 95. Whether you support Windows 95 in your company or just want to know more about it, the MICROSOFT WINDOWS 95 RESOURCE KIT is a valuable addition to your reference library.

Microsoft®_Press_

097-000-680